CHARLES KING

Charles King is Professor of International Affairs at Georgetown University, Washington DC. His numerous books include the *New York Times* bestseller *The Reinvention of Humanity* (published in the US as *Gods of the Upper Air*), which was winner of The Francis Parkman Prize and shortlisted for the British Academy Prize and the National Book Critics Circle Award; *Midnight at the Pera Palace: The Birth of Modern Istanbul*; and *Odessa: Genius and Death in a City of Dreams*, which was winner of a National Jewish Book Award. His writing has appeared in the *TLS*, *New York Times*, *Washington Post*, *Foreign Affairs*, *The New Republic* and other publications.

ALSO BY CHARLES KING

The Reinvention of Humanity
Midnight at the Pera Palace
Odessa
Extreme Politics
The Ghost of Freedom
The Black Sea
The Moldovans
Nations Abroad (co-editor)

Praise for *Every Valley*

'A mesmerising journey of musical genius through one of
the most fascinating and creative moments in human history'
Amanda Foreman

'A book of power and glory, brimming with emotion and
dazzling in its reach' Stacy Schiff

'As compelling as a symphony with a full choir of amazing
characters. Unforgettable' Simon Sebag Montefiore

'Much closer to the teeming panorama of a novel like *War and Peace* than
the narrow focus of most books about music history ... It takes a rare
blend of scholarship, ingenuity and empathy to weave together the stories
of the mostly distressed souls who, one way or another, were connected with
Messiah's creation ... King expertly juggles these individuals' stories and
a lot more besides ... Riveting' *The Times*, Book of the Week

'Charles King's fascinating history of Handel's most famous work shows it
in a whole new light ... His book humanises the work's exalted creators
and demonstrates that the *Messiah* is not a pompous manifesto of faith
but a troubled, often desperate quest for consolation' *Observer*

'By following the links between individuals who are connected by varying
degrees of separation with the work's original creation and promotion,
the author discovers that this one musical piece can stimulate joined-up
insights into almost every significant aspect of its period: cultural, political,
social, economic ... [King's] technique is often cinematic ... A truly
informative, imaginative and engaging work' *Financial Times*

'Fascinating ... King's narrative is wide-ranging, taking in not just the
ailing composer and his circle ... [and] how the *Messiah* coincided with the
birth of the Enlightenment ... In King's telling, the "Hallelujah" chorus
is just one rousing highlight among many' *New Statesman*

'In an engagingly written story ... Charles King explores the background
to a work which he considers the greatest piece of participatory art
ever created. King's discursive and genial approach ... make for
enjoyable reading' *BBC Music Magazine*

'King's story weaves together five parallel plots with imagination,
enthusiasm and erudition ... Engaging' *BBC History Magazine*

'[King is] a splendid writer ... Fascinating' *Atlantic*

'Compelling. King transforms Handel's world into a place we can all recognise and understand as the foundation for our own' *Washington Post*

'Engaging and enthusiastic ... King handles a very large cast of characters and source material with energy, intelligence and aplomb' *Literary Review*

'An adroitly threaded account of Handel's life and achievements [that] opens out to a colourful gallery of eighteenth-century personalities who played a part in making *Messiah* what it was ... Readable, well researched and rich with detail' *Gramophone*

'A book rich with quirky characters living under strange circumstances: eccentric royals, visionary benefactors, financial collapses, theatrical triumphs and career meltdowns ... We are plunged into the hectic mayhem of London life' *New York Times*

'In *Every Valley* Charles King ... sets out to explain the *Messiah*'s enduring popularity ... King interweaves the lives of several people directly or tangentially connected with it [and] accompanies these with analyses of Georgian life and thought ... The result is a densely textured history of the era' *New York Review of Books*

'Smartly written ... In explaining the social and biographical background of the story of *Messiah*, King brings the masterpiece to life – and keeps it alive' *Washington Examiner*

'A work of vivid social and cultural commentary, [as well as] an in-depth study of artistic creation' *New York Times Book Review*

'Charles King shows how Handel's epic work, the *Messiah*, sprang not from one solitary composer's genius but from the dramatic interplay of eighteenth-century lives and their times. Fascinating and accessible to all' Henry Louis Gates Jr

'Vividly depicting life in Britain during the turbulence of the 1700s, Charles King celebrates Handel's *Messiah* as a glorious beacon of hope' Elaine Pagels

'Charles King's erudition is remarkable but never obtrusive, for he is a wonderful story-teller. *Every Valley* is eighteenth-century history as page-turner, evoking both tears and laughter' Archie Brown

CHARLES KING

Every Valley

The Desperate Lives and Troubled Times That Made Handel's Messiah

VINTAGE

1 3 5 7 9 10 8 6 4 2

Vintage is part of the Penguin Random House group of companies

Vintage, Penguin Random House UK, One Embassy Gardens,
8 Viaduct Gardens, London SW11 7BW

penguin.co.uk/vintage
global.penguinrandomhouse.com

First published in Vintage in 2025
First published in hardback by The Bodley Head in 2024
First published in the United States of America by Doubleday in 2024

Copyright © Charles King 2024

The moral right of the author has been asserted

Book design by Cassandra J. Pappas

Penguin Random House values and supports copyright. Copyright fuels creativity, encourages diverse voices, promotes freedom of expression and supports a vibrant culture. Thank you for purchasing an authorised edition of this book and for respecting intellectual property laws by not reproducing, scanning or distributing any part of it by any means without permission. You are supporting authors and enabling Penguin Random House to continue to publish books for everyone. No part of this book may be used or reproduced in any manner for the purpose of training artificial intelligence technologies or systems. In accordance with Article 4(3) of the DSM Directive 2019/790, Penguin Random House expressly reserves this work from the text and data mining exception.

Printed and bound in Great Britain by Clays Ltd, Elcograf S.p.A.

The authorised representative in the EEA is Penguin Random House Ireland,
Morrison Chambers, 32 Nassau Street, Dublin D02 YH68

A CIP catalogue record for this book is available from the British Library

ISBN 9781529942873

Penguin Random House is committed to a sustainable future for
our business, our readers and our planet. This book is made from
Forest Stewardship Council® certified paper.

*In memory of
Pat Ellison*

Contents

Prologue   1
Introduction   5

PART I · Portents

1. "The Famous Mr. Hendel"   23
2. "An Undertaking So Hazardous"   37
3. Jacobites   46
4. Grub Street   55
5. Yahoos   66

PART II · Sorrows and Grief

6. The Hyp and the Prodigious   81
7. Oratorio   93
8. "Dying by Inches"   102
9. A Design for Rescuing   119
10. The Book of Job   131
11. Scorn   151

12. Foundlings 166
13. The Return of a Prince 173

PART III · Resurrection

14. To the Hibernian Shore 187
15. Fishamble 196
16. "Hope Is a Curtail Dog" 209
17. Anthems and Choruses 228
18. Exalted 239
    Epilogue 255

Charles Jennens's Messiah *Libretto* 259
Author's Note 271
Acknowledgments 273
Notes 279
Bibliography 305
Index 319

Every Valley

Prologue

GOPSALL, LEICESTERSHIRE, 1739

Some days he would wander the manor house in a blank stupor, barely able to lift a foot. An ancestor had leveled forests and pried up ore, and within two generations the family had spun pig iron into gold. There were servants and a well-laid table, carriages and gentlemanly privileges, profusion upon profusion. One of his detractors would label him "Solyman the Magnificent," holding court like an Ottoman sultan in a London town house and a country home in the English Midlands. But on the cusp of forty, past midlife for his time and place, he was more like a provincial Saul, the brooding warrior-king, fleeing from the Philistines across a battlefield of ghosts.

Charles Jennens was, by his own reckoning, "puny." He was so afraid of the cold that he lay under six blankets in winter and four in summer. He never married, fathered no children, and made distant enemies more readily than close friends. Most of the people he held in regard would precede him in death, including the man to whom he would make his only discernible statement of love. His smallest agitations could balloon into obsessions. In his will, written and revised as his designated heirs died off one by one, he instructed his executor to return "all the Books in the Cases on that side of the little Room . . . which fronts towards the Windows, and all the Books in the Narrow

Slip between the said Room and the Closet" to the person who had left them there. His Anglican parish priest would sum up his infirmities as "an impetuosity of temper," "an extreme lowness and depression of spirits," and "violent perturbations and anxieties of the mind."

Jennens was born in 1700, at the dawn of a century that would be remembered as an age of rationality and progress. Isaac Newton's laws of motion were still a fresh discovery. The astronomer Edmond Halley was working to chart a particular comet's fierce reliability. In smoky coffeehouses and on the printed page, philosophers and pamphleteers debated the revolutionary claim that the best government was one founded not on the will of God but on a people's right to be governed well.

Jennens's own outlook, however, was a ledger book of worries. By the time he reached adulthood, whatever opinions he held about the future arose from one unshakable conviction: that his life coincided with a wrong turn in national affairs and the initial stages of his country's inevitable decline. On any street, in any town, the fetid churn of modern living was on ready display: men whittled down by politics and faction, country girls painting themselves into city courtesans, public executions, animals tortured for a laugh, wailing children abandoned to their fate. To anyone really paying attention, Jennens sometimes felt, the sum of public life—political conspiracies and scandals, economic scheming, one foreign war bleeding into the next, and all of it amplified by sensational reports in things that printers had recently named "News-papers"—amounted to an ironclad argument in favor of despair.

"'Tis impossible for such a Wretch as I am, surrounded with so many circumstances of inconvenience, which stare me in the face which way soever I take my prospect," he once wrote, "to determine with any certainty upon any Action of my Life." But at Gopsall and in London, Jennens built a private sanctuary filled with evidence of what the world could be, rather than reminders of what it usually was. He piled up newly published books with marbled edges and calfskin binding. In his drawing rooms, he hung pictures by European masters, a gallery that would swell to some five hundred items. He filled cabinets with musical manuscripts sent directly from Venice and Rome, and played the pieces competently on a harpsichord or piano. He was guided by taste and passion, with a consuming desire to be carried away by objects of awe and beauty. In his darkest moments, they were a salvation, like lifelines flung from a receding ship.

One troubled season, surrounded by what had become one of Britain's finest repositories of human creativity, Jennens started pulling down books from his library shelves. He spent days poring over them, scribbling notes, filling up fresh sheets of paper with a sharpened quill. He copied down quotations from the sacred scriptures, some from the Psalms and the Hebrew prophets, some from New Testament epistles. He linked up one passage with another, editing and rearranging them, tying together themes that leaped out at him from the text—the whole of it not so much a story as an archaeology of ancient promises, dug up and dusted off for the present.

What if the way to capture the uses of suffering and the mysteries of living, Jennens began to wonder, was to reenact them in a performance? Seeing the hidden order of things played out before your eyes could be a source of solace, he thought, but even more a route toward enlightenment, with the same direct effect that painting and music had on him. Page after page, what was emerging from Jennens's notes was not a learned dissertation or dry essay but something entirely different: a kind of dramatized philosophy—a script even—visceral and affecting, expressed in words but also, he hoped, transcending them. It took discipline to spin sense out of the surrounding chaos, to imagine a better world and start walking toward it. Perhaps the best vehicle for doing so was not so much an argument as a demonstration.

Jennens could not be sure what, if anything, would become of his "Scripture Collection," as he had started to call it. Even if he ever got around to sharing his vision with anyone, the result could well remain a private folly. He hoped that an aging London composer he called "the Prodigious" might be able to do something with it, he finally told a friend, especially if he could be persuaded to "lay out his whole Genius & Skill upon it, that the Composition may excell all his former Compositions." But then again, maybe not. The maestro's "head is more full of Maggots than ever," Jennens had complained a few years earlier.

Jennens's idea would never bring him fame, which in any case he never seems to have sought. It would add nothing to his already substantial wealth. Even when the grand performance he first imagined eventually found an audience, few people would be able to name him as its source. Yet living differently required thinking differently, he was coming to sense, which is what he hoped his script would be able to show.

Committing his ideas to paper would end up being the most enduring act of Charles Jennens's life, as well as the bravest. "The Subject," he later wrote with a rare hint of excitement, "excells every other Subject." At the heart of his work was not so much a statement of faith as a test of will—an affirmation of something Jennens himself had always found hard to believe in.

It was the staggering possibility that the world might turn out all right.

Introduction

The work of music we now call Handel's *Messiah* has a good claim to being the greatest piece of participatory art ever created. It is heard and sung by more people every year than arguably any other piece in the classical repertoire, from legendary soloists joining renowned orchestras and choirs to strangers singing together from their seats. Its central theme is religious and specific—for Christians, the cosmic meaning of the prophetic birth, suffering, and resurrection of Jesus Christ—with a text consisting entirely of English translations of passages from the Hebrew scriptures and the New Testament. But it has long transcended the commitments that produced it. For a good portion of the planet, experiencing the *Messiah*, especially at the end of the calendar year, has become the most sacred act that a mass secular audience will ever undertake together. It is a piece of music that people not only admire or enjoy but in which they also report finding something like truth—intimate, magnetic, awesome.

That's how it has seemed to me whenever I've heard it, in concert halls, in churches, in high school gymnasiums, and then at home, in the middle of what would turn out to be the worst few years many of us can remember.

Even before the onset of the COVID-19 pandemic, the first weeks of 2020 had been very hard on people I love. Several friends had struggled with their health. Others longed for a child of their own. A beloved uncle sank into a fog of confusion and decline. My wife, Maggie, rushed to be with her mother during urgent heart surgery.

That summer and fall were full of disorder and the tortuous beginning of a national reckoning with racism. Then came a January day when, a few blocks from our home in Washington, D.C., the American political system came very close to breaking. Like people thousands of miles away, we watched the attack on the U.S. Capitol from our computer screens, following the mayor's order to stay home and, more to the point, scared of what might come next. National Guard troops, brought in from all over the country, soon blocked the major streets with armored personnel carriers. For the next six months, part of our neighborhood on Capitol Hill was an armed encampment, surrounded by ten-foot-high fencing topped with coils of razor wire. Through it all, Maggie was dealing with a serious health problem of her own, news of which came unexpectedly while she waited at her mother's bedside. We spent another year worrying and trying to convince ourselves that everything was going to be okay.

Hemmed in, unprepared for what seemed like a dark future—disease, social division, a warming planet, the messed-up state of everything—I wanted desperately to find a way for us to slice through the gloom, to let in a bit of healing light.

A couple of years earlier, I had bought a phonograph for Maggie as a Valentine's Day present. It was a Victor-Victrola VV-50 from around 1924, a windup "portable," meaning a thing that weighs about forty pounds, with no electronics and an iron resonating chamber, and requiring a needle change after every play. Thanks to eBay, we slowly piled up a small collection of early jazz, bits of opera, some shticky comedians, most of the discs dating from before 1935. We sometimes played them for friends, but mainly we liked listening to the records together in our living room, like two time travelers in search of someone else's memory.

Now, surrounded by illness and anxiety, I had an idea. As a writer and singer, Maggie always filled our home with music. If I could find something we both loved, something special I had heard her sing, maybe in the oldest version possible—that seemed like very big magic.

I returned to eBay. It didn't take long to come across the earliest recorded full performance of the *Messiah*, from 1927, with Sir Thomas Beecham conducting the BBC Chorus at Methodist Central Hall, Westminster. A few weeks later, a cardboard box arrived at our house, split and dented after a bad packing job by the owner in Britain. The box contained a grab bag of shellac 78s—literally a bag, a worn canvas tote, as if it had come from the estate sale of a long-forgotten English aunt. Inside was some Percy Grainger, some Rachmaninoff, Sibelius's *Finlandia*, Enrico Caruso in *Pagliacci*. Several of the records were broken into onyx shards, but the *Messiah*, packed in two heavy buckram cases that came with the original purchase on the Columbia label, was miraculously intact.

As it turned out, the *Messiah* recording, in a twelve-inch format, wouldn't fit on the Victrola, which had been built for earlier ten-inchers. So I gave up on half my plan. Instead, I bought a good-enough turntable and speakers, set them up in my home office, and lowered the first disc onto the spindle.

Beecham was the world's first celebrity conductor, with a Vandyke beard and an eye for marketing. I would later learn that his interpretations could be off-kilter, with ponderous tempos and arrangements for modern orchestras that were overwrought and ahistorical, a "technicolor 'Messiah,'" as a reviewer in *The New York Times* once put it. But this performance was quieter and simpler, closer to the way that the earliest listeners would have heard it. A few minutes into the music, as the violins rocked slowly back and forth, then halted before a lone, high voice—sounds that had echoed through London's largest concert hall a few years after another worldwide pandemic, the 1918 influenza outbreak—Maggie and I both burst into tears.

LOTS OF PEOPLE seem to do that.

The *Messiah* is a work of anguish and promise, of profound worry and resounding joy, all expressed in ingenious, irresistible melodies. Its three parts, or acts, run through ancient prophecies of the birth of a rescuer for the world, then his brutal suffering at the hands of oppressors, then his atonement for the sins of humankind and the promise of eternal life for the redeemed—a set of ideas that, for the Christians who made up the *Messiah*'s first audiences, represented the essence of their faith.

In 1741, George Frideric Handel had started out with a stack of pages in English, a collection of short quotations gleaned from across the scriptures that were held to demonstrate that Jesus of Nazareth was the foretold savior. He formed them into solo songs, duets, choruses, and recitatives, the musical connective tissue between the work's various "scenes." He sketched the full musical score in London late that summer, premiered the new work in Dublin in the spring of 1742, and then continued to perform it, or at least attend many of the performances, until he died in 1759.

Handel was German by birth, but he gained his real musical education, in his twenties, in Italy, among composers, performers, and instrument makers engaged in everything from inventing the piano to perfecting what had come to be called opera. He spent his thirties and forties rising from a newcomer to London feeling his way through the city's rowdy theater world to court composer to the British royal family. By his fifties he was his adopted country's most celebrated public musician. But when he began work on the *Messiah*, he was approaching sixty and edging toward the final phase of his career, which made this particular work something of a midlife revival—and an odd one at that. In its sung text and subject matter, the *Messiah* was an anomaly. It would turn out to be wholly unlike anything else Handel ever wrote. Only in the final decade of his life would it became widely known and, even then, with barely a hint of the fame it would achieve long after he was gone.

Other musicians and choral groups, both in Britain and abroad, took it up in the years that followed his death. The earliest documented concerts in the American colonies, featuring selected portions rather than the entire work, came in New York in 1770, at a tavern on Broadway and then at Trinity Church Wall Street. But it wasn't until 1784, at a royal commemoration of Handel's life, held in London's Westminster Abbey a quarter century after his death, that the *Messiah*—or by that stage, often *The Messiah*, even though Handel's original title left out the definite article—began to occupy the position it still holds today: as a piece of music that seems full of meaning to people who treasure it and stealthily familiar to nearly everyone else.

The Westminster event was the first time the work was heard at scale, with "a more numerous Band than was ever known to be collected in any country, or on any occasion whatever," as the public announcement advertised. More than 250 instrumentalists, plus the combined choirs of the abbey, St. Paul's Cathedral, Windsor Castle, and the Chapel Royal, all managed to keep together, a contemporary source marveled, even without "a *Manu-ductor* to regulate the measure" by waving his hands or pounding on the floor with a stick. "I was at the piece call'd the Messiah," Abigail Adams wrote to her niece after seeing a similar performance in 1785, while she and her husband, John, were living in London, "and tho a Guinea a ticket, I am sure I never spent one with more satisfaction. . . . I was one continued shudder from the begining to the end of the performance."

The concerts at Westminster Abbey would stand as the earliest of countless "monster performances" that, by the Victorian era, would become the accepted standard. Audiences and artists increasingly came to see the *Messiah* as the very definition of big music, with large emotions attached, even if many people had a hard time explaining exactly why. Ralph Waldo Emerson, for example, stumbled to express how Handel had somehow captured the essence of wonder, recapitulating even the enormousness of existence itself. "As the master overpowered the littleness and incapableness of the performers and made them conductors of his electricity," he wrote after attending a concert in Boston in 1843, "so it was easy to observe what efforts nature was making, through so many hoarse, wooden and imperfect persons, to produce beautiful voices, fluid and soul-guided men and women." The music had weight, listeners felt. It produced a transporting sense that something cosmic and profound was at stake, even when the cares of this world happened to intrude. "I should have sometimes fancied myself amongst a higher order of Beings," Abigail Adams confided to Thomas Jefferson, "if it had not been for a very troublesome female, who was unfortunately seated behind me; and whose volubility not all the powers of Musick could still."

Only later, in the twentieth century, would music directors and conductors begin performing the *Messiah* as it was heard in Handel's lifetime, with fewer instrumentalists and smaller choirs, sometimes on period instruments and with vocal techniques appropriate to the era. Not that Handel would have minded either way. No two of his performances were exactly alike. He rewrote passages, raised and lowered keys, reassigned parts, cut out entire sections, and changed orchestrations according to the circumstances, as all musicians must. And as a composer who made his living from ticketed stage productions as well as the favor of powerful patrons, volume and spectacle were always part of his toolbox. "Oh, that I had cannon!" he is supposed to have wished about one already thundering anthem.

Yet big or small, history conscious or boldly innovative, the *Messiah* is now everywhere, especially as the calendar year winds to a close. Concerts by orchestras and choirs of different sizes and configurations are scheduled each year in New York, London, Melbourne, Amsterdam, Montreal, Vienna, Milan, Stockholm, Tokyo, and elsewhere. Across the United States, Canada, Britain, and other parts of the English-speaking world, from the Royal Albert Hall to Lincoln Center to small churches and community buildings, audiences show up to sing the work in its entirety, unrehearsed. Carnegie Hall in New York and the Kennedy Center for the Performing Arts in Washington, D.C., host sing-alongs, as do venues in Boston, Atlanta, Los Angeles, Chicago, Salt Lake City, Cincinnati, Houston, Portland, Des Moines, Kalamazoo, and many other cities and towns. According to a blogger who tries to tally them up each year, there were close to two hundred such events in the United States alone in 2023, from a

"Do-It-Yourself *Messiah*" in Waukegan, Illinois, to "Handel's Mess-Cider" at a brewery in San Francisco.

But because the music seems so deeply familiar, it is easy to miss the *Messiah*'s sheer weirdness. Its structure isn't linear or chronological. It has nothing that could be called a plot. Its form is more like that of a found poem, built from Bible verses that have been rearranged and, here and there, edited—a fact that made it an astonishing, and to some listeners even upsetting, innovation at the time. Despite its religious themes, its earliest performances were in secular spaces—a music hall, a theater—rather than where many people thought the holy words most properly belonged, that is, in a church. Parts of the sung text would later become iconic, with melodies familiar to millions, such as the "Hallelujah" chorus, now the universal soundtrack of triumph and jubilation. But other segments can seem by turns mysterious, oracular, or baffling. "How beautiful are the feet of them that preach the gospel of peace," a soloist sings at one point above lilting violins—which turns out to be the *Messiah*'s version of a Christian convert's misquotation of a Jewish prophecy: a passage from the book of Isaiah that the apostle Paul recalled from memory while writing to fellow believers in Rome. Even the music itself represents the oddest possible combination of sacred and profane. It wraps together grand choruses built for a cathedral with arias that were, at the time, most at home in an Italian opera house. Listen to enough of Handel's other compositions, and it doesn't take long to spot the mix of old and new: a secondhand motif, say, or a melody Handel repurposed from another composition.

Given that its biblical text centers on the advent, death, and resurrection of Jesus, the *Messiah* is really a work about Easter—spring-filled, renewing, joyous—for which it was originally written. But over the past two centuries, it has become associated with Christmas. The text is full of passages that evoke the season. "For unto us a child is born, unto us, a son is given," the chorus sings in another passage taken from the book of Isaiah. The melody then bounces stepwise upward—"and the government shall be upon His shoulder; and his name shall be called"—before hitting the explosive refrain:

"Wonderful, Counsellor, the mighty God, the Everlasting Father, the Prince of Peace," an infectious line that people always seem to end up humming on the way home. In another section, a soprano slowly recites the famous scene from the Gospel of Luke, of "shepherds abiding in the field, keeping watch over their flock by night," and the shimmering appearance of an angel with the good news of Christ's birth. The violins, shifting into allegro, build the sense of expectation as the chorus enters again, joined by distant trumpets that conductors sometimes place at the back of the concert hall, proclaiming "Glory to God in the highest, and peace on earth, good will towards men." It is a moment that American listeners of a certain generation often find evokes an unexpected nostalgia—if not for the Bible or the *Messiah*, then for Linus's recitation of nearly the same text in the *Peanuts* Christmas special, first televised in 1965.

The reasons for the work's slide from spring to winter are hard to pinpoint. Hearing the *Messiah* at Christmastime was already a well-established tradition in the early nineteenth century. Performing it then, Emerson worried, shifted the focus away from the glorious resurrection of Jesus and toward his lowly birth, thereby totally missing the theological point—and a sign of how far real faith had declined, he felt, in his "unbelieving city" of Boston. In the twentieth century, the *Messiah* became part of the more general trend of Christmas's outstripping Easter as the primary Christian celebration while also becoming a broadly secular holiday. All of this has cast the *Messiah* in a strange dual role: on the one hand, just another part of the commercialization of Christmas, background music to accompany warm spices and the smell of spruce; and on the other, a tool for rescuing the season from itself—an invitation to worry less about a missed flight or a last-minute gift and more about large, ultimate things. After all, "that's what Christmas is all about, Charlie Brown," as Linus puts it.

Today, the *Messiah* remains the only piece of classical music that reliably brings audiences to their feet, since listeners typically stand, by unspoken convention, at the "Hallelujah" chorus. "When it came to that part, the Hallelujah, the whole assembly rose and all the Musicians, every person uncoverd," Abigail Adams reported already in 1785.

"I could scarcely believe myself an inhabitant of Earth." Yet the reasons for that are more myth than history. There is no reliable evidence to support the usual explanation: that King George II rose at that moment, moved by the holy text and in awe of Handel's genius. Even then, what seems like the piece's choral climax comes not at the end, where a film director might place it—all rolling timpani and fanfare trumpets—but about two-thirds of the way through. At that point in the performance, audience members usually start looking at their programs, reminding themselves that there is still quite a bit left to go. For close to three hundred years, in fact, people have been talking about how, if it were up to them, they might give the *Messiah* a quick edit.

Most remarkable of all, however, is the fact that a confection of spiraling solos and soaring choruses, its words ancient and often opaque, somehow feels like a relevant, grown-up way of engaging with the present. The text is filled with questions that sound wholly contemporary. There is despair at the disorder of the world and exasperation at the lies gobbled up by a gullible public. "Why do the nations so furiously rage together," a bass soloist asks in the middle of the *Messiah*, the words taken from the second Psalm, "and why do the people imagine a vain thing?" There is speculation about the finality of death and the legacies that we leave behind. "O death, where is thy sting? O grave, where is thy victory?" an alto and a tenor sing in a duet based on Paul's first letter to the Corinthians. There are affirmations that we need not think of life as a solo act, that we are lodged inside a universe far vaster than we can understand. "If God be for us," a soprano asks right before the closing chorus, again intoning Paul's words to the early church in Rome, "who can be against us?"

The *Messiah* doesn't so much seek solace in these scriptures as put them to use. Listen closely enough to the words, and what emerges is a set of linked meditations on the proper way of seeing the human predicament. Every performance begins with a promise. "Speak ye comfortably to Jerusalem," a tenor sings in the opening aria, the words again drawn from Isaiah, "and cry unto her that her warfare is accomplished, that her iniquity is pardoned." Take heart, the text says, because real power doesn't lie in force or violence. The sins of the past are forgiven, the long arc of justice already guaranteed. The performance then runs through a gritty, relatable account of everyday hardship, extraordinary agony, and, a little over two hours later, a higher victory. "Blessing and honor, glory and power, be unto Him that sitteth upon the throne, and unto the Lamb, for ever and ever," booms the final fugue of a chorus, before settling into a three-minute-long "Amen."

Even without the theology, the core messages come through. To remake the world, start by rethinking it. This moment is not eternity, this particular misery part of a bigger story. There is comfort in placing yourself in the cosmos. Failing to comprehend the vastness is still a kind of success. An experience that feels like defeat may turn out to be the most glorious moment of your life.

That is perhaps why Martin Luther King Jr. turned to the *Messiah* in one of his most famous speeches. "We must discover the power of love, the power, the redemptive power of love. And when we discover that we will be able to make of this old world a new world," he said from the pulpit of his church in Montgomery, Alabama, in 1957. "We can hear another chorus singing: 'Hallelujah, hallelujah! He's King of Kings and Lord of Lords. Hallelujah, hallelujah!'"

King's message was about loving one's enemies rather than despising them, and he found a similar idea running like a glinting thread through Handel's words and music. In a world of pain and suffering, the triumph of goodness depends on the radical power of acting contrary to expectations. The first step, King taught, is to imagine a world fundamentally different from the one outside your front door. A few years later, when he returned to that theme on the steps of the Lincoln Memorial, in his "I Have a Dream" speech, he used the same text that Handel had borrowed from Isaiah. A more just world, King and Handel both saw, would be one where "every valley shall be exalted, and every mountain and hill made low."

IF THE WORDS, images, and ideas that Handel wove together in the 1740s still seem resonant today, it is in large part because all of us—

you, me, and the *Messiah*—are products of that same era, just not in the way we might think.

At the end of the eighteenth century, the pamphleteer Thomas Paine looked back on his lifetime and named it "the age of reason," a moment that had seen "the general wreck of superstition, of false systems of government, and false theology." Later historians sifted through the thousands of texts published in European cities in this period and selected a canon of writings that seemed to confirm Paine's view of a watershed in human thought: a collective rethinking of the basis of government, the power of science, and the proper understanding of society, produced by writers and talkers from John Locke to Mary Wollstonecraft, Jean-Jacques Rousseau to David Hume. As college courses in a thing called Western civilization would later teach, philosophers and polymaths such as these helped perfect the scientific method. They cataloged universal freedoms and established the ideal of state power constrained by individual rights and law. They affirmed the possibility of progress. As the historian Peter Gay argued in a classic study, their lifetimes framed a historical era that at last witnessed humans' "recovery of nerve" over the "pitiless cycles" of starvation, epidemics, and an early death.

Anyone alive today inhabits a world shaped by the eighteenth century's slow, epochal change in how humans measure reality, relate to one another, and assess the future. But to the people who knew that century firsthand—by living in it—the triumphalist version of their era, full of reasoned debate and cosmic confidence, would have come as a surprise. "If it is now asked whether we at present live in an *enlightened* age," the German philosopher Immanuel Kant wrote, by coincidence in the same year as the Handel commemoration in Westminster Abbey, "the answer is: No, but we do live in an age of *enlightenment*." In one sentence Kant had helped name a historical era while also acknowledging its limitations.

The Enlightenment as most people actually experienced it had fewer wigs and masked balls than we might imagine today, and far more pain and muddling through. Its advances in science and new philosophies of government emerged alongside expansively lethal war making, deepening human bondage, marginalized women, grinding poverty, neglected children, and a host of other private and public ills. By the early eighteenth century, much of Europe had only recently emerged from decades of religious warfare, social collapse, and regicide—the chaotic, interlinked conflicts of the Thirty Years' War on the Continent and waves of civil war in England, Scotland, and Ireland. Individuals and families had close-up knowledge of the failures of human reason and the fragility of social order: a father who never returned from battle, a village burned by an invading army, a church ransacked by people who called themselves Christians.

During Handel's lifetime, his adopted country became the United Kingdom in something like its modern form, with a single parliament and economy. The Royal Navy guarded commercial networks stretching from India to the Americas against the country's chief imperial rival, France—a fact celebrated in the anthem "Rule, Britannia!," which was composed just two years before the *Messiah*. But assertions of great-power invincibility covered up divisions at home and dilemmas abroad.

Politicians and critics traded barbs via pamphlets and cartoons in much the way that social media works now. Insurrections, riots, and rebellions regularly shook the governing establishment. A sizable portion of British society regarded the reigning royal line, the house of Hanover, as illegitimate. An underground conspiracy sought to bring back an older dynasty, the Stuarts, who had themselves been ousted in an earlier plot. At the same time, a series of imperial wars from central Europe to the Caribbean to India swelled the national debt and led to a string of bad decisions that would culminate in the loss of thirteen of Britain's North American colonies. And at the center of it all—family wealth, imperial finances, international trade—lay the horrors of transoceanic slavery. By the last decade of the century, more than a hundred thousand people a year were being purchased or kidnapped in Africa and taken across the Atlantic, a quarter or more of them on vessels flying the British flag. For the youngest on board, born en route, the first thing they saw in the world was the hold of a slave ship.

One way to retrain ourselves to understand the Enlightenment, to see it as complex history instead of our own idealized prologue, is to listen to the people who knew it, sang it, and dramatized it. The truly pressing theme in their art, music, theater, philosophy, and theology was not, in fact, the triumph of rationality. It was instead how to manage catastrophe. In speculative treatises and stage plays, paintings and works of music, one of the Enlightenment's overlooked preoccupations turns out to be the practical grounds for remaining hopeful when the everyday evidence seems to point in the opposite direction. In this way, the *Messiah* matters not just as an epic piece of music but also as a record of a way of thinking, an archive in song handed down from a period of profound anxiety about improving the world whose deepest message is that one nevertheless had to try.

Wade into the words of the *Messiah*, and it isn't hard to find a kind of message in a bottle: a reflection on some of the largest questions of human life, written at a moment—warring, worried, and somehow just wrong—when people could feel the urgency of answering them. In an age supposedly governed by progress, why *do* the nations so furiously rage together? Why do people concoct vain and bizarre versions of the truth? What do we do with the knowledge of our own brokenness—our listless wandering, astray like sheep—and the trail of blood that our actions, and our obliviousness, will leave in the historical record? Adrift in a maddening world, is there really a way to live the advice that Handel set to song from the book of Isaiah: "Lift up thy voice with strength; lift it up, be not afraid. . . . Arise, shine, for thy light is come, and the glory of the Lord is risen upon thee"?

When audiences stand at the "Hallelujah" chorus or belt out their parts in an amateur sing-along, they are participating in some of the foundational problems of the eighteenth century and ones that, in various ways, we still face today. The ravages of markets, the evident failures of human reason, the awfulness produced by well-intentioned schemes for betterment, the sheer contradictions of modern life—all of these things were readily apparent at the time. And if these matters also feel weighty now, at a moment when we are beginning to understand, as never before, the essential connectedness of humans to one another and our frail dependence on the natural world, it is because people three centuries ago were already pioneering how to manage them. One of the major puzzles of that era turns out to be also one of ours: how to live despite what you already know about the world's faults, as well as your own.

The *Messiah* is a piece of modern music built out of very old words, but what it offers is not blind faith in them. It is instead the working out in music of a purposeful, systematic, and moral imagination of things you can't yet see—something that turns out to be as much a product of the Enlightenment as human rights, equality, or progress. In fact, it is this habit of mind that enabled them all: the ability to envision a different reality, full of wonder and promise, and expect that the world as you find it can be nudged in that direction.

Thinking in this way is not really a disposition or a philosophy but more like a skill, something that requires practice as well as a good model. To posit a believable version of a brighter future takes faith—if you want to call it that—or to put it another way, a facility for reasoning contrary to lived experience. The first step is to hold fast to the conviction that the world to come need not look like the one we see before us. That is one of the reasons the *Messiah* continues to move listeners without demanding that they share its religious point of view. At its most profound, the *Messiah* lays out an entire method for seeing the uses of adversity—not by naively claiming that life is easy or always beautiful but by starting from the premise that the world, long before we enter it, is already infused with purpose.

OF ALL THE SECRETS the *Messiah* might hold, however, perhaps the most surprising is that it wasn't Handel's—or at least not *only* his.

The original idea and the selection of sacred texts belonged not to Handel but to the emotionally tormented Charles Jennens, a country squire and political dissident who found solace in the elevating power of awe. The *Messiah*'s record of eliciting powerful emotion starts with the life and talents of Susannah Cibber, an actor plagued by an abusive husband and mired in scandal whose plan for escape involved a risky return to the stage. Its opening night in Dublin hung on none other than Jonathan Swift, the Irish cleric and satirist whose personal demons very nearly wrecked Handel's plans, before his better angels came forward to save them.

Even then, it took close to a decade for the *Messiah* to reach wider acclaim as Handel's most recognizable and important work. That outcome flowed directly from the labors of an Atlantic sea captain and penniless philanthropist, Thomas Coram, a person whose animating mission was not promoting music but rescuing other people's children. In turn, the era's art, wealth, and power all rested on a common source—enslavement—an abstract word for wrecked families and shattered fortunes, like those of Ayuba Diallo, an African Muslim man held captive in the American colonies but working, against all reasonable hope, to return home.

In the middle of these entangled lives was Handel himself, composer to kings but, by his late fifties, in ill health, straining to keep an audience's attention, and on the threshold of a decision that would determine his entire artistic legacy. In turn, his own life and times were shaped by some of the foremost writers, artists, and political figures of the age: the poets John Gay and Alexander Pope; the painter and printmaker William Hogarth; the playwright and theater mogul Colley Cibber; monarchs such as Queen Anne and the first two King Georges, as well as the pretenders to the British throne (or rightful heirs, depending on how one looked at it), the exiled Stuarts; along with an entire cast of composers, instrumentalists, and singers such as the Italian castrati Farinelli and Senesino, male sopranos and altos whose sexual ambiguity made them superstars of the wild, rule-breaking musical period that would come to be called the Baroque.

This book grew out of my search for this deeper *Messiah*, the one built not by a lone genius—what is ever built by a lone genius?—but by a time, place, and group of individuals whose lives resonate powerfully even today. Tracking down their stories involved research in archives, libraries, and landscapes in England, Ireland, Scotland, Italy, and the United States: wending through streets to locate a theater that transformed a musician's future; turning the pages of a private notebook that contained the record of a life's work; holding a map drawn by a kidnapped man on the eve of his freedom; hacking through underbrush to find a lost temple of love; and then, in a windowless room in London, poring over the original manuscript of the *Messiah* itself—a miracle of survival, smaller in size than you might expect, and covered in the musical notes and scribbles that Handel inked onto the staff paper late one summer, with no way of knowing what it would eventually become.

The characters at the heart of this book lived the themes that listeners find in the *Messiah* today: the meaning of suffering, the possibility of justice, the sources of redemption. Handel's earliest audiences lived them as well, which is why they were often divided on whether what they had just heard was magnificent or unnerving or somehow both. Tragedy has causes, and writing about the past is often an inventory of them. But survival, too, has a history—or, more accurately, histories, which might be narrated differently depending on one's language, culture, or religion. This version runs through the extraordinary trials of people whose intertwined lives, set against the backdrop of eighteenth-century Britain, helped create a work that manages to be transcendent art as well as practical philosophy. The *Messiah*'s form is a Christian story of God's plan for humanity's salvation. Its substance, however, is the struggle to think ourselves toward hope.

PART I

Portents

☙ 1 ☙

"The Famous Mr. Hendel"

LONDON, 1717

The Thames was tiled with boats late on a midsummer Wednesday, the kind of liquid English evening where twilight seems to last forever. His Most Sacred Majesty George I, three years into his reign, had set out in a gilded barge around eight o'clock. River craft brimming with duchesses, earls, and other "Persons of Quality," as one witness put it, now jostled for position near him on the water. On another ceremonial barge, fifty violinists, trumpeters, and other musicians cycled through minuets, airs, and hornpipes.

Surrounding the courtiers in silk gowns and powdered wigs, commoners paddled along in their own rowboats and skiffs, laughing and hurling creative insults at one another across the water. "You pimps to your own mothers, stallions to your sisters, . . . christened out of a chamber pot, how dare you show your ugly faces upon the river of Thames, and fright the king's swans?" rowers and wherrymen were known to cry. "You offspring of a dunghill, and brothers to a pumpkin . . . hold your tongues . . . or I'll whet my needle upon mine arse and sew your lips together," might come the reply.

As the raucous procession passed by, onlookers gawked and chittered on dry land. The people, reported a Swiss observer, were *"sans nombre."* Every now and then, a cheer might ripple through the ranks, starting beyond earshot and rolling closer, like a rainstorm combing through a clump of willows.

To any newcomer in the crowd, nature itself seemed to bend to the king's will. From Whitehall to Westminster, past Lambeth and the pleasure gardens at Vauxhall, the slow-moving current was drawing the boats, astonishingly, upriver. A child on the embankment could have challenged the sovereign to a race and won—by running in what would have been, on any ordinary day, the wrong direction.

The entire affair, it turned out, had been planned on a waterman's secret.

Travelers coming to London by sea were sometimes surprised when their sailing ships anchored at the mouth of the Thames and then simply waited—not for a shift in the wind but for a change in the water. Depending on the hour, the river flowed either forward or backward, pushed along by the estuarial tide, carrying lost boots, schools of pike and carp, occasionally corpses, and just now royals and nobility headed toward supper and an evening's entertainment at a garden villa upstream in Chelsea. Early the next morning, with the water returned to its normal state, George floated back home and allowed everyone finally to retire to bed.

Two days later, when a newspaper gave an account of the outing, the most remarkable thing was reckoned to be not the king and his mobile court, swept along by a reversible river, but rather "the finest Symphonies, compos'd express for this Occasion," and the German who had written them. He was thirty-two years old, graced with a royal pension, and comfortable in four languages. He was said to have survived a sword thrust when an opponent's blade landed on a button. He had attached himself to dukes who became princes and princes who became kings. It would take the better part of a century for other people to rearrange his latest work, composed in bright major keys built for the outdoors, and drag it into a concert hall. Its title, *Water Music*, would forever carry a whiff of cow parsley and river mud. But chroniclers were already calling him "the famous Mr. Hendel," and on this splendid July evening, a few months into his thirty-third year, he had every reason to believe one obvious thing: the right river, taken at the flood, could work miracles.

❧

GEORGE FRIDERIC HANDEL—one of the ways he would eventually spell his name—was a native of Halle in Saxony, part of the mosaic of central European kingdoms, principalities, duchies, and free cities that formed the Holy Roman Empire. He was born in February 1685, in the long shadow of conflicts over religion and territory later called the Thirty Years' War. The war had begun with an event that history students would remember for its comical name: the defenestration of Prague, in 1618, when local Protestants showed their contempt for the emperor's Catholic representatives by tossing them from a castle window. Disagreements over political and religious authority exploded into military crises. Other powers, from Sweden to the Ottoman Empire, lined up to defend allies or take advantage of disorder.

What followed was a misery of pitched battles, guerrilla raids, failed harvests, and waves of typhus and plague. The Protestant city of Magdeburg, north of Halle on the Elbe River, was leveled by house-to-house arson. A soldier along the Rhine reported that towns had "neither cat nor dog," since villagers had eaten them all. In Bavaria wolves stalked humans in packs. Across the German lands, mayors ordered the burning of women who were blamed for witching the world into such calamity. Some parts of Europe lost perhaps 20 percent of their populations, a multiple of the casualty rates during the twentieth century's two world wars. In all, as many as eight million people might have died as a result of combat or its consequences. The Peace of Westphalia, which ended the conflict in 1648, promised a war-free future that would be "Christian, general, and permanent." Religious disputes among Catholics, Calvinists, and Lutherans were, in theory, relegated to matters of communal organization and conscience, not pretexts for violence.

Handel's father, Georg Händel, the son of a coppersmith, had grown up amid Europe's forever war. With displaced villagers clogging the roads and cities besieged by foreign mercenaries, he made a living by assuaging human pain. His income came from retainers he was paid as a physician to aristocratic families—their official barber-surgeon, in the language of the day—supplemented by earnings as a pub keeper and public health official. During the era's frequent epidemics, his job was to cordon off neighborhoods and minister to doomed patients. One of them was his own wife, who succumbed to the plague. Georg soon remarried, to a woman some thirty years his junior, Dorothea Taust, the daughter of a Lutheran minister. One of the children they had together, the first to survive infancy, was George Frideric.

The new household was complicated and multigenerational, with crisscrossing relationships that made Dorothea something close to her own great-aunt, when one of her siblings married one of her step-grandchildren. Amid this swirl George Frideric might have been expected to follow his father into the healing business or perhaps advance into a profession such as the law. His interests, however, ran in a different direction.

Even in a provincial city such as Halle, music was everywhere: in the liturgy of the Gothic Marktkirche, the Protestant church where his parents had George Frideric baptized; in the celebrated boys' choir of a local orphanage; in the courtly calendar of the Duke of Saxe-Weissenfels, the local landowner; and in the popular songs that accompanied flagons of wine passed around in the Yellow Stag, Georg's establishment in the town center. Once Georg and Dorothea gave their son an opportunity to pluck a violin string or press down on an organ key, the sound coming at once from nowhere and everywhere, the feeling must have been electric. He was the kind of child for whom fiddling with an instrument was less a parental requirement than a personal fixation. In later life he would apparently say that as a boy he had hidden a clavichord, a small keyboard, in the attic so he could practice without disturbing the family. The story was dubious, given that no one plays an instrument inside a house in secret, but telling in its specificity, like an adult recalling the childhood thrill of reading a favorite book past bedtime.

The boy's ability was immediately recognizable to people who met him. But the world was full of talent. Johann Ambrosius Bach's son Johann Sebastian had been born a few weeks after George Frideric in Eisenach, a two-day coach ride away. The young Johann, however, was reared in a family of established violinists and organists, not bloodletters and pastors. (The two would remain in separate worlds; even in later life, they never met.) For his part, George Frideric's father seems to have had doubts about his son's enthusiasms. At first he practically swatted the boy's fingers away from the keys whenever he had a chance. Yet Georg would have understood that, whatever the line of work, making a living depended on training and patronage. Both were as essential to barber-surgeons as to musicians.

Georg eventually arranged for his son to receive lessons in organ, violin, and composition from Friedrich Wilhelm Zachow, the organist in the Marktkirche, which towered over Halle's market square, a short walk away from the family home. George Frideric slid into an apprenticeship not unlike the ones his father and grandfather would have known: watching a master, learning by doing, copying the best examples of the craft. Over the next several years as Zachow's pupil, he filled up notebooks with musical figures and phrases. He puzzled through which arrangement of sounds produced a particular effect and which ones were amateurish or, by convention, simply wrong. To discover why a composition worked from the inside, you had to touch the welds and pieces, to feel how the seams separated perfection from disaster. He would keep some of these early exercises and sketches into adulthood.

When George Frideric was eleven, his father died suddenly. The household Georg left behind, now headed by a widow, was dependent on frugality and the kindness of relations. Ensuring against an uncertain future seemed a wise course. A few years later, the young Handel began attending lectures at the local university, with no particular specialization in mind, while also taking a position as an organist in Halle's cathedral, the Domkirche. According to his appointment letter, he was required to be present for services before the last peal of the church bells, keep the organ in good repair, mind the elders, and live "Ein Christliches und erbauliches Leben," a Christian and upstanding life. Instead, he chose to leave.

After a year at the cathedral, Handel moved to Hamburg, a dynamic free port on the Elbe. Over the previous century and a half, foreign arrivals—Sephardic Jews, French Huguenots, Dutch Protestants—had swelled the city's entrepreneurial class and expanded its commercial networks. Ships arrived from the Baltic Sea, the Mediterranean, and beyond, laden with raisins, sugar, tobacco, salt, and iron. Hamburg's guilds fiercely guarded their autonomy in the wider empire, and in the decades since the Thirty Years' War they had turned their wealth toward urban renewal. A planned city with grid-like streets and new civic buildings grew up beyond the old town's medieval battlements.

With the patronage of its mercantile core, Hamburg's community of artists surpassed anything Handel had known in Halle. The city's opera house, which opened in the 1670s, was the largest theater in northern Europe. According to Johann Mattheson, a young composer and musician who knew him there, Handel started off playing "a *ripieno* violin in the opera orchestra"—meaning part of the violin section rather than a soloist—"and behaved as if he could not count five; being naturally inclined to dry humour." He occasionally traded lessons for meals and, after a while, began to write his own music.

Among Hamburg's musicians, young men of quick talent and quicker tempers, barely into their twenties, rivalries could be as intense as friendships. After one performance, Handel and Mattheson reportedly took up swords to settle a dispute over command of the harpsichord. Mattheson's rapier landed on a large metal button on Handel's coat (or in another version of the story, a rolled-up score, which is too perfect to be believed). Mattheson would later boast that he had saved Handel's life with his poor swordsmanship.

Hamburg's instrumentalists and occasional composers played where required, in churches or private homes, traveling when necessary, making do. To get to a performance in another town, a musician might squeeze inside a crowded coach next to a pigeon seller and his birds. If no one was available to pump the bellows on a church organ, he could pull in the pastry maker's son down the way. Handel was beginning to settle into a fraternity of itinerant provincial performers, surviving on wits and whim, with no grand plan for what came next. His prospects began to change, however, when he met a visitor bearing the storied name of de' Medici.

FOR PEOPLE OF HANDEL and Mattheson's generation, the kind of artistic life they dreamed of in Hamburg was already being fully lived several hundred miles to the south. In Italy a patchwork of kingdoms, duchies, and city-states had been pitted against one another during the Thirty Years' War. In most fighting seasons, some part of the Italian peninsula was overrun by armies, beset by pirates, or ravaged by plague or smallpox. But over the previous century, Venetians, Florentines, Neapolitans, and others had together set in motion a revolution in sonic common sense: a profound change in the conventions of musical form, perceptions of beauty, and expectations about what counted as obvious or wrongheaded art.

In Venice the organist Giovanni Gabrieli had insisted that instruments should take advantage of their full range of volume. A composer could command them to play boldly or quietly, even in the same composition, to achieve a specific effect. Notes also interacted with the space that hosted them, he pointed out, sounding different to a listener's ear depending on where performers were situated. In Mantua the choirmaster Claudio Monteverdi had abandoned the Renaissance habit of placing voices in competition. Instead of battling one another in a tournament of melodies, some singers might retreat before a single dominant line, their words newly comprehensible above a gentle instrumental accompaniment. In Rome the violinist Arcangelo Corelli was reimagining the principles of harmony and counterpoint. Music could produce something like an idea, with notes moving toward a destination, passing through dissonant, painful pairings, and then resolving into rightness and light.

To think of sound as having a structure—to believe that something as ephemeral as vibrations in the air could be bound by rules or liberated by innovation—was not new. More than two millennia earlier, Plato had written of an Athenian who was disgusted that musicians of his time "contaminated laments with hymns and paeans with dithyrambs . . . and created a universal confusion of forms." But across Europe, Italians were shaping a new mental ordering of music, with a common vocabulary for talking about purposeful sound. A cantata required instruments and voices to operate as a collective. An opera told a story in song. A sonata was built around a theme developed by an instrumentalist. A concerto addressed multiple themes, with responsibility for elaborating them shared among cohorts of musicians. As far away as Halle or Hamburg, it had already become impossible to talk about musical form and style without lapsing into pidgin Italian.

To make music was to chart one's own course through a human-created maze. But practicing inherited conventions, as Handel had learned to do at Zachow's organ bench, was also a way of digging oneself out of them. "So little are they to be learnt by rule," Handel's earliest biographer, John Mainwaring, wrote of the Italian approach to things, "that they are not unfrequently direct violations of rule." The result was an aural world of dictates and requirements that also brimmed with freshness and creativity. Instruments could speak an opinion and then have it echoed back, changed or inverted. Melodies could shift key and wind back on themselves, perhaps repeating da capo, from the top, with a new variation on something a listener had heard only moments before. A composer might hint at a melody, which individual virtuosi had the liberty to spin into a floating improvisation, something subtly original and unreproducible. Alongside the melodic instruments, a company of bass or chordal performers, the *basso continuo*—a harpsichord, organ, or lute, say—might be given general instructions on the progression of chords inside a piece of music, which, like modern jazz musicians, they were then free to realize in their own way.

Living in the artistic realm that Italians had created meant accepting the existing order of the world while also undermining it. You started by imagining a normalcy different from the one outside your window. A woman might sing a man's part as a travesty—*en travesti*, meaning literally a change of clothes—a term that would only later come to mean abnormal or an affront. A man could sing from the edges of his vocal cords and leap into a high falsetto, his false voice. He could do so with even greater range as a castrato, someone whose testes had been removed before his voice had hardened in puberty, a procedure practiced in Italy, the Ottoman Empire, and elsewhere for centuries. Onstage he might play a steel-clad knight, soaring above the battlefield with the voice of an angel. Castrati superstars—Nicolini, Pasqualini, Pauluccio, Momo, Farinelli, Senesino, Guadagni—were paid gargantuan fees for a season's performances. In public they could be swarmed by adoring admirers, both male and female. "Some of them had got it into their Heads, that truly the Ladies were in Love with them," a lengthy French treatise on Italian castrati reported in 1718, "and fondly flattered themselves with mighty Conquests."

In a theater the powerful could sound like women. Ancient gods could walk among men. Wars could end not in gore and death but in communal song. Doing all of this well required intellect and discernment, knowledge of musical form and its effects, and, most important, a sense of sociability. Players and singers were guided by instructions written on a staff, but the notes were suggestions rather than edicts. In a soundscape that allowed uncertainty and impromptu change, musicians had to be both self-aware and neighborly, a skill also necessitated by the technology of the time. A quiet harpsichord could speak comfortably alongside a human voice or a few violins but not more. A lute-like theorbo, with its gentle strings and absurdly long neck, could manage a coiled horn as a partner, but only if its bell were turned discreetly away from the listener. Even a trumpet could cooperate peaceably with other instruments when played in its upper register, where the physics of its metal tubing gave the player more notes to choose from, their timbre more like a warbling bird than a blaring call to arms.

No one had yet given music of this type a label. When they did, the one they chose was also a slur, like punk or grunge. It was the French *baroque*, used in English for the first time in 1765 and perhaps derived from a Portuguese term for a rough pearl or a mouthful of irregular teeth. To its enthusiasts, that was precisely the point. An orchestra of the period was also an intentional community, often assembled for a specific occasion, smaller than in later centuries, and with no need for a conductor—a role covered by the keyboard player or lead violinist and preserved in the modern term "concertmaster." The music they made was solicitous and scrappy, risky and intimate. It soared and swerved, thrilling and dangerous, at odds with everything that had come before, and, to the artists who came after, the perfect example of wildness and excess. But to those who lived it, at the core of their work lay the belief that human creativity could best be used to make an intense, weird, and complicated conversation, sloughing off old conventions while manufacturing bold new ones. "We have freed ourselves from the narrow limits of ancient music," Handel would later tell Matteson.

Among those who understood these attractions best were Ferdinando and Gian Gastone de' Medici, sons of the Grand Duke of Tuscany. Their family's wealth had shaped European culture for three hundred years, and the brothers were passionate stewards of that inheritance. Ferdinando, the grand prince and heir to the throne, was patron to a harpsichord builder from Padua, Bartolomeo Cristofori, who had experimented with replacing the instrument's internal quills with tiny mallets—striking the strings rather than plucking them—an innovation that would evolve into the modern piano. The Medici were collectors, of people as well as art, and they traveled widely in assembling their treasures. On a visit to Hamburg, Gian Gastone apparently saw Handel perform. "A sort of intimacy [developed] betwixt them," according to Mainwaring, and they talked frequently about "the state of Music in general, and on the merits of Composers, Singers, and Performers in particular."

Somewhere in their conversations, Gian-Gastone proposed that Handel come back with him to Tuscany, where "no conveniences should be wanting." For a theater musician from Halle, this new opportunity wasn't just a matter of advancement. Italy promised a leap into another possible life, one of falsetto heroes and unsexed warriors, instruments straining against their nature, an upending of expectations. After some period of time, saving his own money to add to whatever he might receive from his prospective patron, Handel decided to go. By 1706 he had left Hamburg and headed south.

HANDEL TOOK UP a residency of sorts in Florence, receiving food, comfortable lodging, and perhaps a purse of gold coins or other valuable goods in exchange for composing and performing. His acquaintance with the Medici opened pathways toward other supporters and partners as well: cardinals in Rome, republican patricians in Venice, and the very circles of composers and instrumentalists whose work had first captured his imagination as a boy. He wrote and played, offered occasional lessons, and immersed himself in cities that seemed alive with sound, where rustic bagpipers, *pifferari*, wended through the streets at Christmastime. For now at least, Handel could survive on the speed of his writing quill and the condescension—the favor, that is, meted out by one's social superiors—of those willing to pay for it.

He was beautiful, which helped. Handel was "tall, strong, broad-shouldered, and muscular," according to Mattheson. A miniature from the period, thought to be Handel, showed him with a long face and dark, doe-like eyes peering out above a slightly upturned nose. His lips naturally settled into a faint smile that anticipated the punch line of a joke before he even uttered it, an expression that would last into old age. "He always had a dry way of making the gravest people laugh," Mattheson remembered, "without laughing himself."

People could fall in love with him. There were close encounters with women, including a rumored infatuation—hers more than his, apparently—with Vittoria Tarquini, a Florentine soprano and wife of a French violinist who also happened to be Grand Prince Ferdinando's mistress. More often it seemed to be the men who were taken with his vibrancy, his hatred of tameness, his "fire and force," as Mainwaring put it. During rehearsals he was known to snatch an instrument from a musician's hands and render a difficult passage himself. In a social world dominated by men and their passions, it was easy to imagine Handel as the mythical Orpheus, a person who lost out on ordinary love but replaced it with extraordinary, prophetic art.

In older men he could inspire not just admiration but the surrendering awe that comes from witnessing a younger man's potential on the verge of being unleashed. "A graceful youth, / Awakens sweet delight / With enticing tones," wrote Cardinal Benedetto Pamphili in a text that Handel set to music in Rome in 1707. "His hand has wings." (A flatterer and "an old Fool!" Handel would later say of the cardinal.) In Rome he performed in the vaulted halls of Palazzo Bonelli, the home of the city's wealthiest aristocratic patron, Francesco Maria Ruspoli. On Wednesdays he could be found at the weekly assemblies hosted by Cardinal Pietro Ottoboni, a sensualist and connector who gathered performers like statuary. At his Palazzo della Cancelleria, Ottoboni staged grand concerts accompanied by ices and other sumptuous refreshments but "pestered with Swarms of trifling little *Abbés* who come thither on purpose to fill their bellies with these Liquors, and to carry off the Crystal Bottles, with the Napkins into the Bargain," according to one exasperated guest.

By the fall of that year, Handel was back in Florence, then in Venice for Christmas. One evening the Neapolitan composer Domenico Scarlatti saw him exercising a harpsichord while wearing a Venetian mask—identifiable not by sight but by sound, his playing devilish and brilliant, teetering on the edge of his own ability. He was in Rome again in early 1708, possibly Naples sometime later, then Florence and Venice again in 1709. At the end of that year, he presented a new composition, the opera *Agrippina*, at the opening of the Venetian Carnevale. In a city of damp fog and jade-colored canals, crowded with winter masquerades, the work reveled in fading splendor: the story of a scheming mother and a contest for power in ancient Rome, but here played for laughs. *Agrippina* ran for twenty-seven nights straight at the Teatro San Giovanni Grisostomo, not far from the Rialto Bridge. After the first performance, the audience reportedly erupted in wild shouts and cheers, hypnotized and "thunderstruck . . . as if they had all been distracted." Venetian society was now referring to Handel as *il caro Sassone*—the darling Saxon.

Some of Europe's greatest families peered down from five rows of boxes, like swallows clinging to a gilt cliff face. Among those who might have seen Handel that season were members of the princely house of Braunschweig-Lüneburg, the Protestant family that controlled portions of his old homeland in greater Saxony. Their principal residence was in the city of Hanover, on the rich plains of northern Germany. The family's farms had recovered after the end of the Thirty Years' War, and their position rose with the wealth of their domains. After the Peace of Westphalia, they had been elevated from a ducal household to a princely one, with the male head of the family, the prince-elector of Hanover, appointed as one of the nine nobles responsible for choosing the Holy Roman emperor. At the Leineschloss, their palace that backed onto the Leine River, and their country estate at Herrenhausen, with its manicured gardens, French was the language of conversation, tolerant Lutheranism the professed religion, and Italian opera the courtly entertainment.

In the summer of 1710, the prince-elector, Georg Ludwig, offered Handel the role of Kapellmeister, or music director, with responsibility for the family chapel and occasional entertainments arranged by the court orchestra. Among other advantages, the position carried an annual salary rather than the informal favors that came from individual commissions. Handel quickly accepted. It was an opportunity to return home—his mother, in her fifties, had gone blind and was still living in Halle—and to seal a remarkable advancement. In only a few years, the barber-surgeon's son had gone from church organist and sometime university student to personal composer to one of the empire's foremost families.

Yet if Handel had any illusions about what his successes in Italy bought in the world of German nobility and privilege, they were probably dispelled not long after being presented at court. He would have heard whispers of scandal and dark cruelties. Georg Ludwig, short and with protruding blue eyes that threatened to burst from their sockets, had married his first cousin, Sophia Dorothea of Celle. But the union had long ago ended in gruesome fashion. Suspicious that she was having an affair, Georg Ludwig permanently separated the electress from their children and sealed her inside a castle. She was still living there when Handel arrived in Hanover. Her alleged lover had mysteriously disappeared, with no news of his whereabouts and no body ever discovered.

Like a retreating tortoise, the family knew how to harden itself against outsiders. Georg Ludwig's mother, the dowager electress Sophia, wrote to her granddaughter that this new Kapellmeister was a man called "Henling"—the dismissive wave of the hand is almost visible on the page—"who plays the harpsichord so well and who is (so they say) so skilled in music. For myself I know little about it." The dowager electress's daughter had died several years earlier, and since then she found that she had little desire to be entertained. "Music makes me sad," she wrote.

There were others at court who took a stronger interest, however, and their lives would turn out to be tethered to Handel's in ways that were not apparent at the time. The entire Braunschweig-Lüneburg family was about to undergo a change of title. It was a development that would not only transform their fortunes and that of their Kapellmeister but also alter the course of world history.

~ 2 ~

"An Undertaking So Hazardous"

At a time when travel depended on fair winds and bone-rattling coaches, Handel was frequently on the move. Any performer had to stay on the leading edge of musical fashion, which meant seizing opportunities whenever they arose. Handel had accepted the position in Hanover on the condition that he be allowed to pursue other engagements. Given the reception of his latest work in Venice, he was known to prominent families from across Europe, and he had good reason to believe that further invitations would be forthcoming wherever he placed his talent on offer. After a visit to his mother in Halle, he set off across Germany, passed into Holland, and then boarded a ship on the North Sea. In the autumn of 1710, he set foot for the first time in Great Britain.

Foreign observers had long perceived England as something close to a failed state, a "Devil-land" mired in revolution, political conspiracy, and murder. The country was just emerging from more than a century and a half of religious and political disputes similar to those that Handel's family had experienced in the Holy Roman Empire. In the early seventeenth century, the Stuart dynasty, with its roots in Scotland, had drawn together the English and Scottish thrones under a single monarch, James I (or, to Scots, James VI). By the 1640s, however, old resentments over religion and local power had sparked widespread violence in Scotland and Ireland, which radiated into England as a civil war that pitted supporters of King Charles I against the forces of Parliament. Charles was captured and beheaded, and in his place Oliver Cromwell led a parliamentary republic guided by the strict teachings of Puritanism. It was only in 1660 that the Stuart line was restored under Charles's son, crowned Charles II, and a degree of peace, at least temporarily, secured.

The Restoration had changed Britain and its capital in profound and visible ways. By his twenty-fifth birthday, Handel had visited some of the greatest cities on the Continent, but nothing would have prepared him for London—a metropolis of more than 600,000 people, on its way to becoming the largest city in Europe as well as its commercial center. The only built passage across the Thames was the narrow London Bridge, whose roadway was hemmed in by shop fronts. But on the water below, the writer and pamphleteer Daniel Defoe counted two thousand seagoing ships moored or under sail, plus barges, pleasure boats, and other river craft. The Italian painter Canaletto would later render the busy waterscape as a kind of northern Venice, with crowded quays and outdoor staircases descending to the water from palatial riverside homes. "I shall not give you my Opinion of every distinct thing in this City, or an Encomium of [its] Beauty and Ornaments," reported a German visitor, Christian Heinrich Erndl, a physician like Handel's father, "lest the Splendor of so August a City shou'd be diminish'd by my weak Description."

Few places so fully showcased the ability of humans to destroy their surroundings as well as to resurrect them. The Great Fire of 1666 had swept through the oldest quarters of the city, but since then medieval houses and streets had surrendered to new squares and public works that radiated confidence—"a Prodigy of Buildings, that nothing in the World does, or ever did, surpass, except old Rome in Trajan's Time," as Defoe described it. Others were harsher in their assessments. An aspiring writer named Jonathan Swift made a checklist of the things London gutters carried toward the river in a rainstorm: "Sweepings from butchers' stalls, dung, guts, and blood / Drowned puppies, stinking sprats, all drenched in mud, / Dead cats, and turnip tops, come tumbling down the flood." Still, anyone who walked along the Thames could have captured the city's transformation in a single glance along the north bank. In the foreground was the Tower of London, ancient and fearsome, while farther upriver St. Paul's Cathedral, Christopher Wren's masterpiece of lightness and grandeur, presided over new courts and guildhalls. Its dome had been topped out just two years before Handel arrived.

The chance to see all of this would have been enough of a reason to visit, but after Italy, Handel brought with him a special cachet. As soon as other players heard him at the organ or harpsichord, they came away chastened. Ever since seeing him in Venice, Scarlatti was said to have made the sign of the cross in wry homage whenever Handel's name came up. Wealthy families who had heard him there brought back news of an astounding new talent, and few who met him were disappointed. The artist Mary Delany, later one of the century's great letter writers, met Handel not long after his arrival in London. Although she was barely ten at the time, she remembered forever that he had "performed wonders" on her family's drawing-room spinet. English musicians began to exchange testy gossip about his skill and interpretations. "Let him come! We'll handle him," a virtuoso was heard to say, which probably elicited a groan even in the eighteenth century.

Handel's timing turned out to be very good. A generation or two earlier, London's theater world had been virtually destroyed by Cromwell's commonwealth. Puritan officials banned dramatic performances and other frivolities. Sheriffs were commanded "to pull down and demolish all Playhouses within their jurisdiction, and apprehend any Persons convicted of acting, who were to be publickly whipt," according to an early history.

Since the 1660 Restoration, however, theater had been booming. Private performance venues were rising among newly built town houses and churches. Old pasturelands were being paved over, especially to the west of the City of London, the ancient district at the heart of the metropolis. Isolated hamlets were swelling into linked-up neighborhoods that would form London's West End—"the town," as it came to be called, a term that signified a specific geography as well as the city's beau monde, the nobles and gentry who constituted fashionable society. Local playwrights and composers competed with immigrant writers and performers flooding in from across Europe, attracted by the prospect of steady employment. The diarist Samuel Pepys, born in the 1630s, recorded the transformation in public entertainment in his lifetime. "Nor do I dote on the eunuches," he wrote about the Italian castrati who had started to appear on London's stages—which implied that plenty of other people did.

With English tastes changing and a supply of continental artists on hand, theater managers were eager to offer new musical works in the Italian style. One of them was a man of Handel's age named Aaron Hill. People who knew Hill thought of him as a tireless purveyor of projects and schemes, with no particular logic connecting them. As a sometime writer and poet, he would eventually publish a history of the Ottoman Empire, sketch out a biography of Peter the Great, and make a start on an epic in verse about the biblical hero Gideon, which he never finished. He later lost a fortune trying to corner the market in beechnuts. "An imagination as lively as his," recalled one of his acquaintances, "seldom, if ever, [went] hand in hand with solid judgment." But at roughly the same time Handel arrived in London, Hill hit on what he was sure was a brilliant new idea.

The institution he helped run, the Queen's Theatre, had opened only a few years earlier in a bustling district in London's western reaches, on the site of an old stable yard known as the Haymarket. Its builder, the well-known architect and playwright John Vanbrugh, had created a "vast triumphal Piece of Architecture," as a contemporary source called it. Friezes framed the stage. Three-dimensional Corinthian columns faded into flat trompe l'oeil paintings. The theater was not permitted to host serious dramas; that privilege was restricted to two older establishments farther to the east, in Drury Lane and Lincoln's Inn Fields, both with royal patents, or licenses, a legacy of the Cromwell-era ban. But since the Queen's Theatre was allowed to stage works that contained music, Hill proposed to offer a spectacle of grand proportions, capitalizing on the Haymarket's location and showcasing the city's slide westward.

The show, he decided, would be a musical version of a well-known Italian epic poem, a story of love and magic played out in Jerusalem at the time of the First Crusade. The storyline had already proved popular with audiences abroad, since it had nearly everything one could want: a Christian general, his chaste daughter, a valiant knight, a Saracen king, and even a terrifying "Amazonian enchantress." It would be called *Rinaldo,* after the crusading knight, and by the final chord the infidels would be happily converted to Christianity.

Hill vowed to "spare no Pains or Cost, that might be requisite to make these Entertainments flourish in their proper Grandeur." By early 1711 he had gathered a small team to work on the production. He sourced a text from an émigré Italian master. He approached Handel, who was just settling into London society, for a score. He set craftsmen to work building sets and movable scenery. It was a convergence of opportunities that seemed to satisfy everyone, including Handel himself, a visiting composer—the Leineschloss was still expecting his return to Hanover—eager to place his talents before new audiences. Handel raced to make the deadline for rehearsals, recycling older compositions and adapting some of his best material to fit the new words and plot, all in perhaps two weeks.

"My little Fortune," Hill later wrote, now rested entirely on "an Undertaking so hazardous." As with his other projects, things soon began to falter. The tight production schedule, the complex scenery designs, and the performance's sheer ambition threatened to bring everything crashing down before a note was sung. The copyist who had written out the score temporarily hid the sheet music, for fear that he would never be paid for his work. As the opening approached, a newspaper announcement mangled the title, dubbing it "Binaldo," which was gibberish.

When *Rinaldo* finally opened, however, it turned out to be every bit as breathtaking as Hill had hoped. Londoners had never seen or heard anything quite like it: more than two hours of trumpet blasts and timpani, delicate arias and martial entrances, cracking thunder and swirling Furies. Onstage, sceneshifters wheeled out war chariots, unleashed waterfalls, and caused an entire mountain to be cleft in two. According to one source, live sparrows and chaffinches chirped in a sacred grove and then launched themselves out over the seats, taking up residence in the rafters. In keeping with the Italian style, most of the characters were played by castrati or women, who enacted feats of heroism and expressed impassioned, aching love. Handel oversaw it all himself from the harpsichord, exercising the keys with insistent runs and pounding chords.

Inevitably, some of the notices were unkind. It was all pasteboard parody and costumed prancing, reviewers said, not to mention being sung in a foreign language. But even the detractors could not diminish the effect on people who experienced it. "Cara sposa, dove sei?"—my beloved wife, where are you?—sang the celebrated castrato Nicolini as Rinaldo, in a long, writhing mezzo-soprano aria for his beloved Almirena, abducted by the sorceress Armida. In the decades that followed, *Rinaldo* would be performed more frequently in Handel's lifetime than any opera he would ever compose. His melodies were by turns keening and glorious. "Lascia ch'io pianga"—Let me weep— the kidnapped Almirena sang, a slow, simple aria that managed to be both a heartrending lament and an invitation to sing along.

For many listeners, the most surprising thing about *Rinaldo* was how hummable Italian opera turned out to be. A publisher in the Strand, John Walsh, released a simplified version of the score, which meant that someone who had missed out on the spirits and sparrows haunting the theater could now encounter the music and its creator up close. "Signor Georgio Frederico Hendel," Hill had called him in the bilingual wordbook, or printed program, for *Rinaldo,* which rendered Handel more exotic than he was, but evidently to good effect. His music was now available to be tooted on an amateur's recorder or chorded on a clavichord.

Yet Hill ended up burnishing Handel's reputation in another way as well, and the evidence was right there at the front of the wordbook itself. In one of his rare acts of good judgment, Hill had decided to offer *Rinaldo* as a gift to the person whose title graced the theater where it premiered. For the first time, Handel's name was associated not with a ducal or princely family but with a royal one.

※

HERS WAS "the Best of Nations under the Best of Queens," Hill claimed in his syrupy dedication. In fact, Queen Anne had experienced nearly every moment of her adult life as torture. At her coronation in Westminster Abbey, in 1702, persistent joint pain and stiffness, perhaps the symptoms of lupus, required that she be borne aloft in a chair, her regal train trailing behind the bearers. She carried few of her pregnancies—at least seventeen in all—to term. The children who survived never made it to adulthood. A son, William, the great hope as heir and future king, died of a throat infection at the age of eleven. Her husband and consort, Prince George of Denmark, fell to lung disease and dropsy.

In her private life, Anne seemed to oscillate between despair and rage. She became increasingly unkempt and obese, with a taste for wine and spirits. She was frequently covered in sores and bandages, confined to her bed or a wheelchair, and dependent on one of her ladies-in-waiting, Sarah Churchill, Duchess of Marlborough. A brutal falling-out later caused the duchess to suggest that the queen had been involved in an affair with another courtier and one of the duchess's rivals, Abigail Masham, which sealed the image of a palace awash in deviance and sheer oddity. The duchess's rumormongering shaped how Anne would be viewed for centuries to come: as bizarre and broken, a complaining, ermine-wrapped grotesque.

Yet Anne superintended her country's transition away from an old order. The remnants of medieval life were fading into a newly emergent, self-consciously modern society. After her, no monarch would again engage in the ancient practice of using the "royal touch" to cure scrofula, a type of tuberculosis. (The writer and raconteur Samuel Johnson, as an infant, was among the last to receive the treatment; he remembered it only as a solemn meeting with "a lady in diamonds, and a long black hood.") She would be the first sovereign to rule over a genuinely united kingdom, after the English and Scottish parliaments were peacefully joined, in 1707, under a single legislature sitting in London.

For much of her time on the throne, Anne was also a warrior-queen. A month after her coronation, in 1702, Britain joined Dutch and Austrian allies against France and Spain in what came to be known as the War of the Spanish Succession. The British objective was to prevent the French royal family from adding the Spanish Empire, with its troves of silver and other sources of wealth, to France's domains. Reports of battles came in from far afield. "The Sea already swarms with French privateers," a London newspaper declared shortly after the war began. French ships harassed British commercial vessels at the entrance to the English Channel. British and Dutch forces attacked Cádiz, Málaga, and Gibraltar. On the Continent, John Churchill, Duke of Marlborough, commander of British forces (and husband of Anne's confidante Sarah), led allied troops on a long march from the Netherlands, south up the Rhine, then into Bavaria. After a battle near the village of Blenheim in the summer of 1704, as many as twenty thousand French and Bavarians lay dead, along with twelve thousand of Marlborough's own troops.

Blenheim would be celebrated as a national and personal triumph. Anne awarded the Marlboroughs a grand estate in rural Oxfordshire named for the battle, Blenheim Palace, later the birthplace of the duke's direct descendant Winston Churchill. The fighting, though, would rage on land and sea for another nine years. As the war wound on, public performances such as Hill and Handel's *Rinaldo* proved both popular and politically meaningful. Art that portrayed the war as just and forecast a final victory had uses beyond mere entertainment. It didn't take a great deal of imagination for listeners to overlay the triumphant crusaders onstage with the British. Muslim Saracens stood in for French and Spanish Catholics. "I accept your rite," sings the chastened sorceress Armida near the end, tying things up strategically as well as theologically.

Handel was already known to Anne even before *Rinaldo* premiered.

A few weeks earlier, he had composed a cantata to celebrate her birthday, with which she was reported to be "extreamly well pleas'd." The acclaim for *Rinaldo* helped seal Handel's relationship with the palace. Yet when Anne expressed her desire to see him again at court, he gently reminded her of his obligations in Hanover, to which he would soon have to return.

As Handel sailed back across the North Sea, in the autumn of 1711, it was unclear even to him whether he was going for a visit or coming home to stay. All he really knew was that for the time being his life and fortune depended on the two most powerful women he had ever met. One was Anne, in failing health but reigning over an empire growing in power and influence, with a cosmopolitan capital where Handel's name was already recognizable to people who had never met him. The other was the aging grandmother of Herrenhausen and the arbiter of influence in the court that was still, after all, his primary employer: Hanover's dowager electress, Sophia, who misremembered his name as "Henling." All three of their lives were bound together like a sailor's knot, but for reasons that had more to do with religion and politics than with music.

3

Jacobites

Anne was a professed Protestant, but she had come to the British throne amid turmoil over faith and a family betrayal because of it. Charles II had died in 1685 without an heir, which meant that the crown passed to Charles's brother—and Anne's father—James II, who happened to be Catholic. By 1688 it had become clear that he intended his infant heir and Anne's half brother, James Francis Edward Stuart, to be reared as a Catholic as well—an ambition at odds with the interests of the kingdom's largely Protestant political class. "It may be it is our brother but God only knows," Anne had told her sister Mary not long after the birth, sharing in the speculation that the child might be not only religiously suspect but also an illegitimate successor. A future Catholic dynasty now seemed assured, and as if to emphasize the point, James named the pope and King Louis XIV of France as the young prince's godfathers.

In response a coterie of English nobles hatched a conspiracy with James's Dutch son-in-law and Mary's husband, William, Prince of Orange. The plan was to oust James by landing an Anglo-Dutch army in England. When the force eventually arrived, it was a wonder to witness: larger than the storied Spanish Armada, composed of five hundred ships ferrying twenty thousand seasoned infantry and a cavalry of five thousand horses. James's forces melted away with barely a skirmish. Terrified and suffering from nosebleeds, drifting in and out of an opium-induced fog, the king himself rode out to take command of his country's defense, but to little avail. In late November, upon news that the king was retreating to London, Anne scurried down a back staircase in the palace of Whitehall, abandoning her father and publicly siding with her brother-in-law and sister, who would soon accede to the throne as William III and Mary II. Unseated in this Glorious Revolution, as William and Mary's supporters called it, James fled to France and, after an ill-fated attempt to retake the crown by invading Ireland, bided his time in exile. With the succession secure, at least for the time being, English parliamentarians turned to the problem that they believed had necessitated a revolution in the first place: the proper faith of the sovereign. In 1701 Parliament adopted an ingenious solution known as the Act of Settlement. The act established definitively that the monarch would be a Protestant.

That is how Anne came to power the following year when William unexpectedly died in a riding accident, his horse tripped up by a molehill. But the Act of Settlement created its own new problems. Over the centuries, dynastic marriages had produced royal bloodlines that meandered across Europe, running through Catholic branches as well as Protestant ones. In the last thirty years, the British throne had passed from a Catholic, James II, to a Protestant couple, William and Mary, to Anne, the Protestant daughter of a disgraced Catholic exile, who was herself without a living successor. The Act of Settlement was meant to provide a guide for the future by not only reaffirming the Protestant faith of the sovereign but also detailing how that outcome was to be guaranteed: by articulating a new line of inheritance that avoided the possibility of a Catholic monarch's ever returning to the throne at all.

The linchpin of this complex mechanism was something of a surprise. She was the dark presence that hovered over the Hanover court like an aging actor waiting to be called to center stage—Sophia, the mother of Georg Ludwig. The dowager electress's lineage was rooted in the English and Scottish royal houses. She was the granddaughter of James I and the niece of Charles II, two Stuart monarchs whose long reigns had stretched across much of the previous century. She had been raised a Calvinist and had married into another safely Protestant family, the Lutheran house of Hanover. She had even managed to produce multiple heirs—and, unlike many of the Stuarts, legitimate and healthy ones—who were already seeding royal and noble households across the Holy Roman Empire and beyond.

If no direct heirs were available after Anne, the British Parliament specified, Sophia and then her children would accede to the throne. They would become the new "*stock* and root of *inheritance* to our kings," as the statesman and political theorist Edmund Burke later put it, "in order that the monarchy might preserve an unbroken unity through all ages, and might be preserved (with safety to our religion) in the old approved mode of descent." Yet how one got to this arrangement might have strained the memory of even people well versed in royal pedigrees. A published genealogy confirming Sophia's right to reign began with ancient Rome and continued for ten pages down to Anne's day, with the author testifying to its completeness save for people "excluded because of the Popish Religion which they profess." That provision meant that dozens of people with more direct claims were left out of the reckoning. What the plan lacked in elegance, however, it made up for in certainty. Upon Anne's death, the crown would pass to the Hanoverians.

BACK AT THE LEINESCHLOSS, Handel reacquainted himself with the prince-elector's family and perhaps reintroduced himself to Sophia. He was soon at work discharging his duties as Kapellmeister in between family visits to Halle. His mind, though, seemed to be on England. "I have made some progress in that language," he wrote to a correspondent—in French—about his still-halting English. A year after returning to Hanover, in 1712 Handel asked for permission to return to Britain. Once more, the prince-elector granted him leave.

In London, Handel was welcomed with new commissions for the Queen's Theatre and a revival of *Rinaldo*. He presented a new birthday ode in Anne's honor, the spiraling, leaping "Eternal Source of Light Divine," the most movingly celebrated that the ailing queen would ever find herself in her lifetime. He offered a hymn of thanksgiving, a *Te Deum*, in celebration of the end of the conflict with France and Spain. With the Peace of Utrecht, in 1713, Anne's kingdom gained a strategic outpost at the entrance to the Mediterranean, the port of Gibraltar. The French ceded territories in North America and the Caribbean, and the British navy began to emerge as the unrivaled master of the Atlantic.

Later that year, Anne granted Handel an annual pension of two hundred pounds. It was a substantial benefit—although technically illegal, since Handel was not a British subject—and one that came just in time. Georg Ludwig had finally decided that it made little sense to waste money on an absent Kapellmeister, especially one who had aligned himself so readily with another court. Handel was quietly dropped from his official position. Legend has it that this moment signaled a temporary break with his German patrons. Handel had "contracted an affection for the diet of the land he was in," Mainwaring proposed, an explanation bizarre enough to suggest it concealed other motives. Far from being estranged from the Hanoverians, Handel was more tied to them than ever, just in a different role. "Mr. Handel . . . [has] been extremely useful . . . on several occasions," Georg Ludwig's senior diplomat in London, Christoph Friedrich Kreienberg, reported to the Leineschloss in the summer of 1713. "He will continue to tell me all he knows."

Anne had described Handel in her benefaction as "Trusty and Welbeloved," but while he was a musician to her, he was effectively a spy for her designated successors. Knowing the goings-on at court, who was in favor and who out, and, most important, any developments in Anne's health all amounted to valuable intelligence. Handel was only one minor cog in the machine of state, but in the Hanoverians' effort to keep abreast of developments in London, having more channels of information and influence was preferable to having fewer. One of his closest associates at court turned out to be the queen's physician, John Arbuthnot. Handel was "constantly at his house," reported

Kreienberg. News gleaned from a casual talk between a surgeon and a surgeon's son, over dinner or on the margins of a musical evening, would eventually make its way back to the Leineschloss.

Georg Ludwig's principal concern was one that Daniel Defoe stated succinctly in the title of a political pamphlet then making its way around London: "But what if the queen should die?" Despite the Act of Settlement, no one could be completely sure of the answer. Even with the latest war now at an end, the political future still felt insecure. In salons and coffeehouses, conversation seemed to come around inevitably to the same menacing presence, someone whose mere mention could cast a pall over a supper party or cause a tavern table to erupt in a fight. "The main thing which agitates the Minds of Men now, is the Protestant Succession," wrote Defoe, "and the Pretender."

❦

BY THE TIME Anne was crowned, James II, her father, had already died in exile in France. But her younger half brother, James Francis Edward, was very much alive. James had grown up in the Château de Saint-Germain-en-Laye, the birthplace of Louis XIV and a wonderland of regimented gardens and absolutist opulence. He had been taught from childhood, however, that his true home lay in the dominions that had been wrenched unjustly from his family's control. From the suburbs of Paris to the heart of London, a cohort of overt supporters and quiet sympathizers agreed. He was the Pretender who Defoe said haunted the English imagination.

The Jacobite cause—the royal claim of James II and his son, the notional James III, or *Jacobi* in Latin—rallied a loosely connected set of dissatisfactions: with Anne, with the Glorious Revolution, with the crown's embrace of Protestantism, with the English domination of Scotland. The fear of Jacobitism, on the other hand, was an available surrogate for general discontent with the state of the world. Nearly any prejudice could be accommodated inside a loathing of real or suspected Jacobites: hatred of Catholics, Jesuits, priests, libertines, political opponents, the Scots, the Irish, the French, or foreigners at large. Across Britain there was a deep conviction, whispered in private and reaffirmed in pamphlets and newssheets, that Jacobites were secretly everywhere, their principal symbol—a white rose—the telltale mark of an underground network of conspirators and seditionists. Through their dark influence, peace would falter, institutions of public order fail, and political disagreements turn, sooner or later, into civil war.

"At the entrance of this month we find an opposition of Saturn and Mars," noted one almanac. "Now expect to hear from several parts the worst and basest Crimes.... Now another Jacobite plot: Murderies, Robberies, and other such Mischiefs ... as acted in divers parts of this Nation, as well as others beyond the Sea." Experience showed that the stars had sometimes been right. In the late 1680s and early 1690s, Jacobite armies had fought government forces in Scotland and Ireland at places whose mere names—Killiecrankie, Athlone, the Boyne—would later evoke the terror of battle: broadswords hammering against musket barrels, plug bayonets finding their bloody mark. In 1696, Jacobite assassins were foiled in a plot to kill King William. In 1708 rumors of a French invasion in aid of hidden Jacobites had sent Londoners stocking up on food and scurrying for safety until the all clear was given.

Amid these worries, just as Handel was beginning his third summer in London, the flywheels of dynastic succession began to turn. In early June 1714, the dowager electress Sophia was walking in her gardens in Herrenhausen when a rain cloud opened up overhead. She rushed to find shelter and then collapsed, expiring short of her eighty-fourth birthday. In the weeks that followed, Anne was rendered speechless by a stroke, writhed in violent convulsions, and finally died, at the age of forty-nine. "I believe sleep was never more welcome to a weary traveler than death was to her," Arbuthnot told his friend Jonathan Swift.

Anne's death triggered the provisions of the Act of Settlement. Now that Sophia, too, had died, the succession passed to the next generation in her family tree. When the winds cooperated for a passage across the North Sea, Sophia's son Georg Ludwig and grandson Georg August sailed up the Thames to their new stations. They landed at Greenwich in a heavy fog and processed to St. James's Palace. That October, Georg Ludwig, at the age of fifty-four, was formally crowned in Westminster Abbey as George I. Georg August and his wife, Caroline, became Prince and Princess of Wales, next in line to the British and Irish thrones.

Over the coming months, a new wave of fear swept through London on news of an impending invasion by the Pretender, who sailed for Scotland in the summer of 1715, hoping to raise an army of loyalists to oppose the new king. Theaters went dark. The new royal family kept to their palaces. Jacobite forces seized strategic outposts throughout the Scottish Highlands. Rebel infantry pressed across the border, reaching as far south as the English city of Preston in Lancashire. In the end, however, feverish and ill-equipped, defeated in battles and skirmishes with British troops, James was forced to return to the Continent. Arrests and executions of suspected Jacobites followed.

※

HANDEL WATCHED these events unfold from Burlington House, a mansion in Piccadilly, one of a succession of stately homes that he would inhabit as the guest of English patrons, repeating the hopscotch existence he had known in Italy. "There Hendel strikes the strings, the melting strain," wrote the poet John Gay, "transports the soul, and thrills through ev'ry vein." His English was improving, and he was beginning to work more comfortably in setting English texts to melodies. For the rest of his life, though, listeners would joke about the *vee*'s and *dat*'s of his German accent.

Handel was soon informed that his musical service to the houses of Stuart and Braunschweig-Lüneburg would be continued under the new Hanoverian dynasty, along with back pay for the period since he had been dropped as Kapellmeister. Over the next several years, he would be bound ever more closely to the court. The Queen's Theatre was renamed the King's Theatre, which revived *Rinaldo* and premiered even more of Handel's work in the Italian style. The old pension from

Queen Anne was doubled. King George eventually awarded him copyright protection, or a "Royal Privilege," for his compositions—the first time a composer would be able to assert a legal claim of this sort—which at least theoretically blocked his sheet music from being pirated by printers. A few years later he was given the title of "Composer of Musick for His Majesty's Chappel Royal," which wrapped him into the religious rites and calendar of the palace. He would also be appointed music master to the daughters of the Prince and Princess of Wales. "Between 4 and 5 either play the harpsichord or read," went the princesses' daily schedule, "then play with Hendel." That role carried an additional salary of two hundred pounds, five times the pay of the king's rat killer, he might have noted, but slightly less than that of the dancing master. Still, responsibility for the musical education of the younger generation of Hanoverians drew him into the family that, if the Act of Settlement held, would form the rootstock from which all future British kings and queens would emerge.

In the summer of 1717, as Handel ran through the movements of his *Water Music*, floating alongside George I's royal barge on the Thames, he could only have marveled at his own meteoric rise. Only eleven years had passed since he had given up his seat as a theater musician in Hamburg for a risky leap to Italy and then London. Yet he would also have been aware of the precariousness of the regime that now sustained him. The elaborate boating party was in part political, a ploy to enliven public support for a foreign dynasty already showing signs of distress. King George took little interest in government, fumbled disinterestedly with English, and regularly removed his court to Hanover. Access to him ran through a trusted valet who had been the son of an Ottoman bey, then a prisoner of war, then a baptized and renamed Christian, Mehmet von Königstreu—Mehmet the Royalist. For advice the king tended to rely on his mistress, Melusine von der Schulenburg, and his half sister, Sophia von Kielmansegg—the Maypole and the Elephant, as Londoners cruelly dubbed them, after their appearance.

The Prince of Wales, by contrast, just two years older than Handel, appeared frequently in public with his wife, Princess Caroline, radiant and sparklingly intelligent. Their city palace, Leicester House, became a gathering place for artists and intellectuals, as well as the king's political opponents. Inside the family, relations between father and son were tense. Their disagreements ranged from who should be in charge of rearing the king's grandchildren to how to deal with the Jacobites. Beneath them all lay an old tragedy, the fate of the prince's mother, still locked away in a German castle.

Anyone connected with the court was inevitably drawn toward the dangerous crevasses that ran through Britain's royal household. "Inform me once again of the health of yourself, of mamma and all your dear family," Handel wrote to his brother-in-law from London, "so as to relieve my present anxiety and impatience." For now, he told his relatives, he was engaged in business "on which, if I may say so, my fortune depends."

4

Grub Street

At the time Handel first came to Britain, an aging Londoner could measure her life by her country's self-inflicted tragedies: a child during the civil wars that swept across England, Scotland, and Ireland; a young girl when a king was executed and a Puritan oligarchy installed; perhaps a new bride when a king was restored and a matron when another king was violently dethroned; and in her decline witness to a shaky royal succession and armed Jacobites sailing for the coast. In the 1660s, John Milton had invented a word that captured the experience of living through such a string of horrors. At the center of hell, he wrote in *Paradise Lost,* lay a "pandaemonium," an encirclement of demons.

Few societies placed suffering and cruelty so fully on public display. Mobs, riots, and looting were common. Public chastisements, such as being whipped or pilloried, were occasions for entertainment. One German visitor to London in 1710, the same year Handel arrived, was taken by his hosts to see cockfighting near Gray's Inn, dogs attacking a bull on Clerkenwell Green, a sword fight in Southwark, inmates parading at the Bedlam asylum in Moorfields, and a woman on a Thames barge who balanced knives on her eyelids, all of which "vastly delights this nation but to me seemed nothing special."

As many as 186,000 men had been mobilized for the War of the

Spanish Succession, and as with previous conflicts Londoners tended to dread the survivors' return. Peace had its victims, too. Burials typically increased in the years immediately after a peace treaty was signed. Whenever demobilized soldiers and sailors came to town, murders and deaths from fevers always followed, and women tended to be the disproportionate victims. New, more virulent strains of communicable diseases also arrived with London's emergence as a global trading center. Even people who weathered common infections were left with the marks of their good fortune, from faces divoted by smallpox to suppurating wounds that would not heal.

Private misery had its equivalents in public life. The major institutions of state—the monarchy, the Parliament, and the Church of England—were riven and unstable. Under what circumstances violence could be used for political ends, what counted as legitimate authority, when divine will sanctioned secular killing—the entire social and political order seemed built on shifting sand. Catholics were subject to legal and civil restrictions, and among Protestants a panoply of terms identified the excluded, suspect, or merely troublesome: Nonconformists, Deists, latitudinarians, and a host of other categories for Christian minorities, constituting some 8 percent of England's population and more in other parts of the kingdom. The last execution for blasphemy had taken place in 1697. The last alleged witch in England was tried in 1717 and surprisingly acquitted, despite solemn testimony that bees had swarmed from her victims' mouths. A decade later, the last person to be convicted of witchcraft in Britain as a whole, a woman known as Janet Horne, was drizzled with tar in a Scottish village and then set aflame.

In politics people had come to speak as though Britain were naturally sorted into two rival camps. So-called Whigs could trace their lineage back to parliamentary forces in the civil war of the 1640s. They rallied in support of William and Mary in 1688 and, later, the Act of Settlement. When the Hanoverians assumed power, Whigs came up with a version of history tailor-made to justify the new regime: the story that the Glorious Revolution had rescued parliamentary democracy and preserved an island nation safe from the tyranny of Catholic

Europe. The Tories, by contrast, had their roots in the civil war's royalist armies. They were among those most incensed by the unprincipled interruption of Stuart rule and what they saw as the self-interested, corrupt politicking of the Whigs. At their most extreme, Tories even bled into Jacobites, supporting the Pretender's claim and envisioning a Tory-dominated Parliament under a restored Stuart king.

In the House of Commons, the lower, elected house of Parliament, Whigs and Tories would later evolve into modern political parties. Future voters would come to see the competing sides as representing different visions of government and contrasting slates of policies. But at the time, Parliament rested on the votes of fewer than 200,000 male property holders out of a British population of around 10 million. Political rancor was expressed in ways that extended well beyond an election campaign or a debate in the Commons. Factionalism was a repertoire of aspersion, a quick-think rule for knowing whom to blame when things went wrong.

Coffeehouses—more than five hundred in London by the late 1730s, more than the number of inns or taverns—became places where men reinforced whatever profession and outlook on the world they carried in with them. Scholars met at the Grecian in Devereux Court. Barristers huddled at Nando's in Fleet Street. Marine insurers gathered at Lloyd's in Lombard Street, while life insurers preferred Tom's in Exchange Alley. Among the wider public, abstract words—"liberty," "corruption," "constitution," "luxury," "pride"—had the practical power to identify comrades or flush out enemies. Pamphleteers, playwrights, and preachers wielded them like cudgels. "Patriotism, in Days of Yore . . . denoted a Generous Disposition in a Man towards Serving the Publick," wrote one observer, "now, these Times of Reversing are come; it . . . is indiscriminately made use of by each Party when out of Power . . . in order to consecrate their Opposition to that which is in." Even the labels "Whig" and "Tory" had originated as terms of abuse for people whose opinions one happened to dislike. The former came from a Scottish word for a mare wrangler, the latter from an Irish term for an outlaw. In the middle of the century, Samuel Johnson compiled seven examples of the proper use of the word "politician," running from Shakespeare to his own day, for his *Dictionary of the English Language*. All of them were negative.

Anyone with a point of view and access to a print shop seemed to have a plan for fixing everyone else's insanity. Government licensing of periodicals had ended in 1695, and weekly and monthly newspapers filled a market now free from official oversight. "England is a Country abounding in printed Papers," a foreign traveler reported. By one count as many as six thousand polemics, tracts, and commentaries were published in the two decades before the Hanoverians arrived, with little sign of a slowdown once George I was installed as king. Innovations in printing technology and the rapid growth of an urban literate class—by the 1710s perhaps 45 percent of men and 25 percent of women could read—contributed to the flurry of paper. Information was available in ways that seemed new, fast, and out of control. "We had no such thing as printed newspapers in those days to spread rumours and reports of things," remembered the narrator of *A Journal of the Plague Year*, Daniel Defoe's semi-fictional account of a London epidemic half a century earlier, "so that things did not spread instantly over the whole nation, as they do now."

For the first time ever, it became possible to earn a living just from having something to say. A new term—"hacks"—came into use for London's swelling cohort of piecework authors. (The same word also referred to hired carriages and people who sold sex.) The narrow alleyways and courtyards northeast of St. Paul's Cathedral were choked with the lodgings of would-be "novelists," originally meaning someone who reported novel facts and gossip—that is, a journalist— along with the print shops and booksellers that brought their strivings into public view. A young man from the colonies named Benjamin Franklin found work with a printer in Bartholomew Close, where the rowdy apprentices started calling him "Water-American" since he declined their custom of downing pints of ale throughout the workday. Instead of drinking, he tried his hand at hack writing. He used company paper and ink to produce a pamphlet that promised "my *present* Thoughts of the *general State of Things* in the Universe." Franklin's angry employer judged it "abominable."

Not far from the print shop where Franklin worked, another artery of publishers, coffeehouses, and tenements—Grub Street—became a byword for the urge to share one's views and, even more, the ache to have someone take notice. "It fell *dead-born from the press,*" complained the Scottish philosopher David Hume about his first attempt at a book, *A Treatise of Human Nature.* "It came unnoticed and unobserved into the world," he said of another. People of varying social classes found themselves swept up in the first great age of stressing over likes and followers and then, when all else failed, turning to the obscene. The world was flush with creative commentaries on the vulgarity of public life—doggerel that alluded to a public figure's sexual appetites, pornographic allegories, ribald puns, filthy ditties, lewd parodies—which of course also stoked it.

AS AN OUTSIDER dependent on staying on the right side of the powerful, Handel understood the many divisions that snaked through his adopted society. His income, as well as his art, rested on the favor of people who could also easily withdraw it. A generous supporter or advance ticket sales might cover some of the cost of a production, but opening night then dangled on the goodwill of a patron or a public violently sensitive to prices. A change in ticket price could spark a riot, with theatergoers storming the stage and tearing apart sets and chandeliers. When shows ran at a loss, the typical course was for a producer simply "to banish himself from the kingdom" and outrun the creditors, an early historian reported, as one of the King's Theatre managers had chosen to do.

Amid the continuing craze for Italian music, in early 1719 a circle of opera enthusiasts proposed a different model. Their concept was to create a new production outfit structured as a joint-stock company. Supporters would be investors rather than donors, expecting a return on their outlay but also bearing the risk should things fail. A who's who of Handel's landlords and acquaintances signed on, among them Richard Boyle, Earl of Burlington, who owned the Piccadilly home where Handel had lived for a time, and James Brydges, later Duke of Chandos, under whose patronage Handel had begun his first serious attempt at setting English texts. Their hope was to gain a royal charter—the official imprimatur of the king—which could then be used to pull in further partners and paying audiences. By that summer they had persuaded King George to grant the charter and provide a thousand pounds annually as capital. Other investors added perhaps nineteen thousand pounds in all. The company's board of directors named Handel as "Master of the Orchester with a Sallary" and empowered him to steal away Italian singers and musicians from their European engagements.

The Royal Academy of Music, as it was called, was launched the next year with a season that featured a new Handel opera, *Radamisto*. The premiere was overshadowed by politics since the king and the Prince of Wales happened to appear together in the audience, a public reconciliation that likely sent whispers through the stalls. But onstage Handel seemed to have hit on a formula that worked. *Radamisto* was in many ways standard opera fare, a story of heroism and love triumphant. This time, however, he had dispensed with the sorcerers and monsters that had provided fodder for earlier critics. Instead, he offered an imaginary story set in a real place, the ancient Near East, with a tyrannical king, happy and unhappy marriages, a father's love for his son, and—echoing the expectations of the moment—harmonious government at last restored.

Just as Handel's backers had hoped, the opera opened to raves. Scalpers offered tickets at outrageous prices. Women nearly fainted in the stifling crowd. For the productions that followed, Handel was able to secure the talents of some of the leading performers from the Continent. Francesca Cuzzoni, a celebrated soprano, was paid handsomely to give up other commitments and move to London. A playbill that featured the renowned castrato Senesino was enough to guarantee a sellout.

In short order the Royal Academy had shown that Britain had a place for what came to be called opera seria, a sung story on serious, if formulaic, themes. But corralling the cast that sustained it all—a company of large talents and even larger needs—proved to be a challenge. Handel was "addicted to the use of profane expressions," as one account put it, and he often had reason to use them. In rehearsals he was developing a reputation as a demanding taskmaster, fiery when needed, as he had been in Italy. "You may be a real devil," Handel is supposed to have told the temperamental Cuzzoni during one session, grabbing her by the waist and threatening to throw her from a window, "but I will have you know that I am Beelzebub, the chief of the devils!" Rivalries among performers and their backers paralleled the vicious partisanship between Whigs and Tories. During performances people in the audience typically talked and shouted, moving about in their boxes and interacting with what was happening onstage. When singers made an entrance, devotees might break into "Hissing on one Side, and Clapping on the other" before descending to "Catcalls, and other great Indecencies," with the battle continuing afterward in published reviews and private letters.

Grub Street writers intensified the theatrical warfare. "But who would have thought the Infection should reach the Hay-market and inspire Two Singing Ladies"—Cuzzoni and Faustina Bordoni, a Venetian mezzo-soprano—"to pull each other's Coiffs," wrote an anonymous author, inventing a scene that others reported as fact. "It is certainly an apparent Shame that two such well bred Ladies should call Bitch and Whore." Other composers, such as the popular Italian cellist Giovanni Bononcini, competed with Handel for adherents, who divided themselves into factions with a ferocity that could end friendships.

Some listeners found it all ridiculous. "Strange all this Difference should be," went a popular epigram then circulating around London, "'Twixt Tweedle-dum and Tweedle-dee!"—one of the original sources for the names that Lewis Carroll would later make famous in Alice's journeys through the looking-glass. Upon hearing of Handel's *Radamisto*, Isaac Newton reported that going once to an opera was enough for him. The first act he sat through with pleasure, the second stretched his patience, and the third prompted him to run away. Still, with ticket sales brisk and the financial support provided by a royal subsidy and a joint-stock company, the academy seemed exactly the steady foundation that Handel had wished for in his correspondence with his family back in Halle.

❦

IN THE SUMMER OF 1723, Handel finally moved into a home of his own. He leased a brick town house in Mayfair, in London's West End, at 25 Brook Street. (In one of the greatest mash-ups in musical history, nearly two and a half centuries later, Jimi Hendrix would reside for a time in a flat next door, at No. 23.) The house was within easy reach of the theaters and in a neighborhood that bore the visible stamp of the royal line that was now nearly a decade old. The newly laid-out Hanover Square was nearby, as was the columned facade of St. George's church, which Handel would join as his local parish.

The Brook Street house, with three main floors plus a garret and basement kitchen, would become Handel's lifelong residence. His composing room on the second floor and his bedroom on the third were in theory places to which he could repair to work and rest, but the whole house was more like a humming factory than a quiet private home. Downstairs on the ground floor, the front room, or fore parlor, doubled as a public reception space. On any given day, rooms on the higher floors might contain singers and instrumentalists being rehearsed for a performance or people gathering for a small preview of a new work. Along with a small household staff looking after everyday affairs, Handel took on a copyist and assistant, Johann Christoph Schmidt, another German musician settling into London society. He would soon adopt the most English of names, John Christopher Smith, which he in turn passed on to his son. Both Smiths, the elder and the younger, would devote much of their lives to helping manage Handel's engagements and organize his frenetic work schedule.

This new environment of stability and enterprise marked a stunning period of productivity, with Handel producing a string of new operas, all based on historical themes. *Giulio Cesare* sold out its entire run and took audiences to Egypt at the time of Cleopatra as she made a break with her unhinged brother, Ptolemy, and allied her realm and fate with Julius Caesar. *Tamerlano* took place inside the Ottoman Empire at a time of crisis and conquest, with a despot tamed by a father's redemptive self-sacrifice. *Rodelinda,* set in Italy amid war and an uneasy peace, wound through captivity, a couple's enduring love, and a rightful king's restoration to his throne. Since Handel had been given a royal copyright on his own work, John Walsh and other publishers were now obliged, at least in theory, to pay him, an arrangement that could bring in twenty-five guineas for a printed collection of songs and more for an entire score. It was a sum equivalent to about an eighth of his original source of income—the royal pension that ran back to Queen Anne—and, in aggregate, a sizable potential windfall.

Within a few years, the success of the Royal Academy placed Handel in a position to make his life in Britain permanent. In early 1727, King George signed the assent decree that confirmed Handel's naturalization as a British subject. It was one of the last acts George would ever endorse. That June, en route as usual to Hanover, the king collapsed from a stroke and died. Plans were soon made for the coronation of the Prince of Wales as George II. As expected of a composer who had been attached to the prince's household for years, Handel was commissioned to provide the musical grandeur to accompany the royal ceremony in Westminster Abbey.

George was determined that his coronation be larger and more ornate than his father's. A raised walkway was constructed across the grounds in front of the abbey so that crowds could watch the parade of dignitaries without obstructed views. Coffee sellers were on hand to provide refreshment. Tickets were offered for sale to people beyond the usual passel of nobility and upper gentry. The entire procession took two hours to pass, so long that the aging Sarah Churchill was seen to demand that a military bandsman surrender his drum for her to use as a stool.

Not everything on the day went according to plan. Inside the abbey, choristers located in different parts of the vast building couldn't see or hear one another and mistakenly launched into different pieces at the same time. "The Anthems in confusion: All irregular in the Music," the archbishop of Canterbury wrote exasperatedly on his printed order of service. But for one of the coronation anthems in particular, Handel had summoned all of his theatrical sensibility, and the result was astounding.

The text of "Zadok the Priest" came from the biblical story of the prophet Nathan and the Jewish high priest Zadok, who blessed Solomon as king of a united Israel. The music swelled through an undulating prelude, with the tension building across strings and winds. Figures surged upward and forward, then stepped back, then began to rise again, stretching the feeling of anticipation almost to exhaustion. Just at the point of boredom, an explosion of blaring brass and voices echoed through the abbey's soaring space. "Zadok the Priest and Nathan the prophet, anointed Solomon King," the choir sang in full voice, the initial z flaring like an artillery rocket. "And all the people rejoiced and said: God save the king, long live the king!"

No piece of music had ever so powerfully connected biblical Israel and modern Britain, or so explicitly laid claim to the idea that these kings, too—German by birth and British by parliamentary design—were chosen of God. It was a work of cosmic confidence for a family that now fully counted as a dynasty. Every British sovereign to follow (including Charles III nearly three centuries later, in 2023) would choose to have "Zadok the Priest" played at their coronations, as if rubbing a talisman for the security of their own reigns.

The new king and Queen Caroline, by all appearances in love and dependent on each other, had been in London society for more than a decade. In that time they had become comfortably local, more secure in their roles than the previous monarch, who had migrated every summer, like a stork, back to his homeland. The threat of the Pretender and his loyalists was still real. In 1719 a small force of Jacobites and Spanish marines had marched through Scotland before being routed by government troops in a remote Highland glen. Three years later a conspiracy to assassinate leading members of the royal family, led by a senior Anglican bishop, Francis Atterbury, was exposed before it could be set in motion. But no Jacobites rose to contest George II's succession, as they had done with his father's.

Handel, too, seemed more settled than ever. He had multiple sources of income, royal favor, and new seasons to plan at the King's Theatre. He was at the center of a metropolitan society consumed with debates about music and the relative virtues of one composer or performer over another. "People have now forgot Homer, and Virgil, and Caesar, or at least they have lost their ranks," joked John Gay. "There is nobody allowed to say, 'I sing,' but an eunuch, or an Italian woman."

5

Yahoos

The poet Alexander Pope would later describe the era of George II as a new Augustan age, a time that rivaled classical Greece and Rome in its power and grandeur. "Though justly Greece her eldest sons admires, / Why should not we be wiser than our sires?" Pope wrote. "In every public virtue we excel; / We build, we paint, we sing, we dance as well." What read like a celebration, however, was in fact a biting faux tribute to a monarch and a society Pope felt were better at trumpeting their achievements than fixing the country's many problems.

Handel had been part of Pope's circle in his first years in London, a collective that also included John Gay and John Arbuthnot, Queen Anne's physician. The writers among them briefly joined together as the Scriblerus Club, a joke of a name for a group of men who, in plays, poems, pamphlets, and satires, would emerge as the most prescient chroniclers of the ache, grime, and broken beauty of their times. Handel's audiences could not have helped but sense the same concerns playing out onstage. When Handel populated his operas with complicated plots of war, betrayal, loss, and revenge, he was working squarely within the premises and plotlines he had studied in Italy. But his listeners would have seen plenty of parallels closer to home. Their era's signature trait was not so much confidence about what the

Augustan age had built as lingering anxiety about how frequently it all seemed to get knocked down.

"My Mother dear, did bring forth twins at once," the philosopher Thomas Hobbes had written several decades earlier, in the middle of the seventeenth century, "both me and fear." Hobbes had seen normal politics and society dissolve in the English Civil War and had escaped to Paris to wait out the chaos. The age of human history before states existed, he believed, must have looked something like the present: angry, war-ridden, and cutthroat, as Hobbes described it in his *Leviathan*, in 1651, where there was "continuall feare, and danger of violent death; And the life of man solitary, poore, nasty, brutish, and short."

A generation later, John Locke accepted that people seemed shockingly content to suffer inside a "shatterd and giddy nation," as he once put it in a letter, where "warrs have producd noething but warrs and the sword cut out worke for the sword." Locke's father had been a cavalryman in the parliamentary forces during the civil war, and Locke himself had fled to the Netherlands to escape suspicions about his own loyalty to the king. The primitive, stateless, and government-free past that he imagined was more benign than Hobbes's version, but as he wrote in his *Second Treatise of Government*, in 1689, there was simply no going back to a time before countries, armies, and taxes, "a condition, which, however free, is full of fears and continual dangers." His route out of the troublesome present was to ground government in natural rights and the protection of property.

For many philosophers of the era, the remedy to fear was to start with a sober expectation that bad times weren't permanent—that is, to cultivate hope: "an Appetite with an opinion of attaining," as Hobbes had defined it, or "an expectation indulged with pleasure," as Samuel Johnson would describe it in his dictionary in the 1750s. Thinkers differed on whether hope was a passion, a virtue, or a product of calculating reason. Philosophers such as David Hume wrapped discussions of hope into broader speculation about the nature of motivation, or what made human beings strive for some ends but not for others. Yet the common view was that being hopeful was essential to everything from civilized governance to individual survival. Readers who opened Nathan Bailey's *Universal Etymological English Dictionary*, the century's most widely consulted guide to words and concepts, published in 1721, found "hope" described as an "affection of the mind that keeps it steadfast, and from being born away or hurried into despair by the violence of present evils, by a well-grounded expectation of being extricated out of them in time." That was why, Bailey said, hope had long been represented in painting and sculpture as an anchor. It was the thing that secured people and societies against the buffeting winds of fate.

The problem, though, was how to get hope if one didn't already have it—that is, if the rational reasons for being hopeful in the first place proved thin. Given the everyday experience of tragedy and loss, how exactly were people supposed to confront awfulness without becoming prisoners to despair? Christian theologians had long pointed to the promise offered by revealed religion—divine salvation through Jesus Christ—but that assurance would only come to fruition eventually, in a new life after this one. Human experience offered no shortage of reasons for thinking that the opposite was true, both here and in the hereafter. Suffering and damnation seemed entirely reasonable predictions of what was in store in this life as well as in the next. Belief in the reality of hell and the devil, doubts about one's own state of rescue or rejection, warnings delivered from pulpits each Sunday about the likelihood of eternal pain—all seemed to mirror current events and confirm a deep reality of brokenness and unpredictability. If hope was at base a desire to attain something that seemed likely but not certain, as Hobbes had it, what was one to do with circumstances where, on rational reflection, the odds of a decent outcome were minuscule?

For most of the eighteenth century, there was no word for the idea that problems necessarily had solutions at all, whether in one's own life or in society at large. The term "optimism" appeared in English for the first time only in 1759, and it was originally something of an insult. To be optimistic didn't mean to have a sunny outlook or positive disposition. It referred instead to a specific method for wishing away one's troubles rather than facing them: by holding fast to the conviction that this universe, despite the trials and tears, is the optimal one, the best that can be imagined.

Optimism of this sort came from the work of one of the era's most capacious and daring thinkers, the German philosopher and mathematician Gottfried Wilhelm Leibniz. A native of Saxony like Handel, Leibniz had developed new techniques for understanding systems in continuous change, the essence of calculus. He anticipated a machine whose function was not to make things but rather to process information, the basis for later computer science. Just as Handel was arriving in London, Leibniz joined the debate on how to reconcile "the goodness of God, the liberty of man, and the origin of evil," as he put it in the subtitle of his *Essays of Theodicy*, published in 1710.

Even sympathetic readers had to admit that Leibniz's train of thought required some heroic switchbacks. God was all knowing, a fact that any Christian like himself would accept, and thus had the capacity to imagine an infinite number of worlds. God was also all loving, however, and wished only the best for his creation. Therefore, the world that God actually did call into being—the one we experience—must be the one most suited to our happiness, despite the abundant evidence to the contrary.

Had circumstances worked out differently, Leibniz might have ended up as Britain's court philosopher, much in the way that Handel became its court composer. He, too, had been attached to the house of Hanover, as a friend and confidant of the dowager electress Sophia's. But Sophia's death robbed him of a key patron, even as it elevated Handel. Long-running disputes with English scholars—not least with Isaac Newton, over credit for inventing calculus—put Leibniz at odds with Georg Ludwig's newly acquired kingdom. When the family departed for London, they left Leibniz behind. He died in Hanover not long afterward. Later in the century, his ideas would form the target of the greatest satire of the age, Voltaire's *Candide; or, Optimism*, whose Dr. Pangloss deals with tragedy after tragedy—syphilis, an earthquake, the Inquisition—by reminding himself that in the end everything is for the best.

For all the ridicule it elicited, however, Leibniz's unsatisfying answer did help clarify the issues at stake. A contemporary of Leibniz's, Pierre Bayle, spent nearly fifty years coming at the problems of fear and hope through a microscopic examination of history and human folly. His influential *Historical and Critical Dictionary*, translated into English in 1709, was the first major attempt at what would later be called an encyclopedia, and in it Bayle set out to answer the big questions plainly. "Man is wicked and unhappy," he wrote in one of his opinionated footnotes. "Every one knows it by what he feels in himself, and by the intercourse he is obliged to have with his neighbours.... History, properly speaking, is nothing but a collection of the crimes and misfortunes of mankind."

Bayle was a Huguenot, or French Protestant, and had immigrated to the Netherlands when it became impossible to live in Catholic France. Surviving the trials of life, Bayle suggested, required placing one's thought in boxes. Ultimate things—God, morality, truth—had their own logic, which one could piece together by studying the Christian scriptures. By contrast everyday physical processes—the things amenable to observable cause and effect—could be accounted for without regard to grand theories of divinity or justice. The formula for happiness was to train one's brain to recognize the difference between the former and the latter, between the vastness of the created universe and the here-and-now tribulations of simply being alive.

A few decades later, Alexander Pope took a similar line. His philosophical discourse in verse, *An Essay on Man*, from the early 1730s, would be memorized by generations of schoolchildren and adults for its insistence on the underlying harmony in what could seem like mayhem. Even the most terrible occurrences looked different when placed in their proper pigeonholes, he claimed. Some later readers interpreted Pope as a fatalist—"Whatever is, is right," went one line of the poem—but what he was really after was a pared-down theory of hopefulness:

> *Hope humbly then; with trembling pinions soar;*
> *Wait the great teacher Death; and God adore!*
> *What future bliss, he gives not thee to know,*

> *But gives that hope to be thy blessing now.*
> *Hope springs eternal in the human breast:*
> *Man never is, but always to be blest:*
> *The soul, uneasy and confin'd from home,*
> *Rests and expatiates in a life to come.*

Pope had particular experience with seeking consolation where he could find it. A childhood tubercular infection had left him with a severely curved spine that would eventually collapse his rib cage and choke off his lungs. He remained under five feet tall and in near-constant pain throughout what he once called "this long disease, my life."

Other thinkers expanded on Pope's idea of hoping humbly—that is, getting through life by constraining one's line of vision. Since true happiness would forever be unattainable, David Hume advised, the best course was to maintain a temperate, moderate attitude, aiming at "a mediocrity, a kind of insensibility, in every thing." Still other writers speculated that there might even be something appealing in awfulness, if properly understood. A distinct concept, the sublime, came into fashion to describe experiences that were at once elevating and laced with fear. A sublime moment was one that was neither beautiful nor truly dangerous but endowed with elements of both. Peering over a cliff face, for example, might inspire dreadful awe, just as one of Handel's arias, sung by a castrato, could feel heartrending as well as uplifting. You could recognize the sublime, Edmund Burke wrote, when you confronted nature, art, or music that was "in any sort terrible, or is conversant with terrible objects, or operates in a manner analogous to terror." There was something profound at work, his argument went, in the way humans actually experienced something they would otherwise regard as painful.

Some of the core political philosophers of the era—Hobbes, Locke, Bayle—wrote from a position of displacement as *refugiés*, a term newly invented for religious and political minorities who had fled home in order to survive. Already by the 1690s, the word had been anglicized as "refugees." The hidden truth of what would later count as foundational Western philosophy is that much of it was the work of people who, in another era, would have been relegated to an immigrant detention facility. One of the effects of their theorizing about the state of nature was to emphasize how very unnatural the present condition felt. The world was in evident decline. Countries rose and fell, a fact that Edward Gibbon would later confirm in monumental detail in his *Decline and Fall of the Roman Empire*, the first volume of which appeared in 1776. With the painful present always disappearing into history, finding solutions required the creativity and courage of patching a ship already at sea.

IN A TIME OF WAR, political division, and conspiracy, along with everyday cares such as disease and natural disasters, the whole point of studying the inner workings of law, politics, and morality, even the effects of art and music, was remedial—a way of fixing a world out of joint. Thinking systematically was a technique not just for representing reality but for repairing it, an activity not so different from painting an idyllic landscape or making ordered sounds out of cacophony. No one put that technique to greater purpose than someone in Handel's circle whose personal litany of suffering—vertigo, depression, debilitating tinnitus—seemed built for a worried age.

People who knew Jonathan Swift also tended to know Handel, and the two men were sometimes described as versions of the same personality: witty to excess, sarcastic, talented at making ordinary things seem strange and new, and able "to throw persons and things into very ridiculous attitudes." Swift had been born into a comfortable family in Dublin around 1667 (the precise date, as for many people at the time, was uncertain) but fled to England after the Glorious Revolution to escape James II's violent crusade to regain the throne. He was eventually ordained in the Church of Ireland, the established Protestant church in his old homeland, and his hope was to secure a comfortable living as a well-placed cleric. But his satirical writings, which were already gaining a public readership, proved to be an obstacle.

A Tale of a Tub, published anonymously in 1704, was a complicated parable about politics and religion, with Catholics, Anglicans, and Dissenters (Protestants such as Puritans and Quakers who had broken with the Church of England) rendered as nitpicking exegetes. More people read the book than understood it, but anyone had only to turn over the flyleaf to see that Swift was taking on large, even dangerous, themes. The frontispiece engraving was a send-up of Hobbes's *Leviathan*, and the opening paragraph started with a denunciation of all self-important projects for reforming politics and the church. Bookshops were so full of new "schemes of religion and government," Swift wrote, taking aim at just about every Grub Street pamphleteer who had come before him, that most could not help but be like a barrel tossed into the ocean, "hollow, and dry, and empty, and noisy, and wooden, and given to rotation."

Swift's supporters finally persuaded Anne, not long before her death, to appoint him to a deanship, a senior religious position in charge of a cathedral. The one the queen chose, however, was not in England but back in Dublin. From this new position, Swift settled into the tasks of managing a gray pile of a building, St. Patrick's Cathedral, sited on the remains of a swampy meadow. As dean he oversaw a good choir and a devoted set of parishioners in the Liberties, a neighborhood of weavers and market traders. He was joined by a longtime companion, Hester Johnson, whom he called Stella, one of the few people who could match him for wit and wordplay. As he once told a friend, he expected to "die here in a rage, like a poisoned rat in a hole."

In fact, Swift was already on his way to becoming the most incisive social critic of his time. People attended church services just to hear what outrages he might deliver from the pulpit in his high, nasally voice. There were few subjects he failed to cover in published essays, polemics, and sermons, the first collected edition of which, in 1735, already filled four volumes, with much left out. On subjects ranging from the travails of Ireland to the policies of the Whig government, he perfected the deadpan exaggeration and the trolling takedown, parroting the style and argumentation of political speeches and religious commentary. When he had exhausted his store of subtlety and wit, he was not beyond resorting to passages about defecation and other bodily functions as never-fail tools of derision.

Swift's views earned him broad popularity along with the "fierce Indignation" of those he targeted, a phrase that he wrote into an epitaph for his own future memorial in St. Patrick's. Like many writers of the time, he published either anonymously or under one of several pseudonyms, even when the authorship was readily known. He was nearly sixty years old when he invented a pen name that would forever be associated with high parody and, mistakenly, literature for children. What he really offered was the very thing contemporary philosophers had been getting at all along: a method for staring full on at the anxiety of living.

Lemuel Gulliver was the author of a work superior to "the common Scribbles of Politics and Party," claimed the publisher Richard Sympson in the preface to *Travels into Several Remote Nations of the World*, which appeared just as Handel's Royal Academy of Music was enjoying continued success at the King's Theatre, in 1726. Both names—Gulliver and Sympson—were inventions, a double mask for Swift himself. His conceit was that a Grub Street printing house had issued the text that now lay before the reader: a true recounting of several voyages to unknown lands by Gulliver, an obscure ship's surgeon.

After a devastating storm and shipwreck, Gulliver first washes ashore in Lilliput, where he finds himself a prisoner of tiny beings who bind him with stakes and pelt him with arrows. On his next journey, to Brobdingnag, he encounters natives as tall as church steeples, with a language that is as loud as a tumbling watermill. On his third voyage, to Laputa, Glubbdubdrib, and other faraway lands, Gulliver encounters the great Academy of Lagado, where sages have devised a machine for sorting all the words in their language into intelligible sentences, thereby economizing on the composition of philosophical tracts.

Swift's only experience with travel had been on the packet boat, or short-run sailing ship, across the Irish Sea. His approach to travel writing, though, was simply to open the volumes in his own library.

Interspersed with ethnographic asides about the outlandish customs of the people he supposedly met, Gulliver's tales mimicked the travelers' tales that had remained a consistent moneymaker for booksellers, fueled by more than two centuries of European exploration and overseas conquest. His breathless sea voyages and overland adventures also contained a fair amount of detail of particular interest to Swift himself, a non-traveler contemplating the vast abroad: how to find a toilet.

Yet that, in a way, was the point. The *Travels* was not so much about the lure of leaving as the tenacity of home. It was an inventory of the mental baggage that Europeans carried with them, however far they happened to roam, as well as a cutting critique of their own sense of the normal, placed in the mouths of outlandish foreigners. In Brobdingnag, Gulliver is asked to give a description of his homeland to the Brobdingnagian king, which he proudly provides. But to his disappointment, the king's reaction is to pronounce it all "only a heap of Conspiracies, Rebellions, Murders, Massacres, Revolutions, Banishments, the very worst Effects that Avarice, Faction, Hypocrisy, Perfidiousness, Cruelty, Rage, Madness, Hatred, Envy, Lust, Malice, or Ambition could produce"—exactly the judgment that writers such as Hobbes and Bayle had made about their own societies.

By the time Swift got to Gulliver's fourth and final voyage, however, he had come around to something slightly different. This last adventure was a sober culmination of the ideas that Swift had been working toward via the nonsensical hijinks of Lilliputians and Brobdingnagians. The new trip "opened my Eyes and enlarged my Understanding," Gulliver says, and placed "the Actions and Passions of Man in a very different Light." After again taking to sea and then being off-loaded by a mutinous crew, Gulliver washes up in a land of oat fields and grassy meadows. The country is controlled by the Houyhnhnms, a community of beautiful beings who happen to look like the horses of Gulliver's own world (the name was probably Swift's play on "whinny") but with a capacity for reason and virtue that leaves him in awe.

Gulliver is enchanted by nearly everything in Houyhnhnm society. He changes his gait to approximate the noble, confident stride of creatures that have four legs at their disposal. He learns the language under the tutelage of a gentle equine master. He tries his best to explain Britain to his Houyhnhnm listeners but quickly realizes that, to them, he is speaking drivel. It is hard for them to believe a place really exists where people take up arms over "whether *Flesh* be *Bread*" or "the Juice of a certain *Berry* be *Blood* or *Wine*," and where one of the most honorable professions, soldiering, means being "hired to kill in cold Blood as many of his own Species, who have never offended him, as possibly he can."

Before long, Gulliver realizes that Houyhnhnm society, too, has its flaws. The Houyhnhnms share their homeland with hairy, unclean creatures called Yahoos, who vaguely resemble humans. The Houyhnhnms employ Yahoos for menial tasks, but as Gulliver comes to understand, they also secretly fear them. Certain Houyhnhnm leaders worry that Gulliver's middling position—the fact that he resembles Yahoos but has some degree of intelligence—might lead him to organize a revolt by the brutish underclass. Pressed by his mentor to flee for his own safety, Gulliver reluctantly consents to find a way of returning to England, banished from a place he admires and alienated from beings he has come to love.

In his previous voyages, Gulliver had given thanks to God for delivering him from his bizarre trials. But now he comes home chastened and wistful. His entire understanding of himself and his world has been turned upside down. When finally he is reunited with his family, he can barely stand them. Their smell reminds him of the stench of Yahoos. He has difficulty shaking the habit of walking like a Houyhnhnm, which elicits laughs from friends and neighbors. Gulliver's whole change of heart came about, Swift suggested, not through religious faith or philosophical speculation. The route was both more straightforward and more painful: the simple experience of living through misfortune and coming to view oneself differently as a result.

Having a sense of falling short was not the way Gulliver expected to return to England. His first encounter with foreigners, after all, had been with tiny creatures speaking gibberish and launching harmless arrows against him. Where he ended up was as a hairless Yahoo, ill at ease in his surroundings, disgusted by his wife and children, a stranger to everything he once held dear. "When I thought of my Family, my Friends, my Countrymen, or Human Race in general, I considered them as they really were, Yahoos in Shape and Disposition," whose modicum of reason was mainly used to magnify their vices. In this predicament, the worst sin of all, Swift said through Gulliver, was not run-of-the-mill faults like blasphemy, avarice, or dishonesty; pickpockets, fools, and lawyers all had their backstories and maybe even their uses. The only truly shameful thing was to take pride in one's worst qualities. And that was something only Yahoos and humans seemed to manage.

The *Travels*, read and reread for centuries, would make Swift immortal, but much of its core message would, in time, be lost. Victorian publishers tamed the text, scrubbing out the filthier bits—Lilliputians carting away Gulliver's feces in wheelbarrows, for example, or Brobdingnagian maidens using him for their sexual pleasure—while also weakening its central thesis. Generations of readers would encounter what came to be called *Gulliver's Travels* not as a response to its own troubled times but as a benign fantasy and an entertainment for children at bedtime—and, of course, the original source of the word "yahoo."

Yet at its heart was a very adult bit of advice. Knowing your own dark habits was practice for navigating the calamities likely to come your way. Real enlightenment, Swift suggested, came through acknowledging the brokenness of oneself and one's world—not as a route to despair, but as a first step toward correcting the things you had just identified as lacking. Gulliver had even devised a method for making that happen. Toward the end of his narrative, once safely back home, he reported that he had come upon a way of handling the demoralizing fact that he embodied everything he saw as most repulsive in the Yahoos. It was "to behold my Figure often in a glass."

Swift had plenty of quiet moments to do the same. With slim chances of ever being called back to England, he settled into his role as administrator of St. Patrick's in Dublin. His duties included the important job of managing the choristers, which he seems to have detested. Swift could tolerate ballads and popular song—he was an exact contemporary of the blind harpist Turlough O'Carolan, the last of the great Irish bards—but when it came to choirs, organs, and orchestras, his patience quickly wore thin. "Grave D[ean] of St. P.— how comes it to pass," he wrote to himself in a ditty, "That you who know music no more than an ass . . . / With trumpets and fiddles and organs singing / Will sure the Pretender and popery bring in."

"I would not give a farthing for all the music in the universe," he once told a parishioner. It was an art form that he found frequently cheap, overwrought, and boring. If you wanted to write an original birthday song, for example, gather up your inanities and make your way to "Mynheer," or *Mein Herr*, as Swift called him in a satirical poem in 1729.

> *Supposing now your song is done,*
> *To Mynheer Handel next you run,*
> *Who artfully will pare and prune*
> *Your words to some Italian tune.*

What neither man could have known at the time, however, was that their lives would eventually come together in a wholly unexpected way—Swift at the end of his life, and Handel at what would turn out to be a second beginning.

PART II

Sorrows and Grief

6

The Hyp and the Prodigious

Swift used humor not just to reflect the world but also, like the fantastic stagings and high-voiced heroes of Handel's operas, to reorder it. Large was small. Horses were philosophers. Shallower readers laughed at Gulliver's misadventures, but the more discerning also understood that Swift's comedy was always bound to its opposite—not tragedy, but earnestness. Satire worked only because real people lived the things that came into the satirist's line of sight. A society that prized poking fun was also a society working to define the things really worth believing in.

Not long after Swift's *Travels* appeared, an anonymous pamphleteer related the story of a young man who had reached a point of crisis similar to the fictional Gulliver's. Robert Jennens had been born into a well-placed English family, Christian in the normal way, with taken-for-granted piety and an assumption that the Church of England and its rituals were the obvious route to engaging the divine. He had studied at Trinity College, part of Oxford University, before being admitted, in 1723, to the Honourable Society of the Middle Temple in London, one of the Inns of Court for educating lawyers. During the periods he was in residence there, his days were spent fulfilling the obligations of a gentleman pupil, or barrister in training: taking meals in the timber-beamed great hall, watching older advocates argue cases with theatrical flair, perhaps reading case law.

But then came the doubts. At Oxford and now in London, Robert found himself drowning in treatises and tracts, as in Swift's Academy of Lagado, whose random phrasemaking machine calculated every thought that it was possible to think. He wrote to a friend that his reading and reflection had led him to the conclusion that Christianity had done mainly mischief. Leafing through Bayle's *Dictionary*, as his correspondent had done in Oxford's Bodleian Library, led to the conclusion that priests of all religions were the same, tyrannical in their dogma and self-interested in their theology. He flirted with Deism, the belief that reason pointed toward the existence of a supreme being, perhaps a benevolent one, but without the false trappings of miracles and revelation. Once he started down that pathway, though, the road crumbled beneath his feet. What remained of faith was no more than superstition. God was a scheming malevolence. The most damning evidence, as a barrister might put it, was the tormented state of his own heart.

This entire line of reasoning wasn't Robert's own, however. It was his family's reconstruction of it. All that his parents really knew was that in early 1728, Robert Jennens had suddenly given up his plans to be called to the bar and then, in May, he had "destroyed himself," as one account described his death. He had apparently cut his own throat in Middle Temple and then leaped from a window to the pavement below. It was as though he had taken Swift's advice—Look at yourself—and never recovered from the shock.

The family pieced together Robert's torment from letters found in his writing desk after his death. They were later published, apparently with the consent of Robert's father, as a warning against doubt and the dangers of Deism, which was held to be spreading wildly through the universities and Inns of Court, spoiling promising young men with freethinking and hopelessness. Other families reported similarly heartbreaking experiences when their children started questioning dogma and canceling the prophets. "Father, I must to my Confusion, own, that I have been a *Deist* since I came here . . . that

Christian Religion, now profess'd, was no more than the *Comments of the Fathers,* who at best were but a Pack of *Enthusiasts, Persecutors, Immoral, Ignorant,* and *Sanguinary* Villains!" another law pupil reportedly groaned, before being seized with a cough and dying from an ulcerated lung. "I was much surprised at the light-hearted way in which men of this country commit suicide," wrote a French visitor at the time. "I am certain that most Englishmen who put an end to their days are attacked by this terrible malady of the mind, for it is very frequent in London."

Stories such as these circulated widely, and they confirmed parents' fears about the critical theories thought to be indoctrinating Britain's youth, from dissenting religion to overfondness of "the Study of the Mathematicks," as one concerned preacher warned. To Robert's family, the tragedy was painful beyond measure. Relatives set about bringing to account anyone thought to have contributed to it, from fellow students to wayward pamphleteers. (Robert's correspondent, a Trinity College student named Nicholas Stevens, fled abroad rather than face a charge of blasphemy in a university court.)

Instead of bringing the family closer together, Robert's suicide probably widened old divisions. Opinions about government and religion separated different parts of the household like a dark glen, as anyone who heard about Robert's death would have been aware. The two things people knew about the Jennenses were that they were terribly, unbelievably rich and that in the realms of faith and politics some of them trafficked in mysticism and conspiracy.

BY THE 1720S there had been a Jennens at Gopsall Hall, the family's country home in the English Midlands, for less than half a century. The primary estate of more than seven hundred acres stretched across the rolling hills of western Leicestershire. It was first laid out by an earl who had accompanied William the Conqueror during his invasion of England in 1066. From that point Gopsall had trickled down the English social ranks, from nobles to knights and finally to a commoner named Humphrey Jennens—or sometimes "Jennings," as it was probably pronounced—who purchased the manor and farmland in 1685, the same year Georg and Dorothea Händel welcomed a new son in their town house in Halle.

Chroniclers would later refer to Humphrey as "the great ironmaster," as if any informed person would have known who he was. His biography was the history of the industrial Midlands in miniature. He was born the son of a Birmingham metals merchant at a time, the early seventeenth century, when the city was fueling an explosive growth in building and exploration. Birmingham's ironworks sent cannonballs, anchors, nails, hinges, chains, and manacles as far afield as West Africa, the West Indies, and the American colonies. Over time Humphrey built up his own inland empire of furnaces and forests, with smelters scattered across Leicestershire, Shropshire, and Warwickshire and leases on woodlands throughout England. Small trees and brush were slow burned into charcoal, which in turn fueled the white-hot furnaces that turned iron ore into usable metal. In one year workmen could pull down more than six thousand trees from a single worksite; an entire forest could take a dozen years to fell and clean. Among them was the storied Sherwood Forest in nearby Nottinghamshire, which Humphrey helped prune back from thousands of acres to hundreds.

Laundered through hunting parties and strategic marriages, the family's industrial wealth allowed the Jennenses to take their place in English society just below the titled aristocracy. Their name would become infamous through the offspring of one of Humphrey's younger sons, a fantastically wealthy man named William Jennens of Acton Place, Suffolk. When "the Miser of Acton," as he was known, died without a will, the ensuing legal squabbles among his potential heirs carried on for a century. The proceedings and negotiations might even have inspired the fictional case of *Jarndyce v. Jarndyce* in Charles Dickens's *Bleak House*, in which a vast fortune melts away in frivolous claims and attorney fees.

Humphrey's eldest surviving son, Charles Sr., as he was eventually known, was a more prudent steward. He studied law at Middle

Temple before becoming a country squire and justice of the peace, an office of local authority within the crown's legal system. Along with his wife, Elizabeth, he presided at Gopsall over a household of three daughters and four sons. Yet just as the next generation of Jennens children began to move into adulthood, the family was pared down by death. Two of the Jennens sisters fell to illness, as did two of the brothers. Robert then added to the count by taking his own life in spectacular fashion. By 1730 or so, the only remaining son was Robert's older brother, Charles—the prickly, anxious, and sulky squire of Gopsall Hall and a man who, despite being the sole heir to the Jennens fortune, had all the makings of the family's designated failure.

Charles Jennens had preceded Robert at Oxford but seems to have made little mark on the university. He left without taking a degree, and the only record of his time there is a document attesting to his matriculation at Balliol College and possibly a note that he joined the university's music club, where his status was recorded by the secretary as "Member, Non-Performing." For much of his adult life, letters and packages would arrive at Gopsall marked for "Jr." to distinguish him from his father, Charles Sr. It was a form of address that, with its connotation of second-tier status, would hang over him like a flinty ledge. Because of the "ill reception I am able to give my Friends there," he complained well into his thirties, receiving anyone at Gopsall "always gives me as much pain . . . as their Company gives me pleasure." He would be almost fifty years old before his father died and the suffix finally faded away.

Jennens never moved into the law or any position of responsibility. He acquired a good knowledge of music—he could annotate a score and knew his way around a keyboard—and developed a discerning eye for art. But he apparently had no particular ambition other than to lead the life of a gentleman. One of his detractors said that, when in London, Jennens never went out with fewer than four horses pulling his chaise and, when he alighted, employed a footman to clear oyster shells and other debris from his path. That was almost certainly an exaggeration, even a mean-spirited lie, yet everyone seemed to agree that he required tending. Friends would remember him as capable of showing great warmth, but its appearance was always something of a surprise, like a shaft of light illuminating a single spot on heathery terrain, before the clouds gathered again.

By his own telling, Jennens was "tender & sensible," meaning overly attuned to things—art, God, the sniffles—that other people didn't seem to notice. He suffered readily from colds, colic, and other ailments. "I find my Stomach so much dispos'd to breed Wind," he once wrote, "I am forc'd to be very cautious in my Diet," which included "white wine mix'd with hot water at my meals & sack-whey"—a mixture of sherry, sugar, and watery milk—"at night." When that failed to ease his gut, a correspondent reminded him, there was always "your old friend Burgundy." In later life he was said to walk in such an ungainly style that he resembled Swift's Gulliver trying to play a giant Brobdingnagian harpsichord, by leaping from key to key. He could be impetuous and moody, often losing himself to "hasty expressions," as his local Anglican priest put it, that proceeded from "a delicate texture of the nervous system, too liable to irritation." The only surviving correspondence between him and his younger brother Robert, three years before his suicide, is a record of Jennens's own priggishness. In the letter Robert apologized for translating a few sex-laden passages by the Roman poet Horace, something that apparently struck Jennens as immodest and inconsiderate.

If he had no reason to be upset with anyone else, Jennens could make do by being angry with himself. His face was naturally flat and his resting expression blank, even morose, with a high forehead that guarded small, shy eyes. When he judged his worth by looking in the mirror, as Swift had suggested, what he saw most often was despair. Swift himself had coined the popular label for the way Jennens frequently felt. "The hyp," or "the hipps," first used by Swift in an essay in 1710, was shorthand for what physicians at the time called "hypochondria"—not an imaginary ailment, as the term later came to be used, but a state of agitated melancholy. The hyp caused one to forsake social relationships and retreat out of society; it hacked away at the sense of sociability that was thought to undergird civilized behavior and self-government. Philosophers and fictional characters alike reported their own encounters with the disease. David Hume took pills to counteract it. Robinson Crusoe was paralyzed by it.

Some specialists held the hyp to be the equivalent in men of what was known as hysteria in women, perhaps the result of a man's overactive spleen. Others wondered whether it had become more fashion than affliction, "the English malady," as a famous treatise on the subject called it—a result of indulging in luxury, living in large cities, and leading "an unactive, sedentary, and studious life." But when Jennens spoke of his condition, he meant something immediate and real: a sense of entrapped hopelessness that would come over him like a numbing shroud. "Such a Hyppish Wretch . . . I am," he once wrote plainly in a letter. He never seems to have made the comparison explicitly, but it would have been hard to ignore in himself the suffocating doom that had ended his brother's life in one sudden, bloody surrender.

For all these reasons, being around Jennens was like riding a troublesome horse, one of his correspondents wrote in a letter—unpredictable and temperamental, oscillating between high moods and low. "She is finely shaped, well bred, genteel and airy, and is full of spirit; but withal she is a little too frolicksome, and will often fly out and is almost too much for so bad a jockey as I am. But I hope in time she will come off from these tricks." The writer was a poet and translator some fifteen years Jennens's senior named Edward Holdsworth. Over time there was no one Jennens would come to count as a closer friend. Their relationship would be a constant in both men's lives throughout adulthood, with frequent letters and visits where their conversations touched on everything from health and finances to art, classical literature, society gossip, and—crucially, as it turned out—politics.

A popular tutor in classical languages at Magdalen College, Oxford, Holdsworth was remembered by contemporaries as "a very polite and elegant scholar." But when Jennens entered Oxford at the normal age, around fifteen, Holdsworth was already famous not for his academic work but for his steely willingness to risk everything for his political principles. With the accession of the new Hanoverian dynasty, Holdsworth had given up his college fellowship rather than swear loyalty to George I, a requirement for professors and fellows. Holdsworth still retained ties to his old college—an accomplished polymath, he designed Magdalen's striking, colonnaded New Building still in use today—but for a certain set of young men his radical act of dissent made him a hero.

Perhaps influenced by Holdsworth's example, at some point in his youth Jennens, too, came to regard everything that had happened after 1688, from the ouster of James II forward, as a profound mistake. That position put him at odds with his immediate family. His father, as a justice of the peace, had sworn the oath to George I, as had his brother Robert, whose Oxford degree was conditional on a student's professing loyalty to the king. What might have begun as adolescent contrariness, however, developed into a deep conviction. By his twenties Jennens, like Holdsworth, had enrolled himself in a quiet minority of British subjects known as nonjurors: people who refused to pledge allegiance to the crown or—put another way—refused to give up the allegiance they felt they owed to the deposed Stuarts.

By Jennens's day that stance rendered even wealthy, well-placed men like himself ineligible for any position that required a formal expression of loyalty. Nonjurors were barred from election to Parliament, blocked from government appointments, denied service as military officers, and excluded from university honors. A popular play of the era, *The Non-juror*, poked fun at people like Jennens and Holdsworth, portraying them as misguided or, worse, the dark source of the political discord that infused British public life. "Come, come, Clamour is a useful Monster, and we must feed the hungry Mouths of it," declared the lead character conspiratorially, "it being of the last Importance to us, that hope to change the Government to let it have no quiet." Whig historians would paint nonjurors as conservative holdouts, backward-looking nostalgics who stood in the way of social progress and parliamentary democracy. At best they were the tolerated face of an intolerable cabal, people who stopped just on the polite side of Jacobitism. At worst they were potential internal enemies who, if left unchecked, would pave the way for the return of the Pretender.

To nonjurors themselves, however, the stakes were simple but profound. If a Stuart was the rightful king, you couldn't just trade him in for a different one. To be under oath was to make a solemn vow that carried emotional and ethical weight, imbued with the same formality and seriousness, for example, that still accompany the ritual promise to tell the truth on a witness stand. Governments were owed one's allegiance, nonjurors believed, but only so long as they behaved prudently and in principled ways, not by quashing dissent and then calling the result loyalty. That is why it was possible for Protestants like Jennens to believe that dethroning a king, even a Catholic one, was likely to end in disaster. Jennens remained a devout Anglican, but at Gopsall he assembled a gallery of royal portraits of Catholic Stuarts, his own alternative visual history of what he regarded as just government and cosmic rightness. He later painstakingly crossed out the names of all Hanoverians in the printed prayer books that he used in his private chapel.

Jennens spent most of his life either at Gopsall or at town houses in Queen Square and Great Ormond Street, on the border of Bloomsbury and Holborn, London neighborhoods where nonjuring families tended to congregate. By contrast Holdsworth, after leaving his academic post at Oxford, was regularly on the Continent for a year or more at a time. His living came from service as a tutor to young British noblemen making the grand tour through Europe. "He made more journeys to Italy than perhaps any gentleman of his age," recalled one acquaintance who happened upon him amid a gaggle of young men in Florence.

That connection with Europe allowed Jennens to keep up with topics of special interest to any nonjuror. In 1719 the Pretender, the notional James III, had moved to Rome. The pope provided him with a city palace known as the Palazzo del Re, as if to emphasize that Britain's legitimate government was still in dispute. Holdsworth was "notoriously attached to the Pretender," warned a British diplomat, "and is known to debauch the sentiments of the young English." He might first have met the Stuarts in Rome already in 1720. For young nobles and gentlemen on the grand tour—*milordi*, as Italians called them—the palazzo became one of the most anticipated stops on their journeys. Holdsworth's study-abroad business provided a way of experiencing the wonders of Europe, from architecture and new operas to the possibilities of clandestine romance, with women as well as men. But his tours also offered a chance to gather information from the Jacobite court that could be shared with Tory fathers and uncles back home, all under cover of a season abroad. "I suppose you have heard in the publick papers that the Chevalier's eldest son is recovered of the smallpox," Holdsworth wrote to Jennens from Rome in the summer of 1730. "He is so fine a youth, that ev'ry [one] that knows him here rejoices at his recovery, and I don't doubt you have some Jacobite neighbors who are pleas'd with the news." The "Chevalier" was Jacobite code for none other than the Pretender, whose nine-year-old son, Charles Edward Stuart, would soon become the great hope of conspirators seeking a return to Stuart rule.

Jennens and Holdsworth shared more than an interest in politics, however. Jennens was said to be especially nervous among women, while Holdsworth admitted that "I have but little acquaintance amongst the fair sex"—although he felt free to tease Jennens about his family's apparent disappointment with Jennens's reluctance to marry. "But the surest way to keep your self warm will be to secure a good Bed-fellow," he once joked. Their intense friendship would turn out to be the great anchoring fact of both men's lives. "I think myself under stronger engagements to you than to any man living," Holdsworth once told him, "and ought upon proper notice to quit any charge to attend you." Jennens returned the sentiment. "I know of no Honour or Happiness in this world equal to the Friendship of a Virtuous Man," he wrote to Holdsworth after one of his particularly dark periods. "That I have this Honour & Happiness you have given me Demonstration, & as for what goes by those names among the generality of Mankind, I am contented to leave it to those who love the World better than I do."

Male friendships of this sort, full of emotion and effusive regard, were more common among men in the eighteenth century than in later eras, but Jennens and Holdsworth acted in ways that signaled deep mutual devotion and dependence. Jennens paid Holdsworth's bills and managed his finances and literary affairs. He gave him a horse when he was in the English countryside. He advised him endlessly on guarding his health and offered him "my lodgings or any thing else that belongs to me." In return, Holdsworth became the chief facilitator of Jennens's greatest passion—the one thing that, even in his moments of ill temper and paralysis, always seemed to pull him back from the brink.

Over the course of his young adulthood and middle age, Jennens was an inveterate collector. He assembled an unrivaled array of books, paintings, sculpture, musical instruments, and sheet music, which Holdsworth scooped up on his behalf during his frequent journeys around Europe. For Jennens building his collection was all consuming. It was the one thing that in the years following his brother's suicide always seemed to elicit something approaching enthusiasm—or an irritated reaction when things failed to go his way. A piano Holdsworth had sent from Florence, perhaps made by the instrument's inventor, Bartolomeo Cristofori, had been delivered in disrepair and was impossible to tune. Packets of sheet music could arrive with nothing of interest inside. "I am sorry that the loose airs which I sent you from Rome were not to your mind," Holdsworth wrote, "but this comes of employing a blockhead who knows no more of an air than he does of the language of China." Composers sometimes raised their prices when they realized a wealthy collector was bankrolling Holdsworth's purchases. "I had this day some discourse with your friend Vivaldi," he reported from Venice, complaining that the renowned composer had started charging a guinea per concerto.

Jennens seemed happy to spend whatever was required. In his library and drawing rooms at Gopsall and in London he collected pictures by (or at least attributed to) Rubens and Rembrandt, landscapes by Poussin and Bellini, sketches by Titian and Tintoretto, paintings by Raphael, Veronese, and Caravaggio, sculpture in marble and terra-cotta by Louis-François Roubiliac and other masters, and scores by virtually every major composer of the time. "As you know I am perfectly ignorant of Musick," Holdsworth wrote one summer.

"I thought it the best way to buy it as some people do Libraries by the pound, and take my chance whether it prov'd good or bad."

That approach apparently worked. Jennens's music collection was so unlike anything that anyone else would create—an unrivaled repository of songs, sonatas, marches, minuets, cantatas, concertos, and operas copied at the time they were made—that it would help to define the Baroque as a distinct period in musical history. Among the treasures preserved after Jennens's death and later passed down to a British library was a new piece Holdsworth happened to pick up from the quarrelsome Vivaldi. It would turn out to be one of the earliest surviving copies of *The Four Seasons*.

Of all the artists and composers Jennens collected, however, there was one whose work he approached with purpose and planning. He bought every piece of music as soon as it became available. He bound them in leather volumes labeled with shelf marks and gave them pride of place in his library. Their creator was Jennens's political opposite—a German servant of a German regime that both he and Holdsworth regarded as illegitimate—but that did little to dampen his enthusiasm. Still, Jennens and Holdsworth knew that government agents, on the lookout for treasonous plots among nonjurors, were likely to read their correspondence. That is perhaps why, to shield the maestro from any mention of Jacobite intrigue, they referred to him as "the Prodigious" or sometimes simply as "H——l."

∼ 7 ∼

Oratorio

Jennens had barely reached adulthood by the time the Royal Academy of Music was founded, but after his brother's suicide he became one of Handel's most loyal subscribers. A few years later, in the summer of 1733, he might have met Handel for the first time when both men happened to be visiting Oxford. Before long, he stood out as something close to a fanatic. "I shall rejoice to hear of your good health, & of the good success of the Prodigious," Holdsworth wrote to him, "which I doubt not will keep you in big spirits." Jennens would later state his devotion in the clearest possible terms. "Every thing that has been united with Handel's Composition becomes sacred by such a union in my eyes; unless it be profane in [its] own nature."

Each autumn Jennens would arrive in London from Leicestershire and chart his stay by the performances he was able to attend, like a sailor reckoning a course toward a safe port. The town house in Queen Square, where he was living at the time, shared with his brother-in-law, was northeast of Covent Garden and the Haymarket and within easy reach of the theaters. Handel's house, too, was only a short ride away, and by the mid-1730s visits to Brook Street seem to have become a regular part of Jennens's annual stay in London. Over time he came to feel a testy sense of investment in whatever the Prodigious happened to be creating there. He would report to Holdsworth on each new work that he heard or saw in manuscript form, accompanied by biting reviews of any compositions he found unworthy of Handel's genius. Whenever the maestro had failed in his eyes, with a hackneyed melody, say, or a wobbly pairing of notes and words, Jennens felt the disappointment to be deeply personal, even an insult. The sentiment would only grow as he came to know Handel better.

Each summer, though, as he made the return journey from London over rutted roads and into the muddy fields of the Midlands, Jennens's heart inevitably sank. The landscape around Gopsall could seem gloomy and forbidding, so much so that villagers would later think it the perfect place to erect a gibbet, a post for hanging the bodies of the executed. It was one of the last landmarks future visitors would pass before the manor house came into view. There would be no more chance of "delight," as Holdsworth put it, until the next opera season, and even that depended on whether Handel was offering fresh compositions or merely reviving older work. "I hope that will raise your spirits another winter," Holdsworth said after a spare season, "as I fear his silence contributed to sink them this." The problem was that just as Jennens was coming to rely on his annual pilgrimage south, Handel's own fortunes were beginning to darken.

The same year as Robert Jennens's death, in 1728, London newspapers announced the opening of a new work conceived by John Gay, the poet and a friend of Swift's. Gay was among the smart set of artists and literary men whom Handel had met not long after coming to London. But while Gay was known as a sharp-tongued raconteur within this elevated circle, he had so far achieved little in the way of public fame. That all changed with his script for a stage performance that premiered at a theater run by the producer John Rich in Lincoln's Inn Fields, a rival to Handel's Haymarket. Gay called the work *The Beggar's Opera*—probably from an idea originally suggested to him by Swift—and the name gave away the joke up front. How would the stylized conventions of Italian opera look, Gay proposed, if they were set not in a fantasy kingdom or Eastern empire but in the world that audiences knew lay not far from their theater seats, in London's cutpurse alleys and rat-ruled prisons?

Gay's plotline was a hilarious mess. Polly Peachum, the daughter of a corrupt thief catcher, marries a highway robber, Macheath, who is at first imprisoned, then briefly set free by the jailer's daughter, then recaptured and condemned to the gallows, where he receives a last-minute pardon from the king. The music was supplied by an acquaintance of Handel's, the German composer Johann Christoph Pepusch, who borrowed widely from popular ballads as well as from Handel's own catalog. Discerning listeners could pick out bits from *Rinaldo* and the *Water Music*. The songs were interspersed with witty banter and veiled references to public figures, from celebrity criminals to prominent Whigs. Most remarkable of all, ticket holders arriving at the theater door could expect to understand everything that happened onstage, since the entire production was sung and acted in English.

The response was overwhelming. The show continued for sixty-two performances. No stage production had enjoyed a longer initial engagement, with revivals in future years assured. By the end of the second season, *The Beggar's Opera* had earned a little more than five thousand pounds in profit, the equivalent of a decade's worth of income for a reasonably situated gentleman.

It was also the first stage production to develop its own line of merchandise. Sitting in the audience one night was a young artist named William Hogarth, the son of an impoverished Latin teacher. He had grown up near Grub Street and made his living as a painter and engraver, taking his subjects from current events and society happenings such as Gay's raucous new production, for which he made sure to secure a ticket. From his seat, he turned the action onstage into sketches—he had brought along large sheets of paper, tinted dark blue so as not to disturb anyone with any glare—and then, back in his studio, the sketches into full-scale paintings.

One of them showed the cast during a crucial scene when the imprisoned Macheath, awaiting execution, sees his luck begin to turn. Hogarth peppered the painting with insider knowledge, such as the fawning attention paid by Charles Powlett, Duke of Bolton, to Lavinia Fenton, a player who everyone knew was also his mistress. Widely available as a print, the work would turn out to be Hogarth's first major sales success—the earliest of many viciously observant paintings that, over the next decade, would make him the essential visual chronicler of his time.

Hogarth had shown *The Beggar's Opera* as audiences experienced it: clever, biting, and oddly hopeful. For decades to come, there would never be a London theater season without it. In an era that prized satire on the page, the playwright and the producer had excelled at putting it on the stage. And with a souvenir to collect, theatergoers who had been doubled over in the stalls could laugh once again whenever they looked up at a Hogarth print on their drawing room walls. The astounding triumph, people quipped, had made Gay rich and Rich gay. In the process, what had been thrilling a few years earlier—the imaginative settings, predictable storylines, and sheer spectacle of Italian opera—now became an object of parody. *The Beggar's Opera* "gave such a turn to the Town," remembered a prominent patron and philanthropist, the Earl of Shaftesbury, "that Opera's were generally neglected."

In taking aim at the most fashionable entertainment of the moment, Gay and Rich had also targeted its leading practitioner—Handel himself. Audiences began to fall off for the Royal Academy's performances. Investors, seeing their capital withering away, made no plans for renewing the joint-stock company that had underwritten the academy's work. Handel quickly pivoted, as he had done before, and launched a new partnership at the King's Theatre, again with a royal subsidy but without secure investor backing. At the end of 1730, word came from Halle that Handel's mother had died. He arranged to pay the funeral expenses but, with new openings needing his attention more than ever, decided not to attend in person. "Ich kan nicht umhin allhier meine Thränen fliessen zu lassen," he wrote to his brother-in-law later that winter. "I cannot help but let my tears flow here."

※

IN AN ODD WAY, *The Beggar's Opera* was as much a work of homage as ridicule. Gay and Rich had shown the power of English words adapted to the conventions of opera, even if their aim was to play them for laughs. In fact, Handel had experimented with something similar a decade earlier. He had first tried setting English texts while residing at Cannons, the home of a patron, James Brydges, later Duke of Chandos. His earliest attempt at a dramatic work in English, *Acis and Galatea*, based on a story of tragic love by the Roman poet Ovid—and with a text devised, ironically as it would turn out, in part by John Gay—dated from this period. Gradually Handel had developed greater skill in marrying melodic lines with the natural rhythms of the language, an ability he would hone with biblical anthems such as "Zadok the Priest." While at Cannons he had also explored something rather different: the idea that a story drawn from the Bible need not be just a pious tale or a collection of poetic phrases, but a complex narrative, with scope for the kind of romance and heroism typically seen on an opera stage. The year after his mother's death, Handel returned to the stacks of compositions from his Cannons days and pulled out a set of pages that he believed might be given new life.

Esther took its plot from the biblical story of a Jewish orphan who became queen of Persia and saved the Jews of the kingdom from destruction. The idea was lifted from a play by the French dramatist Jean Racine, and the English text was likely supplied by the men in the Cannons orbit, such as Handel's old friend John Arbuthnot, Alexander Pope, or perhaps even, once again, Gay. Its appeal lay in its unusual stock of drama: an unlikely queen, a villainous courtier, an appeal to the heart of a besotted king, and a nation saved, all through Esther's revealing her true identity as a member of a persecuted people. The result was a work that built tension and sympathy by placing at the center of the action a woman with a choice to make: acquiesce to injustice or expose a secret, using her intelligence and quiet power to forestall a massacre.

In May 1732, Handel launched a new, extended version of *Esther* at the King's Theatre. It was billed as "an oratorio, or sacred drama," and the announcement supplied advance instructions for anyone who might not know what exactly an oratorio was supposed to be. "N.B.," warned an advertisement in the *Daily Journal* newspaper: "There will be no Action on the Stage, but the House will be fitted up in a decent Manner, for the Audience. The Musick to be disposed after the Manner of the Coronation Service"—that is, as a concert with several soloists and a chorus but no costumes, stage effects, or running about.

In Italy an oratorio was a way of skirting the Roman Catholic Church's prohibition on dramatic performances during Lent. The term itself had come from the place where music of that type was first performed, in a lay community of pious brothers, or Oratorians, of St. Philip Neri in Florence. It was a musical form that Handel knew well—and had already turned his hand to composing—as a young man in Tuscany. But as a working artist and effective stage producer, he would also have understood that oratorio had a financial advantage. With no tailors or set carpenters to pay, producing an oratorio was far less expensive than mounting an opera, a fact that promised to elevate his own bottom line.

The advance notice seemed to work. Virtually any listener would have remembered the basic plotline from childhood Bible lessons, although it might have seemed odd to see biblical Persia transposed to a secular theater, with a cast made up almost entirely of Italians. Even Senesino, the famous castrato, appeared onstage as Assuerus, the king. But the simple fact of being able to make sense of the words being sung by the company—now in English rather than Italian—was arrestingly fresh. George II and Queen Caroline were in attendance on opening night, where they might have recognized at one point in the music a recycled version of "Zadok the Priest." "This being a new Thing set the whole World a Madding," a contemporary account reported. "Han't you been at the *Oratorio*, says one? Oh! If you don't see the *Oratorio* you see nothing, says t'other; so away goes I to the *Oratorio*, where I saw indeed the finest Assembly of People I ever beheld in my Life"—even if the Italians tended to garble the words. "But for the Name of *English*," the reviewer felt, "it might as well have been *Hebrew*."

Unlike *The Beggar's Opera*, *Esther* was the kind of performance one could leave feeling not just entertained but educated, even edified, since listeners knew that the storyline was inspired by true events, as later scriptwriters might put it. The glow from opening night did not last long, however. Another group of musicians, perhaps getting wind of Handel's plans, had already offered their own patched-together Esther story more than a week before Handel's premiere—and even giving Alexander Pope top billing as the supposed author of the sung text. Near the end of the run, an upstart theater just across the street in the Haymarket announced that it would stage a "pastoral opera," which turned out to be a pirated version of *Acis and Galatea*. In the months that followed, however, Handel had bigger worries than policing his own creations.

The field was now crowded with producers, composers, and performers seeking to capitalize on Handel's innovations, as well as to exploit whatever enthusiasm yet remained for Italian opera. One of them was Senesino, whose career in Britain Handel had helped to launch. He soon emerged as the headliner of a company later called the Opera of the Nobility. In addition to the star power of Senesino himself, the company was able to contract Farinelli, the most sought-after of the great Italian castrati. In due course the Opera of the Nobility stole away almost the entirety of Handel's singers and orchestra, in the same manner that Handel had earlier lured away performers for his academy.

Senesino's company enjoyed the added advantage of its own high-level patronage. Just as George II had staked out his position in English society by opposing his father, so too his own son Frederick used the partisanship of music and theater as a lever against whatever his father had endorsed. Living debt-ridden and debauched in Hanover, Frederick had been effectively kidnapped and dragged to Britain to take up his duties as Prince of Wales. "If I was to see him in hell," his mother, Queen Caroline, once said, "I should feel no more for him than I should for any other rogue that ever went there." Now in his early twenties, the prince aligned himself with Senesino's company as patron, providing a royal endorsement to counter the one the king had provided to Handel.

A few years later, in 1734, the King's Theatre refused to renew Handel's position as resident composer, ending a relationship that stretched back two decades. He soon found another venue, in Covent Garden, but Grub Street writers had already begun to circle, sometimes using Handel as a foil for attacking foreign singers, Whig politicians, or anyone who came in a commentator's sights. "Let it suffice to say that he was grown so insolent upon the sudden and undeserved Increase of [power and fortune], that he thought nothing ought to oppose his imperious and extravagant Will," complained *The Craftsman*, the leading opposition newspaper. "This Excess and Abuse of Power soon disgusted the Town; his Government grew odious; and his *Opera*'s grew empty. However, this Degree of Unpopularity and general Hatred, instead of humbling him, only made him more furious and more desperate."

Handel could be found in "a *deep Melancholy,* interrupted sometimes by *raving Fits* [and] frantick, incoherent Speeches," *The Craftsman* reported. The claim was probably more allegorical than factual—a commentary on the sorry state of public life delivered as a swipe against a prominent artist—but still an example of the stories eagerly circulated by Handel's growing set of detractors. His compositions had once "pleased our Ears and touched our Hearts," reported another newspaper in early 1735, but "this Winter [he] sometimes performed to an almost empty Pitt." His friends, too, had started to sense that something had changed, if not in Handel himself, then in the world around him. "I am sorry to hear of the ill success of the Prodigious," Holdsworth wrote to Jennens consolingly.

AS HANDEL WAS beginning to worry more intensely about how to fill seats in future performances, an anonymous pamphleteer carried news of one of his unlikely rivals: the small company across the street that would soon offer a cut-rate *Acis and Galatea*. "I left the *Italian* Opera, the House was so thin, and cross'd over the way to the English one, which was so full I was forc'd to croud in upon the Stage, and even that was throng'd." The really surprising thing was to find "an *English* Tradesman's Daughter [spring] up all of a suddain, and rival the selected Singers of *Italy*." She was "very young, and very pretty," with a voice that was "exceeding small, but exceeding sweet."

Few people in London society knew the performer's name, but she would soon take up residence a short walk from Jennens's town house in an alleyway called Wild Court. Before long anyone who read a newspaper or frequented a bookseller would feel more intimately acquainted with Susannah Arne, or "Mrs. Cibber" as she would come to be known, than with any other public entertainer of the time—just not in the way she might have hoped.

8

"Dying by Inches"

Susannah Maria Arne was born in 1714 to Anne Arne, a midwife, and her husband, Thomas, who made a comfortable living as an upholsterer and undertaker at the Two Crowns and Cushions, his business near Covent Garden. Thomas's father and brother had died as paupers, both of them confined to infamous debtors' prisons, the Marshalsea and the Fleet. But Anne and Thomas had built their own household on skills that provided insurance against down markets: birthing babies, often burying them not long afterward, and, in the middle of London's construction boom, outfitting theaters, clubs, and fine homes with expertly crafted soft furnishings.

Living near wealth if never with it, Anne was eager for her two eldest children who survived infancy—Susannah and her older brother, Tom, born in 1710—to have a place in society. She took pains to introduce both of them to music, languages, and art. New Handel operas and other productions were on offer not far away from the family home in King Street, and Tom would sometimes borrow formal clothes from his father's funeral wardrobe and take advantage of cheap seats reserved for liveried servants. When the King's Theatre was dark, members of the orchestra were available for private lessons. Anne arranged for Tom to take instruction in music theory and violin, and in turn he passed along some of what he learned to his sister.

Thomas Sr. seems to have done little to encourage Anne's plans, preferring instead that his son help secure the family's standing by moving into the law. But Tom would later tell the same story as Handel: that he had acquired a clavichord and practiced it quietly at night to avoid the disapproval of his practical-minded father.

A chance encounter seems to have brought Thomas Sr. more in line with his wife's view of their children's future. One afternoon he called at the London town house of a wealthy client, perhaps to plan a funeral or arrange for a chair to be reupholstered. He was invited upstairs, where he found himself in the middle of a society party and concert. There, confidently bowing a violin, was his son Tom. From that point forward, the elder Thomas exchanged his disregard for a doting insistence that both children find ways of pursuing music, if not for art's sake, then for profit's. Within a few years, he had supplanted his wife as the font of the family's ambition. He refashioned himself and his children into entertainers, eventually setting up a small production company, with Tom as composer and arranger and Susannah, not yet twenty, as onstage ingenue.

In the spring of 1732, the Arne family began to put on operas and other performances in English just across the street from the King's Theatre. Reviews of the Arnes' productions were kind, even enthusiastic, not least because of the sheer drama of an upstart company's daring to challenge the great Handel in his own neighborhood. Susannah in particular, although the least musical of the ensemble, was gaining a reputation for quality—a mere "Tradesman's Daughter" who was somehow able to command attention.

She was reckoned to be attractive if not conventionally beautiful, with dark, almond-shaped eyes and a nose that, in every later depiction of her, always seemed pasted from someone else's face. Despite instruction from Tom, she never learned musical notation. She memorized a score without seeing it, by having each line plunked out on a keyboard. Her voice was a soprano that would later deepen to an alto but forever "a thread," small and thin, as the music historian Charles Burney described it. Onstage, however, she knew how to take up space, filling a character's persona and drawing the audience's gaze.

"In grief and tenderness her eyes looked as if they swam in tears," a contemporary later recalled, "in rage and despair they seemed to dart flashes of fire."

Even Handel seemed to be moved by her talent, untrained and inexpert at this point but still evident to anyone who happened to come across Miss Arne, as she was then known. Only a year after her debut, in 1733, Handel offered her a secondary role in a new oratorio he had been working on, *Deborah*. The performance turned out to be overshadowed by an audience revolt at a ticket price increase, when subscribers "forc'd into the House & carry'd their point," according to one viscountess in attendance. But Susannah's name now appeared in notices alongside some of the great Italian figures of the London stage, the start of what her father hoped would be a long and profitable career.

Yet in a family that valued hedging its fortunes, Thomas Sr. was not content with his daughter's being merely employed in the theater business. A safer bet was for her to marry into it. If there was a model for what a craftsman dazzled by the footlights might dream his own family could become, it was the household headed by a playwright and actor named Colley Cibber, author of *The Non-juror*, the popular play that had parodied the brand of politics espoused by Charles Jennens.

Cibber's life had paralleled the rise of theater in London. In many ways his life *was* the history of English theater. His career ran from the revival of stage plays after the Puritan closures through the era of renowned actors such as David Garrick and Kitty Clive, whose names would become synonymous with drama in the Augustan age. Over thirty-six straight years, he never missed a season in costume and then spent nearly twenty more in cameo roles—close to three thousand performances over his lifetime. Voltaire saw Cibber onstage in London and pronounced him "an excellent player" and a good comic writer whom the king had elevated to the post of poet laureate, "a title which, how ridiculous soever it may be thought, is yet worth . . . some considerable privileges to the person who enjoys it."

Pugnacious, witty to excess, and dogged in the pursuit of his vision of art, Cibber was also one of the managers of the theater in Drury

Lane, near Covent Garden. He was a person for whom the word "impresario" might have been coined—that is, if it weren't Italian. The fashion for Italian performers and musical theater, he believed, had been for the worse. Much of his life was spent defending the simple claim that, as he put it in his memoirs, "a good play, well acted, [is] the most valuable entertainment of the stage." The problem was that Cibber had only a shaky understanding of what "good" might mean. He passed on producing works that turned out to be hits. He created his own derivative plays that ended up as duds, including a version of Shakespeare to which he applied his own edits, then shook his fist when a cretinous public failed to recognize genius.

Whenever receipts were down, Cibber turned again and again to broad comedy, the one place where his taste was always on the mark. Audiences seemed to have an inexhaustible appetite for his clowns. The most famous was Lord Foppington, whose name gave away the type. Cibber would appear in a velvet coat and an enormous old-fashioned wig, borne aloft in a sedan chair, all fey twists and hand waves, and then deliver punch lines with a trademark grimace and a turn downstage. Intellectuals debated whether he was so bad he was good or just unquestionably awful. He would later become the butt of Alexander Pope's *Dunciad*, a withering faux-heroic poem about the pretensions of terrible art. *The Dunciad* would go on to become the most dazzling publishing phenomenon of the century, sold and resold in multiple editions, quoted and discussed, and generally considered uproariously funny in its dissection of a culture that seemed to worship inanity. Cibber would be remembered the way Pope cast him: as the "Antichrist of wit."

For Thomas Arne Sr., however, all of this was the very definition of success. The same year his daughter first appeared in a Handel oratorio, Thomas came up with a plan for moving into Colley Cibber's orbit. Cibber's son, Theophilus, was already following in his father's footsteps as a budding theater manager and stage actor. He had developed his own signature role, an even cheaper version of Lord Foppington based on Ancient Pistol, a minor Shakespeare character whose most important contribution to theater history had been to debut the phrase "The world's mine oyster." Theophilus was more than a decade older than Susannah and a recent widower. His face was ravaged by smallpox. Each of these qualities, Thomas might have reasoned, made him particularly susceptible to his daughter's charms.

Theophilus and Susannah had already met in the small world of the London theater, but now her father encouraged them to see more of each other. She was lithe and demure, always pliable to her family's will and presumably to a suitor's as well. Theophilus seems to have been genuinely smitten. In the spring of 1734, he proposed marriage, and Susannah agreed. Thomas was ecstatic. His family tree was now entwined with that of genuine stage royalty.

To Anne, however, the marriage could only mean the failure of everything she had hoped for her daughter. Theophilus had been born during the Great Storm of 1703, a monumental cyclone that pulled down chimneys, sank ships at sea, and killed notables such as the Anglican bishop Richard Kidder, ironically the author of a popular tract on the rightness of God's divine plan. As Anne knew, Theophilus thundered his way through the world: drinking to excess, sleeping his way around a cast, and gambling and spending himself into debt. "I pity you," Colley Cibber once said with a shake of his head, confronting his son about his extravagant lifestyle. "Don't pity me," Theophilus replied curtly. "Pity my tailor."

Faced with the inevitability of her daughter's marriage, Anne came up with her own hedge. She had an attorney draw up a prenuptial agreement, unusual for the time, that protected Susannah's future earnings from her husband and his creditors. Susannah gave no hint that she would ever enforce it.

After the wedding in April, the new Mrs. Cibber, barely twenty-one, was soon pregnant. She lost a baby girl not long after giving birth, but she had little time to recover. Her new husband, like her father, realized that Susannah's talents could be spun into a steady income. About this time, the younger Cibbers came to the attention of the same person who had made Handel's career in London years earlier. Aaron Hill was still planning and scheming, adapting foreign works for the stage in an effort to shape public taste to his own skittish interests. In late 1735 he began to gather artists for a translated production of a work by Voltaire, *Zara*, the story of a noblewoman torn between religion and love, set against an exotic, orientalized backdrop. At Theophilus's urging, Hill cast Susannah in the title role.

Opening night at Drury Lane, early the following year, was cobbled together and strange. The male lead, Hill's nephew, bolted at the last moment, so a stand-in had to read his lines from the script. Still, the production ran for fourteen nights, and the reception was beyond encouraging. *Zara* was a spoken play rather than an opera, with incidental music supplied by Susannah's brother Tom, or Thomas Arne, as he was now known to the public. Yet anyone in attendance could immediately see what Hill had intuited during casting.

Susannah didn't so much declaim her role as inhabit it. In earlier Arne family productions, she had shown a tendency to talk her way through an aria rather than nail every note, but few people seemed to care. It turned out that she was not really a singer at all. "I thought her voice not the best, and if not the best, 'tis nothing," said her father-in-law, but "in forty years experience that I have known the stage, I never knew a woman at the beginning so capable of the business." Her real gift was to make an audience empathize with tragedy by recalling, just for a moment, their own familiarity with pain. It was a talent that would soon be sharpened by experience.

SUSANNAH'S FIRST GREAT TRIUMPH as an actor happened to coincide with the realization that her marriage had been exactly the trap her mother had feared.

The success of *Zara* led to further performances, now carefully superintended by Theophilus. He pocketed Susannah's earnings, an annual salary of two hundred pounds from Drury Lane, and basked in her reflected glory. He stoked public interest by manufacturing feuds with other female actors, including Kitty Clive, slightly older than Susannah and the obvious rival for a rising star—"the apple of Contention the Part of Polly in the Beggar's Opera," according to one observer. These minor scandals brought his wife even greater fame, which in turn made her a magnet for anyone wishing to be close to a celebrated talent: stage-door hang-abouts, spongers, flatterers, rakes. When Theophilus wasn't arranging his wife's engagements, managing access to her became his sideline pursuit. He assembled a cadre of wealthy young men drawn by the chance of meeting Mrs. Cibber in exchange for a small consideration, such as paying Theophilus's tavern bill or floating a loan.

Despite these income streams, Theophilus's debts rose along with his ambition for his wife. Thinking back on the earlier prenuptial agreement, Susannah quietly sought to have more of her earnings flow directly to her, rather than to her husband and his creditors. But when news of her plans reached Theophilus, he showed up at her dressing room in Drury Lane in a drunken rage. He pushed through her door, grabbed her stage costumes, including finely tailored garments and expensive jewelry, and promptly sold them. From now on, he told her, keeping a roof over their head would depend on how well she treated his friends. Among them was a young country squire named William Sloper, to whom Theophilus was already indebted for hundreds of pounds. In the late spring of 1737, he told Susannah that the family would move out of central London to a villa in Kingston-upon-Thames. He also informed her that Sloper—but not Sloper's wife, Catherine, and their two children—would be joining them.

The Sloper family owned an estate in Berkshire, which they oversaw from a redbrick mansion sited within a lushly landscaped idyll. William Sloper's father, William Sr., was a Whig parliamentarian who managed colonial projects overseas and handled the budget for George II's household, which meant that some of Handel's pay might well have passed through his hands. In Kingston, both Theophilus and the younger Sloper took pains to hide their identities. When other people were around, Theophilus referred to Sloper as either "cousin Thompson" or, out of earshot, "Mr. Benefit." But the fact of a mysterious young man's keeping company with a married couple soon set whisperers to work.

Servants would later report that Theophilus and Sloper always chose nearby bedrooms when they were lodging together. In a ritual enacted each evening, they said, Susannah would first undress in her husband's chamber, after which Theophilus would accompany her to Sloper's door and hand her over to his creditor. She usually took along her own pillow, which she would return to the marital bed the next morning. Whatever the suggestive details, the emergence of this trio coincided with a rise in Theophilus's net income. His debts, at least for the time being, no longer seemed to be a concern.

After a summer in Kingston, the three moved back to their own houses, with Theophilus and Susannah making a home together in Wild Court in Holborn. Theophilus remained fully in charge of Susannah's stage appearances. He decided where she would perform, with whom, and in what role.

In the summer of 1738, perhaps to escape a new wave of debt collectors, Theophilus left suddenly for France. When he returned, he learned something that seems genuinely to have shocked him. Susannah and Sloper were continuing to meet in secret. His wife and his creditor, despite the origins of their relationship, had apparently fallen in love. Sloper had even taken a room in the city, in Blue Cross Street, near the king's stables, the Royal Mews, so that he and Susannah could be conveniently alone—without Theophilus in tow.

On the few occasions Susannah had stood up to her husband, Theophilus had always responded with tears and entreaties, occasionally with shouts and threats. Now he tried gentle persuasion. He wrote to his "sweet Numps," his "Little sweet Naughty Child" and "dear, saucy Pug," and begged her to understand the many sacrifices he had made on her behalf. He had never wanted anything but her security, which she was now threatening by making what had apparently been a business arrangement into an illicit affair.

When this approach failed—Susannah gave no indication she was prepared to drop Sloper—Theophilus turned from keening to calculating. Even as he continued to manage Susannah's public life, he encouraged neighbors to spy on his wife and her lover. The proprietor of the house in Blue Cross Street, a Mr. Hayes, stepped into a closet in an adjoining room and drilled a spy hole through the wall into the rented room next door. On lazy afternoons or evenings when Theophilus was busy onstage, Mr. Hayes watched through the wainscoting as Susannah and Sloper slipped into bed.

Soon, the entire arrangement Theophilus had concocted with his wife and benefactor came crashing down. Susannah was pregnant again, this time almost certainly with Sloper's child. A relationship of his own confection Theophilus now interpreted as a matter of blatant infidelity. His response, however, was not to file for divorce. Ending a marriage was difficult and expensive, and in any case Susannah's own convictions—her middle name, Maria, pointed to the quiet Catholicism she had inherited from her mother—would have prohibited it. For Theophilus, moreover, dissolving the union would have meant giving up the very thing that had placed bread on the table and covered his gambling chit.

Instead, he decided to run straight at the problem by suing Sloper for damages. The sum he sought was extraordinary—five thousand pounds: a figure that equaled, for example, the earnings in salary and gifts that a superstar like Farinelli was said to receive for a year on the opera stage. To a middling actor, it was a lifetime's fortune, but as Theophilus saw it, a fair estimate of his loss. After all, in his view, Sloper had destroyed his principal source of income by enticing his wife into abandonment, like a covetous neighbor leading away a prize cow.

BY THE TIME Theophilus lodged his complaint, British men could satisfy themselves that they had come around to an enlightened understanding of women's nature and their proper role in public life. "Bless us! what care do we take to breed up a good horse, and to break him well! . . . And why not a woman?" Daniel Defoe had written at the turn of the century in his first published work, *An Essay upon Projects*, which contained a plan for women's education. "I cannot think that God Almighty ever made them so delicate, so glorious creatures, and furnished them with such charms, so agreeable and so delightful to mankind, with souls capable of the same accomplishments with men, and all to be only stewards of our houses, cooks, and slaves."

Plenty of women would have agreed. Female authors published Grub Street tracts, philosophical treatises, and works of fiction. Female actors like Mrs. Cibber appeared onstage to enthusiastic crowds of both women and men. Women of means created charitable societies, patronized musicians and artists, and sponsored the education of children. Widows and unmarried heiresses owned as much as 20 percent of Britain's real estate and other taxable property. Those without means did the cleaning, serving, sewing, cooking, vending, nursing, and tending that kept Britain and its empire functioning amid war, epidemics, and political upheaval. If women later seemed sparse in the historical record, lost amid generals on the battlefield and savants thinking up Western civilization, it was because male historians worked very hard to miss them.

Still, as a class, one important thing set women apart: their exclusion from the state. Women were denizens of their country, but its citizens, in a practical sense, were exclusively men. Women were blocked from voting, standing for political office, and working as lawyers, civil servants, justices of the peace, or clergy in the established church. By attaching themselves to a man through marriage, they gave up most civil rights as well. After her wedding a woman simply disappeared in a legal sense, occupying a status not unlike enslavement. The ability to hold property, manage her finances, determine her heirs, and offer testimony in a court case—since a husband and wife were considered one person, a wife testifying against her husband was the judicial equivalent of self-incrimination—all became radically diminished. Even controlling her own body—for example, the choice of when, or whether, to have sex with her husband—was more of a privilege than a right, with the terms set by the man to whom she had surrendered her whole being at the time of their legal union.

The courts had long ago established that a husband owed his wife care and protection but also correction when she misbehaved, with the right to *flagellis et fustibus acriter verberare uxorem*, as English common law had it, "to beat his wife energetically with whips and sticks." Her period of servitude ended only with the manumission of widowhood. That was the point behind Anne Arne's failed prenuptial agreement for her daughter. If she were to marry without a contract explicitly laying out her rights, Susannah would cease to exist as a person visible to officialdom. There were exceptions, of course. Women could reign over the state, as Queen Anne had done, and could be held responsible for committing acts against it. Even then, however, the law made adjustments for gender. A woman sentenced to death for treason could choose to be burned alive rather than eviscerated.

For many women, the early eighteenth century actually witnessed the narrowing of opportunities previously open to them. Migration from the countryside had swelled the populations of London and other cities—by mid-century perhaps 75 percent of Londoners had been born elsewhere—which in turn increased labor competition. Men pushed into trades where women had long carved out places of their own, from milliners and tailors to hairdressers and wigmakers. Even midwives like Anne Arne were faced with new male competitors—whose first task was usually to point out how poorly women had mastered their craft. Men were pioneering new techniques designed to make childbirth easier on the attending physician, such as prone birthing and the use of forceps, even if they proved murderous for mothers and babies. "If such are the triumphs of the men's learning over the women's ignorance," wrote Elizabeth Nihell, a midwife who worked just down the street from Handel's theater in the Haymarket, "may the women continue their ignorance still of such curious practices!"

Men generally agreed that all these arrangements made sense. They differed only on why. Some rooted civic inequality in the dominion God had given to Adam over Eve. Others constructed elaborate theories of natural difference, which usually required generalizing from some sample of the female type. Jean-Jacques Rousseau, writing in the 1760s and widely read in English translation, held that in his experience women were less capable of rational thought than men, more sluggish of mind, overly concerned with appearance and finery, and best suited to the affairs of home. Still other writers, such as

Locke and Defoe, allowed that women had the power of reason and that there was no sense in preventing them from being educated and occupying useful places in society. But their delicacy of frame and unique sensibilities, as well as their preferences for modesty and mothering, meant there was an obvious order in society that marked off separate spaces for the two sexes. In any case, as any husband of a headstrong wife knew, what a woman might not gain by power in the public sphere she could readily attain by quiet persuasion in the private. Spending too much time thinking about women in public life, therefore, was to worry over rights that women neither wanted nor needed. "Consult the women's opinions in bodily matters, in all that concerns the senses," Rousseau wrote, summing up nature's fundamental division of labor, "consult the men in matters of morality and all that concerns the understanding."

"What nonsense!" wrote Mary Wollstonecraft, whose *Vindication of the Rights of Woman,* published in 1792, would become the century's signature argument to the contrary. Rousseau, like most men, had mistaken effect for cause, Wollstonecraft said. If women were relegated to "a state of perpetual childhood, unable to stand alone," that was where they were likely to remain. Women should not be placed in a position where, rising in society through a well-formed marriage, they also took themselves out of the world. "The laws respecting woman," she wrote, "make an absurd unit of a man and his wife; and then, by the easy transition of only considering him as responsible, she is reduced to a mere cypher." Whatever agency women might have by nature was trumped by the laws and techniques men had devised to domesticate it. So for women to change their lot, they merely required the thing that men had reserved for themselves: a "civil existence in the state." Everything else—personal virtue, private achievement, public benefit—would fall into place once women were treated as civic beings as well as physical and moral ones.

If anyone needed an example of what a woman freed from manmade constraints looked like, she was right there among Susannah Cibber's in-laws. Theophilus's younger sister Charlotte was one of the great outrages of her time. She was born late in her mother's life, and people who knew her felt she had arrived in the world as a fully formed person as a result. In childhood she insisted on wearing breeches instead of a dress. She handled a horse's currycomb with more expertise than she wielded an embroidery needle. By the time she was in her teens, she reckoned herself to be "equal to the best Fowler or Marksman in the Universe." These "strange frolicks" born of "a wild and ungovernable disposition," according to a contemporary account, infuriated her father, Colley. His only recorded comment about his daughter, upon watching her lead a parade of giggling children from astride a beribboned donkey, was "Gad demme! An Ass upon an Ass!"—a quip that seems to have crushed her.

When she was sixteen, Charlotte married a prominent violinist, Richard Charke, but eventually separated from him. She requested that her acquaintances now refer to her as Charles. Thereafter, he—or sometimes she—usually appeared in public wearing a coat and periwig and swearing frequently and creatively. Charles made a serial living as an actor, grocer, pork trader, pub keeper, valet to a lord, farmer, copy editor, pastry cook, and master of a puppet show. His memoir, or hers, *A Narrative of the Life of Mrs. Charlotte Charke,* was published to scandalous acclaim in 1755. Readers who opened the first page found that, true to form, she had dedicated the book to a person she called "a Nonpareil of the Age"—that is, herself.

Susannah was keenly aware of her sister-in-law's choices, as well as the rough road she traveled because of them. More than once in later life, Susannah would use her theater salary to pay Charlotte's debts when pubs and puppets failed. She might well have seen their predicaments as oddly similar. For all that separated them—Susannah in miserable bondage to a husband, Charlotte a bold refugee from one—their fates were not so far apart. Wellborn women could chart their course in life according to a set of accepted virtues—elegance, propriety, civility, prudence, fortitude—the maintenance of which had consequences for everything from social standing to the likelihood of contracting an appropriate marriage. But female actors lived along the hazy boundary between being of note and being notorious. They were generally considered only a few ranks above women who provided sex at a price, which meant that their public personas had to be carefully engineered and protected. Women performers had to be relatable and accessible yet never within too easy reach—exactly the line of arbitrage that Theophilus had exploited to his profit.

William Hogarth had captured the problem in an engraving that first appeared just as Theophilus was filing his legal complaint against William Sloper. *Strolling Actresses Dressing in a Barn* showed a company of traveling female actors backstage, readying themselves for an allegorical play. A dress slips to reveal a breast. Calves and thighs emerge from shifts and gowns. Cats run riot. A monkey pisses in a helmet, and someone's toddler guzzles a tankard of beer—all of it showcasing the riotous reality of everyday life among the acting set. In a visual aside, Hogarth also hinted at a radical change then afoot. Peeking out from among the stage props was a piece of printed paper, the text of a new licensing act passed by Parliament in 1737, which sought to quell the chaos of the theater world. All spoken stage plays were now required to be preapproved by a government censor, the better to ensure that "players" did as little damage as possible to public morality and political stability.

Susannah's reputation, as well as her livelihood, depended on staying on the right side of respectability. Her grandfather and uncle had known the inside of a poorhouse. The fear of falling was a family heirloom. Susannah was married to a person who behaved like a monster and in love with a married man who could not save her. With Theophilus's legal case now pending, she faced a public airing of her most intimate relations. From her doting father to a terrorizing husband, her worth had always been whatever a man said it was. All Theophilus had done was tally up the sum: precisely five thousand pounds, the damages he sought from Sloper.

A woman who could channel the pain of others so powerfully that she could move an audience to tears had disappeared inside a character wholly scripted by the men around her. It was around this time, though, that a shift seems to have begun in Susannah. Until this point, none of the written sources on her life had recorded her own words. Now, at the age of twenty-four, her voice at last appeared on a page.

In May 1738 she wrote a letter to Theophilus begging him to leave her alone.

Something had to change, she insisted. She had to be allowed to take control of her own affairs. Otherwise, her life would continue to be, as she put it, a "dying by inches."

※

IN THE SUMMER OF 1738, to prepare the ground for his legal case, Theophilus tried to publish a series of open letters to Susannah giving his side of the story. He portrayed her as sex mad and irreligious, given to perverse "private Meetings . . . at Chapells, Masquerades, and Places that shock me to think of." He had lifted her out of penury, he claimed, the daughter of a "poor unfortunate Family" unworthy of his beneficence.

"I chuse to smile, Madam, because I scorn to be angry with what is beneath my Resentment." Even booksellers interested in salacious gossip found the letters overwrought and refused to take them on. When that avenue failed, Theophilus tried another. He would convince the public of his devotion by "asserting the Husband"—that is, by claiming his ancient right to correct a wife who had gone astray.

By this time Susannah had moved with Sloper to a house in Burnham, a village in Buckinghamshire. She had given birth to, and then lost, a son. In early September, Theophilus showed up at their home with a carriage and two hired men named Fife and Watson. Brandishing pistols, they burst through the front door and led Susannah outside. Sloper looked on in horror as the men bundled her into the carriage and sped away on the high road to London.

When he had gathered his wits, Sloper leaped onto his own horse and easily caught up to the carriage, trotting alongside and demanding that Theophilus and his associates release their captive. It was only when Susannah complained of being ill from the jostling and general mayhem—she was pregnant again, she soon declared—that the kidnappers agreed to stop at an inn in the village of Slough. To the bewilderment of the drinkers and coach drivers on hand, the whole company trudged indoors: a famous woman of the stage, a parliamentarian's son, two thuggish henchmen, and the man known to theatergoers as Ancient Pistol, now actually carrying one.

For Sloper there was no way to resolve the situation on his own. Any effort he made to liberate Susannah by force would only have strengthened Theophilus's contention that Sloper was alienating her from her lawful husband. That claim, backed up by the evidence of his own actions, would put Sloper—married and of considerable social standing—in legal jeopardy. Instead, Sloper took the wiser course of fleeing Slough and alerting Susannah's family, the Arnes.

Meanwhile, the next morning Theophilus and his men continued on with Susannah to London, where they stashed her at rented rooms in Bow Street. There Susannah was placed under the care of a Mr. Stint, a candle snuffer at the nearby Drury Lane Theatre. Theophilus was due soon onstage, so he turned over his brace of pistols to Stint and promptly left the scene. The reason for the firearms might have been unclear to Stint—at least until someone started banging on the bolted door, demanding to be let in.

Before he realized what was happening, "an hundred mob," as the baffled Stint later described it, pushed through the door. From his day job, Stint would have immediately recognized their leader, however incongruous the context. It was the well-known composer Thomas Arne, Susannah's brother, along with a band of rescuers he had assembled since receiving Sloper's urgent call for help.

Stint, confused and quickly disarmed, was sent reeling beneath a hail of fists and kicks. Thomas and his aides spirited Susannah away to safety, placing her in the care of her mother, Anne, who might well have felt she had seen all of this coming.

News of the bizarre affair—a rural abduction, a carriage chase, a heroic brother liberating his sister from an armed captor—spread quickly across London. That evening, when Theophilus stepped onto the stage at Drury Lane in a reprise of his father's character Lord Foppington, the crowd hissed and booed.

But as Theophilus knew, his well-being no longer had much to do with capricious audiences or condescending critics. His future now depended on a court of law. If a group of right-thinking jurymen did their business as he hoped, the reward would sustain him comfortably into old age.

All he had to do was wait for a trial date and, in the meantime, collect as many witnesses as possible who would swear to his wife's ongoing betrayal.

9

A Design for Rescuing

The public scandal surrounding Theophilus and Susannah Cibber was a true-life version of the unlikely plots and shocking betrayals that wound through a Handel opera, the drama heightened by the fact that the protagonists were already in the public eye: Colley Cibber's stage heir, a beguiling ingenue, and the son of a member of Parliament. The difference, of course, was that the stakes were real, for the central characters as well as for their families. For William Sloper's father, William Sr., for example, the whole affair could not have come at a worse time. Its sheer tawdriness aside, the threat of Theophilus's legal vendetta was taking attention away from an ambitious project the elder Sloper had been nurturing since the time his son's future mistress had launched her stage career competing with Handel in the Haymarket.

In the spring of 1732, Sloper had been among a group of twenty-one gentlemen who had formed a trust and received a charter from George II to create a settlement in North America. More than half a century had gone by since the establishment of a new British colony there. This one, sited in the borderlands between South Carolina and Spanish Florida, would be the thirteenth on the Atlantic coast south of New France. The trustees had argued that the region's temperate climate would provide a suitable environment for farming and manufacturing, especially the production of silk. Nearly twenty years earlier, conflicts with indigenous communities had devastated South Carolina. But since then relations with tribal leaders had improved, and there was reason to believe that the people living near the coast, members of the Muscogee Confederacy, would accept a foreign settlement between the Savannah and the Altamaha Rivers. Planting English-speaking colonists there would also serve as a buffer against Spain, should the animosities that had fueled the War of the Spanish Succession ever return. In honor of the king, Sloper and his fellow trustees proposed to call it Georgia.

The new colony was to be peopled with smallholders and craftsmen, not plantation owners, with the trust working to recruit incarcerated debtors who wished to begin new lives overseas. In helping to finalize plans for Georgia, Sloper might well have realized that the project had come around a few decades too late. Had the option of emigrating been available to Susannah Cibber's bankrupt ancestors, locked up in the Marshalsea and the Fleet, her embarrassing affair with Sloper's son would never have taken place.

At the center of the Georgia plan was a business partner of Sloper's who was considered Britain's foremost expert on North American affairs. Thomas Coram was "the honestest, the most disinterested, and the most knowing person about the plantations, I ever talked with," according to Horatio Walpole, the brother of the Whig prime minister, Robert Walpole. People knew him as one of the most hopeful men of his time, not from any great evidence of success—his modest living came from his work as a factor, or commercial agent—but rather because he had a reputation not unlike that of Handel's old producer Aaron Hill: as a dogged purveyor of proposals, in Coram's case, in the practical realm of business. He tended to present his projects "without any Art but that of disclaiming it," an acquaintance remembered, but "once he made an Impression, he took care it should not wear out; for he enforced it continually by the most pathetic Remonstrances." His disarming plainness—a tendency to swear, an approximate understanding of higher learning, and a broad, burred accent that later listeners would associate with cartoonish pirates—somehow made his enthusiasms seem all the more genuine.

Coram was born around 1668 in Dorset, on the southwestern coast of England. His father had sent him to sea at the age of eleven and a half. (Coram would still emphasize the "half" into old age, like a child straining toward twelve.) As a young adult, he served as an auditor of ships ferrying soldiers across the Irish Sea to quash the Pretender's resistance in Ireland. He later spent a decade in Massachusetts, married a Boston woman, Eunice Waite, and drew up plans for exploiting fisheries and felling forests, none of which he saw come to fruition. A foray into shipbuilding ended in legal disputes with business partners and threats against his life. After returning to England, saddled with debt, he signed on as cargo manager of a short-run transport ship, the *Seaflower*, laden with wheat and bound for Hamburg. In the summer of 1719, the ship was driven by the wind onto a sandbank off Cuxhaven on the North Sea. Coram watched as German villagers brought out axes and wagons, plundered the grain, and hacked away at the masts and decking until the *Seaflower* was reduced to a hull.

Despite this record, Coram's connections and experience in North America recommended him to investors such as Sloper. The broad outlines of the Georgia proposal were in fact Coram's, although he had originally imagined placing the colony in Nova Scotia and settling it with industrious Germans like those who had chopped up the *Seaflower*. At trustee meetings, surrounded by men far above him in social rank, he advised on everything from Christian missions to the Indians to budget estimates for travel and supplies. To underwrite the costs, he helped secure subscriptions from the governors of the Bank of England and the directors of the East India Company. In November 1732, only a few months after Handel premiered his first English oratorio, *Esther*, the first wave of 114 colonists set out for Georgia. Coram was standing dockside at Gravesend on the Thames to see off the group, headed by the charismatic soldier and parliamentarian James Oglethorpe. He watched as the trust's ship, the *Anne*, sailed downriver toward the English Channel and the open sea.

Coram and other trustees imagined Georgia as an egalitarian society founded on principles of charity and common assistance. Among other innovations, it was the first colony purposely designed to be free from slavery. But in the swamps and coastlands of America, things quickly took a different turn. Enslaved people from South Carolina were imported as servants and laborers to clear land and build the first planned settlement, Savannah. To skirt the ban, colonists sometimes drew up "hundred-year contracts" with Carolinian planters, who would dispatch people they claimed to own to work in Georgia's fields and forests.

The colony's leader, Oglethorpe, had a reputation as a social reformer. One of his earlier causes had been the appalling conditions inside debtors' prisons, which had led him to initiate a public investigation of a particularly gruesome tragedy: the death of Susannah Cibber's uncle, Edward Arne, who had perished from cold and starvation in the dungeon of the Fleet. Oglethorpe even invited an energetic young Anglican clergyman, John Wesley, to serve as rector of the new church in Savannah—the first step on Wesley's path to founding a reconfigured form of Christianity later called Methodism. But Oglethorpe was also developing his own sense of the practicalities of colonial management. Compromises had to be made, and in his view Georgia's main benefit was as a strategic outpost, not a social experiment. "Carolina has above 40,000 negroes, and not 4,000 white men that can bear arms, and those mere militia," Oglethorpe would later write to another Georgia trustee, Handel's patron the Duke of Montagu. "If [the Spanish] remove us, all that country is at their pleasure."

A year before the first colonists arrived, Spanish coastguardsmen had forcibly boarded a British merchant ship, the *Rebecca*, and in the process allegedly cut off the ear of its captain, Robert Jenkins. Back in London, Coram watched as the case was given mythic proportions by British newspapers and the Tory opposition. Naval reprisals were ordered against Spanish assets in the Atlantic and Caribbean, which would escalate into the full-scale War of Jenkins' Ear, as it later came to be called. Tensions were also emerging over whether the Georgia colony's statutes should mirror English law, particularly regarding traditional restrictions on women's ability to inherit property. When the board took up the matter of women's rights, Coram found himself nearly alone in insisting on parity with men. He walked away from the trusteeship in protest.

Coram would come to refer to Georgia as "that Wretched Colony." As his participation in the project dwindled, he proposed a colonization effort in the Bahamas, then a plan to educate Native American girls, then a relief fund for destitute New Englanders in London, ideas that came to little more than stacks of paper. As an agent for the titled and powerful, Coram traveled in much the same company as Handel. He walked the streets Charles Jennens knew well, in the neighborhood of Queen Square and Great Ormond Street, although the two men left no record of ever having met. Yet within a few years, all their lives would turn out to be braided together in the most unexpected way, through yet another of Coram's many schemes—"my Darling Project," as he described it to a correspondent. Rather than establishing new communities on the other side of the Atlantic, however, this one involved redeeming the damaged society Coram found right outside his front door.

VIRTUALLY ANYONE who passed through eighteenth-century London noticed an undeniable fact about the capital city: it seemed awash with children. "Proud Coaches pass, regardless of the Moan/Of Infant Orphans, and the Widow's Groan," John Gay wrote in his poem *Trivia; or, The Art of Walking the Streets of London,* a decade before he turned his sights on Handel with *The Beggar's Opera.* Among the poor and working classes, children were employed as manual laborers as soon as they were able to bear a burden. They toiled as street runners, delivery boys, seamstresses' assistants, servants, and small-shop manufacturers. Others were put to begging or fell into the hands of street gangs, a problem in cities across the kingdom.

From his dean's lodgings in Dublin, Jonathan Swift wrote that it was "a melancholy object to those, who walk through this great town, or travel in the country, when they see the streets, the roads, and cabbin-doors crowded with beggars of the female sex, followed by three, four, or six children, all in rags, and importuning every passenger for an alms." Rather than have the children "turn thieves for want of work, or leave their dear native country, to fight for the Pretender in Spain," Swift wrote in 1729 in *A Modest Proposal*, his satirical broadside against ineffective schemes for public improvement, they might simply be "stewed, roasted, baked, or boiled . . . in a fricasee, or a ragoust." Hogarth would later capture the reality of childhood poverty, at least as imagined by the wealthy, in a popular print. In the despairing and destitute swill of a fictional Gin Lane, an infant boy plunges headlong over a staircase while his mother, dazed and syphilitic, concentrates on her snuff tin.

The mistresses of dukes and earls could fall pregnant as unexpectedly as haberdashers and fishwives, of course, and England's great families were riddled with people whom the prevailing rules of inheritance rendered illegitimate, even if they might be given a title and a palace as compensation. (The eldest son of Charles II and his lover Lucy Walter—James Scott, 1st Duke of Monmouth—would produce a family line that wound through the network of patrons and business partners that sustained both Coram and Handel.) But public attention tended to focus on women who became pregnant out of wedlock and without the means to care for the children they bore.

Abandonment could at times be its own "morbid morality," as a contemporary source put it, "by which an unhappy female, who fell a victim to the seductions and false promises of designing men, was left to hopeless contumely, and irretrievable disgrace." Even then, the lines of class and power always ran crooked. In the 1720s, a plurality of London men arrested for paying a woman for sex gave their status as "gentleman." Their female partners, by contrast, tended to be under the age of nineteen and in circumstances frequently described as "mother dead; father at sea." The majority of unmarried pregnant women, however, were neither selling sex nor victimized by wealthy libertines. They were ordinary working-class women whose relationship with a friend or acquaintance had produced a baby. In one count later in the century, when a woman gave birth alone, she was most likely to list the occupation of her child's father as "Servant," "Journeyman," or "Soldier," or even the indeterminate "Gone to sea" or "Gone to America."

Most of the children who resulted from these relationships—regardless of social class—never even survived long enough to fall into delinquency, however. By some estimates, at the beginning of the century, perhaps 45 percent of infants died within their first year of life, with the figure rising steadily through the 1720s and 1730s. By mid-century in London, 75 percent of children might have died before the age of five. Even for parents whose children were brought into the world with the care of an experienced midwife like Susannah Cibber's mother, Anne Arne, odds were about even that a baby would ever see a birthday at all.

Stillbirths, congenital anomalies, and fatal injuries were common, as was infanticide, although probably not as common as Grub Street stories about it. Early-childhood mortality was so expected, in fact, that in official documents "infancy" was itself understood to be a cause of death distinct from infectious diseases such as consumption and smallpox. Four of Susannah Cibber's five siblings, for example, had died while infants, as had at least two of her own children. Orphanages and other institutions had little effect on this grim accounting. Just as in the general population, 75 percent of girls and boys in institutions perished while still babies, with many already suffering from malnutrition and disease when they were first handed over or picked up from the street. By the 1730s more than a third of all burials in London were in child-size coffins.

Eunice and Thomas Coram never had children of their own, but even as Coram launched the Georgia project, the plight of a specific category of parentless child—one known as a foundling—had already become his consuming obsession. Orphans, or children whose parents had died, had long been the concern of churches and charitable societies. Foundlings, however, were different. They were the children of someone very much alive. A parent had abandoned them on a street or dropped them off at a wealthy home. Foundlings might be sent to a workhouse, where they would be looked after haphazardly if they were infants or employed to perform menial tasks as soon as they were able. More often, as Hogarth had depicted them, lolling about on a trash-strewn street, they had few pursuits besides begging, stealing, or simply dying—the objects of both fascination and fear, with little to be done about their fate but pity it.

As he walked around London, on his way to trustee meetings or an audience with a well-placed client, Coram had begun to imagine an institution that would care for foundlings rather than ignore or warehouse them. His "Designe of Re[s]cuing," as he once called it in a letter to a correspondent in Boston, had at its heart not only an institutional innovation but a moral one as well. What was needed was a body that would take as its aim not so much eliminating a social ill as remaking a real person at a crucial way station: the moment, in infancy, when they were all potential. If reimagined when the years to come were still malleable, a child's future could be shaped differently from its past.

The parents who were unable to care for their children, Coram sensed, were not at all like those depicted by Hogarth or satirized by Swift. Most mothers were victims of chance and burdened by shame, powerless to care properly for their children yet unwilling to surrender them to a bleak future in a workhouse. Given an opportunity, these women might choose for their children to be reared happily and safely by people who could "foster" them—an ancient word derived from the same Old English root as "fodder," suggesting that a child's truest parent was the person who fed them. Under British law there was no provision for a family to adopt a child, a condition that would not be established by statute until the twentieth century, although a child could become the "ward" of an adult through the courts. But distressed mothers, Coram felt, might find comfort in knowing that able strangers would see to the child's well-being, providing a pathway to adulthood that she herself was unable to offer.

Coram's concept was not just to stave off the ill effects of a lowly birth, nor simply to build a bulwark against bad parents and unwanted babies. It was to redraw the arc of individual lives, one at a time. Yet his plan faced one very large obstacle. "The inconvenience to be apprehended from such an asylum," noted an early account of Coram's ideas, "is the encouragement that may be given in some instances to the licentious habits of life, *by the people providing for the consequences of it.*" It was no use tending to foundlings, the logic went, if saving them meant relieving wayward women of the results of their own wicked behavior. The first step in caring *for* foundlings, Coram concluded, was to get people of means to care *about* them. They had to be rendered visible in ways other than as a public blight, with wealthy supporters—the same kinds of people who had established the Royal Academy of Music and whom Coram had buttonholed for his colonial schemes in North America—made to believe that a story of hopelessness could be recast as redemption.

To do all that, Coram reckoned, he would have to transform the rescue of foundlings from an exercise in piety or good works into something much more radical: a fashion. It was an untried strategy, and for it to work, the first people he would need to convince were not dukes, earls, and gentlemen of rank, as he had done with the Georgia project.

He would have to turn, instead, to their wives.

❦

PROPOSALS FOR SOCIAL BETTERMENT were common in Georgian Britain, a great "age of benevolence," as it was called at the time. The sheer volume of projects, petitions, and charitable subscriptions could seem as overwhelming as the social ills they aimed to solve, which was why Swift's *Modest Proposal*—to deal with abandoned children by eating them—hit its satirical mark.

The engine of social change was thought to be the cultivation of sensibility, which was understood as a deep appreciation for the moral and emotional weight of things. Sensibility was as tangible as taste or sight. It enabled profound engagement with art and music. It was thought to form the structure of polite society and to orient the mind toward beauty, perhaps even to undergird civilization itself. If not properly balanced, sensibility could turn into a debilitating oversensitivity, the source of Charles Jennens's depression. But when managed by individuals with an eye to the commonweal, sensibility was the antecedent of hope: a visceral response to unwarranted suffering that could spur action to alleviate it.

Using his network of colonial contacts, Coram arranged to visit the town houses or country estates of distinguished women, to whom he hoped to present his idea. He had a printer compose a formal petition to which the women could add their names. As he had always done, to get across the urgency and necessity of a project, he ratcheted up the stakes where required, adding pathos and gravity.

A new charity was essential, Coram wrote as a preamble to his petition, "for preventing the frequent murders of poor miserable infants at their birth; . . . for suppressing the inhuman custom of exposing new born infants to perish in the streets; . . . [for halting] the putting out such unhappy foundlings to wicked and barbarous nurses, who . . . either turn them into the streets to beg or steal, or hire them out to loose persons, by whom they are trained up in that infamous way of living; and sometimes are blinded, or maimed and distorted in their limbs, in order to move pity and compassion."

One by one, Coram insinuated himself into the drawing rooms of just about any woman of rank he happened to know, carrying a quill, ink, and paper. He would then move on to someone else who might be persuaded to help if they recognized the signature he had just acquired. He noted their names and dates of contact inside a ragged, repurposed pocket almanac—a real-time record of a life's work coming into being.

He had begun, on March 9, 1729, with Charlotte Seymour, Duchess of Somerset, whose husband controlled estates across the length of England, from Northumberland to Sussex. Next, on April 22, he moved on to Anne Vaughan, Duchess of Bolton, whose husband happened to be the figure besotted with a player in Hogarth's painting of *The Beggar's Opera*. Three days later, he made his way to her stepmother-in-law, Henrietta Paulet, the dowager duchess, herself the product of a liaison between an unmarried woman and Charles II's illegitimate son, the Duke of Monmouth. On December 22, Coram called on Sarah Lennox, Duchess of Richmond, and, after the Christmas holiday, Isabella Montagu, Duchess of Manchester. He rode out to meet Frances Lee, Countess of Lichfield, on April 27 and then, on May 19, Dorothy Boyle, Countess of Burlington, whose husband had been one of Handel's hosts before he leased the house in Brook Street.

As his engagement with the Georgia project wound to a close, in the early 1730s, Coram moved on to the ladies' male counterparts. He approached another Handel patron, the Duke of Montagu. He set up a meeting with the Duke of Richmond, whose wife he had seen in December. Then came the Earl of Albemarle, the Duke of Manchester, the Duke of Kent, the Duke of Bedford, the Duke of Portland, alongside a parade of surgeons, apothecaries, merchants, and well-heeled gentlemen. Over more than a decade, Coram copied down the names of some 375 persons of influence, either in his notebook or on drafts of his petition—including 25 dukes, 57 earls and other ennobled peers, the prime minister, and Frederick, Prince of Wales.

A "hospital" for foundlings, as Coram described it, would require a royal charter, which in turn would enable a parliamentary bill authorizing the charity to take in children. All of that demanded considerable sums of money for paying legal fees, copying documents, and eventually constructing a building. Along with his signature gathering, Coram had been laboring to collect funds that would set the entire enterprise on a firm foundation, taking in donations where he could get them and planning for a future when the hospital might become a reality.

For financial support, the logical place to go was to the families who made their money in the place he knew best, the colonies. Their wealth, in turn, had come from the one source that knit together an otherwise fractious and divided British society: the commerce in human beings. "I thank God I have more love towards Mankind than to have any hand in Introducing Slavery upon Children unborn," he once wrote to a correspondent in Massachusetts. More than any of his other projects, however, this one was coming to depend on the profits that slavery produced. The truth was that at the time nearly everything did.

10

The Book of Job

"I am oblig'd to you for purchasing the 200 [pounds in] S. S. Annuities, which I shall herewith send you an order to accept for me," Edward Holdsworth wrote to Charles Jennens in the spring of 1734. Jennens managed Holdsworth's investments, as he did for several of his friends, and Holdsworth's abbreviation would have been clear to him, as it was to anyone who hoped to increase the value of their portfolio. "S. S." referred to the South Sea Company, whose annuities were a source of guaranteed income.

The company's stock, on the other hand, inevitably soared and sank, and when the share price plummeted suddenly, in 1720, well-placed families had found themselves bankrupt overnight. Cannons, the Duke of Chandos's great manor house in Middlesex, where Handel first experimented with English oratorio, later had to be liquidated, with contents and architectural elements sold off in a marathon auction. But for those who had the stomach to invest for the long term, the South Sea Company would turn out to be one of the most lucrative bets in the market. Eventually Holdsworth would come to hold at least a thousand pounds in South Sea assets. Jennens himself would purchase twelve times that amount in stocks and annuities, which paid dividends as high as 8 percent.

The company had been created at the end of Queen Anne's reign as a joint-stock firm, much like Handel's future employer, the Royal Academy of Music. It took in private capital, turned it toward a profitable business, and then paid out interest to shareholders and other investors. But the South Sea Company was also a version of what would later be called a public-private partnership. A royal charter granted the company a trading monopoly in "the kingdoms, lands, etc., of America . . . or which shall hereafter be discovered." In return the company's profits financed major British state operations—essentially an enormous debt-equity swap before anyone had invented the term.

The company cooperated with another similar venture, the Company of Royal Adventurers Trading in Africa, or simply the Royal African Company, which had been created under Charles II and rechartered under James II to explore the west coast of Africa and organize new commercial operations there. The Royal African Company established a string of fortifications along the coast, taking some from their original Portuguese or Dutch builders and erecting new ones where required. A royal charter empowered its agents to use military force against non-Christian African powers, seize any land not belonging to Christian princes, and control trade between England and the entire Atlantic coast of Africa.

The business of both these companies was aided by an innovation that came about through the Peace of Utrecht, the peace agreement that Handel had celebrated with one of his earliest works for the British royal household, the hymn of thanksgiving for the end of Anne's war with Spain. Under the terms of the treaty, British ships were given the right to carry goods across the Atlantic and unload them for a profit throughout Spain's overseas dominions. One key aspect of that change was known in Spanish as the *asiento de negros.* Through the *asiento*, or contract, Britain obtained the right to supply enslaved laborers in the Spanish Atlantic. The government in turn subcontracted that opportunity to the South Sea Company, which made use of the forts and trading networks pioneered by the Royal African Company. With the granting of the *asiento*, the slave trade became the South Sea Company's signature moneymaking venture and, by extension, a principal source of public and private wealth in Britain overall.

The two companies helped to shape the market in the involuntary transport of human beings—the Royal African Company alone would force more enslaved Africans across the Atlantic, nearly 150,000 people, than any other single institution—but by the early eighteenth century neither could any longer claim a monopoly on purchases and shipping. Their enormous success had created its own competition. More and more private shipowners began to organize triangular journeys out of London, Liverpool, Bristol, and other ports: taking manufactured and industrial goods, from cloth to iron, to West Africa; hauling Africans to the Caribbean and the coastal Atlantic; and then bringing sugar and tobacco back to Europe. By the middle of the century, a third or more of all people forcibly taken to the New World were arriving on British ships, which in turn produced its own effective lobby for protecting, and even escalating, the free trade in unfree labor. The same year Jennens purchased Holdsworth's South Sea annuity, upward of fifty thousand people were forced onto ships in African ports and river outposts, some eight thousand of whom would die before reaching their destinations in the Caribbean and North and South America.

Slavery was so woven into British politics and society that its sheer ordinariness could render it invisible. Isaac Newton owned shares in the South Sea Company. John Locke owned stock in the Royal African Company. In 1719, when readers first opened *Robinson Crusoe*, Daniel Defoe's fictional tale of a civilized Englishman remaking himself from scratch, the premise of the storyline was believable precisely because it was so commonplace. Defoe's castaway ends up shipwrecked on a desert island because of a business venture to buy Africans on the coast of Guinea, sell them in Brazil, and pocket the proceeds. "And they offer'd me that I should have my equal share of the *Negroes* without providing any part of the stock," Defoe had Crusoe recount.

Handel, too, circulated in a world where empire, enslavement, and art were mutually dependent. Nearly a third of the Royal Academy of Music's investors were also investors in the Royal African Company or had close family members who were. Some of them, such as the Duke of Chandos, had derived much of their wealth from Caribbean plantations. Chandos's principal family holding in Jamaica—the Hope Estate—would still hold 379 people in bondage a century later, with their collective value assessed at a little under seven thousand pounds. Handel himself held perhaps two hundred pounds in South Sea Company stock, buying in as early as 1716, but liquidated most of it before the crash of 1720. Until 1732, he received portions of his salary from the Royal Academy of Music, and briefly his royal pension, via annuity accounts held by the South Sea Company and the Royal African Company, where he was listed as one of its "Adventurers," the latter company's term for investors. Those arrangements provided a substantial cash account—twenty-three hundred pounds—from which he withdrew funds for the rest of the decade.

The evidence suggests that Handel's accounts were mainly a banking mechanism, a convenient way to receive his regular income not unlike a modern direct deposit system, rather than a calculated investment in the slave trade as such. But even in this sense, he was in much the same category as anyone of means at the time. The money and financial systems that sustained him—before and after moving to Brook Street, gaining copyright protection for his compositions, and becoming a naturalized subject—were in one way or another entwined with the trade in people.

At the time, one only had to look around and listen to find this reality on public display. William Hogarth's paintings and prints showed what forced labor had built: images of country estates and London town houses in which Africans and Afro-Caribbeans were as much an indicator of fashion-conscious wealth as a silver teapot or Oriental carpet. Black servants attended to the needs of white families from the edge of the frame, sometimes wearing a silver collar as a sign of ownership. The person who put the entire machinery of empire and exploitation to music was none other than Susannah Cibber's brother Thomas Arne. "Rule, Britannia!" Arne wrote in 1740, adapting words by the Scottish poet James Thomson, "Britannia, rule the waves!/Britons never, never, never shall be slaves." In one sung line, Arne's work would come to define both British identity and British imperial might. The first phrase lauded the power of Britons' globe-spanning commerce and navy. The second named what—and who—had enabled it.

※

IN THE EARLY EIGHTEENTH CENTURY, the components that would later define slavery in popular memory—the fusion of enslaved status and race, the inevitable passing of bondage from parent to child, even the sharp distinctions between slavers and abolitionists—were not firmly in place. Sea captains who had trafficked people could later work to free them. Artists and thinkers who abhorred the idea of inherited captivity could accommodate themselves to the reality of it. Scholars and pamphleteers still debated whether skin color marked an essential difference among human types or represented merely an accident of environment or parentage, without any deeper meaning. Women and men of visibly African descent could live in London not just as servants but, in greater and lesser degrees, as free members of society.

Social caste, in certain instances, still trumped color. John Montagu, Duke of Montagu, patron to Handel and Coram, was one of the wealthiest landowners in Britain. He had married Mary Churchill, daughter of the Duke of Marlborough and Sarah Churchill, the former lady-in-waiting to Queen Anne. In addition to employing black servants, Montagu became one of the most important facilitators of African and Afro-Caribbean advancement. He took under his protection Ignatius Sancho, a composer and playwright who had been born on a slave ship. Sancho would become perhaps the first formerly enslaved man to vote in a British election, and his posthumously published writings, *Letters of the Late Ignatius Sancho, an African,* would help fuel the antislavery movement.

Other British writers such as Olaudah Equiano, kidnapped in

what is now Nigeria, and Ottobah Cugoano, seized as a child in present-day Ghana, would later emerge as essential public voices in the campaign to end the trade in human beings. Families, too, could stretch across the divide of race. When Theophilus Cibber launched his legal case against William Sloper Jr., he turned for representation to a young lawyer on the rise named William Murray. Years later Murray would become not only an earl but also the great-uncle and guardian of a woman named Dido Elizabeth Belle, whose mother had been enslaved in the British Caribbean. Her portrait, painted by the Scottish artist David Martin, still stands out as one of the most entrancing images of the time—with Dido herself, wry and playfully smiling, rushing across the canvas behind a seated white cousin.

In the American colonies, however, things were developing differently. Legal systems were in a state of flux, as Coram discovered when he lost out to his fellow trustees on the matter of women's equality in Georgia. New laws would soon reshape local society. Many of the colonies were putting in place the rudiments of a rigid structure of intergenerational bondage that targeted Africans and their descendants. New legislative acts confirmed that being baptized a Christian did not preclude slave status. Colonial assemblies came to define runaway "Negroes" differently from escaped European servants. White settlers were given the legal right to apprehend black runaways, with guaranteed immunity if an enslaved person were killed in the process. Officials ruled that children born of mixed parentage, free and enslaved, were assumed to be enslaved, too.

Slavery as a human institution was ancient. From the Egyptians and Aztecs to the early-modern Venetians and Ottomans, it was practiced in many forms and for many reasons, from a way of working off a debt to a consequence of losing a battle. But racialized enslavement—in which a human being identifiable by physical appearance became an economic unit with a defined monetary value and exchangeable for other goods similarly priced—was a modern innovation. Its essential features were still being fleshed out as Handel received his salary via the Royal African Company and Jennens and Holdsworth purchased their South Sea annuities. To different degrees, colonies along the

Atlantic Seaboard were developing from societies with slavery into slave societies: economic and administrative entities that not only practiced enslavement but relied upon it. By the 1730s the normalcy of it all had become so unremarkable that the same colonial newspapers that carried faraway news of a royal birth or an opera premiere in the Haymarket also ran, a page or two later, announcements offering cash rewards for the forced return of an absconded Negro.

Enslavement as practiced by European empires grew out of an economic system designed to transfer wealth across continents, from Africa to Europeans' colonies in the New World and then back to their home ports and capitals. It depended on the military and commercial power of modern states. It was backed up by evangelizing Christianity and the presumed logic of science, both of which located the origins of slavery not in history but outside it, in the will of God and the timeless facts of natural hierarchy. Its legality rested on sources as varied as English common law, court cases, parliamentary legislation, and the edicts of colonial assemblymen who were in the self-interested position of claiming to own other human beings. The result was a transoceanic system of organized bondage that, over the span of four centuries, shipped an estimated twelve and a half million people from Africa to the New World—more than half of whom were seized in the century that Europeans would later remember as an age of reason and enlightenment.

Of the forty British colonies throughout the wider Americas, only thirteen would eventually rebel to form a new country, the United States. When they did, they emerged with a political economy in which about half of all debt was secured by collateral in the form of enslaved individuals and families. Even once slavery was formally abolished—in Britain's remaining colonies in 1833, in the United States in 1865—its makers gave it a stealthy afterlife. In the United States, Jim Crow laws kept alive many of the political practices, social hierarchies, and everyday violence of enslavement for another century. Antimiscegenation laws and other segregation measures, adopted even in states that had no direct link to the slave system, extended the traditions of the old South to the American Midwest and western plains. In Britain, the government took the remarkable step of using public funds to reimburse enslavers for their erstwhile property. In granting freedom to more than 800,000 people on Caribbean plantations and elsewhere, Parliament also allocated twenty million pounds—nearly two billion pounds today—to indemnify slave owners for the resulting loss of labor. Paying out money to aristocratic families, merchants, bankers, and other leading figures in British society, the program amounted to the largest direct reparations program ever created—in this case, compensating not the victims of a vast historical wrong but rather its beneficiaries.

In all these ways, Enlightenment-era enslavement was the product of a specific moment. Its origins lay in an early-eighteenth-century change in what constituted white common sense—the growing conviction that the most naturally enslavable individual was one who happened to be black. In that shift lay the essential awfulness of racialized bondage. It was a process observable across a single lifetime: the intentional cutting away of the rights and privileges of people who, not long before, might have been full subjects and citizens of the places they had been forced to inhabit.

THAT IS HOW, in early 1731, just as Thomas Coram was gathering signatures for his foundling project and Thomas Arne Sr. had begun to make plans for his daughter Susannah's debut on the London stage, a man named Ayuba Diallo came to be standing on the deck of the *Arabella*, a British-flagged ship recently arrived in West Africa.

The *Arabella* had anchored at Joar, a settlement on the north bank of the Gambia River at the edge of low, wooded hills. For nearly two centuries, Joar had been a busy trading post, or factory, and an inland partner of the Royal African Company's fortress on James Island, nearer the river's mouth. Now, in the dust and bustle of caravans arriving and riverboats crowding the banks, Diallo was talking as fast as he could—remonstrating, pleading, literally begging for his life.

In his late twenties, Diallo was the privileged son of an *almaami*, or local Muslim judge, and educated in Islamic law and texts. He had come to Joar from Bundu, a fertile lowland farther north along the Senegal River, a place "flowing with milk and honey," as the Scottish explorer Mungo Park would later report. Home to several languages and cultures—Fulbe, Malinke, Soninke, Wolof—Bundu had been conquered in the 1690s by Fulbe farmers and herders in a series of conflicts with the Malinke, or Mandinka, not unlike clashes in Europe over religion, land, and power in the Thirty Years' War. Since then, Bundu's new rulers had turned geography to their advantage. To the north lay the meeting place of the savanna and the Sahara Desert, leading to the sultanates of North Africa. To the west were the Atlantic coast and the European empires beyond. For the *almaami* elite, long-distance trade—in iron, guns, textiles, and silver—opened up opportunities for levying taxes on the caravans that traveled between these two borderlands. By the early eighteenth century, however, the Bundu pathway had also become an important route for the commerce in people.

In Joar, Ayuba Diallo's plan had been to offer the *Arabella*'s captain, Stephen Pike, two boys he had taken captive from among his non-Muslim neighbors, hopefully in exchange for something Diallo considered even more valuable, writing paper. As he knew, captains like Pike seemed to have an insatiable appetite for kidnapped laborers. Pike's employer, a prominent London merchant named William Hunt, operated a commercial and slaving firm with his brother Henry. He would dispatch Pike and the *Arabella* on at least nine slave voyages across the Atlantic—a venture so remunerative, in fact, that William would eventually sign on as a philanthropic supporter of Coram's foundling project.

But as the *Arabella* strained against its cable, Diallo found himself in a position he could never have imagined. To his astonishment, he and a friend or servant, Loumein Yoai, had been shaved and shackled and herded on board with another 167 women, men, and children.

Through an interpreter, Diallo protested to Pike that there had been a terrible misunderstanding. Pike had not been interested in the two boys, so Diallo had traded them for cows on the other side of the

Gambia River. But on his way home, he had been seized by a group of Malinke men, who had in turn sold him to the British. Pike explained that the *Arabella* would soon set sail, making for the mouth of the river nearly two hundred miles downstream.

As an experienced river slaver, Pike wanted to leave as soon as possible after his human cargo was loaded and secured. Mutiny by the captives, who had to be superintended above decks for meals and toilets, as well as the possibility of tropical diseases laying low his twenty-man crew, put a premium on departing swiftly. This particular journey was expected to take six weeks or more, and the Hunts' factor across the sea, Vachel Denton, was eager to add a fresh intake to "a parcel of choice Country born and other well seasoned Negroes," as one of his sale bulletins would later declare.

Once the *Arabella* was supplied with water, meat, and fruit, with perhaps sacks of ground maize and broad beans for the captives, Pike was disinclined to wait. However, if Diallo's family were prepared to offer a ransom—two adults, say, in exchange for the tiresome man who now stood before him, protesting that he had been wrongfully seized—the slight delay might be worth it. After some thought, Pike agreed to allow Diallo to pass word to a local villager, who set off at a run, hoping to cover the distance to Bundu, which could take up to two weeks under regular conditions, before the captain set sail.

Pike waited for a time, but with no word from Diallo's relatives he eventually ordered the *Arabella* turned downriver. At some point after April 11, 1731, the ship put in at James Island for final restocking. On April 18 it reached the open Atlantic, with Diallo and Yoai in the hold.

The first person from sub-Saharan Africa ever recorded as enslaved by Europeans—a woman taken by the Portuguese in 1441—was from Diallo's geographic region, Senegambia. But by the time Diallo was led onto the *Arabella*, people from Senegambia accounted for a relatively small proportion of those seized and sent across the Atlantic, less than one-twelfth of the total. Most people began their forced journeys in the Bight of Benin and the Bight of Biafra, the elbow of the African continent, or in west-central Africa, in what is today

Angola. The kidnapped typically ended the first leg of their ordeal, if they survived it, by being unloaded in Brazil or the Caribbean.

But things were beginning to change. Developments in sailing technology were cutting voyage times. Fewer crew members were required to maneuver the ships. Larger vessels could carry more people. With costs falling, private merchants such as the Hunt brothers were dispatching more and more captives westward. By the middle of the century, the number of individuals forcibly shipped across the Atlantic had increased sevenfold as compared with a century earlier. Within a few decades, enslaved people would come to account for more than 95 percent of the value of trade between the Old and the New Worlds.

Their destinations were increasingly not just plantations in the Caribbean but also British colonies along the North Atlantic coast—which is where the *Arabella* was now headed. Sharks would have followed the ship, attracted by the trail of waste that heavily laden vessels scattered behind; they were sometimes known to haunt a slave voyage all the way across the ocean. Belowdecks, people exchanged information in multiple languages, sharing their names, speaking of where they had come from and the families they had left behind, speculating about where they might be headed, sometimes singing. There would have been brutality, sickness, and possibly new births. On the *Arabella* nineteen people died along the way, their bodies tossed overboard, unless they had killed themselves by choosing to jump.

After roughly forty days at sea, Diallo next stepped onto land in the port city of Annapolis in Maryland. Colonists could open their local newspaper, the *Maryland Gazette,* and read news from London of "the Voices hired by Mr. Hendel, for the Italian Operas in the Hay Market." But the vital information that had already filtered back to Bundu was that Ayuba, husband to Finda and Umm, father of Samba, Dimba, and Fatimata, had been taken by the Christians and would almost certainly never be seen again.

MARYLAND WAS ALREADY a hundred years old by the time Diallo arrived. Its capital was named for Queen Anne, and much of the colony was run essentially as the property of the Calvert family, the barons Baltimore, despite the political risks posed by their Roman Catholic faith. Given the wealth to be derived from tobacco farms along the Chesapeake Bay, London merchants were also attracted by the business opportunities there. William Hunt, for example, owned significant tracts of land on the Chesapeake and later served as trustee for the Maryland government's banking interests in London.

Once the *Arabella* arrived in Annapolis, Vachel Denton, the Hunts' factor and also the city's mayor, arranged for Diallo's sale. A planter, probably named Alexander Toulson, paid forty-five pounds for his claim to ownership. Toulson farmed land on Kent Island, a low rise of fields and timberland in the Chesapeake, where he put Diallo to work in the plantation's tobacco rows. Diallo—or Simon, as Toulson started calling him—could read and write Arabic and spoke as many as six languages, including Fulfulde and Wolof, yet had to make do with signs and pointing when he tried to understand what Toulson required him to do.

Toulson likely held title to other people as well, who were made to plow, plant, and serve. When he compiled his will five years later, he listed women and men called Philis, Sue, Pompey, Crocus, Ceeser, and Darkey among his possessions—the last of whom, should there be any "increase of the said negro woman," was to be separated from her children, who were bequeathed to a different heir. But from what Toulson or his overseer could tell, Diallo seemed to have little experience as a field hand. He soon fell ill and was transferred to working as a cattle herd, an occupation he knew well from Bundu. When out with the cows, he found it easier to keep up his daily prayers, which he managed to do by stealing away to a quiet stand of trees.

On at least one occasion, the young son of a white American colonist happened to see him there. The child mocked the strange ritual, taunting Diallo and throwing dirt in his face. Before long, Diallo made plans to escape. He left Kent Island, possibly swimming the narrow strait to Maryland's Eastern Shore, the mainland peninsula that separated the Chesapeake from the Atlantic. He crossed through swamps and cattail forests. He forded slow-moving creeks and worked his way around inlets fingering in from the bay, avoiding every rise in the landscape that gave an excuse for a house or church.

Not quite a decade earlier, in 1723, the Maryland colonial assembly had passed legislation making it lawful for white people to "shoot, kill and destroy such negro or negroes, or other slave" who ran away from their professed owners and refused to surrender. Rewards were offered to any citizen who successfully detained a runaway until the claimant could be informed. Toulson apparently never took out an advertisement in the *Maryland Gazette* to try to retrieve Diallo, as other slaveholders routinely did when their property fled. "Run away from Samuel Peel's Quarter, call'd Turkey-Island in Anne-Arundel County, on Sunday the 27th of April last," ran one notice, "a Negroe Fellow call'd Limehouse, about Thirty Years old. He had on when he went away, a new felt Hat, a new grey Fear-nothing Coat, one new and one old Cotton Jacket, . . . a pair of old Cotton Breeches, a pair of white Coventry made Yarn Stockings, a pair of good Negroe Shoes." The reason was that Toulson's quarry had already been captured.

At some point not long after leaving Kent Island, Diallo had been spotted in a field or along a road. He was seized by a passerby and taken nearly sixty miles away, to Dover, then part of Pennsylvania, where the St. Jones River meandered across the coastal Atlantic plain. He was placed in the local jail, which is where a traveling lawyer and clergyman, Thomas Bluett, happened to hear of the newly arrived runaway. Apparently out of curiosity, Bluett asked to meet him in the local tavern, located in the same building as the jail. Diallo was led in, and Bluett began questioning him in English. When Diallo responded in the languages he knew, the only words Bluett could make out were "Allah" and "Muhammad."

Through another enslaved man in Dover who spoke Wolof and English, Bluett managed to jot down Diallo's story—a tale of misfortune and, as Bluett understood it, wrongful imprisonment. "By his affable Carriage, and the easy Composure of his Countenance," Bluett later recalled, "we could perceive he was no common Slave." That is also probably how the authorities connected him back to Toulson. Landowners talked about their property, and the troublesome, voluble Diallo might have been identified just by asking around. Toulson soon arrived in Dover to return him to the plantation. But Diallo's encounter with Bluett had opened up the thinnest of hopes, the mirror image of what had happened on the *Arabella:* that he could make himself understood, that a person could listen, and that, moved by his story, someone might offer him a way out.

The thought that now seemed to occur to Toulson was something that would be nearly impossible for American slaveholders to imagine in future decades. Perhaps he had made a mistake in buying Diallo, apparently a highborn, literate man who might be redeemed, for a price, by his family in Africa or by the Hunt brothers in London. Once he had returned to Kent Island with his captive, Toulson allowed Diallo to draft a letter to his father and family.

"I am Ayuba bin Sulayman," Diallo wrote, the Arabic script curling leftward on the page. "I am Ayuba bin Sulayman," he repeated, giving his name again and again, insisting on the person he had been. He begged a reader to believe him. "There is no strength or power but with God Almighty," he told his family, offering peace to all of them, naming them one by one, asking after his children, and asking that his wives not take new husbands, since he was making every effort to come home. "Believe, Muslims of Bundu," he wrote.

Toulson transmitted the letter to Vachel Denton, who tried to get it to Stephen Pike, the *Arabella*'s captain, who he thought would be in the best position to carry it back to Bundu. But the *Arabella* had long since set sail. Instead, Denton placed the letter on another ship bound for London, inside a package addressed to Henry Hunt, the *Arabella*'s co-owner, who opened it at some point in his firm's offices in Little Tower Street. From there it was a short walk to Leadenhall Street, the headquarters of the Royal African Company, where, in the same circle of merchants and colonialists Thomas Coram was soliciting for support of his foundling project, Diallo's appeal came into the hands of the associate of Coram's who would soon lead the first colonists to Georgia: James Oglethorpe.

In addition to his work on the Georgia project, Oglethorpe was deputy governor of the Royal African Company as well as a major shareholder. When he received the package containing Diallo's letter, he had the text translated and was immediately taken with the story. Oglethorpe might have been moved by the plight of a noble "prince"—the way Diallo was coming to be seen, based on Bluett's interview with him in the Dover jail—who had been mistakenly seized and put to work on a plantation half a world away. He might equally have reckoned that a well-placed Muslim man, if rescued and returned home, could be useful in the company's trade with inland states in West Africa.

Through the Hunts and Denton, Oglethorpe sent word that he wished to purchase Diallo's freedom on behalf of the company. When news of the offer finally reached Maryland, Toulson was apparently "very willing to part with him, as finding him no ways fit for his Business," according to Bluett. Denton arranged for Diallo to live with him in Annapolis until a new ship could be readied for the voyage eastward. In the spring of 1733, two years after being seized on the Gambia River, Diallo departed Annapolis above deck, unchained, bound for London, and in the company of Bluett himself.

DURING THE JOURNEY Bluett worked with Diallo on English so that, over the intervening weeks, he was able to make himself understood in yet another language. Somewhere along the way, Bluett also discovered that Diallo was not only an educated Muslim but perhaps also a hafiz, a person who had memorized the Qur'an in its entirety, or at least someone with more than a passing knowledge of the text and its interpretation. Once their ship arrived safely in England, in early May, Bluett became Diallo's minder and guide. There was to be no meeting with Oglethorpe, who was by this stage already in Georgia and taking the colony in a direction that would infuriate Coram.

But Diallo quickly fell into the wider circle of nobles and gentlemen who seemed charmed by the idea of a foreign prince rescued through their own generosity.

London society had frequently swooned at unusual visitors and public curiosities. Thomas Arne Sr., Susannah Cibber's father, had hosted a delegation of four Iroquois leaders who visited Queen Anne in 1710 and lodged them at his business, the Two Crowns and Cushions. John Arbuthnot, the Scottish physician and Handel's old friend, had been the guardian of "Peter the Wild Boy," a child whom George I brought to London after finding him living feral in a Hanover forest.

But Diallo's story was special. It seemed a real-life reenactment of a popular stage play, *Oroonoko,* a fictional tale of an African prince tricked into slavery. *Oroonoko* was familiar to anyone who frequented the theater. It had been adapted by the playwright Thomas Southerne from a work by Aphra Behn, one of the earliest women to write what would later be called a novel. Even though it dealt with the horrors of plantation life, Southerne's play was not an argument against slavery so much as a demonstration of its naturalness—but only if one were careful to get it right. Audiences who saw *Oroonoko* could come away convinced that some African societies were very much like Britain's own, all part of a God-ordained hierarchy of savages and nobles, the former destined to servitude, the latter enslaved only by misfortune. It was thus easy to think that Diallo's captivity, like Oroonoko's, had simply been a mistake—a wrinkle in the universal order of servants and lords, now in the process of being set smooth again.

Lodged at the Royal African Company's headquarters, Diallo found himself swimming in invitations. He became one of the capital's most sought-after celebrities. In town houses and Bloomsbury dining rooms, he met everyone from fellow Muslims such as the envoys of the bey of Tunis to the Duke of Montagu, Handel's patron whom Coram would soon sign up for his foundling project. George II and Queen Caroline received him at court and presented him with a watch as a token of their regard. In the swirl of London society, intimate and kaleidoscopic, it was wholly possible for the same people who had attended a Handel opera one evening to find themselves face-to-face with Diallo the next, a man whose captivity had, in a roundabout way, helped pay for the action onstage.

The fact that Diallo was a professing Muslim was of particular interest at the time. Handel had located some of his operas in Islamic landscapes, or at least a musician's fantasy of one. Many of his patrons, as well as his audiences, had family fortunes wrapped up in Britain's burgeoning commercial interests in the Near East and India; what they saw onstage was often a make-believe version of places with which they were already familiar. But philosophers and pamphleteers were also coming to use Muslim societies as a counterpoint to their own, a position from which to critique the perceived deficiencies of Christianity and the self-satisfaction of European empires, much as Swift had done with Gulliver's fanciful travels.

A friend of the Duke of Montagu's, the French philosopher Montesquieu, turned the fictional correspondence of two Muslim noblemen into a slicing satire of European politics, fashion, and manners in his *Persian Letters,* published in 1721. Pierre Bayle, the encyclopedist whose radical views Robert Jennens had encountered at Oxford, argued that Islam was in fact more tolerant than Christianity; if one were using reason alone to reach a conclusion about the divine, he felt, the best course was to become a Muslim. English naturalists and geographers, too, had a fascination with the Islamic world, not only in what would later be called the Middle East but also in West Africa. The region's renowned centers of Islamic learning provided powerful evidence against the belief that Europeans were the only people to engage in scholarship, reasoned debate, and science.

In all these matters, Diallo proved a rare informant. He was soon put to work translating Arabic texts for the royal physician, Hans Sloane, a slaveholder by marriage whose private collection of cultural artifacts and natural specimens would later form the foundation of the British Museum and British Library. Diallo might even have created three handwritten copies of the Qur'an, apparently from memory, two of which went to Sloane and the Duke of Montagu. When asked about his homeland, he drew a map with annotations in Arabic script showing the river systems of West Africa, the site where Captain Pike had seized him, the political boundaries of Bundu and other powers, and the place where he had bizarrely ended up—England—which he rendered as a tiny circle diminished by the vastness of Africa.

As he had done in Maryland, Diallo continued to write. He corresponded with his new associates in London, instructing them in the Arabic alphabet and the cultures of his homeland. He dispatched letter after letter back to his father in Bundu, sending word of his whereabouts just as he had first done from the deck of the *Arabella*, without ever knowing whether his messages were received or what might have become of his wives and children. He endorsed an application to join the Spalding Gentlemen's Society, an English provincial association of scholars and learned amateurs, adding his own greeting and signature to a text prepared by one of his supporters.

"His Youth was taken up in Learning, so that he could repeat the Koran by memory at 15 years of Age," wrote Joseph Ames, an antiquary and typographer, in proposing Diallo for membership. "He hath Learned Three Languages ... [including] the English. In his more advanced Years he taught Youth Arabic & dealt for Negroes &c. [and] hath 2 wives, 4 children, 18 servants, 3 Houses, 73 Head of Black Cattle, besides Asses and other Things." As Ames pointed out, Diallo was notable not only for being a former slave but also for having been, back in Senegambia, a slave trader, something that the membership board must have regarded as yet another marker of the ways in which he was not that different from prominent Britons. When he was admitted as a member, he joined a long list of British polymaths and literary notables, from Isaac Newton to Alexander Pope, most of them enmeshed in the same imperial networks that had both doomed Diallo and rescued him.

At the time he arrived in Britain, Diallo was still considered the property of the Royal African Company. Some of his patrons, such as Hans Sloane, thought it the best place for him to remain. He was more likely to be safe and well treated if he were kept as a ward of the company, Sloane believed, and cared for by paternalistic benefactors who were also, in a purely legal sense, his owners.

Thomas Bluett, however, felt differently. Not long after returning from Maryland, he helped organize a campaign to secure Diallo's freedom and took out a public announcement to spread the word. Subscriptions "to redeem" Diallo, as Bluett put it, soon poured into the hands of trustworthy keepers at Hamlin's Coffee House near the Tower of London. Within a few months, sufficient funds had been collected to pay off the chain of debts—from the Hunts to Denton to Toulson, then back to Oglethorpe—that had determined Diallo's worth. As with Theophilus Cibber's reckoning of the cost of his wife's affair, the value could be stated precisely: fifty-nine pounds, six shillings, and eleven pence. In December 1733, with the debt at last settled, the Royal African Company authorized a signed and sealed certificate confirming that "Simon . . . the Gambia Black lately brought from Maryland" was now a free man.

Diallo's growing circle of acquaintances and supporters asked a tailor to create an outfit more closely resembling what he might have owned in Bundu. He wore the new clothing to his audience with George II and perhaps again when other admirers commissioned a portrait. Painted by the Bath artist William Hoare, the image showed Diallo wrapped in a West African silk boubou, his head topped by a winding turban. Hanging around his neck was a leather amulet containing Qur'anic verses that he had written out himself. He looked straight out at the viewer, his face serene, with a natural, confident expression that was markedly at odds with the depiction of black servants in Hogarth's paintings.

Diallo had been reluctant to have his image made, probably on religious grounds. He was astounded when Hoare insisted on examining Diallo's boubou and turban so that he could get everything exactly right. "Why do some of you painters presume to draw God, whom no one ever saw?" Diallo asked. But the picture would stand as something of a rarity: likely the first full portrait ever created of a formerly enslaved black man.

Diallo was now in a condition that Alexander Pope had described with precision in his *Essay on Man*, the first part of which appeared only a few weeks before Diallo arrived in London. "Where slaves once more their native land behold," Pope wrote, "No fiends torment, no Christians thirst for gold." From his position as a newly liberated man, Diallo soon made a hopeful and startling admission to his hosts. His goal was to live not in London, feted as a prince of the imagination, but to return to Africa as the real Ayuba bin Sulayman—the Arabic form of his given name and his father's name—Job, the son of Solomon. The next step would be to figure out how exactly to start the journey home.

11

Scorn

As a public figure, Handel offered his name and reputation to causes like those that inspired Thomas Coram and delivered Ayuba Diallo from bondage. Later in the 1730s, he was one of the organizers of a campaign for down-and-out performers called the Fund for Decay'd Musicians. Performing artists tended to live on the frontier of poverty. Handel's principal trumpeter, John Grano, would be known to history not for his playing but for the fact that he wrote one of the most detailed memoirs of life inside the Marshalsea debtors' prison, the same place that had killed Susannah Cibber's grandfather. It was the death of another musician, an eminent oboist whose orphaned children were seen begging around the Orange Coffee House in the Haymarket, that had prompted Handel and a group of associates to set up their new charity. Through concerts and donations, they raised money to carry an unlucky violinist or organist through illness or a financial downturn. Toward the end of his life, Handel would bequeath a thousand pounds to the fund's coffers.

At the time, however, he might have worried that the line between benefactor and beneficiary was often uncomfortably thin. He was secure, if not rich, as an individual. Each year he garnered six hundred pounds in royal pensions and appointments: two hundred granted by Queen Anne, two hundred added by George I, and a further two hundred for overseeing the musical education of George II's daughters. His operas brought in additional receipts, as did active stock and annuity accounts and, notionally at least, the copyright on his printed music. All of that was more than enough to employ a manservant, Peter le Blond and later John de Bourk, a cook, and at least two maids, some perhaps accommodated in the garret at the top of 25 Brook Street. To an artist, though, money was a constant concern. On at least one occasion, he found himself unable to pay his performers, which caused a singer's irate husband to threaten him with arrest. One of the largest single boosts to his bank account came from a benefit concert that friends organized on his behalf at the Haymarket, which netted perhaps a multiple of his annual pension income.

Handel's health had also begun to falter. A profession that demanded frenzied labor, strict deadlines, and constant socializing had exacted a price. Now in his early fifties, Handel had become an "epicure," as an acquaintance called him, an expansive gourmand. He was known for overindulgence, even among the gentlemanly set that expected a full table and free-flowing port. He had grown round, even obese, and "unwieldy in his motions," according to another friend, with prominent jowls and a chin that stairstepped down into his cravat.

Stories circulated about his appetite and the comical behavior it could produce. Once, at a meal with his principal performers in Brook Street, Handel exclaimed, "Oh—I have de taught!" He then rushed from the dining room into his composing room, closing the door behind him, supposedly so that he could commit his musical thoughts to paper before they scurried away. A guest who peeked through the keyhole found him not scribbling on a staff but making his way through an expensive hamper of burgundy. On most days, however, his discomforts were real: colic, constipation, joint pain. The old flashes of anger, familiar to friends and musicians under his direction, were now harder to explain and sometimes targeted at no one in particular.

In the spring of 1737, Handel was struck with "Rhumatick Palsie," as an acquaintance put it, likely a mild stroke that affected the fingers on his right hand, "though I fear . . . he will loose a great part of his execution so as to prevent his ever playing any more Concertos on the Organ." The condition would turn out to be temporary, but later that year friends reported that "his senses were disordered," in what became a recurring bout of mental confusion—perhaps a result of lead poisoning, a common danger from wig powder and fortified wines and spirits stored in leaded vessels. A cartoon would later circulate depicting Handel as many had already come to view him: as a pig in a wig and scarlet coat, seated on a firkin and tooting away at an organ draped with a ham and game fowl. "The Charming Brute," read the caption.

Despite his ailments, Handel could still compose furiously. When Queen Caroline died that autumn, the victim of a hernia exacerbated by an ill-considered surgery, his anthem "The ways of Zion do mourn" accompanied the funeral procession in Westminster Abbey. It was a searing farewell to a woman he had known for almost thirty years— "the finest Cruel touching thing that ever was heard," according to one of the queen's daughters. He was busier than ever with ticketed performances, working first out of the new opera house in Covent Garden and then again at the Haymarket, although now without the stability of a long-term contract.

In the spring of 1738, he premiered a new opera, *Serse*, based on the life of the Persian king Xerxes, which closed after five performances. Audiences at the time might have been baffled by the head-scratching opening, in which Xerxes sings a gentle ode to a shade tree by rhyming the Italian words for "friendly" and "vegetable." The reception gave no hint of how "Ombra mai fù," or "Handel's Largo," would be seen centuries later—as one of the most gorgeous arias ever written. Italian opera was clearly "not a plant of our native growth," Colley Cibber quipped in his memoirs not long afterward. Handel could at least take consolation from the fact that his chief rival, the Opera of the Nobility, would soon be on its way to collapse.

The same year a statue of Handel was unveiled in the gardens at Vauxhall, a popular venue on the Thames for supper parties and fresh-air ambling. Carved in marble by Louis-François Roubiliac, later one of Charles Jennens's favorite sculptors, it showed Handel reclining and with his legs crossed, plucking a lyre while dressed in an open shirt and slippers. The statue was unprecedented not only in the casual way Roubiliac portrayed his subject. It was also a public monument to an artist who was still alive—a signature honor, to be sure, but also a reminder that statues were usually erected to people once they were past their prime. Handel continued to produce original Italian operas or revive old ones, reaching back to the previous decade in hopes of building an audience-pleasing schedule. Few were unqualified successes. Even George II had decided to stay away from the theater, part of an extended mourning period for his deceased queen.

With new work closing after a few performances, Handel found himself at risk of being frozen in time, an eminence to be venerated rather than a font of originality. Even Jennens and Holdsworth had started to worry. "He wou'd do very well I think to lay quiet for a year or two, and then I am perswaded that his enemies will sink of course, and many of them will court him as much as now they oppose him," Holdsworth told Jennens. "But I am chiefly concern'd for you, for I fear whilst Handel retires you'll have the Hyp."

IN THE YEARS SINCE he had first met the great man, Jennens had come to feel an increasing sense of possessiveness toward Handel and his work. Reading Virgil was one way to "keep off the Hyp" in Gopsall, he told Holdsworth. The other was to "go to London, & there Mr. Handel will do it for me." His opinions about Handel could swing from worshipful attention to impatient irritability and then back again, sometimes in the space of a single season. When the composer failed to deliver, Jennens nursed the disappointment like a wounded limb. Dependent on Handel's work while also frustrated with it, Jennens gradually came around to a new and perhaps surprising realization: that the solution to the Prodigious's troubles could well be Jennens himself.

Handel relied on other people to provide the concept for a new piece of theater as well as the specific text that underlay the music—"the book," as producers from London's West End to Broadway would later refer to it in English, or the libretto, as musicians knew to call it in Italian. Decades earlier in Italy, cardinals and patricians vied with one another to suggest words or stories that Handel might render into song. Later in England, Aaron Hill had brokered the relationship with the librettist who had created *Rinaldo,* while Alexander Pope or John Arbuthnot had perhaps written the text for his first English oratorio, *Esther.*

Jennens had known some of the men who made the leap from Handel's acquaintance to his collaborator. It was easy for him to imagine doing the same. He had been immersed in classical Greek, Latin, and biblical sources since childhood, as was expected of a gentleman. He was a person of taste and discernment. He had assembled one of the greatest musical libraries in Britain. There was nothing to stand in the way of proposing new performances that Handel might translate to the stage.

From the mid-1730s, bundles of paper filled with Jennens's angular handwriting began to arrive at Brook Street. In fact, the first documented contact between the two men—in July 1735—was a letter from Handel in which he thanked Jennens for sending along an unnamed, and unknown, oratorio that Jennens had apparently drafted. As he got to know Handel better, the volume of ideas seemed to increase.

To anyone who knew Jennens well, his own preoccupations leaped from the pages. He took the story of the biblical Saul, a king beset by worries, and spun it into a pageant played out in Israel at a time of war and dynastic collapse. At its center was a triangle of love and jealousy involving three men—Saul, David, and Jonathan, the king's son—pulled apart by incompatible devotion. He likely helped create a text, based partly on the book of Exodus, about the deliverance of the Israelites from Egyptian bondage, in which the tyrannical captors bore more than a passing resemblance to a nonjuror's vision of the Hanoverians. He contributed to a project drawn from the work of John Milton, an abstract drama of energy, reflectiveness, and moderation, with the last of these—the carefully managed life—hailed as a model for survival and flourishing. "Kindly teach, how blest are they,/ Who nature's equal rules obey," went the libretto, a gloss on Jennens's own attempt at keeping on an even plane, "Who safely steer two rocks between,/And prudent keep the golden mean."

The texts were especially suited to Handel's new pared-down production style, where the drama lay in the stories, the ideas, and the musical composition itself, without the complex staging required of opera. Handel engaged them with renewed energy. The oratorios *Saul* and *Israel in Egypt* and the pastoral ode *L'Allegro, il Penseroso ed il Moderato* opened in 1739 and 1740. With the focus now purely on the music, the works were scored for larger orchestras, more voices, and more rafter-rattling choruses than anything Handel had yet produced. "He opens with the Loves of Saul & Jonathan, Then follows another on the ten plagues of Egypt (to me an odd subject)," noted a friend, Katherine Knatchbull. "He says the storm of thunder is to be bold & fine, & the thick silent Darkness to be express'd in a very particular piece of Musick."

Audiences bought tickets. Members of the royal household attended the premieres. But most productions also closed quickly. Other new works followed, but they ranged in Jennens's view from a "tolerable success" to "the worst of all Handel's Compositions." Few would be performed again in Handel's lifetime. In February 1741, Handel premiered an opera at Lincoln's Inn Fields, *Deidamia*, based on the story of Achilles and his secret love, whose union provided a haven in a time of war. The production closed after three performances. It would turn out to be the last Italian opera Handel ever composed.

Later that year rumors began to circulate that Handel was considering a return to the Continent, perhaps even quitting Britain for good. Jennens could not help but feel his efforts to revive Handel's career had all been a sad, depressing waste. "I could tell you more of his Maggots," he had said to a relative sometime earlier, a judgment that now seemed all the more apt. "But it grows lat[e] & I must defer the rest until I write next; by which time, I doubt not, more new ones will breed in his Brain."

Scorn

IF HANDEL'S CREATIONS HAD lost some of their power to entertain, for many Londoners the deficit was more than made up for by the trial of *Cibber v. Sloper*, which began in December 1738, just a few weeks before the opening of *Saul*.

Theophilus Cibber's lawsuit against William Sloper Jr. was argued at the King's Bench, the most senior court in England, with the esteemed trial judge William Lee presiding. The solicitor general, John Strange, the second-highest-ranking attorney in England, led a team of experienced barristers sitting on Cibber's side of the courtroom. Sloper was the named defendant, but for all practical purposes Susannah Cibber was the person on trial. The attorneys for her husband promised to bring forward witnesses who would testify to Sloper's "Assaulting, Ravishing and Carnally knowing Susannah Maria Cibber," as the court documents put it, "to be done at three several Periods of Time, at divers Days," which in turn had caused Theophilus to lose "the Company, Comfort, Society, Assistance, &c." of his beloved wife.

The barristers for the plaintiff unwound their case slowly and with care. Colley Cibber was called to confirm that Susannah and Theophilus were husband and wife. He swore that they were in fact married, adding that Susannah's low estate had turned him against the union from the start.

"Did Mr. Cibber, the plaintiff, during that time support her well and liberally, as became an affectionate husband?" Theophilus's counsel asked.

"He did," Colley Cibber said, "even to profusion. I often admonished him about it; and advised him to retrench his expenses. . . . He made her several valuable presents of rings and jewels."

Charles Fleetwood, the manager of the Drury Lane Theatre, was then called to confirm Susannah's substantial salary and other income. The defense quickly objected. Surely her finances were irrelevant to the matter at hand. On the contrary, the plaintiff's side countered, Fleetwood's testimony would demonstrate just how much money Theophilus stood to lose because Sloper had distracted his wife from the affairs of home. With the questioning allowed to proceed, Fleetwood testified that Susannah had been earning 200 pounds in salary, plus another 150 as a bonus, "for she grew much in favor of the town, and 'twas a very good benefit."

The lawyers for the plaintiff next called Mrs. Hayes, proprietor of the house in Blue Cross Street where the encounters between Susannah and Sloper were said to have taken place. Mrs. Hayes swore that she had let rooms in her house to a Mrs. Hopson, who would occasionally be visited by two friends, a man and a woman. Mrs. Hayes said she had no knowledge of just who Mrs. Hopson was, only that she seemed to be a quiet lodger and presented her landlord with no problems. She did find it odd, though, that Mrs. Hopson never seemed to spend the night in the rooms. Instead, she would sometimes leave her two friends alone while she went elsewhere.

One day an acquaintance of Mrs. Hayes's happened to be visiting and immediately recognized Mrs. Hopson. As Mrs. Hayes testified,

> "How do you do Mrs. Hopson," said he. So after she was gone, I asked him who Mrs. Hopson was, and he told me she was Mrs. Cibber's maid; so I gave her warning, and let my lodgings to another; for I did not like their coming. . . . One day after I gave warning, Mr. Sloper was in a great passion above stairs at something, and Mrs. Hopson came to me, "You have made a fine kettle of fish of it," says she.

Mrs. Hayes surmised that Sloper was enraged over the fact that he and Susannah had been identified as the lodgers for whom Mrs. Hopson had been the intermediary. From that point, Mrs. Hayes said, she wanted nothing more to do with whatever Susannah and Sloper had been getting up to under her roof.

Theophilus's attorneys had managed their witnesses expertly. They had unrolled a compelling story of surreptitious meetings and hidden identities. It was now time to solve the deepest mystery of all: what actually happened when Susannah and Sloper were in private. For this purpose the attorneys had an ideal witness in Mrs. Hayes's husband.

Like his wife, Mr. Hayes had grown suspicious about Mrs. Hopson's odd behavior in Blue Cross Street. "When Mrs. Hopson had my lodgings," Mr. Hayes said, "Mr. Sloper and Mrs. Cibber used to come often to her, and she used to leave them together two or three hours at a time. They used to go away at one, two, or three o'clock in the morning, in coaches or in chairs."

Blue Cross Street was a small alley just to the west of what would later become Trafalgar Square. It was not the obvious place for a romantic hideaway, since it was right next to the king's stables. But it did have the advantage of being midway between the houses where Cibber and Sloper lived. To get back and forth, they could each take a sedan chair, a small enclosed seat carried between two runners, or chairmen.

Sedan chairs could be picked up from stations throughout the city, like cabs at modern taxi stands, or hailed on the street by a servant. Since the chairs were transported at speed, just a few inches off the ground, accidents were common. But in London's warren of side streets and alleys, they were usually faster than carriages, not to mention more private—a fact that prompted the attorney's next question: How precisely had Mr. Hayes come to know that the two lodgers were in fact Mrs. Cibber and Mr. Sloper?

Mr. Hayes had a ready answer.

"I dogged them both home in their chairs," he said.

As soon as his renters stepped into the street, cloaked against the night air, Mr. Hayes had made a point of following them. He hoped to check what Mrs. Hopson had said about the woman and, with luck, establish the identity of the man who, he noticed, wore a fashionable bagwig: a wig with longer hair in the back encased in a silk covering—an obvious sign of a person of means.

On different evenings Mr. Hayes trailed them each in turn. He wended through crowds and stole around corners, staying far enough back not to be noticed. For fifteen minutes or so, Susannah's chairmen had headed northeast, past the new church of St. Martin-in-the-Fields and the opera house in Covent Garden. Once they had come to Holborn, they turned into the narrow confines of Wild Court. A quick conversation with a neighbor presumably confirmed that the woman was indeed the famous stage actor, just as Mrs. Hopson had said.

On another night, Mr. Hayes puffed along just out of sight as Sloper's chairmen took their passenger roughly the same distance, but to the west. They bore the sedan chair toward the wealthier streets of Handel's Mayfair neighborhood. They edged along the buildings of St. James's Palace and the green expanse near the villa of the Duke of Buckingham, which would later become the most famous royal palace in the world. At last, when the chairmen stopped outside a new town house in a narrow street known as St. James's Place, Mr. Hayes waited for the passenger to alight and walk inside. He then sidled up to the chairmen while they were catching their breath.

"After he was gone into the house," Mr. Hayes stated in court, "I asked the chairmen whose house that was? and they told me, Old Mr. Sloper's." It was the home of Thomas Coram's old associate, the parliamentarian and Georgia trustee William Sloper Sr. From that fact, Mr. Hayes easily deduced that the person in the bagwig must be the distinguished gentleman's son, William Sloper Jr.

That was not the end of Mr. Hayes's amateur detective work, however. Besides stalking his wife's lodgers through the streets of London, he decided to inform himself about what was happening within his own home.

"I have a closet on the same floor, adjoining to the room where they used to sit," he testified. One day, he gathered up a brace and bit, stepped into his own closet, and "bored holes through the wainscot." From that vantage point, he "could see them very plain."

Sloper would meet Susannah in the room and then proceed "to kiss her, and to take her on his lap," Mr. Hayes recounted. On December 22 of the previous year, Sloper "lifted up her clothes, and took down his breeches, and took his privy member and put it in his hand, and put it between her legs." The same scene played out again the following

January 12. Sloper again "took her upon his lap, took up her clothes, took down his breeches, and put his privy member between her legs." On that occasion Mr. Hayes had decided to remain at the spy hole for the entire afternoon. Between five and six o'clock, he saw Sloper "let down the turn-up bed softly." Susannah lay down on her back and "pulled up her clothes." Mr. Hayes remembered that Sloper then removed his bagwig and placed it on a candle sconce, an odd detail that lent credence to his account. Then, he said, Sloper "let down his breeches, took his privy member in his hand, and lay down upon her."

Over and over again, Mr. Hayes delivered the same line about legs and privy members—almost as though he had been coached by someone with an eye for story and stagecraft. After several rounds, Justice Lee finally stopped him. "There is no occasion to be more particular," Lee said. "We are not trying a rape."

Next, it was the turn of Sloper's team to address the jury. Their opening statement made it clear that they planned to take a novel strategy in their client's defense. The matter at hand was not whether indecent relations had occurred, Sloper's counsel said. The stories of trysts and assignations—all vividly described by people who swore on good authority that Susannah and Sloper had met with immoral intent, in secret, and on multiple occasions—amounted to little. There was nothing illegal at stake even if these things had happened just as described, the defense argued. The only matter before the court was whether Susannah's husband had been harmed in the process. And the best way to prove that he hadn't was to show that "the plaintiff had certainly encouraged it, and had no pretense to come to a jury for damages."

The defense called to the stand a string of witnesses—including Mrs. Hopson, Susannah's maid who had first given away Sloper's identity—to confirm not only that Theophilus knew of the meetings between Sloper and his wife but that his finances saw an uptick as soon as Sloper came into the couple's lives.

"Mr. Cibber was then very bare of money, and afraid of his creditors," Mrs. Hopson testified. "But one day he told me: Anne, says he, I shall have a good deal of money soon and you shall have some. And

I know he soon after had a good deal of money, and he paid me five guineas."

Mrs. Hopson further testified about what had happened when the threesome took lodgings together: the nightly ritual of Theophilus's handing over his wife to Sloper, the story of Susannah's taking her pillow with her to Sloper's bedchamber, even the cordial "Goodnight, my dear" that Theophilus would utter as he closed the door. Mrs. Hopson's conclusion—that the unconventional arrangement was Theophilus's doing—was backed up by other witnesses called by the defense. "I thought it no business of mine," said a Mrs. Carter, the wife of another landlord, "if the husband consented, and was satisfied."

After this testimony, the defense had only to summarize the facts as they had been presented. How bizarre that Theophilus takes money from Sloper and "resigns his wife to him," said one of Sloper's attorneys, the young barrister William Murray, in his closing speech, "and then comes to the Court of Justice, and to a jury of gentlemen for reparation in damages." Theophilus had clearly known of the affair, benefited materially from it, and conspired in first creating it. He could not now claim to be its victim. "Certainly the plaintiff cannot be injured," Murray said, "if he has not only consented, but has even taken a high price."

The jury was then sent out to deliberate. After only half an hour, they returned to the courtroom to report that they had found in Theophilus's favor. Sloper had, after all, slept with another man's wife, a fact that seemed beyond dispute. Theophilus had evidently experienced some degree of injury as a result, given that he and his wife were now estranged.

But that was as far as the jurors were willing to go. In delivering their decision, they awarded Theophilus damages that were ludicrously small: just ten pounds, a far cry from the five thousand he had sought.

❧

THROUGHOUT THE TRIAL, the one person conspicuously absent from the courtroom was Susannah Cibber. There was no point in her testifying. If she admitted to the affair, her reputation, and likely her stage career, would be damaged beyond repair. If she denied it, she would be committing perjury, not to mention giving evidence against her husband, which English common law regarded as a judicial impossibility. In the end, however, none of that mattered. Both Theophilus's original complaint and Sloper's defense against it had the same effect: destroying the woman each man claimed to love.

The trial had been of such intense public interest that someone, sensing an opportunity, had taken down notes on the proceedings. As soon as the verdict was in, the pages were rushed to a printer in Fleet Street. The full account appeared as a booklet a few days later. The text was filled with graphic details: the comic voyeurism of spy holes, secret witnesses, and servants afforded the chance to speak candidly about what their fancy masters and mistresses got up to behind bolted doors.

The transcript was accompanied by engravings purporting to show the scenes Mr. Hayes had described in court. There was Theophilus, depicted in his Ancient Pistol costume with oversize tricorn and drooping cavalier boots, looking on as Sloper climbed atop a naked Susannah. The booklet would be reprinted again and again for more than a century. Other publishers pirated the original copy and included it with collections of sensational trials and society scandals, a riveting story of illicit love with a dollop of the pornographic. People who had never seen Mrs. Cibber onstage could find out as much about her as they needed to know, all of it straight from eyewitnesses who provided rare insight into the lives of the rich and famous.

For Susannah, the trial was a public humiliation from which it was hard to imagine recovering. The most intimate facts of her sexual life, aired in a Middlesex courtroom, were now hawked on printed pages from Grub Street to the Strand. The devoted wives she had played onstage, the virtuous maidens, the long-suffering heroines—all of them now melted like greasepaint in summer. Beyond that, she was nearing the end of yet another pregnancy, in ill health, and, because of her notoriety, impossible to cast, even if a producer agreed to let her return to the stage.

Fearing further harassment by Theophilus, she moved from friends' houses to acquaintances' spare rooms, sometimes introducing herself as "Mrs. Archer," a thin ruse to prevent gossips from giving away her whereabouts. The next February, she gave birth to another child, a daughter named Molly. Her landlords noticed that she was visited regularly by a "Mr. Wheeler"—Sloper again in disguise—who seemed devoted to her and the new baby, who was healthy and thriving.

By that summer, though, Theophilus was back. He had somehow tracked Susannah to a London suburb, where he stripped her room of anything of value, from gloves to bed linens. He soon hauled Sloper back into court. He demanded even more money than before—ten thousand pounds—for Sloper's continuing liaison with his wife. In December 1739 it took another jury less than half an hour to find in his favor, even if the jurors once more whittled down the award, this time to five hundred pounds. For Theophilus the profit from his litigiousness, though still small, was clearly moving in the right direction.

Nearly everyone had been making money from the affair. "Henceforth, business poured in upon me from all quarters," recalled William Murray, later the 1st Earl of Mansfield and lord chief justice, the kingdom's preeminent jurist. His leap into the law as a younger barrister had begun with service as Sloper's junior counselor. Grub Street booksellers now had two trial transcripts to publish, which they issued in a repackaged double set. Printers took interest in Theophilus's old pretrial letters, which also found their way to market.

It was not difficult for Theophilus to spot the bright seam waiting to be mined. If nothing else, the trials had confirmed that an offense had been committed against him. Every moment Sloper and Susannah were together, they were committing it again. His wife's love for another man, he realized, could be the vehicle of his own perpetual enrichment.

Susannah must have reckoned that the serial disgrace might well continue forever. Theophilus could just keep on suing, especially now that the fact of her affair had twice been established in a court of law.

Westminster Bridge, with the Lord Mayor's Procession on the Thames, by the Venetian painter Canaletto, 1747. The bridge was not yet built when Handel had debuted his *Water Music* thirty years earlier, but a crush of boats was commonplace on the Thames during royal celebrations and public holidays.

Attributed to Balthasar Denner, this portrait is thought to be the earliest verified depiction of Handel, ca. 1726–28. By his early forties, Handel had become a naturalized British subject, premiered some of his most important operas, and created soaring anthems for the coronation of George II. But rivals and critics were beginning to gather.

Jonathan Swift, as painted by Charles Jervas, ca. 1718. People who knew Swift thought of him and Handel as similar personalities: witty, sarcastic, and talented at making ordinary things seem strange and new. As dean of St. Patrick's Cathedral in Dublin and in charge of the cathedral's choristers, Swift would play a central role in the premiere of the *Messiah*.

A view of Gopsall Hall, Charles Jennens's family home. Because of the "ill reception I am able to give my Friends there," he once complained, hosting guests "always gives me as much pain . . . as their Company gives me pleasure." He undertook a massive redesign, shown here, after the death of his father. The memorial he built to his friend Edward Holdsworth is visible on the left.

Charles Jennens was born into wealth, but "the hyp"—bouts of deep depression—could drive him to despair. "'Tis impossible for such a Wretch as I am . . . ," he wrote in 1746, around the time this portrait was painted by Thomas Hudson, "to determine with any certainty upon any Action of my Life." By this stage, his "Scripture Collection"—the basis for the *Messiah*—had already been performed in Dublin and London.

Susannah Cibber, as painted by Thomas Hudson, 1749. Wed to actor Theophilus Cibber, who controlled her finances as well as her most intimate relationships, she described her life as a "dying by inches." Her performance at the premiere of the *Messiah* would mark a watershed in a public life marked by stage triumphs as well as painful scandal.

Strolling Actresses Dressing in a Barn, by William Hogarth, 1738. Hogarth showed a company of traveling actors readying themselves behind the scenes—a window into the chaos and scandal thought to define the lives of "players" such as Susannah and Theophilus Cibber.

Hogarth's 1728 rendition of a scene from *The Beggar's Opera* by John Gay, produced by John Rich. In taking hilarious aim at the most fashionable entertainment of the moment—Italian opera—Gay also targeted its leading practitioner: Handel himself.

In Hogarth's *Gin Lane,* 1751, an infant boy plunges headlong over a staircase while his mother, dazed and syphilitic, concentrates on her snuff tin. Hogarth captured the reality of poverty, at least as imagined by the wealthy. By mid-century, an astonishing 75 percent of children may have died before the age of five.

Ayuba Sulayman Diallo, as painted by William Hoare, 1733. "Believe, Muslims of Bundu," Diallo wrote to his family from enslavement in Maryland, urging them not to give up hope for his return. After the Royal African Company granted his freedom, friends commissioned a London tailor to make clothing similar to what Diallo had worn in West Africa. The amulet around his neck contained Qur'anic verses he had written out from memory.

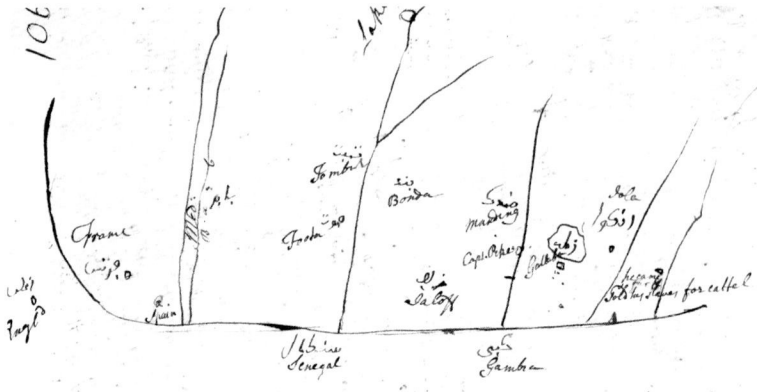

Diallo's patrons—who were also his captors—were eager to make use of his knowledge of geography and languages. At some point he helped produce a rough map of his homeland in West Africa showing major features of the landscape, political influences, and, just offshore, a tiny dot representing England.

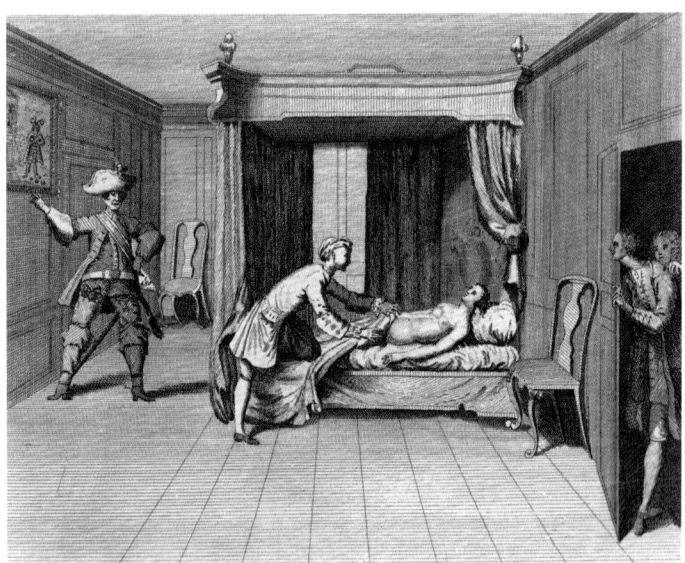

Pistol's a Cuckold, or Adultery in Fashion, 1738, a cartoon depicting Theophilus Cibber (in his stage costume as Ancient Pistol), William Sloper, and a naked Susannah Cibber, with Mr. and Mrs. Hayes, their landlords, looking on. The Cibber-Sloper trial was of such public interest that a transcript, with titillating and embarrassing illustrations, would stay in print for years to come.

Thomas Coram, as painted by William Hogarth, 1740. Hogarth's portrait highlighted Coram's varied career as a sea captain and purveyor of projects on both sides of the Atlantic. His contacts among Britain's wealthiest families were essential to his late-life proposal to build an institution for indigent children in London.

The Charming Brute, 1754, published anonymously but based on an earlier design by the engraver Joseph Goupy, was a complicated satire, in part a reference to Handel's legendary appetite for food and drink, in part a critique of his perceived pigheadedness— a frequent source of ire to Jennens and others who knew him well.

The first page of the original wordbook, or printed program, to the *Messiah*, 1742. Jennens said that it was "full of Bulls," or printer's errors. Only two copies of the original printing are thought to exist today, one in the British Library and this one, from the Library of Congress.

Handel worked quickly and furiously on the *Messiah*, as he usually did when a deadline loomed. At some point in the flurry of activity, Handel or someone else upset an ink pot onto the manuscript, here at the end of the recitative "Behold, a Virgin shall conceive." But they quickly wiped up the ink before it fully penetrated the paper.

The "Hallelujah" chorus from Handel's original composing score of the *Messiah*, 1741. Handel jotted a note that he had reached this point on September 6, along with a circle with a dot in the middle, the astrological symbol for a Sunday.

William Neale's music hall in Dublin was squeezed between existing buildings, where Fishamble Street jerked down to the river Liffey. But already in its opening season, it trumped more established venues by featuring *"Mr. Handel's new Grand Oratorio, call'd the MESSIAH,"* as a newspaper announced.

Prince Charles Edward Stuart, as painted by Louis Gabriel Blanchet, 1739. Decades after Charles landed in Scotland to retake Britain for his father, old men would wax lyrical about the scene of bagpipers, kilted clansmen, and the Young Pretender. Life and politics should return to normal "when the Hurly-Burly's done," Jennens assured Holdsworth, "but if not, we live under the care of Providence, & that is my best security."

March of the Guards to Finchley, by William Hogarth, 1750. Hogarth depicted the Jacobite rebellion of 1745 in an amusing light, with British guardsmen marching off to camp after news that Bonnie Prince Charlie had reached Derby. But the early success of Charles's army set Londoners on edge and shook the reigning House of Hanover.

The Battle of Culloden, April 16, 1746, the end of the Jacobite rising, in a print from 1750. The Duke of Cumberland, sword drawn, looks on as an aide's horse tramples Highlander corpses.

George II regarded "fidles . . . and violeens" as insufficiently martial, so Handel scored his music celebrating the end of the War of the Austrian Succession for brass, percussion, and woodwinds. The festivities in London in April 1749 featured minuets and fanfares, exploding cannons, and a mechanical sun emblazoned with "Vivat Rex," "Long Live the King."

Thomas Coram was remembered as one of the century's greatest philanthropists, here depicted, in a print based on a painting by Balthazar Nebot, in the act of rescuing an abandoned child. But he faced persistent suspicions that his foundling project would encourage the "breeding of Rogues and the increasing of Whores."

The cornerstone for the Foundling Hospital was laid in the autumn of 1742. The design called for two wings, alongside schools, dining rooms, dormitories, and offices. A large chapel united the two wings, forming a visual centerpiece as visitors approached the building over playing fields and parkland.

When mothers or guardians delivered children to the Foundling Hospital, they sometimes passed along a "token" that would help identify a child in the hospital's files. Tiny expressions of hope, the tokens are today held in a London archive and form one of the world's largest collections of everyday objects and period textiles from the eighteenth century.

"There are many circumstances which concurr to sink my Spirits at certain times," Jennens wrote to Edward Holdsworth while working on the *Messiah*, "but I have learnt of you to trust Providence, & I hope that will never suffer me to be much or long dejected." The Gopsall Temple he erected to Holdsworth eventually collapsed, but today the columns are still visible on the original site.

Over the centuries, bits of the Holdsworth memorial were separated from the decaying structure and moved to new locations for safekeeping. As of 2022, this statue, an allegorical image of Christian faith that once stood on the domed roof, resided in a museum warehouse in Leicester.

In an undated portrait, apparently the last one made of Jennens, the English painter Mason Chamberlin showed him with one of his editions of Shakespeare. The publishing project would create professional jealousies that overshadowed his role in the *Messiah* and would color how Jennens was seen for centuries afterward.

The so-called Gopsall portrait of Handel by Thomas Hudson, 1756, was likely commissioned by Jennens. Hudson depicted the aging composer with what had become his most famous work. The *Messiah* sits on the table, but Handel would not have been able to read the music. By this stage he was completely blind.

As soon as the second trial was over, she, Sloper, and Molly again fled. Their location went unrecorded and was apparently unknown to people in their old circle.

It was as if Mrs. Cibber had exited the stage and simply disappeared. Two years would go by before she was heard from again.

～ 12 ～

Foundlings

While Theophilus was dreaming of the money to be made in future rounds of *Cibber v. Sloper*, Thomas Coram had good reason to feel that his foundling project was going the way of his previous schemes. He had secured pledges of help with legal fees and other expenses associated with obtaining a royal charter. He had even identified a plot of land where a building might eventually be constructed. But what he had to show for nearly two decades of canvassing was mainly a bundle of signatures.

Queen Caroline's sudden death in 1737 had ground government business to a halt. The king and the entire nation entered a period of mourning. Her passing had also robbed Coram of a behind-the-scenes patron who might have persuaded the court at last to grant the charter. "I was in hopes from her late Majesty's so much talked of extencive Goodness and Charity that the Expence of passing a Royal Charter would have been defrayed," he wrote to a friend, "but I soon found myself Mistaken." He sought the help of other members of the royal family, only to come up against the same domestic infighting that had frustrated Handel. Virtually anything that the king and queen supported seemed anathema to their children, as well as to those who attended them. When Coram turned up at St. James's Palace to present his petition to one of the princesses, a lady-in-waiting "gave me very rough words and bid me be gone," he scribbled in a note.

Coram was even beginning to have trouble in his traditional hunting ground for patronage, among the nobility. It was one thing to add one's name to a petition but quite another to pay for an ambitious building project, assuming royal assent ever came. Trying to persuade wealthy people to support the offspring of impoverished parents was like asking them "to have putt doun their Breeches and present their Backsides to the King and Queen in a full Drawing room," he wrote. In addition, Coram found himself once again confronting the perennial complaint that helping foundlings was, in fact, a sop to immorality. At one dinner in 1739, he attempted to convince the husband of a recent heiress that her wealth might underwrite the good work of rescuing children. The gentleman countered that his wife had already flatly refused since "she would by no means encourage such a wicked thing."

Coram was already in middle age by the time he started filling in names and dates in his black notebook. He was now in his seventies. Eunice, to whom he had been married for forty years, would soon be dead. A portrait from the time by William Hogarth showed Coram dressed in the simple rust and black wool of a frugal factor rather than the brocade of a gentleman. His face was ruddy and weathered. His white hair—his own rather than a wig—cascaded to his shoulders. Whatever power of persuasion he still had rested on pity and embarrassment—not for the needy children, but for Coram himself. "Even People of Rank," a witness recounted, "began to be ashamed to see a Man's Hair become Grey in the course of a Solicitation by which he was to get nothing."

He had little energy to send out handwritten letters and make personal appeals, as he had once done. Instead, he printed five hundred circulars to distribute to anyone who had previously signed his petition or otherwise contributed to his efforts, urging them to help push to completion a project that seemed, on Coram's telling, always on the threshold of success. Using his own meager resources, he commissioned an artist to design a seal, hoping that it would make his prospective hospital for foundlings appear more official. The image showed Pharaoh's daughter discovering the infant Moses, "the first Foundling we read of," as Coram described it. But as he and everyone else knew, it was an imprimatur for a wholly imaginary institution.

PEOPLE WHO KNEW Coram found his principal virtue to be a relentless sense of possibility, even when a project seemed to have been cast adrift. Still, it must have come as a surprise even to him to learn, in the autumn of 1739, that his foundling idea had suddenly been rescued.

In mid-October he received news that George II had finally signed the charter of a "Hospital for the Maintenance and Education of Exposed and Deserted Young Children," written on a massive piece of parchment and fastened by silk cords to a six-inch wax seal. Energized by the official support of the king, Coram's network of patrons now sprang into action.

A meeting was called the next month at Somerset House in the Strand, the London residence of Coram's first signer, the Duchess of Somerset, to inaugurate the institution and set up an administrative structure, vested in a president, general committee, and board of governors. The leadership was to be drawn from among Coram's extensive list of supporters, which read like a directory of English notables: more than three hundred dukes, earls, viscounts, knights, soldiers, gentlemen of action, global merchants, politicians such as Robert Walpole, clerics such as the archbishop of Canterbury, and even artists such as William Hogarth.

At some point, Coram or one of his patrons had approached William Hunt, the owner of the *Arabella* and the ultimate reason for Ayuba Diallo's kidnapping. The minimal contribution for being included on the list of governors was fifty pounds—which meant that the amount Hunt donated to Coram's effort was slightly less than the money he and others received in compensation for freeing Diallo. For this sum, his name would sit alongside those of the Duke of Montagu, the Duke of Chandos, and Hans Sloane—all, like him, beneficiaries of the sale of one kind of human being and now benefactors for rescuing another.

The very last name on the charter was Coram's own, and at the organizing meeting he was given the honor of reading the document aloud. He followed with his own speech about what had turned out to be a seventeen-year project, perhaps the most sustained charitable effort ever undertaken in Britain by a single person. "I can now rest satisfied," he said, at the outcome of "expensive labour and steady application."

In the months that followed, the governors worked through the details of what precisely the Foundling Hospital, as it was coming to be called, would look like. Staff had to be hired. An administrative system had to be designed for tracking children who might come under the institution's care. The governors devised a plan for parceling out infants to nurses or foster parents in the countryside, while older children were to be cared for in London, where they would benefit from a program of education, practical training, and Christian instruction.

Two years later, in the spring of 1741, the Foundling Hospital officially opened in a house in Hatton Garden, to the east of Colley Cibber's Drury Lane Theatre and Charles Jennens's town house in Queen Square. In early March the governors published a written announcement that the admission of children would commence later that month. Coram had worried that "my declining years will not permit me to hope seeing the full accomplishment of my wishes." In fact, at the age of around seventy-three, he was there to witness the first intake on March 25.

By eight o'clock in the evening, a large crowd had gathered at Hatton Garden. A porter was placed at the door to manage the multitude. One by one, the adults on hand, mainly women, were invited forward. Each of them presented a child to waiting nurses and other staff, who made a note on a ledger of any items that the women had handed over, such as a blanket or clothing. Many of the children were ill or too weak to nurse, "as if Stupefied with some Opiate," as one observer put it. Any child in clear distress or likely suffering from a communicable disease was turned away. "A more moving Scene can't well be imagined," the governing committee's minutes reported on the first night. "The Expressions of Grief of the Women whose Children could not be admitted were Scarcely more observable than those of some of the Women who parted with their Children."

Every time a new intake was announced, crowds would quickly assemble, with women pushing and shoving to get closer to the front door. Plans were under way for a larger, permanent building not far away, but after nearly two decades of entreaties, Coram worried that he had drained the pool of sympathy dry. William Hogarth was drafted to design an illustrated subscription letter that could be distributed more widely, beyond the governors. It showed a kindly man—Coram himself—leading distressed women and their children toward a house of refuge.

But despite the endorsement of leading members of society, and a governing board that represented some of the most well-placed men of the time, there was a persistent suspicion that something tawdry lay at the bottom of the entire project. As a Grub Street poet later put the matter cuttingly, addressing Coram directly,

> *The* Hospital Foundling *came out of thy Brains.*
> *To Encourage the Progress of vulgar Amours,*
> *The breeding of Rogues and the increasing of Whores.*

Even some of the governors seemed to agree with that assessment. Later versions of the hospital's code of operations would place education at the center of its mission, but the board approved an initial plan that provided for instruction in reading but not in writing. Instead, foundlings were to be put to work in trades, if they were able, so that they would be kept in the station to which they had been born. It was a provision adopted apparently over Coram's objections.

Disagreements on the board were soon compounded by scandal. Stories filtered up to Coram of corruption in the nursing staff, perhaps even an unsettling relationship between a laundry maid and a gentleman governor. When Coram raised the issue with the board, the response of his fellow governors was to censure him for spreading rumors about honorable men.

Coram responded as he had done before. A little more than a year after the first intake of children, in May 1742, he resigned his membership of the hospital's general committee. His last vote was to approve the purchase of 400,000 bricks for the new hospital building, a project that had not yet broken ground. He relinquished any formal role in the administration, repeating his behavior with William Sloper Sr. and the Georgia trustees years earlier.

"But thou'rt in thy Projects so wonderously nice," the same Grub Street poet wrote, "Thou quit'st them as soon as they're set to a Price."

CORAM NOW SETTLED into what might have been the closest he ever came to retirement. His project was only partially complete. There was no dedicated building, no secure stream of funding, and no space at Hatton Garden for more than a fraction of the children who were presented there. Of the first 30 children taken in, 23 died within the first few months. Only 135 children were admitted in the entire first year. Of those more than 100 perished.

When mothers, fathers, or guardians delivered children to Hatton Garden, they sometimes passed along a sealed letter or a small object—a token, as they came to be called—that would help identify the children in the hospital's files and connect them back to a parent, should a family member ever wish to retrieve them from the hospital's care. The tokens would survive down to the present, tucked away in a London archive: strips of serge or gown silk cut from dresses or skirts, squares of upholstery, needlework, a medallion broken in two, an ace of spades, a hazelnut—a material record that, among other things, would eventually form the world's largest collection of period textiles.

In addition to preserving the objects, hospital officials created billets, or data sheets, giving descriptions of their new charges, written out on the spot, by quill, in a careful hand. "A female child two months allmost naked a paper with it a pink ribband knot," a staff member noted on one of the earliest intake forms. "A female child about 5 weeks a fine holland cap . . . tied with a black ribband a pair of fine White holland sleeves a pair cotton stockings and a pair white brocaded silk shoes tied with a white ribband and a paper," someone wrote of a different child. "A male child in convulsions about five weeks old a paper given with it, a damask bib red callicoe sleeves," a nurse or clerk said of another.

It is unlikely that Coram ever read the billets himself, but if he had, he would have found something remarkable: a quiet confirmation of his earliest beliefs about foundlings and the circumstances that produced them. When staff members described the appearance of a newly arrived child, the word they used most frequently was not "ill" or "weak" or "dirty." It was "neat."

"Very neat," a hospital official jotted down about one child in April 1741. Then "Exceedingly neat" about another one. Then, a few more lines down the ledger, "Very neatly dressed" about yet another. It turned out that the children brought to the Foundling Hospital were not uncared for or simply abandoned. The fact that they had made it to the front door was, like the tokens attached to them, a profound expression of hope.

For Coram's new institution—crammed into temporary quarters, dependent on a limited set of patrons, and now at odds with its founder—the future would hang on making the public at large understand that reality. On the makeshift seal he had commissioned years earlier, Coram had intuited the right way to represent them. Like the infant Moses, the foundlings had been set adrift not because they were unwanted but for precisely the opposite reason. They had been given away in order to save them—left behind because they were deeply, heartbreakingly loved.

13

The Return of a Prince

Ayuba Diallo was the kind of distinguished guest who might have been brought along to see the early workings of the Foundling Hospital, but by the time the first children were being examined and recorded, he was no longer in Britain. Diallo had been clear with Thomas Bluett and other supporters that his real desire was to go home. In the summer of 1734, the Royal African Company agreed to help arrange a return journey.

A company ship, the two-masted *Dolphin,* was already scheduled to make a voyage to the west coast of Africa. Diallo's name was added to the ship's manifest, and a letter of safe passage was secured from the French government in case he should fall into French hands once he reached his destination. The considerable gifts he had received while in Britain were packed into chests and hauled to the port of Gravesend. Before he left, Diallo also secured a commitment that should the company come into possession of any Muslims in the future, they would be freed upon the payment of two non-Muslim captives—essentially the bargain he had attempted to strike years earlier with Captain Pike of the *Arabella*.

At last, on June 28, the *Dolphin* turned down the Thames, bound for the Gambia River. As the company's leadership wrote to the governor of James Fort, Diallo was to be accorded all assistance in his journey, not least because "he might be able to do the Company good Service."

The voyage turned out to be easier than might have been expected, with fair winds and calm waters, and by early August the *Dolphin*'s crew began to notice the characteristic change of water, from blue to brown, that signaled the outflow from a major river. On August 7 the *Dolphin* put in at James Island. A British traveler and clerk for the company, Francis Moore, reported that the people stepping ashore included the ship's captain, a selection of passengers and company employees, "and one Black Man, by name *Job Ben Solomon*, a *Pholey of Bundo* in *Foota*," which wrangled Diallo's identifying features into a vocabulary that made sense to the company's administrators. It was the first time Diallo had set foot in Africa since being sold into bondage more than three years earlier.

His first aim was to try to find some way of getting word of his arrival back to Bundu. Moore was due to take up a post as the company's agent in Joar, the river port where Diallo had been abducted. Once he learned more of Diallo's story, Moore decided that they would travel together upriver, since Diallo would be able to send news more easily from there than at the mouth of the Gambia.

On August 23 they set out together in a sloop loaded with supplies for restocking the Joar factory. They made slow headway but finally arrived on September 1. Through a Fulbe man in the village, they sent a message to Diallo's father, telling him that his son had miraculously returned and requesting that one of Diallo's children come to Joar, from where they would journey together back home.

Diallo waited for months, first in Joar, then back at James Island, then back again upriver. In the meantime, some of the gifts he had brought from London were lost or stolen. The region had been engulfed in a fratricidal war over control of cattle herds and trade routes. Communication in the countryside slowed to silence. Finally, in February 1735, a group of Fulbe men whom Diallo knew arrived in Joar. They had come to greet him and to bring news of everything that had happened in his absence.

His father, Sulayman, he learned, was dead. Diallo's only consolation was that before Sulayman died, he had been able to satisfy himself that his son was miraculously alive and well. He had in fact received the letters Diallo sent from London. Information about Diallo's fate had come too late for one of his wives, however. She had already remarried, certain that Diallo, even if he was still alive, would never be seen again. Over the years Bundu had been racked by warfare, part of a long-running struggle to consolidate a larger Muslim state centered on the Futa Jallon highlands to the north. The cattle herds were now gone, killed or seized by marauders.

According to Moore, who was there at the time the news arrived, Diallo "wept grievously" when he heard of his father's death. He "forgave his Wife, and the Man that had taken her," since Diallo had been spirited away to a land from which no one had ever returned. For the next four days, Moore reported, Diallo did nothing but talk with his old acquaintances, pausing only to eat and sleep, and plan the next leg of his journey farther inland.

Moore's account of Diallo's odyssey was published three years later, in 1738. *Travels into the Inland Parts of Africa* would become one of the most detailed studies yet written of the politics, economy, and cultures of West Africa, not least the sophisticated system of Muslim education that had produced someone like Diallo. "They are more generally learned in the *Arabick,* than the people of *Europe* are in the *Latin,* for they can most of them speak it," Moore would write about the Fulbe people of Bundu.

But powerful individuals in Britain already knew of Diallo's whereabouts. Diallo had kept in contact with Hans Sloane and the Duke of Montagu, sending greetings and keeping them apprised of his present condition—aware of the fact that they might prove useful to him, as they hoped he might be to them. He had been a captive, then a curiosity, and now an intermediary who could well further British business interests along the Gambia, if politics and warfare allowed new ventures to be established. "All the Muslims here pray for you," he wrote to the duke from Joar.

He had extracted a significant concession from the Royal African Company—that Muslim captives could be ransomed—and there seemed to be hope that one in particular, Loumein Yoai, who had been taken at the same time as Diallo, might be able to return. Bluett, now back in Maryland, soon wrote to the Duke of Montagu that "Job's man" had in fact been located, but since he had turned out to be "an Excellent Slave," the American planter who claimed to own him would be loath to let him go. Bluett informed the duke that the old slave trader Vachel Denton had "promised to buy him, as Cheap as Possible for me," and place Loumein Yoai on the next ship to England.

In January 1736, Hans Sloane received a letter from Diallo, in Arabic, that gave the final chapter of his story. In the intervening months, Diallo had traveled upriver and then overland back to Bundu. When he first walked into his old village, everyone who saw him burst into "floods of tears," since few people had believed the earlier news that Diallo had returned from the dead. For Diallo's part, it was impossible to explain all that had happened to him, "from such distant parts as are beyond their capacity to conceive, from Maryland to England, from thence to Gambia Fort, and from thence . . . to my very house." He sent greetings to Queen Caroline, to the Duke of Montagu, and to everyone else whom he had met in London. "All with me praised God for his providence and goodness." As a public acknowledgment of his fortune, he announced a month's fast in thanksgiving. By 1738, Loumein Yoai, too, had arrived back at James Fort on the Gambia River.

News of Diallo's return was of special interest back in London. "We often think and speak of you with esteem, and we are oblig'd to you and the Mussulmans of your nation for the prayers you make to God for our prosperity," the Duke of Montagu wrote to him. "God Almighty is Great. He is the Common Father of us all." But Diallo's return home came at a price—not to him, but to some of his African neighbors. "In the morning [I] set Mr. Job out into this Country," Thomas Hull, a Royal African Company representative, reported from Bundu, "in order to look for Slaves, Cows or Corn."

Diallo not only resumed his role as a local notable but now, just as his liberators had hoped, he became an informal agent of the company. In the shifting imperial politics of West Africa, he became a fixer and facilitator inside Britain's network of iron traders, shippers, gold merchants, and slavers. Freed from captivity, he was still caught up in a commercial system that, by now, bound his homeland closer than ever to Britain's interests overseas. "About Noon came home Mr. Job & brought the news of all the Countrys being well pleased with the Company & would stand by them against the French or others, & that the Company should have all possible Security & encouragement for their Servants and effects," Hull wrote.

Information about Diallo's new life also reached the Spalding Gentlemen's Society. Since his election to the esteemed fellowship, Diallo's papers had been preserved in the membership files, including his original application with his signature, a recommendation by one of his London acquaintances, and details of his biography and achievements. The membership list, published later in the century, amounted to a directory of the foremost intellectuals, men of science, and polymaths of the time—including a certain Leicestershire landowner, industrialist, and investor in a slaving firm, who had a particular passion for collecting.

An accident of spelling placed his name very near Diallo's. Two lines below "Job Jalla, Priest, at Boonda in Africa," as Diallo's name and status were rendered, was "Charles Jennens, Esq., Gopsall, Leicestershire."

But for the canyon of enslavement, the circles that Diallo and Jennens inhabited in London were not that far apart. It would not have been unusual to see Diallo walking past Jennens's town house in Queen Square. In fact, he would have been hard to miss. "He was an Open, Candid, humane & Good man Spake English well enough to be understood, was Skilful in and wrote Arabic well & fast or very readily and Six other Eastern languages Dialects thereof used in differing Kingdomes of Africa," remembered the president and founder of the Spalding Gentlemen's Society, the antiquary Maurice Johnson. "Wore the Alchoran [Qur'an] of his own writeing in a ribband hung on his breast a White Cotton long robe & a White Muslin Turban the Capp Crimson Velvett." Hans Sloane's home in Bloomsbury was a short distance away, as was one of the city residences of the Duke of Montagu, in Great Russell Street, the site that would later become the British Museum. Diallo might even have attended a musical evening in Covent Garden or the Haymarket, given that his English hosts laid out the achievements of their own civilization before him as they might welcome a visitor from an alien world.

If Diallo and Jennens never happened to meet—and there is no evidence they did—it was one of history's great missed opportunities. For in a strange twist, just as Diallo was reassembling something of his old life in Bundu, Jennens had begun to imagine his own story of boundless hope, tenacious belief, and a returning prince. "Handel says he will do nothing next Winter," he would later write to Holdsworth, "but I hope I shall persuade him to set another Scripture-Collection I have made for him, & perform it for his own Benefit in Passion Week." Jennens gave few details at the time, but the subject had been weighing on him for years.

JENNENS HAD AN EYE for suffering and its remedies, but he tended to express his generosity close to home. To Holdsworth he was a financial planner, literary executor, and overall life manager. To the nonjuring community at large, he was a patron of first and last resort. Portions of his estate later went to support Christian missionaries, the widows of Leicestershire clergymen, several parish churches, six London hospitals, and a school for indigent children. In his own collecting, he spared no expense at all. "I have been glutted with the Italian Theatre," he wrote to Holdsworth one summer when his friend was traveling in Italy. He instructed him to start turning his attention in a new direction, since he had "not yet had so much as a Tast[e] of the Church."

That was true only as far as Italian music was concerned. Jennens had in fact long been steeped in the sacred. In his work on Handel's oratorios, he had drawn his subject matter from the Anglican liturgy and its associated texts. His librettos for *Saul* and other works were in effect original epic poems, built in part from rhymed passages of quatrains and couplets, most of them inspired by biblical stories that were intimately familiar not only to a person of Jennens's convictions and social standing but to the British public at large.

The most recent major edition of the Bible had been published a little more than a century earlier, in 1611. It had been the product of a royal commission charged during the reign of James I. The commission had been tasked not with reworking everything from scratch—multiple serviceable translations were already in use—but rather with establishing an agreed-upon version, revising where necessary to render the original Hebrew and Greek as accurately as possible.

More important, the newly standardized English, reviewed for clarity, was to remove infelicities of expression derived from earlier Latin translations, such as the Vulgate used by Roman Catholics. All of it would then be presented in a clean version, with no margin notes that might suggest interpretations at odds with what the established church actually preached. In these ways the updated edition would also serve as a brake on "the most dangerous increase of papistry and atheism," as one of the project's authors put it.

For sheer poetry and memorability, the newly authorized version, or the King James Bible, as it came to be called, was an astonishing achievement—but not because it was fluent or easy. The commissioners hewed to the literal renderings of the original languages, which often ended up as stilted and verbose in English. They chose to retain words from previous translations that were, by that stage, a century or more old. Already by the time it was published, the finished text was a "Noah's ark for English words and expressions," as one modern scholar has described it.

Yet when the new edition found its way into the liturgy of the Church of England, later in the seventeenth century, preachers reading a passage as well as villagers recalling one from memory were speaking words that were both comprehensible and just ancient enough to be mysterious. According to Jonathan Swift, the King James Bible had become by his day a "Standard for Language, especially to the common People"—a stark contrast, he believed, to hack writers who used "the newest Sett of Phrases, and . . . all the odd Words they have picked up in a Coffee-House." Far from being arcane or archaic, biblical imagery and phrasings blessed as definitive by the King James text were seen as a kind of ideal—a demonstration, sentence after sentence, not just of what language could mean but of what it could do.

For Jennens, the King James Bible was an innovation that magnified a constant: the unalterable reality of divine truth, as inherited from past generations. His understanding of religion paralleled his Jacobite political sympathies. Faith, like royal majesty, was at its core a mystery. The promise of salvation, available to any Christian, was not something that could be arrived at through calculation. To subject the truths of Christianity to rational justification or, even worse, unmoored critique was to fall into the endless, looping questions that had doomed his brother Robert. Picking and choosing which bits of religion one felt like believing in—admitting the existence of a watchmaker God, as the Deists did, who set the world in motion but then left it to tick along on its own—was to miss the totality of truth. Awe and an appreciation for the intangible, not ad hoc sense-making or secular rationality, were the only proper ways to approach the divine.

That was why, like any nonjuror, Jennens also believed one owed allegiance to the inherited institutions of the day. Religion and government were both local interpretations of something vast and universal. They were methods for ordering cosmic reality. To require that either one accord with individual will or fiat was to take away the thing that made them work in the first place: the enigmatic idea that human inventions such as a liturgy or a king still deserved our loyalty and obedience. Take away the mystery, and what remained was chaos.

For Jennens, however, none of this was an argument for naive faith. It was in fact the opposite. An open-eyed, anchoring sense of reality was a requisite for living, he believed. Steadfast conviction about the deep structure of existence, wound through with purpose and revealed in specific lives and stories, was what sustained individuals as well as entire societies through turmoil. Jennens would later have a redolent image carved into one of the mantelpieces at Gopsall Hall: a depiction of the biblical Daniel in the lion's den. You might suffer for the things you believed, but in your darkest moments they could also be a ladder out of despair.

The problem for Jennens was actually living the things he professed. By 1741 his hyp and other ailments had returned in abundance, and it was not difficult to locate the sources. His work with Handel had found only limited success. Cooperating with the Prodigious had tried his patience and convinced him that working together required an exhausting diligence to make sure Handel stayed on course. "Mr. Handel has his fits of hard Labour," he complained to a friend and fellow enthusiast, "as well as idleness." Jennens hated one half of the year because of the weather, and the palliative that helped get him through the other half—music—depended on a composer who was nursing his own worries and infirmities. "I am sorry you cannot brag of your health," Holdsworth wrote that June from Rome. "I hope the country exercise this summer will make you quite stout, that we may rejoice together on my return."

In his libraries in Gopsall and London, Jennens had assembled a substantial collection of the latest works on Christian faith. He regularly bought new volumes by subscription, meaning that he was among the readers who paid in advance for the cost of producing them. Many of the works, not surprisingly, were directed against doubting Christians and rationalizing Deists. There was Richard Kidder, the bishop who had been killed by a collapsing chimney during the Great Storm of 1703, just as Theophilus Cibber was being born, on proofs for the divinity of Christ and God's plan for humanity. There was Henry Hammond's *Paraphrase and Annotations upon the Books of the Psalms*, which pointed out specific inaccuracies in the King James translation and suggested alternative wording. Jennens owned Edward Wells's *Help for the More Easy and Clear Understanding of the Holy Scriptures*, Edward Pococke's *Commentaries on Hosea, Joel, Micah, and Malachi*, and William Nicholls's *Commentary on the Book of Common Prayer*—all of which would have been more at home in a theologian's study than in the private library of a gentleman.

Sometime between the autumn of 1739 and the summer of 1741—

the precise timing is uncertain—Jennens turned to these texts in earnest. He spread the volumes across tables, perhaps using long wooden bars to keep a passage at the ready. He copied down specific phrases on fresh sheets of paper, noting passages that his sources had quoted from the King James Bible or the Book of Common Prayer, the basic liturgy used in the Anglican church, sometimes with slight rewordings rather than the biblical originals. He drew out the explicit connections the theologians had made between the prophecies contained in the Hebrew scriptures and, as he understood it, their fulfillment in the New Testament.

Kidder and other writers had been concerned with proving the status of Jesus Christ as the deliverer from the travails of the world, the savior promised by the prophets. Their audiences were other theologians, doubters, or, in Kidder's case, observant Jews, who rejected the idea that their entire faith was no more than a prelude to someone else's religion. Jennens, though, was animated by themes that were both universal and intimate. At some point, he began to sort his reading notes into three large parts. The first was to cover the prophecy of God's plan for redeeming mankind and the future events through which that prophecy would unfold. Jennens started with the promise that the ephemera of life were not random, that there was a reason to be at ease in the world and confident about the future. The second part showed the suffering and tribulation of the world and narrated the traditional story of the passion of Jesus Christ, but in a swerving, episodic way, rich in violent imagery, shifting again and again between the biblical storyline and the challenge of contemporary belief. The third part was a grand hymn of thanksgiving for God's erasure of human faults and the final triumph over death—the assurance Jennens had announced at the beginning.

What he had been scribbling was not a straightforward statement of belief, although it tracked the standard Anglican view of prophecy, Christ's atonement, and heavenly redemption. It was more like a journey of ideas "more to my own tast[e]," as he wrote to a friend at the time, than might "please the town"—something that he knew London's fashionable society just wouldn't get. The pages formed his own working out of the deep meaning of everything he claimed to believe, both about the world to come and about the troubled, inconvenient one around him.

He was taking a run at the same problem that had exercised thinkers such as Hobbes and Swift, that had lain at the core of the fantastic storylines of heroic opera, and that had pushed his brother Robert into self-negation: how to live bravely in the face of disaster and defeat. The place to start, he felt, was not with a statement of human insufficiency and brokenness, or with a listing of the articles of faith from which one might derive reasons to be hopeful. It was rather to posit a hopeful worldview and then to work backward—to tell a story about existence that would make sense only in light of the vision one began with up front.

Sometime before midsummer 1741, Jennens at last sent his pages to Brook Street. Making something of his creation, he believed, would require Handel to summon a new burst of energy. Given its large, complicated themes, his text would amount to something only if the Prodigious unleashed his entire talent on it—although the prospect of the maestro's doing so was at best uncertain. There was no storyline in any of it, no named characters, and only one episode that could be called a scene or incident: the announcement of the birth of a savior to a group of shepherds. Moreover, Jennens was using not just incidents drawn from the Bible but the sacred words themselves, re-stitched from across the Hebrew scriptures and the New Testament, edited here and there by his own hand for meaning and clarity—and nowhere a rhyming couplet or anything that resembled the text of an actual song.

On July 10, 1741, in a letter to Holdsworth, Jennens at last named the thing he had recently dispatched from his writing table. It was the first time its title would ever appear in a written document.

"The Subject," he wrote, "is Messiah."

PART III

Resurrection

14

To the Hibernian Shore

"I can't help telling you I don't like your Winter Journeys," Jennens wrote to Holdsworth in early December 1741. "You have recovered your Health beyond all reasonable Expectation, and now you are going to put it again to the Hazard." For almost as long as Jennens had known him, Holdsworth had suffered a string of recurring ailments—"faintness, lowness of spirits, want of sleep, pain in my back, and the rest of that dismal catalogue of Horrors which that filthy town of London brought upon me." Treatments regularly drew him to spa towns, from which he would regale Jennens with stories of the characters he happened to meet along the way. "And I am lodg'd in the same house with a famous Presbyterian preacher," he once wrote from Bath, "and our chambers join so close, that when the Spirit moves, I can hear him belch & fart as I am in bed." Now Holdsworth was planning a trip across the Alps, to spend another winter in Rome and southern Italy, and Jennens was concerned that the severe weather en route would do him in.

He had good reason to worry. The winter of 1739–40 had been arctic, the coldest and longest in modern European history. The next two were nearly as bad, with early snowfalls and heavy rains. The Thames froze over. Coal shipments were blocked from reaching their distributors. Prices for heating fuel soared. In Scotland cows and sheep perished for lack of fodder, heightening a food crisis brought on by floods and harvest failures. More time indoors meant a quicker spread of seasonal respiratory illnesses, such as influenza, and raised fears of another outbreak of plague. In Ireland people in the countryside had given their suffering a name: *bliadhain an áir* in Gaelic—the year of the slaughter.

Back in London, Jennens was steeling himself against the wet, ache-inducing months to come. But he had also experienced quite a different shock to the system earlier that autumn. "I heard with great pleasure at my arrival in Town, that Handel had set the Oratorio," he wrote to Holdsworth. Many months had gone by since Jennens had sent his pages to the Prodigious, with apparently no word about what had happened to them.

What he learned next, however, was devastating: Handel was nowhere to be found. He seemed to have fled the capital without warning. What was even more galling was that he had taken Jennens's new text, and whatever music he had written for it, along with him. "It was some mortification to me to hear that instead of performing it here," Jennens wrote indignantly, "he was gone into Ireland with it."

ALTHOUGH JENNENS DID NOT know it at the time, Handel had in fact sat down that summer in his house in Brook Street to see if something could be made of Jennens's unsolicited scripture collection.

Handel usually worked on small, horizontal sheets of paper, roughly nine by twelve inches. A printer or one of his assistants lined the pages, front and back, with staffs, the five horizontal lines of musical notation. The preparer first drew two vertical lines on the page in pencil, to mark the margins, and then used a rastrum, a device with ink quills or nibs set to draw multiple staff lines at once. Each page had enough space to write out up to ten musical parts, but Handel needed only four or so to set his ideas for the strings, for the vocalists, for the *basso continuo* musicians who would improvise around the underlying chordal structure of the piece, and for any special instruments that might be required.

Handel had a habit of noting on his manuscripts when he started and finished specific portions, all in a clear, compressed script and in a liberal mixture of languages. In the late summer of 1741, he had gathered a sharpened quill, an ink pot, and a sheaf of staff paper. On August 22, according to his own annotation, a Saturday, he began to write.

He prefaced the new work with a short overture, a "sinfony" as he called it. On the pages that followed, he unrolled fresh melodic lines to be sung by soprano, alto, tenor, and bass voices. He sketched original violin parts and chordal figures to be realized by a harpsichord or other instruments in the *basso continuo*. Handel's speedy hand caused the stems of the notes to slope severely to the right, his crotchets and demisemiquavers—quarter notes and thirty-second notes—curling up like weevils. When he had an idea that would not fit fully on the prepared staff, he hand drew five new lines himself, corralling the notes before they could scurry away. Sometimes he would just place a dot on the staff to indicate a musical pitch, without completing the full notation, a reminder to himself or a copyist of the basic idea, with the expectation it would all be filled in later.

As the days went by, Handel followed Jennens's scenario closely, dividing the music into three distinct parts, or acts. He interspersed arias to be sung by soloists with short, free-flowing recitatives, a wisp of transition to connect the longer pieces. Here and there he provided choruses, built for a number of voices, that emphasized a major scriptural passage or gave a bit of dramatic contrast to a work that had no real narrative line.

From time to time, he did what he had always done as a composer: thinking back to motifs that had worked well before and putting them to new use. On occasion he recycled melodies from lyrics originally sung in Italian, nudging the English of the King James Bible into the available rhythmic space. For the words "For unto us a child is born," which Jennens had selected from the book of Isaiah, Handel repurposed a duet he had written earlier that summer, "Nò, di voi non vo' fidarmi," or "No, I will never trust you," a self-borrowing that placed a strange emphasis on the first English word, "for," rather than the more natural "us" or "child." When he matched an Italian musical line from the same duet to another phrase from Isaiah, "All we like sheep have gone astray," the ready-made melody ended up with a pause after the fourth English word—which could make the scripture seem less a metaphor for humanity's sinfulness than a declaration of affection for livestock.

On August 28, Handel completed work on the first part of Jennens's text and turned his attention to the second. In the first week of September, he was designing a chorus to fit material Jennens had drawn from several chapters in the book of Revelation: a grand moment of rejoicing when the kingdoms of heaven and earth unite in rightness and glory. For the biblical words "Hallelujah" and "forever," he applied rhythms just enough at odds with the English to be interesting. His "Hallelujah" stressed the first syllable, rather than the more natural third, and then hammered the others like a tocsin. He approached "forever" with the insight of a foreign-language speaker reveling in the sound of a favorite English word. He created a syncopated phrase that started on the offbeat and then emphasized the middle syllable—for-*ev*-er and *ev*-er. Handel repeated it over and over, just as he had done years earlier in his coronation anthem "Zadok the Priest," measure after measure, until he sensed the musical point had been made.

Next, he added two beats of total silence, drawing rest marks through all the parts on the page. His quill then inked fat, round circles onto the paper, the chorus's final notes. Below the staff lines, his handwriting now became broad and open, taking up half the page as he copied Jennens's libretto, with plenty of space between the letters. When he wrote out the final word—"H—a—l—l—e—l—u—j—a—h"—it was the musical equivalent of a long, full exhale. The text stopped well shy of the page's edge, as if he had finished the longest leg of a race with time to spare. He jotted a note that he had reached this point on September 6, along with a circle and a dot in the middle, the astrological symbol for a Sunday.

Fables would later circulate about Handel's recollection of that moment. "I did think I did see all heaven before me, and the great God himself," he is supposed to have recalled, according to a source from nearly a hundred years after the fact. But even if Handel had a sense of divine inspiration—and there is no evidence he felt that way at the time—he still had work to do. A full third of Jennens's text had yet to be set to music. Handel carried on composing for another week. He added abbreviated instructions for John Christopher Smith Sr. or another copyist to repeat a section or fill in missing notes, expecting him to know what was intended.

At one point, in the hurly-burly of Brook Street, a maid, trying to tidy up, might have bumped into his writing table. Perhaps Handel himself, in the throes of composition, was careless in laying down a new sheet of staff paper. In any case, someone knocked over a pot of ink onto the manuscript. Whoever was there immediately reached for a piece of cloth or paper and tried to wipe up the mess. Their quick thinking saved Handel's work. The fat black smudge stained the page, but the ink never fully soaked into the paper. The underlying notes were still just visible underneath.

After twenty-four days, nearing mid-September, Handel had filled up both sides of at least 130 pages, a stack of paper around two inches high. On the reverse of the last page, at the bottom, he wrote "Fine del oratorio." He had completed it, by his own assessment, on September 12, 1741, a Saturday, with the missing sections filled in, or "ausgefüllt," as he noted, two days later.

There was no title page or florid introductory note, nor did Handel ask Smith to bind the sheets together. They remained a loose sheaf, the top page eventually bearing the grime of sweaty fingers and perhaps the traces of more than a few dinners. At the top of the first page of music, near the left margin, he scribbled an unceremonious title: *Messiah, an Oratorio.*

HANDEL HAD SPENT his entire adult life working quickly and fiercely. Composing for the theater required speed, especially when a deadline loomed—as one did now.

In the months since Jennens had delivered his new libretto, Handel had received an unexpected invitation. It possibly came from William Cavendish, Duke of Devonshire, who also held the title of lord lieutenant of Ireland, the viceroy of the British king. The request was apparently that Handel come to Dublin to stage a series of concerts to lift public spirit in the face of failed harvests and bitter cold. There would be no shortage of devoted listeners, who would be afforded the rare opportunity of hearing the great master perform outside London.

The timing could not have been more fortunate. Handel had planned nothing new for the coming season. He now had Jennens's libretto, which, given its theme of suffering and resurrection, could play well in Passion Week, the period just preceding Easter, if the initial Dublin run warranted extending into the spring. And if the pull of Dublin wasn't enough, there was always the push of London's artistic factionalism and society infighting. "At a Time when Party runs so high, and Politicks seem to have taken up not only all our publick Papers, but the Attention also of the Bulk of Mankind," a letter in the *London Daily Post* had claimed that spring, Handel was suffering "the cruel Persecution of those little vermin, who, taking advantage of their Displeasure, pull down his Bills as fast as he has them pasted up, and use a thousand other little Arts to injure and distress him."

Handel decided to leave. As the autumn chill set in, Peter le Blond packed Handel's traveling trunks with warm clothes and a woolen overcoat. Smith turned the new composing manuscript into a full score, rendering page after page of rushed handwriting into neat, careful notation, with plenty of space for future amendments and conducting notes. Other copyists created parts for singers and instrumentalists. Smith might have overseen arrangements for a carrier to transport musical scores, a chamber organ, and other requirements for a trip expected to last at least a few months, perhaps even longer.

In early November, Handel set off by coach, probably bringing Smith and at least one other assistant, and headed north. It would be weeks before he got around to telling Jennens about the music that now lay somewhere in his baggage.

⁂

HANDEL'S FIRST DESTINATION was Chester, four days by coach from London and the normal stopping place for travelers catching the Dublin packet boat. He took up residence at a local inn, the Golden Falcon in Northgate Street.

While in Chester, according to a story later circulated by the music historian Charles Burney, Handel supposedly polished the vocal parts for Jennens's new oratorio. Burney, then a boy, reported seeing Handel rehearsing singers he had drafted from Chester cathedral, just down the street from his lodgings, using amateur singers and musicians to sight-read passages that he and Smith were still in the process of editing.

"You shcauntrel!" Handel was said to have screamed at one wobbly bass, a printer named Janson. "Tit not you dell me dat you could sing at soite?"

"Yes, sir," came Janson's reply, "but not at *first sight*."

Burney's story was perhaps too good to be true, but Handel might well have had time on his hands. It was not uncommon to wait in Chester for days or even weeks, especially in late autumn and winter, for favorable winds to allow passage to Ireland. The city was unusual in having most of its medieval walls still intact, and visitors passed their time promenading along the ramparts among half-timber Tudor homes, taverns, and market squares, all in various states of disrepair. "The church and clergy here, no doubt, / Are very near a-kin," wrote a testy Jonathan Swift, who had come through Chester years earlier on his way to find a London publisher for *Gulliver's Travels*. "Both weather-beaten are without, / And empty both within."

The packet boats to Dublin ran from Parkgate on the river Dee, twelve miles from Chester, and from Holyhead, more than eighty miles away in Wales, "a straggling confused Heap of thatched Houses, built on Rocks," according to one traveler. The choice of port depended on time, money, and where the winds appeared more cooperative, as well as one's ability to handle a horse. Jonathan Swift had journeyed with a guide along the "rough, rocky, broken road" to Holyhead, a mountain path whose "sudden inequalities" left backs sore and legs aching. Handel likely opted for the easier journey to Parkgate, where he would have boarded the small ship waiting to take on passengers.

From the crossings he had earlier made between Holland and England, Handel knew what to expect on a packet journey, but the sailing would nevertheless have been arduous. Icy winds sliced across the Irish Sea. Storm clouds could rise up on the western horizon with shocking speed. Ships could founder in high swells, even under the hand of an experienced captain.

Since the packet boats carried the Royal Mail and other valuable cargo, they were obvious targets for French privateers in times of war, which is why government officials usually chose to take an armed Royal Navy vessel rather than the unarmed commercial packets. If everything went smoothly, an uneventful crossing still meant at least a full day of tossing, tacking, and thumping. For Handel and his traveling companions, the ordeal finally came to an end, perhaps on November 18, when the packet safely reached the Irish coast.

Around 120,000 people lived in Dublin, "a fair and well built City, of great Antiquity, pleasantly seated near a large Harbour," according to a contemporary survey. It was the second-largest urban space in the British Isles after London. Four stone bridges stretched across the river Liffey, which separated the older districts from the newer northern suburbs. South of the river, two Protestant cathedrals, Christ Church and St. Patrick's, rose near the castle, seat of the lord lieutenant, Ireland's governor. Other landmarks lined the quays or defined the skyline on the low hills above, from the Customs House and Four Courts, the main legal complex, to the Royal Hospital for injured and aging soldiers and the gray edifice of Trinity College, "all noble Buildings, and aptly contrived for their several Purposes."

It was the first time Handel had ever been to Ireland. Yet despite the grand and picturesque scene that greeted him, it would have been hard not to think of the journey as a kind of self-banishment, a season in the provinces for a performer who had spent the last thirty years mainly in the seat of empire. In the capital his departure was the subject of gossip and worried conversations among his friends and admirers, all of whom seemed uncertain about exactly how long this unusual absence was supposed to last. "Till He comes, this Town will be a very dull place to [me]," Jennens remarked. Charles Burney would later attribute Handel's flight to "the joint effects of anxiety, mortification, distress, and disappointment." Alexander Pope offered a more poetic explanation in one stanza of his *Dunciad*. It was simply the dullness and bad taste of London society, he wrote, that "drove him to th' Hibernian shore."

15

Fishamble

Dublin was dominated by the Ascendancy, the network of Protestant nobles, landowners, and merchants who controlled Irish politics, the church, and economic life. Protestants still held a slim majority of the city's population, which was just at the point of tipping decisively in favor of Catholics. They prided themselves on a local parliament that met every other year, a viceregal court, and a renowned university, which even London lacked. They viewed their own contributions to culture as comparable with the capital's, if on a smaller scale. Whatever roughness remained they attributed to "papists, converts or known Jacobites," who gathered each June on St. Stephen's Green, the parklike common south of the Liffey, to mark the Pretender's birthday.

Two public theaters, in Smock Alley and Aungier Street, offered drama and music, sometimes even hosting major London artists for the season. A new "musick hall" had recently opened in one of the oldest streets in the city. Medieval records had labeled it Vicus Piscatorius, or fish row, but Dubliners knew it as Fishamble Street, a lane flanked by attractive houses and wending from Christ Church to the river. Squeezed between existing buildings, the hall was tucked nearly out of view in a bend where Fishamble jerked downhill. Still, the manager, William Neale, trumped many of the more visible venues in his opening season.

Neale was a music publisher and treasurer of the Charitable Music Society, a group accustomed to meeting in the nearby Bull's Head Tavern and whose fundraising had made the music hall possible. He and his associates might have been the original source of the invitation delivered to Handel by the Duke of Devonshire, or they might have been in touch separately once it became clear that Handel was planning a visit to Ireland. In any case, in mid-December a newspaper carried an announcement that tickets would soon go on sale at a house in Abbey Street, where Handel had taken up residence, for a series of performances in Neale's new hall.

Featuring some of his older work, such as *Esther*, *Acis and Galatea*, and *L'Allegro, il Penseroso ed il Moderato*, which Jennens had helped create, the series was planned to run into mid-February. Skilled instrumentalists were easy to find in Dublin, and choristers from the cathedrals were recruited to form the chorus. Handel had even persuaded a celebrated German soprano, Christina Maria Avolio, to come to Dublin to join him. The available seats filled up in advance, some six hundred per performance, "so that I needed not sell one single Ticket at the Door," he wrote to Jennens gleefully on December 29—at last beginning to fill Jennens in on what had transpired in the months since he had suddenly exited London.

The Irish public's reaction gave a needed boost to Handel's spirits. The audience at an early performance, he told Jennens in his chancy English, was "composed (besides the Flower of Ladies of Distinction and other People of the greatest Quality) of so many Bishops, Deans, Heads of the Colledge, the most eminents People in the Law as the Chancellor, Auditor General, etc." If things continued in this vein, he hoped to extend his stay and schedule another round of concerts, "passing my time with Honnour, profit, and pleasure."

Dubliners seemed delighted to have Handel in town, and he repaid their enthusiasm with his familiar dry humor, even in the middle of a concert. On one occasion, his principal violinist, Matthew

Dubourg, a talented English musician who was master of music for the lord lieutenant's official band, launched into a meandering improvisation, looping through passages that went on longer than Handel thought was tasteful. Just as Dubourg settled into the final shake, a trill that punctuated the end of his solo, Handel commented, loud enough for everyone to hear, "You are welcome home, Mr. Dubourg!" The audience was charmed, and Handel himself could not have been more pleased. "As for the Instruments they are really excellent, Mr. Dubourgh being at the Head of them," he told Jennens, "and the Musick sounds delightfully in this charming Room . . . (and my health being so good) that I exert my self on my Organ with more than usual Success."

AS IT TURNED OUT, the smooth opening to Handel's season was about to come to an end. In late January 1742, a new obstacle arose, and it came from an unexpected and powerful source—the aging dean of St. Patrick's Cathedral, Jonathan Swift.

Now in his mid-seventies, Swift had grown even more irascible in the decade and a half since *Gulliver's Travels*. His renown as a satirist, commentator, and preacher had never translated into a change of fortune. The Hanoverian court continued to hold him at arm's length. His mail was routinely opened by government censors seeking evidence that his disregard for authority drifted as far as Jacobitism. He suffered from tinnitus that was at times debilitating, leading to almost complete deafness in one ear. Frequent bouts of vertigo left him disoriented, and nothing that a doctor might prescribe—tinctures, boluses, emetics, a cloth cap stuffed with cloves and nutmeg—provided relief. Swift's companion, Stella, had wasted away from tuberculosis and died in 1728. He had spent the last dozen years battling mental confusion that left his parishioners baffled when his sermons seemed to go weirdly astray. "My giddiness is more or less constant," he told Alexander Pope. The "rage and rancour against persons and proceedings," as he described his condition to another friend, seemed inescapable.

In the middle of Handel's first concert series, Swift circulated a memorandum to the senior clerics under his authority. He directed them to prohibit their choristers from participating in any future Handel performances. "And Whereas it has been reported, that I gave a Licence to certain Vicars to assist at a Club of Fiddlers in Fishamble Street," Swift wrote, "I do hereby declare that I remember no such licence to have been ever signed or sealed by me, and that if ever such pretended Licence should be produced, I do hereby annull and vacate the said Licence." Any church musician who appeared at such a venue, Swift continued, his anger mounting word by word, "as Songsters, Fidlers, Pipers, Trumpeters, Drummers, Drummajors or in any Sonal Quality, according to the Flagitious aggravations of their respective Disobedience, Rebellion, Perfidy & Ingratitude," would be punished to the fullest extent allowable.

It was unclear whether Swift's missive was aimed directly at Handel or at any performers who might lend their angelic voices to a secular cause; perhaps the ban was simply a product of Swift's own increasingly tormented mind. But since the end of the run was within sight, Handel chose to carry on. He could always cut out a chorus here and there if he had too few singers to mount a choir. After all, he was well practiced in rearranging a score and improvising to fit the performers he had on hand. Still, it was one thing to struggle toward the conclusion of a concert series but quite another to plan for additional performances without a full complement of talent—much less in the face of public disapproval by one of Dublin's most voluble, and volatile, clerics.

By this point, though, a second series of concerts had already been announced, with an unspecified program. There was also the music he had composed for Jennens's new scripture collection, still unused and especially well suited to the Easter season, if he could fulfill his other commitments and stumble toward the spring. The only choice was to find new singers and adapt as best he could.

Before long Handel's attention settled on someone working only half a mile from Fishamble Street, in the company of the Aungier Street Theatre. Her advantage was that she had sung Handel's work many years before, in London. The drawback was that the gossips had surely set to talking as soon as she stepped off the packet boat—about her gentleman lover, her willing cuckold of a husband, and her breathtaking, scandalous trials.

SUSANNAH CIBBER HAD COME to Dublin perhaps two weeks after Handel, on December 3. For two years she had been living in England under various aliases, with William Sloper and their daughter, Molly. Whenever information came that Theophilus had discovered her whereabouts, she and her new family promptly packed up their belongings and moved on once again. The invitation to appear at Aungier Street had come through an old contact of hers from Drury Lane, and as with Handel it must have been something of a relief to be so far away from the capital. She took up residence not far from the theater, possibly with Sloper and Molly in tow, and was scheduled to begin her run before Christmas.

Once he started thinking about how to manage his second series of concerts, Handel reached out to Cibber, perhaps calling on her personally or asking Smith to make the arrangements on his behalf. He would have realized the additional work he was taking on. Since Cibber did not read music, he would need to work with her individually, helping her to learn a part by heart. Her health was a concern, too. She had been frequently ill with fever since arriving in Ireland, a condition that would eventually cause her to cancel stage appearances and rack up a debt of work to her primary employer. But Handel was in no position to worry about any of it. Subscriptions for the new series were already on sale, and his commitment to offering something original this time around had only grown.

When she received the invitation, Cibber agreed to perform. There was only a week between the closing of the first series and the opening of the second, which gave little time for Handel to take her through the intense preparation she required, one note at a time. But in the end, the second series went off nearly as planned, with a revival of

Esther and other works, interrupted only by an unspecified illness that would plague Cibber throughout the spring.

In the meantime, two other dramas had been playing out offstage. Handel's plan was to remain in Dublin, at least through the spring. For the upcoming Easter season, he had been at work revising and amending Jennens's new oratorio, which he had carried with him from London. He shortened various portions, perhaps worrying that the melodies were winding on too long without a dramatic payoff, and adapted the music to the complement of musicians and soloists he had on hand, including Cibber. A great deal had happened to her in the decade since she first appeared as a soprano in her father's small-scale productions, and she now sang lower than before, in the range of a passable alto. Handel lowered the keys of arias he had first laid down in Brook Street to make sure that Cibber, whom he intended to cast in the new oratorio, could hit the high notes.

A parallel set of preparations had been going on for months at St. Patrick's Cathedral. With the public clamoring for more chances to hear Handel, a delegation of Dublin leaders had approached Swift, imploring him to release his choristers from the prohibition on their performing at Fishamble Street. Despite the dean's irritability, a tentative deal had been struck to allow singers from St. Patrick's to join Handel's musicians, but only if the dean of neighboring Christ Church agreed. Yet just at the point of sealing the agreement, Swift had reneged, a development that had occasioned his threatening missive in late January. Everyone now seemed to take a hand in trying to persuade the dean to relent: public officials, trustees of charitable societies, friends, perhaps even his publisher, George Faulkner, who also happened to own *Faulkner's Dublin Journal*, a prominent newspaper that had been advertising Handel's concerts.

No one knew precisely why or when, but sometime that spring Swift apparently changed his mind. He might have been persuaded by the fact that proceeds from Handel's new work were to be used specifically in aid of worthy causes, such as paying off the private debts of incarcerated paupers. On March 27, Faulkner's newspaper finally reported that "the Gentlemen of the Choirs of both Cathedrals," St.

Patrick's and Christ Church, would participate in a special, previously unannounced concert:

> For the relief of the Prisoners in the several Gaols, and for the Support of Mercer's Hospital in Stephen's Green, and of the Charitable Infirmary on the Inns Quay, on Monday the 12th of April, will be performed at the Musick Hall in Fishamble Street, Mr. *Handel's new Grand Oratorio, call'd the MESSIAH.*

A full rehearsal was scheduled for less than two weeks later, on April 8, but another obstacle soon fell in Handel's path. Cibber was ill again, as she had been for much of March. Several performances at Aungier Street had to be canceled. To make up for the lost revenue, she now owed the theater—which, after all, was bankrolling her attempt at a return to the stage—additional appearances. In order to allow her to recover and to discharge her other duties, Handel decided to postpone the rehearsal by a day, to April 9.

In addition to Cibber, Handel had gathered a cohort of eight or nine soloists, among them Avolio and someone called Mrs. Maclaine. For the choir, at least sixteen choristers were selected from across St. Patrick's and Christ Church, most likely all men rather than choirboys (whose appearance on a secular stage would almost certainly have sent Swift into another angry spin). Countertenor, tenor, and bass soloists were probably drawn from among their number, with the expectation that they would step out to sing their parts and then recede back into the chorus. For instrumentalists Handel could call on people who had already been performing in his two concert series. Matthew Dubourg would serve as concertmaster since, beyond his own considerable talent, he came with his own orchestra—the state ensemble that played for military and ceremonial occasions in Dublin—which also turned out to be a good place to source two unusual requirements that Handel had written into the score: trumpets and timpani.

It was as patched together a company as Handel had ever assembled—the notorious and feverish Cibber, a German soprano, two amalgamated church choirs, and the equivalent of an army band—tasked with performing a collection of sacred scripture, in English translation, with no plot, all of it set to music that drew from the conventions of Italian opera, and with the concert's profits going to pay other people's debts. The whole cast of performers probably met only once before the premiere, and even then, to heighten interest for the main event, the organizers had arranged for the rehearsal to be open to the public.

The original announcement had given the premiere date as April 12, but yet another complication arose when several people pointed out that the timing clashed with an already scheduled cathedral celebration. The vicars would be forced to withdraw their support, since the holiday was immovable and the choristers would be required to sing at the planned events. To accommodate the choir and rescue his grand choruses from being cut from the score, Handel rescheduled the opening for April 13, a delay that had the additional advantage of allowing everyone one more day to look over their parts.

ON THE TUESDAY before Easter, carriages began lining up early on Fishamble Street. The concert was set to begin at midday, and given advance ticket sales and the enthusiasm generated by the public rehearsal, the crowds were expected to be large. Two newspapers had printed requests that gentlemen leave their rapiers at home and ladies "not to come with Hoops," in order to be able to pack in as many people as possible.

When the doors were finally opened at eleven in the morning, "Lords, Justices, and a vast Assembly of the Nobility and Gentry of both Sexes," an observer reported—more than seven hundred people in a hall Handel estimated could reasonably hold only six hundred—crowded through the arched entryway, elbowing their way toward whatever seats remained free.

Over the past several months, Jennens had gotten over his "mortification" at Handel's sudden departure from London, perhaps because Handel had kept him apprised of plans for the first performance of his oratorio. Jennens had responded by sending Handel two epigraphs to adorn the top of the wordbook, the *Messiah*'s libretto and scenic structure, which had been printed by Swift's publisher, George Faulkner. "MAJORA CANAMUS," one of them read in Latin—"Let us sing of greater things"—a quotation from Holdsworth's favorite poet, Virgil. The other contained short passages from the New Testament, including from the apostle Paul's first epistle to his younger colleague Timothy, in which he laid out the foundations of the new Christian faith. "And without controversy great is the mystery of godliness," Paul wrote, from the manifestation of God in the person of Jesus to his resurrection and ascent into heaven. Jennens was credited nowhere in the wordbook—he gave no hint that he wanted to be—but anyone in Fishamble Street could now follow along with the text and sense the same large themes he had distilled from the sacred words.

The audience calmed down as Handel's music began with the expected overture. From that point, the musicians wound through the three parts that Jennens had imagined, with responsibility passed back and forth among soloists, choristers, and instrumentalists—a rainstorm of images and feelings, rather than a narrative that a listener might be expected to track from beginning to end. At the front of the music hall, singers related a prophecy about redemptive motherhood, a virgin conceiving a son whose very name—Emmanuel, or God-with-us—confirmed that hope still lived in the world. Rough places would be made plain. Crooked things would be pulled straight. Good tidings flowed from the joy of a child born warm and safe. Voices were lifted up, fearless, skipping lightly and even carelessly, as in a country dance. Later came a calming, satisfied confidence, the child now grown into a man, a rescuer who feeds his flock like a shepherd.

But then a disorienting darkness rolled in, like storm clouds brewing over a swaying wheat field. The momentary happiness was extinguished in a flurry of fists, the pummeling of oppressors, an inescapable wave of ridicule, defamation, and shame, with a mother tragically fated to outlive her own son. Fixing this world would require reimagining the moral order, the text suggested. What seemed normal in this life—the everyday pain, the casual suffering—was in fact the opposite of justice and right. A correct universe would be an upended one. "Ev'ry valley shall be exalted," as a tenor had explained near the top of the performance, "and ev'ry mountain and hill made low."

Jennens had selected passages from Isaiah and the minor prophets, then from the Gospels and the book of Revelation, sometimes paraphrasing in order to draw out a dramatic idea. But at every turn, it would have been impossible to miss the connections between the cosmic and the contemporary. A voice crying in the wilderness proclaimed a new truth: that across a desert would come not a judging God but a deliverer, who would seal up war and forgive every wrong. A light would shine on those who walked in darkness. A lame man would leap like a deer. A just government would at last rule the land. But there were still tribulations to endure before the great peace. "Yet once in a little while and I will shake the heavens and the earth, the sea and the dry land," a bass sang in the first part of the oratorio, glossing the prophet Haggai.

Amid the promises and prophecies were also questions that sounded as if they were somehow made for the moment. "Why do the nations so furiously rage together," Jennens had written, basing his text on the second Psalm, "and why do the people imagine a vain thing?" If there really was a power that could set the world aright, how would you recognize it? "Who is the King of Glory?" the choristers sang, intoning the twenty-fourth Psalm. Now and then, hints of an answer to Jennens's questions came into view, sometimes as another question, sometimes as a cryptic truth. "Behold, I tell you a mystery," the bass sang from Paul's first epistle to the Corinthians. "We shall not all sleep, but we shall all be changed in a moment, in the twinkling of an eye, at the last trumpet."

Handel's score connected the many disparate threads. He had used Jennens's scriptural selections in ways that sometimes made the English literal and at other times struggled boldly against the words themselves. When the text spoke of valleys being raised up, the singer climbed higher and higher, as if scaling a cliff face, then traveled back down when mountains and hills were cut low. "And I will shake all nations," another soloist sang, turning the word "shake" into a long run of rumbling seas and tumbling edifices. Yet when Isaiah predicted the birth of a redeeming prince, Handel set the prophet's vision not as a solemn declaration delivered by a wizened seer but as an erupting chorus—"Wonderful, Counsellor, the Mighty God, the Everlasting Father, the Prince of Peace"—like the blasting entrance of the full choir and orchestra at the coronation of George II. Even the *pifferari*, the wandering bagpipers he had probably first heard in Italy, made an appearance in a pastoral movement that recalled the shepherds who first learned of the birth of a savior. The recycled musical phrases he had written down in Brook Street, drawn from his life as well as his own art, were now an accompaniment to Jennens's mirroring of past and present.

Cibber had been onstage since the beginning of the performance. Near the top of the second part, she stepped forward to sing openly of suffering and its consequences. Virtually anyone in the audience would have known of her hopeless marriage and debilitating scandal. As she traded places with Avolio and other soloists, it would not have taken a great deal of imagination to see another storyline emerging from within Jennens's sacred text, delivered in the lowered range of Cibber's small voice. One aria in particular showcased her talent as well as her predicament. It demanded little in the way of dexterity or vocal mastery but everything in terms of raw emotion and sensibility.

The orchestration was spare. Handel had written the aria so that the soloist would exchange keening, drawn-out phrases with the violins, or float above the other instruments without battling them for attention. Cibber likely watched Handel for a cue as he, perhaps mouthing the opening words, prepared to take her through the melody, just as he would have done at a keyboard in the weeks before.

"He was despised, rejected of men," Cibber began, singing the words Jennens had taken from the book of Isaiah. The tension built at the end of the next phrase—"a man of sorrows and acquainted with grief"—then circled and resolved, settling calmly into the end of a musical idea. Over the next several minutes, Cibber returned again and again to the same bleak description of an outcast life, before plunging into the graphic details of pain and disgrace. The tempo picked up slightly, the tone darkening to a minor key, as she sang of how a man willingly placed himself before those who tormented him, not acquiescing to violence, but drawing it closer, taming it. "He gave His back to the smiters, and His cheeks to them that plucked off His hair," Cibber sang from Jennens's libretto. "He hid not His face from shame and spitting." She then returned to the top of the aria, da capo, just as Handel had instructed opera singers to do hundreds of times before. She sang again of a man who knew sadness without being drowned by it, someone who taught that the opposite of fear was not bravery but understanding.

The audience would have understood the text as pointing toward the suffering of Jesus Christ and his road toward self-sacrifice. But any listener would also have recognized the obvious parallel with Cibber's own life—despised, rejected, a person of sorrows, acquainted with grief. With a slight rewording, she could have been singing about herself.

The effect must have been wrenching. By the end of the aria, it was wholly possible to believe that the greatest heroism was simple survival, that transcendence might even depend on knowing horror from the inside. It was the strangest possible formula for hope but one that, by the final notes, one could begin to see clearly: that the way to overcome one's enemies was to shock them into witnessing their own cruelty—to force them, like Swift's Gulliver, to confront their worst, ugliest selves.

A later account would place Swift's godson, a Trinity College student named Thomas Sheridan, in Neale's music hall as a witness to Cibber's performance. Beside him was one of Swift's friends, the cleric Patrick Delany, chancellor of Christ Church, there perhaps to ensure that his choristers made their parishes proud. On the day of the performance, stonemasons were preparing to set the tombstone of Delany's wife, who had died only a few months earlier. He had ordered it inscribed with words about her remarkable ability to subdue evil with good. Given the circumstances, he was primed for emotion. After Cibber had finished the last words of her aria, perhaps mimicking the violins with a grace-note flourish on the final syllables—

"acquainted with grief"—Delany reportedly exclaimed from his seat, "Woman, for this, be all thy sins forgiven!"

For the rest of the performance, it was as if Cibber had taken Delany's words to heart. Handel had assigned the parts so that after "He was despised," she receded into the background, with other soloists taking pride of place as the music wended through Jennens's text. When Cibber finally stepped forward again, she had nothing more to say about captivity, scorn, and abuse. The entire audience knew that these were the realities of her life in London, from her dead children, to her public humiliation, to being relentlessly pursued by a cruel husband. But here, onstage in Dublin, she was living the very admonition Jennens had found in the ancient prophecies: to gain a new life, face forward and speak into being the world you want to see.

Now every line out of her mouth was a triumph. "If God be for us, who can be against us?" Cibber sang, using Jennens's quotation from Paul's letter to the Romans. "It is God that justifieth, who is he that condemneth?" A few minutes later, the entire choir joined in for the closing chorus—voices, strings, trumpets, and timpani together in one spiraling, glorious, exultant amen.

∽ 16 ∾

"Hope Is a Curtail Dog"

In the days and weeks after the Dublin concert, the public reaction to the *Messiah* was astonishment and wonder. "The whole is beyond any thing I had a notion of till I Read and heard it," reported the Irish bishop Edward Synge, who left one of the few eyewitness accounts. "It seems to be a Species of Musick different from any other."

The audience was "uniformly grave & decent" throughout the concert, Synge remembered, "tho the young & gay of both Sexes were present in great numbers" and would normally have carried on more boisterously in a playhouse or music hall. To others who recalled being there in Fishamble Street, the combination of words and music seemed "elevated, majestick and moving," according to one observer, "the Sublime, the Grand, and the Tender" together, which "conspired to charm the ravished Heart and Ear." The fact that the proceeds went to charities only increased the sense of piety connected with the work. In the end 1,223 pounds was raised for various good works, which among other things allowed 142 debtors to be released from local jails.

But this was Dublin, not London, and Handel knew he must soon return home. He continued with further performances, including a reprise of the *Messiah* in early June. At some point, however, he suffered another "Paraletic stroke," which a surgeon treated with "violent bleedings & other evacuations." He remained in Ireland, recovering, for much of the rest of the summer.

Once he began to feel better, Handel presented himself at St. Patrick's Cathedral to thank Swift for allowing his choristers to perform in an unusual venue. At the dean's lodgings, a servant ran to tell Swift of the distinguished visitor who had just arrived. It took some time for Swift to understand who was at his door, but once his mental fog cleared, he was ecstatic. "O! A *German*, and a Genius!" he exclaimed. "A Prodigy! admit him."

Once Handel came into the drawing room, according to a contemporary source, he could do little more than "behold the Ruins of the greatest Wit that ever liv'd along the Tide of Time, where all at length are lost." There is no record of the words they exchanged, but it was apparently the last intelligible conversation Swift would ever manage. After the meeting his delirium grew. He refused to eat unless his food was cut up into chunks. He soon forgot the names of friends, colleagues, and servants. He carried on in that fashion until he died, a little over three years later. He was buried in St. Patrick's Cathedral, the place, just as he had predicted, he was destined never to leave.

On August 13, Handel, likely accompanied by Smith, set off on the packet boat to Parkgate and through the north of England. He took the occasion to stop at Gopsall, hoping to inform Jennens in person of all that had happened in Ireland, but no one was at home. A few weeks later, by then back in London, Handel at last wrote to Jennens to tell him of the resounding success of his oratorio, now several months beyond its premiere. He enclosed Bishop Synge's ringing testimonial, which lavished praise on the *Messiah* for its spiritual depth and emotional effect. "It was indeed Your humble Servant which intended You a visit in my way from Ireland to London," Handel told Jennens, "for I certainly could have given you a better account by word of mouth, as by writing, how well Your Messiah was received in that Country." It was the last time nearly anyone would refer to their joint creation as something other than Handel's alone.

NEWS OF SUSANNAH CIBBER'S RETURN to the stage in Dublin quickly filtered back to London. "O wondrous girl!" ran a poem in the popular *Gentleman's Magazine* already that March, "how small a space / Includes the gifts of [the] human race!" But with her starring role in Handel's sacred oratorio, it was as if she had fully escaped the slough and muck of the last several years.

She began the journey back home on August 23, and by the time she arrived, her life had been set on a wholly different course. On the packet boat, she met David Garrick, the most renowned actor of the day, who was completing his own run in Dublin. It was a connection that held the promise of future appearances alongside someone who counted as stage royalty. She soon signed a contract to appear at Covent Garden, the first of what would turn out to be regular engagements on the London stage. What was more, she had news from her brother Thomas that the tide of public opinion had turned wholly against Theophilus. He was now widely perceived as a difficult partner and a risky investment for any producer. Few playhouses seemed willing to take him on.

While she had been away, another legal case was in the works, but this time with Susannah and her mother as plaintiffs. They brought suit against Theophilus to enforce the old prenuptial agreement the couple had signed. Under the terms of the contract, Theophilus was to have turned over hundreds of pounds in Susannah's earnings to designated trustees, something he had persistently failed to do. The money was long spent, of course, and in any case the outcome of the lawsuit, if it ever went to court, seems to have been lost. But the act of forcing Theophilus to account for his own profligacy was a way of striking back at his propensity to sue.

His deposition in the case was one long denial of everything the public knew to be true of the Cibbers' marriage, from Theophilus's control of Susannah's assets to his seizure of her personal property. He compiled his own account of the origins of the Sloper relationship, but it amounted to little more than a pathetic inventory of the ways in which he had been wronged. "She eloped from this Defendant on account of her having committed Adultery [and] has continued to live from him ever since and entirely left performing on the Stage," he swore, "and this Defendant is an entire Stranger to and can give no manner of account of what gains or perquisites she has made at any time or by what means she has supported herself." His words were also a confirmation of what the public at large was now coming to see: that Susannah's Dublin appearances had begun to put her reputation, as well as her earnings, back on an even keel. "This Defendant hath heard that she has for some time been resident at Dublin in the Kingdom of Ireland and performed as Singer and Actress upon the Stage of the Theatre there where she has acquired large sums of money."

That autumn Mrs. Cibber appeared at the Covent Garden theater as Desdemona in *Othello*. When she delivered her final lines—"[My sins] are loves I bear to you . . . O banish me, my lord, but kill me not! . . . let me live tonight!"—the audience erupted in "a burst of applause seldom heard in a theatre," according to a witness. Reverend Delany's flash of compassion had been borne out. All did seem to be forgiven. Cibber's reclaimed glory was a magnet for theatergoers as well as managers. She would soon be powerful enough to insist that Theophilus be barred from the premises of any venue where she happened to be performing.

The January after Cibber returned to London, William Sloper Sr., Coram's old associate, died at his town house in St. James's Place, leaving his son as his sole heir. The younger Sloper's change of fortune lifted Cibber as well. Although still only his mistress, she was now openly connected to a gentleman of substance rather than a young rake who had to steal away from an assignation in the dead of night. He succeeded his father as a member of Parliament for the same constituency and was able to establish a kind of second household with Cibber and their daughter, Molly, even though he still had a wife and other children lodged elsewhere.

Cibber divided her time between Sloper's Berkshire estate and her own London town house in Scotland Yard. In February 1743 Handel launched a new oratorio based on the life of the biblical Samson. He cast Cibber not as the treacherous Delilah but as Micah, Samson's virtuous friend, who urges him on to his true calling of rescuing an embattled Israel. "For my part, [oratorios] give me an idea of heaven, where everybody is to sing whether they have voices or not," noted the dyspeptic Horace Walpole, son of the former Whig prime minister. Still, he had to admit that oratorios were "thriv[ing] abundantly." Before long, a new invitation arrived on Cibber's doorstep. It was another offer from Handel, asking if she would consider performing again with him in the work she had helped premiere in Dublin, but this time for the fickle, fractious audiences of the imperial capital.

THE FIRST LONDON PERFORMANCES of "A Sacred Oratorio"— the *Messiah*, but unnamed in the published announcements—were scheduled for March. The person who had effectively created Italian opera in London, only to fall its victim, was now hailed as master of the English oratorio. Handel "is more esteemed than ever," Faulkner's newspaper reported from Dublin. Yet the fact that the *Messiah* was now being advertised in London without its title was an indication that things were not going well.

The previous autumn Jennens had been buoyed by the information he had been able to glean from Handel and others about the Dublin concerts. "His Messiah by all accounts is his masterpiece," he told Holdsworth proudly. Since then, however, his feelings had changed. When Jennens finally saw the score for the *Messiah*, possibly sometime after he made his regular autumn return to the capital, his judgment was unequivocal. "His Messiah has disappointed me," he wrote to Holdsworth.

He distanced himself from the work by calling it Handel's alone, "being set in great haste; tho' he said he would be a year about it, & make it the best of all his Compositions." He had obtained a copy of the wordbook that George Faulkner had produced in Dublin and found it "full of Bulls," or printer's errors, "& if [Handel] does not print a correct one here, I shall do it my self, & perhaps tell him a piece of my mind by way of Preface." Jennens surely also spotted some of Handel's salvaged melodies, as if the composer could not be bothered to set Jennens's text to music that was wholly new. Handel had recently borrowed a dozen new manuscripts from Jennens's library that Holdsworth had sent from Italy, "& I dare say I shall catch him stealing from them," Jennens complained. He resolved never again to put "sacred words into [Handel's] hands, to be thus abus'd."

Besides dealing with an upset Jennens, Handel soon found himself swimming in a new public controversy. Critics railed against the prospect of mixing scripture and stagecraft—the same amalgam that had perturbed Swift—in a work that seemed too pious for the drawing room and vaguely wrong when performed in the same theater that might host *The Beggar's Opera* on another evening. "I am a profess'd Lover of *Musick,* and in particular all of Mr. *Handel's Performances,* being *one* of the *few* who never *deserted* him," wrote an anonymous correspondent in one London newspaper. But "an *Oratorio* either is an *Act* of *Religion,* or it is not; if it is, I ask if the *Playhouse* is a fit *Temple* to perform it in, or a Company of *Players* fit *Ministers* of *God's Word.*" Not using the title of the oratorio in the public announcement, Jennens told Holdsworth, was Handel's way of dulling the "clamour about Town, said to arise from the B[isho]ps, against performing it," and avoiding a violent public reaction if such a weighty term— "Messiah"—were printed on a playbill.

The London premiere of the *Messiah* took place at the Theatre Royal in Covent Garden on March 23, 1743. Matthew Dubourg had come over from Dublin to serve again as concertmaster, and Susannah Cibber was on hand to reprise her parts from the Fishamble Street performances, a casting that likely heightened public curiosity about the work despite the unease over its subject. A story would later circulate that George II was in attendance and was so moved by the "Hallelujah" chorus that he stood in reverence—the supposed origin of the modern practice of an audience's doing the same. There is no contemporary evidence, however, to confirm such a thing ever happened or, indeed, that the king was even present. Given the uproar over the mixture of sacred and profane in the run-up to the opening, in fact, he might well have decided that a king's primary job was to identify controversy and then walk briskly in the other direction.

Jennens, on the other hand, seems to have made a point of being there. He vacillated between hating what he heard and reluctantly approving of it. At some point, he had marked up his copy of the score with suggested musical rephrasings, realigning words and notes in ways he found more pleasing and natural. "He & his Toad-eater Smith," he wrote to Holdsworth the day after the London premiere, taking aim at both Handel and his assistant, "did all they could to murder the Words in print; but I hope I have restor'd them to Life, not without much Difficulty." The result, Jennens felt, was "in the main, a fine Composition, notwithstanding some weak parts, which he was too idle & too obstinate to retouch, tho' I us'd great importunity to perswade him to it."

The tumult surrounding the work's unveiling in London had been "a Farce," Jennens complained, "which gives me as much offence as any thing relating to the performance can give the B[ishop]s, & other squeamish People." Handel managed only two more London performances of the *Messiah*, on March 25 and March 29. Compared with the reaction in Dublin, they barely made a ripple. "But partly from the Scruples, some Persons had entertained, against carrying on such a Performance in a Play House, and partly for not entering into the genius of the Composition," the Earl of Shaftesbury recalled, "this Capital Composition, was but indifferently relish'd." Cibber's performances would be remembered rapturously by some who saw her—"He was despised" seems to have been as moving in London as it had been in Dublin—but for other commentators her return was an opportunity to dust off old gripes. It was hard to understand, Walpole wrote cuttingly a few weeks before the *Messiah* was introduced to the capital, why Handel insisted on putting aside virtuosi with voices in favor of "a girl without ever an one."

By April, Handel's paralysis was back, this time affecting his head and his speech. He had reportedly told Jennens's cousin that the cause was his dispute with Jennens over revising the *Messiah*. Their disagreement seems to have caused another wave of ill health in Jennens himself, a condition that usually meant lashing out at those closest to him. "I don't yet despair of making him retouch the Messiah, at least he shall suffer for his negligence," Jennens told Holdsworth cruelly. "Nay I am inform'd that he has suffer'd.... This shews that I gall'd him: but I have not done with him yet." Holdsworth knew Jennens well enough to see when his hyp was raging. "This is really ungenerous," he wrote back soothingly, "& not like Mr. Jennens. Pray be merciful; and don't you turn Samson, & use him like a Philistine.... This all proceeds from your staying so long in that dismal melancholick country Leicestershire."

Over the next several months, Handel recovered sufficiently to resume composing and to plan a full season. He and Jennens continued their negotiations over the future of the *Messiah*, and by the following spring Handel had again relented on some unspecified points of composition and phrasing, at least according to Jennens. He was always reworking and rewriting, however, depending on which singers he had available for any performance. Given the customary on-the-spot improvisation by harpsichordists and other virtuosi no two performances of a piece were ever alike. "Handel has promis'd to revise the Oratorio of Messiah," Jennens finally told Holdsworth in the late spring of 1744, "& He & I are very good Friends again."

Handel would eventually oversee two more performances of the *Messiah*, in April 1745, this time advertised by name, but he had already moved on to other things. He was once again creating new work at breakneck speed, launching or reviving a string of musical dramas and oratorios, some again drawn from biblical themes but, unlike the *Messiah*, with original texts narrating a discernible plot. He and Jennens resumed their cooperation, producing an oratorio based on a Jennens text, *Belshazzar*, about the fall of a Babylonian ruler and the freeing of his Jewish captives through the intervention of the Persian king Cyrus—yet another field on which Jennens could exercise his interest in bad sovereigns and heroic saviors.

Overall, audiences were weaker than Handel had hoped. In frustration, he did something that marked a performer's slide toward desperation: he threatened to abandon future appearances unless he was shown more gratitude and respect. His whole aim in recent years, he said in an advertisement he took out in *The Daily Advertiser*, had been to show what could be achieved by "joining good Sense and significant Words to Musick." Yet "I have the Mortification now to find, that my Labours to please are become ineffectual, when my Expences are considerably greater." He ended with a cloying plea: "In the mean time, I am assur'd that a Nation, whose Characteristick is Good Nature, would be affected with the Ruin of any Man, which was owing to his Endeavours to entertain them."

When petulant performers threaten to quit the stage, an audience's response is often to call their bluff. But in Handel's case, his gamble seemed to work. A few days later, he published another advertisement announcing that out of duty to his gracious subscribers he would resume his performances. Jennens thought his behavior was a sign of madness. It was all part of "a new & hazardous Experiment," he told Holdsworth, born of Handel's inability to manage his expenses and keep up with public taste. By May 1745, expenditures had begun to outstrip income in at least one of Handel's bank accounts. While he was never in danger of being thrown out of Brook Street, he was more concerned than ever about how to cover the costs of producing a full season's worth of performances.

Both Handel and Jennens had more to worry about than the next oratorio, however. For years Jennens had known that because he was a prominent nonjuror, his letters were subject to government review. A thick parcel of classical translations he had sent to Holdsworth in Venice, for example, had raised the suspicion of censors. "Your letter . . . being swell'd to an extraordinary bulk was I suppose suspected to be full of Politicks, and therefore was open'd, for so it come to me," Holdsworth reported. "And those who had the curiosity to look into it probably took the Greek characters for Cyphers." At the moment, it was more important than ever to keep their friends and acquaintances "off Politicks," Jennens said. The best course, Holdsworth suggested, was for people to "mind their own business."

The reason was that, in the summer of 1745, the British political system was on the verge of revolution. A change of power had come to seem more plausible than at any point since Daniel Defoe had written of the Jacobites' haunting the public imagination during the reign of Queen Anne. For the first time in more than three decades, what had once seemed like an old exile's pipe dream—the restoration of the Catholic Stuarts—was looking more and more like a prophetic return.

❦

"THEY ARE, I am afraid, more numerous than most gentlemen imagine," Robert Walpole had told the House of Commons in 1738. "I am not ashamed to say I am in fear of the Pretender." While there had been no widespread rebellion since 1715, talk of plots was frequent. Ordinary brawls and riots provided an occasion for denouncing George II. Crowds that had gathered over some other grievance would end up shouting slogans in support of the Jacobites. Domestic politics and international crises were also more entangled than ever. The War of Jenkins' Ear, which had threatened the Georgia project that Coram, Sloper, and Oglethorpe worked to get off the ground, had bled into a new round of conflict among European powers.

In what would later be called the War of the Austrian Succession, at the end of 1740, Prussia had invaded Austrian Silesia, a disputed territory. France, under King Louis XV, came to Prussia's aid, while Britain and Hanover—both ruled by George II as king and elector—aligned with Austria. In 1742, George ordered a British expeditionary force to Flanders, hoping to counter French moves against the Austrian Netherlands. The next year, British, Hanoverian, and Austrian troops pushed into Bavaria, a Prussian ally.

George and his second son, William Augustus, Duke of Cumberland, departed for the front with a personal retinue of more than six hundred horses, thirteen coaches, and nearly a hundred wagons and carts. In June 1743, at the Battle of Dettingen, George personally led his infantry into battle on horseback, then on foot, sword drawn, when his horse bolted. It was the last time a reigning British monarch would appear in a military engagement—and the occasion for a new Handel *Te Deum* celebrating the king's battlefield victory.

In time the war spread to wherever British and French assets came into contact, from North America and the Caribbean to West Africa and India. A British patrol sailed up the Gambia River and destroyed a French factory opposite James Island, where the *Arabella*, the slave ship that carried Ayuba Diallo, had put in before charting a course for Maryland. In London, French diplomats monitored the political undercurrents and sought routes of influence via Tory politicians and nonjuring gentlemen. If their allegiance could be tipped slightly in favor of the Stuart cause, Britain's old factionalism could be turned to France's strategic advantage.

"I have brought a Drawing of a person for whom you have a great respect," Holdsworth wrote to Jennens cryptically after returning from Italy. It was in fact a pencil sketch of the Pretender himself, in profile, his aquiline Stuart nose shown off to regal advantage, which Holdsworth had likely acquired from the court in exile in Rome. At any point since the Glorious Revolution, possessing a portrait of James Stuart would have been a powerful symbol of one's political commitments, but now the lines of allegiance were more distinct than ever. In early 1742, Walpole had resigned as the leader of the House of Commons and effective Whig prime minister. In his place came yet another Whig government. It was a change without a difference that served only to inflame discontent among the opposition Tories. Jacobite sympathizers increasingly became overt supporters of the Stuart cause. A movement that for decades had been formed of nostalgia and whispers seemed suddenly immediate and real—not least because of its new and mesmerizing leader.

James's son Charles—"so fine a youth," as Holdsworth had described him more than a decade earlier—was by this time nearing his mid-twenties. Handsome and well connected across Catholic Europe, he had become the diplomatic mouthpiece for his father, the "Old Pretender," as he was now usually known. Seeking to capitalize on the political energy of wartime, Charles led secret negotiations for a French and Jacobite invasion of Britain in 1744. The plan might have succeeded but for the changeable weather in the English Channel, where days of gale-force winds snapped the masts of French ships preparing to embark.

The following year, the timing was more propitious. That May, British, Hanoverian, and Austrian forces suffered a signature defeat at Fontenoy in the Austrian Netherlands, a strategic loss that strengthened France's hand in the wider war. Charles now plotted a new invasion, apparently without the prior sanction of either his father or Louis XV. He departed on two hired ships, the *Du Teillay* and the *Elisabeth*, one of them captained by a privateer and slave trader, Antoine Walsh, whose father had commanded the vessel that spirited away James after his own ill-fated expedition to Ireland in 1690. Their holds were filled with muskets, broadswords, and gold.

Charles's plan was to foment a rising in Scotland, his family's ancient homeland. Loyal Highland chieftains could be expected to rally clansmen and cattle herders on their expansive upland estates. With a domestic rebellion set in train, Charles hoped, the French king would launch a full-scale invasion in support. From the French coast, Charles's ships sailed northwest to the Outer Hebrides and then to the mainland, quietly spreading word of the prince's mission along the way. "I am come home, Sir," Charles had told one of the first clan leaders he happened to meet in the western isles, a claim that was initially met with skepticism. Within a matter of days, though, reluctance tipped toward expectant possibility.

On August 19, Charles gathered a group of loyalists at Glenfinnan, at the head of the long, picturesque Loch Shiel in the west of Scotland. Unfurling the royal banner, a white square on a red background, he formally launched his bid to take back the entire kingdom in his father's name. Decades later old men who had been present would wax lyrical about the scene of bagpipers and kilted clansmen and tell stories of the sheer charisma of the Young Pretender—the Chevalier's son, as Jennens and Holdsworth had referred to him in their letters, now *Tearlach Mac Sheumais*, Charles, the son of James, to the Gaelic-speaking Highlanders, and, as word of his arrival spread to villages and towns farther inland, increasingly Bonnie Prince Charlie.

Charles had little military experience, but as he and his companions began a steady march to the south and east, his flair for political theater was studied and effective. He sported tartan trews and a blue cap, or bonnet. He stopped to dance at a Highland ball. He cultivated an image as a true field soldier, riding among the troops and mucking his way across burns and through heather, now in its full purple bloom. "He never dinn'd nor threw of[f] his cloaths at night, [nor] eat much at Supper," recalled Lord Elcho, a Scottish noble and head of Charles's cavalry escort, "used to throw himself upon a bed at Eleven o'clock, & was up by four in the morning." The legend that grew up around him—of a prince come to do his father's will, a story resonant with biblical overtones—fueled what was quickly becoming the Stuarts' greatest chance of reclaiming the throne in more than half a century.

His supporters, by now an actual army, marched into Perth on September 9 and then Edinburgh on September 18, both with barely a skirmish. Government troops garrisoned in Edinburgh castle, perched on a craggy outcropping above the city, sent word that they would not surrender. Rather than attacking, Charles allowed them to remain there, an airy irrelevance above an ancient capital that had suddenly turned Jacobite. A few days later, on September 21, Charles's army met its first significant resistance at Prestonpans, on a flat expanse to the east of Edinburgh. Surprising the government infantry at daybreak, the Jacobites attacked with a musket volley followed by a charge on foot, the clansmens' broadswords slicing through the redcoat lines.

The battle was over in a matter of minutes, but its meaning was enormous. Charles's army now swelled with new recruits—Lowland farmers, sons of city merchants, Irish infantrymen, and more than a few Englishmen, Protestants as well as Catholics—drawn by Charles's claim that he was not a conqueror but a liberator, come to wipe away Whig corruption and the illegitimate Hanoverians in one go. Success on the battlefield brought the foreign support he had hoped for, if not a full invasion. A French ship soon arrived with muskets, cannons, and more gold. In October, Louis XV formally recognized Charles's father, James, as king of the Scots.

By mid-November, Jacobites had taken Carlisle, their first city in England. From there, they pressed south to Preston, then Manchester, and then, by early December, Derby, less than thirty miles from Jennens's estate at Gopsall. To people living in London, history seemed to be unrolling with disorienting speed. With the Jacobite army now less than a week's march away from the capital, any Londoners with a country house and a private carriage packed up and left town. Public coaches were fully booked. Jennens, then at Gopsall, advised Holdsworth, stuck in London, to collect the dividends on his South Sea Company investments as quickly as possible. "If some Politicians are not mistaken, all this"—meaning his entire portfolio—"may quickly vanish into Air."

For all these precautions, Jennens was reasonably sure things would blow over, one way or the other. Given how far things had gone, it was not hard to imagine a Jacobite victory. "Credit will revive when the Hurly-Burly's done, & Bank-notes be as valuable as before: but if not, we live under the care of Providence, & that is my best security, as I believe you think it yours too," he wrote. In fact, Jennens was less enthusiastic about the Jacobite rising than his nonjuring beliefs might have suggested. Refusing to swear allegiance to an illegitimate king was a matter of principle, but this was "Politicks," for which he cared nothing, especially when the form it took was a tartan dandy on horseback.

As the autumn of 1745 wound on, public anxiety continued to rise. Letters to newspapers called for a ban on Italian operas, which were thought to be an unnecessary trifle during a national emergency, not to mention being foreign. Perhaps they were even a subtle form of cultural warfare controlled by the Old Pretender from his palace in Rome. Other writers, however, urged the opposite: that singing was exactly what was required in a crisis. "Then, hey my dear Friends, since plainly we're sinking," went one new ballad.

> *Still let us be gay, and damn all dull Thinking;*
> *And if we must go, we'll still raise our Notes,*
> *And die, like the Swans, with our Songs in our Throats.*

In London gentlemen formed volunteer detachments to defend the capital. Militias were called up. The government soon began arresting not just professed Jacobites but also some nonjurors, including people close to Jennens. "I am glad to hear my Friend is so well under his confinement, & I always thought he had Resolution enough to bear greater misfortunes," he wrote to Holdsworth about someone he dared not name in writing.

Some theaters were still operating, and Colley Cibber's old play *The Non-juror*, more wincingly relevant than ever, returned to the stage. Audiences could once again laugh at political dissenters, even as the government was busy rounding them up. Even Jennens's own household had descended into rebellion, with his servants apparently taking advantage of the uncertainty and disorder. "You see by some parts of my Letter, that I am not in very good humour: & to add to my Chagrin, I have lately discover'd my Man Dick to be a Rogue," Jennens complained to Holdsworth, "which has brought me into another dilemma, either to continue a Rogue in my Service till I can get an honest Man, (if there be such a thing to be found) or to be some time without any Servant; which to such a helpless Creature as I am is a great misfortune, but I believe I must submit to it as to the lesser Evil of the two."

EARLIER THAT YEAR Susannah Cibber had appeared for the first time onstage with David Garrick. The play was Shakespeare's *King John*. At the point when Cibber's character, Constance, learns of the capture of her son by the evil king, played by Garrick, Cibber delivered her reaction with "piercing notes of wild, maternal agony," shrieking and collapsing to the floor. Other members of the cast were stunned into silence. Some had to be fed their next lines. When it came to singing, she still had her critics, but as an actor Cibber was hailed as Garrick's natural partner, the perfect theatrical companion for the greatest male lead of the age. "I desire you always to be my lover upon the stage," Cibber wrote to him, "and my friend off of it."

Now, in the middle of the Jacobite emergency, Cibber lent her own restored reputation to the government's cause. In late September she took to the stage at Drury Lane to lead the audience in a secular hymn arranged by her brother. "God bless our noble King / God save great George our King," the people sang, joining soloists and a choir in Thomas Arne's setting of new words to a traditional melody. It was the first time a version of what would later become the British national anthem was ever sung as an expression of popular unity. "The universal Applause it met with, being encored with repeated Huzzas," reported *The Daily Advertiser*, "sufficiently denoted in how just an Abhorrence [the people] hold the arbitrary Schem[e]s of our invidious Enemies, and detest the despotick Attempts of Papal Power."

Evening after evening, crowds came out both to be entertained and to convince themselves that the crisis would pass. Candle makers illuminated the theaters for free. Actors donated their salaries to a charity for soldiers. Cibber contributed her pay as Polly Peachum in a revival of *The Beggar's Opera*. "The Rebellion is so far from being a disadvantage to the playhouses," she wrote to Garrick, "that, I assure you, it brings them very good houses; and the masters receive so much profit from *The Non-Juror*, that I wish it does not give them a respect for the name the rest of their lives."

Soon there would be even more reason to celebrate. Just at the point of pressing his advantage, with the capital on edge and the markets shaky, Charles Stuart made a fateful decision.

British troops led by the Duke of Cumberland—at twenty-four years old, exactly the same age as Charles—had been recalled from Flanders with the aim of countering the Jacobites. Charles might have ordered his forces south, moving toward London before Cumberland's forces could position themselves to defend it. But Charles's advisers were divided on what to do next. Some were worried that the prince had grown overconfident, guided more by hopeful ignorance than military logic. His supply lines were thin, Cumberland's men already hardened by battle, and a French invasion either delayed or nonexistent. "He thought himself sure of Success," Lord Elcho remembered, "and his Conversation ... at Table was, in what manner he should enter London, on horseback or a foot, and in what dress." Others urged him to seize the historic moment. The mobs of London would greet him with cheers, some of his officers claimed, since George II was "a hated Usurper who would be deserted by every body upon the Princes appearing."

In early December, in a move that surprised nearly everyone, Charles chose to turn his army around. "Damn me, Vaughan, they are going to Scotland," an English supporter said to one of Charles's bodyguards. "By God I had rather be hanged than go to Scotland to Starve." When news of the retreat reached the Duke of Cumberland, he could hardly believe his luck. "Of a sudden they quitted Derby," he wrote with amazement. Charles made the journey north on horseback rather than marching in front of his men, feeling dejected and "out of humour," and convinced that his advisers had somehow betrayed him. It was the first time he had retreated since landing in the kingdom he had pledged to reconquer for his father.

The news was greeted in London as nothing short of miraculous. In the weeks that followed, theater performances became excuses for exultant cheers that the threat seemed to have passed. In Scotland the Jacobites, now pursued by government forces, retreated farther north. Later that spring, on April 16, 1746, the Duke of Cumberland's army caught up with the Young Pretender's troops on a boggy expanse outside the garrison town of Inverness. As many as fourteen thousand men faced off across moorland at Culloden, buffeted by wind and heavy rain. The Highlanders' charge that had worked at Prestonpans was now slowed by the waterlogged ground and scrub. It was halted altogether by cannons loaded with grapeshot and the newfound willingness of government soldiers to hold their ground.

In under an hour, Cumberland's men had put the Jacobites to flight. Charles quit the field with a detachment of French and Irish cavalry, while the wounded were bayoneted where they lay—"So that I never Saw a Small field thicker of Dead," recalled a British private. For days and weeks afterward, redcoat patrols hunted down the survivors. Charles, disguised as a female servant, escaped westward to the Isle of Skye. He was soon headed back to France.

❦

LATER THAT SUMMER, the Duke of Cumberland and his forces returned to London in triumph, ushered in by bonfires and the pealing of church bells. High-placed rebel sympathizers were put on trial and executed. Parliament passed the new Act of Proscription, which disarmed Highland men and banned the kilt and other cultural symbols perceived as synonymous with disloyalty, although some of the act's restrictions proved impossible to enforce. Further reforms reduced the hereditary powers of the clan chieftains who had rallied to Charles Stuart's cause and increased state supervision of schools, the better to guard against "the rising Generation being educated in disaffected or rebellious Principles," as the Act of Proscription put it.

Even committed nonjurors might have realized that the prospect of a Stuart return was now effectively extinct. Despite the failure of the Jacobite rising, however, Jennens would never take the oath of allegiance. At midlife and secure in his wealth, he had no reason to do so. "As Antient Pistol says, Hope is a Curtail Dog in some affairs," Jennens had told Holdsworth in the middle of the crisis, quoting the Shakespeare character whom Theophilus Cibber had tried to make his own. In life there were some things that worked out brilliantly and others that, no matter how much one wished, simply didn't.

He had seen Holdsworth earlier that summer in London. When he went back to Gopsall as usual for the warmer months, Holdsworth lodged at his town house in Queen Square. Jennens was in uncharacteristically good spirits. His gas had subsided, he reported, and he was feeling surprisingly well except for a new toothache. "Here I am, safe sound & jolly, having smok'd away the ventosity of my stomach in 10 pipes since I saw you," he wrote from Gopsall. Still, he was concerned for Holdsworth's needs and chastised himself for failing to lay out the drinking chocolate, which he knew Holdsworth liked.

If letters passed between them that autumn, none have survived.

Then again, it would have been hard for Holdsworth to write. He had been ill, as he often was when the weather turned cool, but this time was worse. His limbs had weakened, and he soon found himself unable to use his hands and legs at all. After leaving London, he stayed with friends in Warwickshire, not far from Gopsall. Jennens might have visited in person, since he seems to have remained in the north of England for the whole season, rather than spending it in Queen Square as usual.

It must have come as a great shock, in the early winter, when Jennens received word that his dearest friend was dead. Holdsworth had slipped away on the morning of December 30, 1746, at the age of sixty-two. His hosts were concerned that "as his blood appear'd to be in a mortifying state just before he died he will not keep long." He was buried quickly, without great ceremony, in the nearest village church. If a funeral was ever held, Jennens did not record attending it. He helped settle Holdsworth's affairs, serving as his literary executor and also dealing with a voluble brother and sister-in-law who had appeared on the scene to divide up the meager estate.

There was simply no one "more sensibly affected" by Holdsworth's death, according to his final hosts, than Jennens himself. He apparently made no written mention of the loss. But of all the paper that a gentleman of means and intellect might naturally accumulate—household accounts, reading notes, drafts of his librettos, even the original pages of his "Scripture Collection" that became the *Messiah*—the only things Jennens made an effort to preserve were his vast collection of sheet music and his documentary link to Holdsworth. He kept their letters safe, the ones he had received as well as those he had sent off to Venice, Rome, or wherever Holdsworth happened to be, retrieved at some point from his dead friend's effects. He held on to them—at least one hundred eleven in all—for the rest of his life.

17

Anthems and Choruses

The victory over the Jacobites was followed two years later by the end of the War of the Austrian Succession, the continental conflict that had pulled Britain into a global war with France. The growing mood of security and confidence—or at least George II's eagerness to nudge public sentiment in that direction—played to Handel's advantage. In the spring of 1747, he had premiered a new oratorio, *Judas Maccabaeus,* which drew its theme from Jewish history. A tale of resistance to foreign rule and the struggle against false gods, it was dedicated in the wordbook to the Duke of Cumberland—hero to Whigs, "Butcher" to Tories and Highlanders. Handel later inserted an easily singable chorus, "See, the conquering hero comes," which would rival Arne's "Rule, Britannia!" as the emblem of a newly assertive Britishness.

The Treaty of Aix-la-Chapelle, in October 1748, formally returned Britain to peace with France, Prussia, and other belligerent powers. It would turn out to be more of an armistice than a lasting settlement. Britain and France would go to war again only six years later, a conflict sparked in part by an attack on French positions in the Ohio River valley led by a young lieutenant colonel named George Washington. But Aix-la-Chapelle did manage to weaken the link between domestic politics and foreign intrigue. France undertook to expel any remaining Stuarts. No Jacobite rising would ever again threaten the succession. Charles Edward Stuart would make one further clandestine visit to Britain, but his cause was effectively at an end. By the time he died several decades later, in 1788, diminished by alcohol and disappointment, even most nonjurors had come around to accepting the reality of a Hanoverian dynasty.

George placed the Duke of Montagu, who served as master of the ordnance, in charge of plans to celebrate the hopeful new era. It took months to organize an event of suitable scale and grandeur, something that would both please the king and mark the first time in years that no grenadiers or cavalrymen were called to battle. Handel was commissioned to provide a musical prelude. An outdoor stage and set, consisting of a hundred-foot-high temple of wood and canvas painted to look like stone, now rose in the flower meadow in Green Park near St. James's Palace. In an attempt to control the expected carriage traffic, newspapers gave careful instructions for arrival and departure. People planning to attend were warned that thieves would no doubt lurk in the crowds.

In April 1749 an audience of thousands arrived to witness the nine-hour spectacle. A hundred musicians—woodwinds, trumpets, horns, and drums, but no strings, Montagu insisted, since the king regarded "fidles . . . and violeens" to be insufficiently martial—formed the largest and loudest orchestra Handel had ever commanded. The royal family looked on from the palace. Other people leaned out of windows or climbed to their rooftops. The festivities featured minuets and fanfares, booming cannons, whirring fireworks, and a mechanical sun emblazoned with "Vivat Rex"—"Long Live the King"—which workmen cranked up above the temple to illuminate the entire scene. The whole thing was impressive beyond measure, although "Irregular & in Confusion," as one witness reported. Rain clouds threatened. Falling fireworks set a woman's clothes ablaze. The faux sun burned for nearly a full minute as planned, but an errant rocket caused part of the stage to catch fire.

Still, the "Royal Fireworks," as the event would be known afterward, confirmed Handel's place in what would later be called national identity. When Handel first came to Britain, its unified Parliament was only three years old and its rightful royal line in dispute. Now the kingdom was forging a public story that cast Britons not just as subjects of a common king but as members of an emerging nation, defined by some combination of official Protestantism, naval power, a global empire, and most important not being French.

Part of that sense of the commonweal was also coming to mean having a tune by Handel occasionally running through one's head. He was now more publicly adored than at any point since he had arrived in London more than thirty years earlier. His position as his adopted country's premier public composer was unrivaled, with an annual routine that involved English-language oratorios during Lent and spectacle when required by the crown.

Some of the old energy was back. "The old Buck is excessively healthy and full of spirits," a friend reported. In rehearsals he was known to suddenly cry, "Chorus!!!" at the end of a quiet aria, inspiring his singers while also terrifying them. He had maintained a signature style of dress left over from his youth, including an old-fashioned white wig, large and full, that bounced as he played and nodded at his singers. Audiences could tell when things were going well by how vigorously the curls shook during a performance.

As for the *Messiah*, it was, if not the least of his creations, then by the late 1740s among the least performed. Few people had ever had a chance to hear it. He had conducted it eight times and, of those, only once since 1745. He never published the full score. Pirated copies of arias and choruses circulated, as they always had, but with their words drawn straight from scripture, they were not the sort of thing one sang around the spinet after supper. The whole invention now seemed the product of an odd parenthesis, one winter and spring when a harried composer fled briefly into an Irish exile.

Even Handel's collaboration with Jennens was at an end. After Holdsworth's death, Jennens would never again work with the Prodigious on a piece of music. Their labors together had always been a three-way affair, in spirit if not in name, at least as far as Jennens was concerned. Handel had "made me but a Scurvy return for former obligations," he had complained to Holdsworth the year after the first London performances of the *Messiah*. Now, without his friend and confidant, his tireless listener and bucker-up, what was left of his old passion seems to have withered.

But the work Jennens and Handel had created together was now, at the end of the 1740s, on the cusp of an astonishing renewal. An unexpected possibility would soon come Handel's way. It was a chance to assist a growing, fashionable charity dedicated to the relief of children in need. The occasion would bring the *Messiah* into the one place that, surprisingly for a work on sacred themes, Handel had never performed it before: a church. The charity and its irascible founder would be the unlikely vehicle for making the work—and its composer—close to immortal.

IN SEPTEMBER 1742, the month after Handel returned from Dublin, the governors of the Foundling Hospital had laid the cornerstone for a permanent building. Around the corner from Jennens's residence, a new structure began to rise on fifty-six acres in Lamb's Conduit Field, a place where urban London dissolved into meadow and countryside. The design called for two wings, for girls and boys, alongside schools, dining rooms, dormitories, and offices. A large chapel would unite the two wings, forming a visual centerpiece as visitors approached the building over playing fields and parkland.

Coram had been present for the cornerstone ceremony, his disagreements with other members of the governing body temporarily patched over. Hogarth's portrait of him, circulating as a print, would cement the image of the hospital's champion and truest builder as an indefatigable advocate for a noble cause. The governors even allowed Coram to retain the physical copy of the king's charter. By the autumn of 1745, he could walk across the expansive site to see workmen completing the building's first wing and children already being moved out of Hatton Garden into their new quarters.

With each new admission, however, five times the number of children would be presented at the door as could be accommodated inside. To manage the demand fairly, the governing committee instituted a lottery system. Women drew colored balls from a box—white for accepted, red for rejected—to determine whether their child would be allowed into the inspection room. Around a hundred children were being accepted per year, but that was only a tiny fraction of those still "drooping and dying" in inadequate care, as a contemporary source put it. Funding receipts were also down. Coram's relentless beseeching could open purses and bank accounts, but now that the hospital was a formal charity overseen by well-heeled dukes and earls, among them some of the largest landowners in Britain and overseas, any sense of urgency had begun to fade.

In 1749 the governors hit upon the same idea that had occurred to Coram more than two decades earlier. Making a charity into a fashion was the surest route to its survival, and there was perhaps no one better to aid that transformation than the country's foremost composer, his reputation now refreshed in a time of peace. Were Handel to hold a concert for the hospital's benefit, the governors reasoned, their cause would be fused with someone now regarded as close to a national treasure. Some of Handel's closest friends were members of the governing body, and he himself had already contributed to the charity by donating an organ, which would later be assembled in the chapel. It seems to have taken little persuading for him to agree to stage a special concert. In the late spring, newspapers carried an announcement for a performance featuring a selection of his music from the Royal Fireworks and other unnamed pieces.

There were no windows yet installed in the chapel and little in the way of furnishings. But the advertisement assured the public that the shell of a building would be "Sashed and made commodious." On May 27, the program went off just as expected. A thousand people had purchased tickets. The Prince and Princess of Wales were in attendance. Handel premiered a new work that came to be known as the "Foundling Hospital Anthem," one element of which was simply the recycled "Hallelujah" chorus from the *Messiah*. In fact, the Foundling Hospital concert might have been the first instance of listeners' rising to their feet at the chorus, since Handel placed it exactly where one might expect a jubilant wrap-up: as the final movement. The event was considered such a resounding success that the governors invited Handel to return the following year.

Money, as it had always done, followed endorsements. Handel's association with the hospital was part of what would turn out to be a rush of artists toward the hospital's efforts. Hogarth and others had already contributed to the hospital's interior decoration, adding ornate biblical scenes to the court room, or meeting chamber, for the hospital's governors: Moses in the bulrushes, the outcast Hagar and her fatherless son Ishmael, Jesus inviting the little children to come unto him. Now the hospital was increasingly functioning not only as a concert space but also as a public gallery.

Hogarth donated his portrait of Coram, and a lottery brought in his *March of the Guards to Finchley*, a boisterous take on the dispatch of redcoat soldiers to confront the Jacobites. The picture collection grew to include many of the preeminent painters of the century, including work by portraitists such as Joshua Reynolds and Thomas Gainsborough. Displayed in the hospital's public rooms, the paintings would form what amounted to Britain's first public art museum—an outcome that Coram could hardly have imagined when he set out collecting signatures for his proposed charity decades earlier.

In the spring of 1750, an announcement circulated for a new concert under Handel's direction, now in the completed Foundling Hospital chapel. The program included the full "sacred oratorio" that he had felt unable to name publicly only a few years before. The *Messiah* had first been performed in aid of debtors, and it was now to have a kind of second premiere, in a chapel dedicated to the rescue of needy children. Paid choristers and boys from the Chapel Royal formed the choir. Hogarth offered his services to design the tickets. They featured an image he had created as the hospital's new coat of arms: an infant with a hand outstretched, above a motto that said simply, "Help."

When the doors opened on May 1, more than twice the number of people showed up as for Handel's concert a year earlier. Thousands pushed and elbowed to get inside. So many prominent donors were left without a seat that Handel agreed to perform again on the following day. "Two or Three Bishops were there," one attendee reported, "so that I hope, in a little while, that Hearing of oratorios will be held as orthodox." The minutes of the Board of Governors soon recorded that Handel had joined their number as a Foundling Hospital trustee.

Coram was most likely absent from the *Messiah* concert. He had earlier been left off the guest list for people invited to see the opening of the court room with paintings by Hogarth and other esteemed artists. Recognized as the hospital's founder but no longer considered quite fit to circulate in the rarefied reaches of London society that now ran it, Coram would soon be close to penury. Some of his remaining friends organized a public subscription to help support him.

Coram told a friend that it was something of an achievement to have managed one's finances so well, with generosity of purpose and no self-indulgence, that one could move toward death in satisfied poverty. He was now in his eighties. On many days, he could be seen sitting outside the Foundling Hospital in his rust-colored coat, smiling among the children. He died not long afterward, in March 1751. Only then did the governors make his connection to the Foundling Hospital permanent. After a solemn, well-attended service, he was buried under the altar of the chapel, steps from Handel's organ, which was at last fully installed and tuned.

CORAM HAD LIVED long enough to see a monumental expansion in the hospital's operations. The year he died, records showed that a total of more than 800 children had been admitted to the institution. That figure would swell in the years to come. Within a decade, 270 children were residing in the main building in Lamb's Conduit Fields, while more than 6,000 others were placed in the care of foster families and wet nurses throughout Britain.

For years, communicable diseases would continue to take an appalling toll. At mid-century the infant mortality rate was 63 percent, although already less than the 75 percent in other institutions. In time, however, the hospital would turn out to be a pioneer in reducing childhood death. A program of mandatory childhood inoculation against smallpox would stem one of the era's greatest killers. Nurses and other employees were required to have had the disease before beginning work. The mortality rate gradually came down, and infants grew into young girls and boys recognizable by the brown wool uniforms, designed by Hogarth, that marked them as Foundling Hospital residents. When they came of age, boys could expect to be apprenticed or sent to sea, girls to work in manufacturing or domestic service. Many would move into their adult lives, start families of their own, and work throughout Britain and overseas in skilled trades, as weavers, tailors, and shopkeepers, even the occasional singer or organist.

Over the course of the 1750s, the Foundling Hospital's "Annual Musical Festival of Messiah," as the organizers called it, became one of the most anticipated events of the London season. The concerts brought in nearly seven thousand pounds in all, an enormous sum for a charity. If the *Messiah* now seemed intimately familiar to thousands of people, it was because many of them had heard it in that venue. "It was afterwards consecrated to the service of the most innocent, most helpless, and most distressed part of the human species," wrote John Mainwaring in his early biography of Handel. Susannah Cibber apparently never participated in the hospital concerts; she had moved on to other engagements onstage and last sang for Handel in 1745. But for the first few years at least, audiences could expect to see Handel himself in charge, conducting the choir from the keyboard, a role that he later ceded to John Christopher Smith Jr., son of his old assistant, in his capacity as the Foundling Hospital's official organist. Now and then, if the weather were fair and the crowds bearable, an astute visitor might even have recognized Charles Jennens, well dressed and dour, seated among the listeners, having made the short walk from his town house. The association with Handel made the chapel a popular destination even outside the annual performances. The pious tourism of attending a Sunday morning service became so popular that the hospital began offering pews for rent. Visitors could gaze up at the gallery to see Coram's children, as they came to be called, in their crisp uniforms, sitting patiently through the liturgy.

From his coronation anthems to some of the greatest works of public spectacle ever created, Handel had become nothing short of the architect of British musical sensibility. The concerts at the Foundling Hospital provided a regular occasion for popular adulation unlike anything he had ever experienced. His music was inseparable from a cause as well as a moral sensibility: helping indigent children and knowing the deep tangibility of hope. After the London premiere of the *Messiah* in 1743, Handel is supposed to have told a noble patron, "My Lord . . . I should be sorry if I only *entertained* [an audience]; I wished to make them better." The quotation was probably a later invention, but to his listeners the story came to express something real. Handel's music did well because people now expected it to make them good.

Handel performed the *Messiah* more frequently than any other oratorio he ever composed, thirty-six times, most of them after the age of sixty. But for many of his admirers, the Foundling Hospital concerts were what made the *Messiah* his greatest creation—a fact so seemingly obvious that the details barely warranted a mention. "It is needless to enlarge upon particulars, which are easily remembered, or to give a minute account of things generally known," wrote Mainwaring. The *Messiah* was now established as "the favourite Oratorio," he said. "So that it may truly be affirmed, that one of the noblest and most extensive charities that ever was planned by the wisdom, or projected by the piety of men, in some degree owes its continuance, as well as prosperity, to the patronage of HANDEL."

The old typesetter from Bartholomew Close apparently agreed. Benjamin Franklin, who had returned to London in 1757 as colonial agent for Pennsylvania, was in the audience at one of the chapel concerts. Writing to a young friend afterward, he felt no need to describe it as anything other than "the Oratorio in the Foundling Hospital." By that stage, anyone would have known what he meant.

IN THE WINTER OF 1751, Handel noticed a problem with his left eye. "So relaxt"—it's weakening—he jotted in German at the bottom of another oratorio he had been working on, along with the date, February 13. He was just turning sixty-six. For the past fifteen years, busy performance seasons had left him plagued by recurring illnesses, including bouts of unexplained paralysis. Now his eyesight seemed to be fading as well, the same affliction that had rendered his mother completely blind in middle age.

Bach had died the previous year, and Handel might have been aware of how the great composer had ended up: as a pitiable colossus who had to be led to the keyboard by an assistant. Only a few months after first noticing his eye problems, Handel found himself following the same course. Each time he instructed a lawyer to update his will, his signature became noticeably less legible, trending toward a scrawl. He started attending prayers twice a day at St. George's church near Brook Street and pulled back on his swearing, for which he had once had a particular gift. He found some relief in taking the waters in spa towns such as Bath or Tunbridge Wells, but each time he returned to the manuscript pages on his table, the lines on the staff had become less distinct.

He still composed, now with the help of Smith Jr., but his performances increasingly depended on recalling things from memory or relying on his legendary gift for improvisation. He practiced incessantly during oratorio season, working to keep his skills sharp and the impromptu passages fresh. He might give out only sketch parts to his musicians, playing all the solos himself at the keyboard and then using a final trill to signal the rest of the orchestra to join him again. His fingers had grown puffy and dimpled, like a baby's, but his hands, as a Roman cardinal had once put it, still had wings. "To see him . . . led to the organ . . . and then conducted towards the audience to make his accustomed obeisance," remembered Charles Burney, "was a sight so truly afflicting and deplorable to persons of sensibility, as greatly diminished their pleasure, in hearing him perform."

In 1756, Jennens persuaded Handel, around the age of seventy-one, to sit for the portraitist Thomas Hudson. He wore a dove-gray coat with gold brocade that stretched over his substantial midriff. The painting showed Handel to be more jowly than ever, his eyebrows bushy, his head turned slightly to look straight out at the viewer. But the full-on gaze, focused at middle distance, hinted at what everyone knew: that his sight had totally gone. The printed score that Hudson placed on the table before him—the trailing letters of *Messiah* just visible in the frame—was now unreadable to the man who had composed it.

~ 18 ~

Exalted

By the spring of 1759, Handel's health had worsened. He had been able to travel to Tunbridge Wells for a water treatment the previous summer, but now he found it impossible to attend performances, much less conduct them. An attempted surgery to correct his eyesight—carried out by the same traveling oculist, John Taylor, whose gruesome ministrations had led to Bach's death—was a failure.

In early April an announcement appeared for the annual performance of the *Messiah* the next month at the Foundling Hospital. Handel would not live to hear reports of it. He died in Brook Street on April 14, 1759, the Saturday before Easter. He had bequeathed his clothes to a servant, a copy of the *Messiah* to the Foundling Hospital, his music manuscripts to John Christopher Smith Sr., two paintings to Jennens, and—now, at last, a wealthy man—generous sums to relatives, friends, and the Fund for Decay'd Musicians. He was buried a short time later in the south transept of Westminster Abbey.

In his will, Handel had specified that his funeral take place "in a private manner," but at least three thousand people were said to have attended the service, even though it was not formally open to the public. A statue by Roubiliac, which Handel had paid for himself, was later unveiled as his memorial. The likeness was reckoned to be one of the truest ever created. It showed him in a casual pose, bareheaded and wigless, his body curled around a page from the *Messiah* score, the aria "I Know That My Redeemer Liveth."

The scheduled performances continued at the Foundling Hospital chapel, now solely under Smith Jr.'s direction. A rumor soon began to circulate that Handel had in fact died on Good Friday—a fitting end, his admirers insisted, for a composer whose most memorable work was already considered something close to sacred. "I went to the cathedral to hear Mr. Handel's *Messiah*," reported the old Savannah vicar John Wesley—by now a leader of the Methodist movement—after attending a concert in Bristol. "I doubt if that congregation was ever so serious at a sermon as they were during the performance."

Twenty-five years later, in May 1784, King George III and an audience of four thousand gathered in Westminster Abbey to celebrate the centenary of Handel's birth. The *Messiah* capped off the three-day tribute. "And from that time to the present," Charles Burney noted in a published account of the concert, "this great work has been heard in all parts of the kingdom with increasing reverence and delight; it has fed the hungry, clothed the naked, fostered the orphan, and enriched succeeding managers of Oratorios, more than any single musical production in this or any country." At the "Hallelujah" chorus, Burney remembered, he couldn't help imagining the orchestra and singers merging with the saints and martyrs in the abbey's stained-glass windows, a celestial band of musicians more "ecstatic and affecting" than anything he had ever heard. At one point or another, everyone he looked at in the audience had tears in their eyes.

Much of the income from the Westminster celebration, some six thousand pounds, went to the Fund for Decay'd Musicians, which, in the decades since Handel had helped found it, had effectively become the world's largest insurance program for professional performers. The donation swelled the fund's coffers to twenty-two thousand pounds, an astonishing figure in support of the performing arts. But it also brought the connection between music and empire full circle: the fund's managers promptly invested the money in the South Sea Company. The company's annuities, paying dividends of 3 percent, would continue to be one of the fund's major sources of revenue until, graced with a royal charter, it evolved into what is today the Royal Society of Musicians.

By the time of the Handel commemoration, the *Messiah* had become so widely popular that the guardians of the original manuscript kept it close and safe. After receiving the stack of pages from Handel in his will, John Christopher Smith Sr. carefully preserved it alongside the other original manuscripts—not just an artifact of a storied composer and a signature episode in the history of music, but also a kind of relic of universal spirituality. Upon his death, it passed to his son, Smith Jr., who in turn gave his father's massive Handel collection to George III, allegedly in exchange for a lifetime pension.

The *Messiah* manuscript then resided in the library of the royal family at Buckingham Palace for a century and a half, before being placed under the stewardship of the British Museum in 1911. During the Second World War, rare volumes and priceless artifacts from the museum were relocated to the London Underground or outside the capital, saving them from the German bombs that damaged or destroyed much of what was left behind. In 1957, Elizabeth II donated the royal music collection to the public trust. The *Messiah* is now kept in a basement strong room in the British Library, one of its principal treasures, still showing the ink stains, smudges, and rewrites that Handel applied furiously as he made plans to depart for Ireland.

JOHN MAINWARING'S *Memoirs of the Life of the Late George Frederic Handel* was published a year after Handel's death. Mainwaring was a Cambridge theologian, and his only connection to his subject was possibly an acquaintance with the Smiths, whose stories and recollections might have informed his biography. What made the book compelling, however, was the author's nose for a good anecdote, regardless of whether it was verifiable. Because his account was the first one off the printing press and nearly contemporary with the composer's life, it would remain hugely influential for centuries to come. Most of what people thought they knew about Handel came from Mainwaring's telling.

Soon after *Memoirs of the Life* appeared, Jennens acquired a copy. He filled it with his own annotations and disagreements, a running commentary on a story he was certain the biographer had misunderstood. "Explain your self, if you can!" he wrote in the margin in response to one of Mainwaring's judgments. He shelved the marked-up volume in his library, a hidden remembrance of a man he had worshipped and battled for much of his life. By this stage, Jennens had only a scant role in the public memory of the great master. Wordbooks to the *Messiah* were occasionally printed with his name at the front, acknowledging him as the librettist, but that practice soon fell away. His name appeared nowhere in Mainwaring's text.

Jennens was now master of Gopsall Hall. His father had died in 1747, and he had at last come fully into his inheritance. Yet the person who might have given his newfound freedom greater meaning—Edward Holdsworth—was also gone. In the years that followed, Jennens undertook an expansion of the manor house, with new wings and a reimagined facade. On the far edge of the grounds of Gopsall Hall, he hired workmen to dig out a wide, deep ditch. They used the excavated dirt to build up a mound at the center. The inside of the ditch was lined with bricks to create what landscape designers called a ha-ha, a steep trench that kept away cows and sheep, with no fence to interrupt the view.

Jennens commissioned an architect to draw up a structure to be sited atop the mound: an open-sided octagon consisting of Ionic columns connected by arches, all supporting a dome of considerable weight and proportion. He paid Roubiliac, who had just completed Handel's monument in Westminster Abbey, to shape a piece of Carrara marble that would surmount the dome, a more-than-life-size image of Christianity personified, in the form of a classical maiden supporting a large cross and holding a scroll representing the Gospel. Under the dome, he placed a funereal urn on a cenotaph carved with complex images of grief and loss: a broken temple, a winged genius at rest, the ruined tomb of Virgil entwined with a bay laurel. The whole edifice was a tribute to Holdsworth.

Jennens wrote a long inscription in Latin to accompany the monument, although, true to form, he spent much of his available space complaining that the person he originally asked to compose it never came through. But its principal message was praise for Holdsworth's faithfulness and purity of heart, his character and genius, along with a subtle nod to his Jacobite study-abroad tours:

> *He tutored the sophomoric youth*
> *in his own craft and furnished them*
> *with mores against an age debauched*
> *by vices both private and public,*
> *no less through his example than through his advice.*

The inscription occupied two sides of the cenotaph, all of it rolling toward a summary of Jennens's feelings in a final phrase: "indignata Amicitia," his "indignant friendship" in defense of a man he felt no one but himself had truly known.

By the time the monument was finished, in 1764, Holdsworth had been dead for eighteen years. To visitors walking the grounds, the "Templum Gopsaliensis," as Jennens grandly referred to it, loomed in the distance, a pleasing focal point when they looked out past the estate's lake and paddock, toward the fields and woodland beyond. But the point of the temple was not to be admired from the manor house. It was rather to provide a place from which to look back on Gopsall Hall. The hillock on which it sat was left to grow wild, with a short pathway leading up through the undergrowth. To anyone who followed the footpath and then stepped up into the columned rotunda, the whole estate suddenly opened up to its finest advantage—the house, the gardens, the new wings—the crooked now straight, the rough places plain.

"There are many circumstances which concurr to sink my Spirits at certain times," Jennens had written to Holdsworth while he was working on the *Messiah*, "but I have learnt of you to trust Providence, &

I hope that will never suffer me to be much or long dejected." For the rest of his life, gazing out from Holdsworth's temple at least, he could be assured of one remarkable thing. From that point of view, he looked not like Swift's Gulliver, the hairy Yahoo he so often felt himself to be, but as Holdsworth always saw him: at his absolute, splendid best.

※

FOR NEARLY TWO CENTURIES after Thomas Coram's death, his body remained in the chapel of the Foundling Hospital. But the old sailor and cajoler turned out to be as restless in death as in life. As the hospital survived and flourished, its population of children outgrew the premises. The old building in Lamb's Conduit Field was abandoned for newer, larger quarters. Each time the hospital moved, as it would do several times, Coram was dug up and moved with it: from Bloomsbury to Hertfordshire, then back to London. His body was finally placed in St. Andrew's Church in Holborn, not far from Hatton Garden, where his foundlings had first been given a second chance. His most notable quality, a friend remembered, was that he had "lived above the Fear of every Thing but an unworthy Action."

As Coram's design for rescuing hardened into a lasting institution, it lost some of the hopeful glow that had surrounded the early Handel concerts there. The *Messiah* performances ended in 1777 as organizers lost interest and other opportunities arose throughout the year for hearing Handel's work. In the Victorian era, the hospital's reputation would darken. There were stories of coldness and cruelty, of toddlers torn away from the families who had fostered them as infants. Salvation sometimes came to look more like exploitation, with children farmed out as factory workers and laborers—an alternative to the workhouse but still regimented and limiting, meant to keep children in the social station into which most had been born. Yet because of Coram's legacy, generations of young people conquered the greatest obstacle of their time: making it to adulthood.

The original building Coram had dreamed into being fell to urban developers and later became a park. As the decades wound on, however, the Foundling Hospital returned to something closer to his original vision. It updated its name and mission while also rooting both in the past—no longer a single physical space, but a network of helpers and services known as the Thomas Coram Foundation for Children. A statue of Coram himself, based on Hogarth's painting, now stands outside the foundation's national headquarters in central London, adjacent to the site of the chapel where the *Messiah* became Handel's most famous creation. Today, the foundation—called simply Coram—is Britain's largest charity devoted to adoption and foster care.

AFTER THE DUBLIN *Messiah*, Susannah Cibber's reputation was no longer defined by court cases and public scandal. She had reclaimed her life, and at its center was not a father or a husband but her own searing talent. "This air," wrote Charles Burney, who once heard her sing "He was despised," "has been often sung by Italian singers of the greatest abilities, but never, I believe, in a manner so truly touching to an Englishman. . . . By a natural pathos, and perfect conception of the words, she often penetrated the heart, when others, with infinitely greater voice and skill, could only reach the ear." Cibber had become so associated with the *Messiah*, in fact, that people came to assume that Handel had written portions of it for her, although he hadn't. It was her own interpretation of Jennens's libretto, set to Handel's melodies, that had brought down the house.

Thomas Sheridan, the Irish student who had perhaps seen her in Fishamble Street, soon to become an actor in his own right, would later describe her *Messiah* performances as an experience notable not for what she did onstage but for what she did to an audience. She had the power to elevate public taste and calm discontent, a kind of universal balm to the disorders of politics and society at large. "No person of sensibility who has had the good fortune to hear Mrs. Cibber in the oratorio of the Messiah," he wrote, "will find it difficult to give credit to accounts of the most wonderful effects produced from so powerful a union."

After the mid-1740s, Cibber became the most celebrated tragedienne in the history of English theater. She earned perhaps seven hundred pounds a year in salary—comparable with Handel's six hundred pounds in base income from his royal duties—augmented by bonuses and other occasional revenue. She was reckoned to be the most highly paid actor of her generation, second only to a man, David Garrick, with whom she had an onstage relationship that the public followed as intensely as social media would later track celebrity marriages. Whenever she was cast as Desdemona or Juliet, audiences clamored for seats. Theatergoers found she had the extraordinary power to make the low into the high, a debased character achieving, by the final curtain, some measure of victory.

On Sunday evenings she hosted one of the most fashionable salons in London, a meeting place of artists, actors, writers, and politicians. She and Handel had become close friends, and it was not unusual to find him at the harpsichord or to see the two of them together inside a gaggle of guests, sharing a laugh or a confidence. What did Handel think of the composer Gluck, she once asked. "He knows no more of contrapunto as mein cook, Waltz," came Handel's reply, apparently punctuated with a bawdy swearword. Still, given Cibber's ongoing relationship with Sloper—she lived with him for the rest of her life, at least when he wasn't living with his wife, Catherine—she could never be admitted to the society of women of position and distinction. Sloper apparently never sought a divorce. Catherine would eventually destroy every piece of documentary evidence she could find of her husband's second family.

Cibber continued to suffer the recurring illnesses she had experienced in Dublin—digestive problems and debilitating pain, later attributed to "stomach worms"—which would sometimes cause her to cancel appearances or postpone openings. Sea bathing in frigid waters at Scarborough, in North Yorkshire, was a doctor's prescribed treatment, to which she submitted with annual dread. In December 1765, she starred in a play called *The Provoked Wife*. The plot had a familiar theme—about a woman who wrenches free from her brutish husband and seeks solace with a new love—only now played as a wild farce, a comic version of a story Cibber had actually lived, publicly and horribly, thirty years before.

She died the next month, at the age of fifty-one, at her town house in Scotland Yard. The theaters in Drury Lane and Covent Garden went dark for the evening, a tribute never before seen. The poet George Keate, a friend of Voltaire's, circulated a new work to the memory of "the celebrated Mrs. Cibber":

> *By Death's cold Hand those Features now are bound,*
> *That once could ev'ry Change of Passion wear!*
> *Mute is that Voice, whose more than magic Sound*
> *Stole like soft Music on the ravish'd Ear!*

In her will she left everything to Sloper in trust for their children, of whom Molly remained the only one still alive. (Molly would pass her adult life in security, happily married to a country vicar.) That February, Cibber was buried in the North Cloister of Westminster Abbey—an unusual honor, given that she was a lifelong Catholic—and a wall away from Handel's resting place in the sanctuary. The exact site remains unmarked to this day.

As for Theophilus, while Mrs. Cibber was performing tragedies, he was living one. After two lackluster trials and his wife's redemptive performance in Ireland, he never again brought a legal suit against her. He had tried his hand at writing, but the plays that resulted—*The Lover*, *The Harlot's Progress*—were cheap farce or derivative twaddle, with plenty of implied sex. For his own version of *Romeo and Juliet*, he cast himself and his fourteen-year-old daughter from his first marriage in the title roles. He turned in a more serious direction by publishing a five-volume *Lives of the Poets*, but it turned out to be the work of a ghostwriter. There were drunken rants onstage, the occasional volley of vegetables from the stalls, a stint in prison for indebtedness, and recriminations with producers, which meant theaters sometimes barred him for a whole season. He came to believe that Cibber and

Garrick were conspiring to wreck his career, a claim he indulged in rambling essays that he marketed to newspapers and publishers.

He became the kind of actor other actors mocked, a catchphrase comedian with a reputation for shouting his lines. "Possessed of talents that might have made him happy, and qualities that might have rendered him beloved," noted a contemporary encyclopedia of stage personalities, "his life was one scene of misery, and his character made the mark of censure and contempt." In 1758 he accepted an invitation from the Smock Alley Theatre in Dublin, perhaps hoping to use an appearance in the city to launder his reputation, just as his wife had done years earlier.

That October he boarded the packet boat at Parkgate, along with a tightrope walker who had been booked by the same venue. En route the ship foundered in a rogue wind in St. George's Channel. He and all the other passengers were lost at sea. The only remnant, washed up on the west coast of Scotland, was a chest containing some of his books and papers. His life, said Daniel Defoe's grandson, who knew him, was "begun, pursued, and ended in a storm."

JENNENS LIVED ON for another quarter century without Holdsworth and more than a decade without Handel. His collection of Handel's music would swell to 368 volumes, but once there was no more music to collect, his interests turned in a different direction. In his sixties, he embarked on an ambitious project to create new editions of all the plays of Shakespeare.

His method was visionary and modern, if controversial at the time. The idea was to publish each play separately rather than as part of a collection. He would take care to make the texts as accurate as possible, using earlier editions that were produced in Shakespeare's lifetime or that could otherwise be verified as authentic—the antithesis of the rewrites that Colley and Theophilus Cibber had tried to turn into a trademark industry. Numerous footnotes contained scholarly excursions on alternative wordings and possible stage directions, even here and there hints about Jennens's own deeper beliefs and passions. To say that a bruised heart could be pierced through the ear, Jennens remarked about one passage from *Othello*, was a poetic way of memorializing something that was "touching, affecting, comforting" all at once, "as with musick."

In addition to *Othello*, he got around to *King Lear*, *Macbeth*, *Hamlet*, and *Julius Caesar*, but the project turned out to be a nightmare. As a later account put it, "He imprudently thrust his head into a nest of hornets." In making the case for his own contribution, Jennens applied his usual ill temper and impatience to the labors of other writers and would-be authorities. One of them, the publisher George Steevens, a friend of Samuel Johnson's, took such offense that he dedicated part of his own writing career to destroying Jennens's.

"The chief error of Mr. Jennens's life consisted in his perpetual association with a set of men every way inferior to himself," Steevens wrote. "By these means he lost all opportunities for improvement, but gained what he preferred to the highest gratification of wisdom—flattery in excess." Jennens's obstinacy was equal to his vanity, Steevens said, and "what he had once asserted, though manifestly false, he would always maintain."

Steevens's version of Jennens's life and work, born of his own professional jealousy, would largely shape how he was seen forever after: Jennens's eye for art was inferior, his taste in books even worse, his attainments in any field negligible. Later, an encyclopedia of the century's eminent personalities would follow Steevens's line, casting doubt on Jennens's principal achievement while also diminishing it. "He is said to have composed the words for some of Handel's oratorios, and particularly those for 'the Messiah,'" the encyclopedia entry concluded, "an easy task as it is only a selection from Scripture verses."

Jennens fell ill at some point in the late autumn of 1773, a time of year he always dreaded. On November 20 he called for his chaplain, who administered last rites, and then threw himself back into his chair, dying instantly. He was buried at the parish church in Nether Whitacre, a Warwickshire village not far from Gopsall, in the Jennens family chapel just off the main sanctuary. Two years after Jennens's death, his nephew and executors placed a carved memorial in the wall. It listed the many bequests he had made in his will and the specific amounts in sterling that he donated to charities. There was no mention of the *Messiah*.

The vault is now used as a vestry and storage room for the small church, an austere space attached to a Gothic tower of local sandstone that can glow kiln red in the right light. The congregation plans to raise enough money to move the memorial to a more prominent spot, away from the aluminum ladder and cardboard boxes that share the same space. Over the centuries, whenever new plaster went up or scaffolding was taken down, bits of the memorial were chipped away. But an inscribed motto is still just visible at the top, inside a small roundel. "Non omnis moriar," it reads, quoting a line from the Roman poet Horace.

"I will die, but not all of me."

THE SAME YEAR as Jennens's death, news filtered back to the Spalding Gentlemen's Society from the Gambia River. Another of its members, the "Priest, at Boonda in Africa," had died as well. Little was known about what had happened to Ayuba Diallo in the intervening decades, other than that he had continued to work with the Royal African Company, at least until 1752, when the company was dissolved. He had helped extend the company's reach into the interior. His assistance had furthered not only the trade in products extracted from the forests and hills, especially gum arabic, an essential ingredient in ink making and dyeing, but also the commerce in people. One of his first recorded acts when he returned to the Gambia River was to trade some of the presents he had received in England for "a Woman-Slave and two Horses." A few years later, when Diallo proposed that the company bring him back to England to renew his acquaintance with Sloane, the Duke of Montagu, and others who had helped him, the company sent clear instructions to its outpost on James Island:

"We would have you by all means discourage the same." From the company's point of view, Diallo's place was in Africa.

In Britain, however, a version of Diallo's life story had already become famous. Thomas Bluett had written up his account of Diallo's sale and redemption, from West Africa, to America, to Britain, and then back home again. *Some Memoirs of the Life of Job, the Son of Solomon, High Priest of Boonda in Africa,* using Bluett's English version of Diallo's name, appeared in 1734. Bluett had made Diallo's father into a senior cleric, which was a Christian's fumbling attempt at categorizing what it was like to be an *almaami* in Fulbe society. But the work included details of the recent past of Bundu and other states and empires, their political and religious structures, and the customs of Islam in West Africa, as accurate as a European at a distance could make them. It also had the distinction of situating an enslaved person in history—not as a beast teetering on an auction block, devoid of a past, but as an actual human being, with a family lineage and hopes for the future.

Bluett's pamphlet would turn out to be the first widely available narrative compiled from the actual testimony of a transatlantic captive. Even people who had never met Diallo in a city salon or country estate could now feel they knew something of his life and fate, and the humanity that had been stolen from him by specific, named people: the Hunts, Pike, Denton, Toulson. It would be followed by many similar accounts of grisly capture, the Middle Passage, auction pens, and plantation terror. Future abolitionists would point back to his biography, in Bluett's telling, as one of the sources of the entire movement. In an era that prized sensibility—a feeling of empathy and the motivating power of emotional connection—it was a story that helped train white readers to see the things that Diallo's life, for all its complications, fully represented: the intentional horrors and absences created by centuries of Atlantic bondage. Much later, when Alex Haley retold his own family's history of captivity and freedom in the novel *Roots*, the early life of his first traceable ancestor, Kunta Kinte—born in a Muslim village in Senegambia and sold into slavery in Annapolis, Maryland—would bear a striking resemblance to Diallo's own.

Diallo was one of the victims of slavery and one of its abettors, and in the end also one of its destroyers. His life intersected with nearly everyone of consequence in the capital city of a colonial empire that had stolen him, sold him, and also redeemed him. Scholars are still finding traces of him tucked away in archives and libraries: letters, reminiscences by friends, a page from a Qur'an apparently written out in his own hand, a language lesson that he supplied to one of his many London associates. The map of his homeland that he drew in London—the one that showed England as a tiny dot off the coast of West Africa—survived amid the correspondence of Hans Sloane. To anyone who now has the chance to handle it, safeguarded in the rare books and manuscripts room of the British Library, it is an illuminated pathway back to a moment when empire, faith, terror, and hope were wound together in one extraordinary life.

Diallo's portrait by William Hoare disappeared from public view at some point after it was created, but in 2009 it came up unexpectedly for auction in London. Its beauty and rarity—an eighteenth-century black man viewed not as a servant but as a dignified subject in his own right—caused a sensation. Curators around the world began scouring their collections for other versions. A print turned up at the Royal Academy of Arts. Another oil portrait, similar to Hoare's, surfaced in a private collection in the United States and was acquired by the American Revolution Museum at Yorktown. Hoare's original was purchased by the government of Qatar, but the new owners allowed it to stay in Britain on long-term loan.

Diallo's image now hangs in the National Portrait Gallery near Trafalgar Square—at the center, it turns out, of a kind of shadow geography of the *Messiah* itself. The location of Cibber and Sloper's secret hideaway is literally around the corner. Farther on, a visitor can call at Handel's home in Brook Street, now an intimate and moving museum. In the opposite direction lie the sites of Jennens's town houses in Queen Square and Great Ormond Street, which are themselves not far from a children's park that sits on the grounds of the old Foundling Hospital. Nearby, the Foundling Museum houses Hogarth's portrait of Thomas Coram and other treasures from the hospital's two centuries of work.

Even at the farthest point Diallo's epic life ever took him, the past still echoes into the present. Three thousand miles away, back in Maryland, the area of Kent Island where he was held captive is crossed by a road called Plantation Lane. Among the small farms and rural businesses is a company called Jailcraft Inc., whose website describes the firm as "a certified detention equipment contractor able to assist you with any aspect of your detention equipment needs."

THE JENNENS FAMILY'S Gopsall estate had been built on the iron trade. It was sustained in part through South Sea Company investments. After Charles Jennens's death, it passed to a niece's husband and their descendants, then to an earl, a baron, and finally the Crown Estate, the property-holding office of the British monarchy. Gopsall Hall eventually followed the path of other English country houses too large and expensive to maintain. It became a radar station during the Second World War and was finally pulled down in 1951. The grounds are now a glamping site and RV storage park.

The Holdsworth temple collapsed in 1835, a casualty of weather and neglect. Bits and pieces of it, the Roubiliac statue and the urn, found their way to a Leicester museum and the garden of a stately home. Some of the ruins, however, are still in place. A few broken columns jut up out of a thicket of bracken and brambles, nearly invisible at the edge of a beech wood and a wheat field. As the estate declined, visitors started leaving graffiti on what became known locally as a monument to love. Norman and Tess stopped by in 1942. Dave and Zoe visited in 1967. L. Jones, Woodcutter, was presumably taking a break from his work in the forest. In 1948 a man named Zachert carved both his surname and his condition: "German P.O.W."

Over the decades, the ruins became so much of a local landmark that a legend grew up about their most famous association. If the temple was a tribute to the power of human connection and universal optimism, and if Handel had ever visited Gopsall, as he had, what better place for him to have created something that can still make an audience feel, just for a moment, what it's like to be wrapped in love?

Today, a fading tourist placard gets its history spectacularly, exquisitely wrong: "George Frideric Handel is said to have closeted himself inside the Temple for 3 weeks in August/September 1741 to write his masterpiece 'The Messiah.'"

Epilogue

In Dublin the instrumentalists had already begun tuning up, adjusting gut strings and cane reeds sensitive to spring mists and chill. Handel took his place at the organ and arranged the conducting score. Matthew Dubourg, the concertmaster, eyed Handel for a cue to begin. Dubourg was to oversee the instrumentalists while Handel concentrated on Susannah Cibber, the other singers, and Jonathan Swift's choristers. With seven hundred people rustling and settling, Dubourg lifted his bow, and the music stirred into motion.

The performance began with a dark, hesitant processional in a minor key, a "sinfony" as Handel had named it, pitted with moments of silence. From there, it drifted into an insistent fugue, rippling, wavelike, and wholly familiar to anyone who had ever heard a Handel opera. Next came another short introduction, more stately, building toward what seemed like an expected entrance.

A singer stepped forward from the choir.

Charles Jennens had based the first portion of his libretto on the fortieth chapter of the book of Isaiah. In the passage he copied down, Isaiah had been in the middle of a finger-shaking rebuke of Hezekiah, king of Judah, attacking him for his complacency and greed. But then his words changed. They became less thunderous and more composed, like the sayings of a confident oracle. They had been rendered by the King James translators as a stream of images and analogies. There are things that wither and things that remain. All princes will one day be brought low. Whirlwinds will shake every field into stubble. But the universe offered a pathway through, Isaiah had prophesied, a way to walk without fainting and to run without growing weary. Humans, too, could feel what an eagle felt: the moment when its wings spread out on the wind, taking flight.

A wisp of a tenor voice arced over the musicians. He pronounced two words crisply, more spoken than sung, and now in the brightest possible major key. He then reached up toward a longer, higher note, not so much soaring as summoning, addressing his listeners directly, and pulling the rest of the orchestra along with him. The strings entered again, as if lifting his arms to urge him on.

To tell the greatest story he could imagine—of a love so powerful it not only conquered death but promised to return to the scene of the crime—Jennens had decided to lead not with a complication or a predicament but with a resolution. If you could envision a future world where warfare was finally accomplished, where iniquity was pardoned and valleys exalted, it might just be possible to live as if *this* world worked that way, too. He had borrowed the words from an ancient text, yet to those who recalled being there in Fishamble Street, they seemed wholly urgent and original—built both from and for the time in which they were now being sung.

Everyone in Neale's music hall had lived through war or disease. A seething political conspiracy threatened to upend the established order or, depending on one's politics, to restore it. An unexpected change in the weather had recently left families frozen and starving. Many of the women would bury more children than they saw into adulthood. But onstage Susannah Cibber would soon help proclaim that death had been swallowed up in victory. Back in London, Thomas Coram, who had nearly resigned himself to being a voice crying in the wilderness, would soon have proof that a single life really can repair a corner of the world. And thousands of miles away, Ayuba Diallo, back from an unimaginable odyssey, was still recounting the story of how his bonds, against all hope and expectation, had been broken asunder.

Epilogue

It took a universe of pain to make a musical monument to hope. Some of the early Enlightenment's foremost philosophers were refugees dreaming about what a just government might yet bring. The Baroque era's art and music were things of shards and tempests that would be remembered for their power to calm and awe. Great powers leveled civilizations while also building one. Their naturalists and mathematicians perfected a style of thought that, in generations to come, would make the whole of the cosmos more knowable but also more mysterious and beautiful. Their principal religions placed suffering, rejection, and brokenness at the core of their teachings yet still clung, knuckle hard, to the promise of something better. Their merchants shipped other humans into bondage, people whose descendants would, again and again, bend the powerful toward justice.

In line after line of song, the *Messiah*'s main message still comes through: a key to living better is practicing how to believe more. The cynics are wrong, but so, too, are the naive optimists, a point that Jennens emphasized over and over again in his selection of scriptures. There is no sorrow like this sorrow, no heaviness like the one that only we can know. Darkness really does sometimes cover the face of the earth, and we are all, in our ways, astray. But the route out of despair, he concluded, lay on the pathway toward it.

His method was to take the words of the prophets seriously, the essence of which soloists and choirs have been proclaiming, in Handel's version, for nearly three hundred years. Be not afraid. Dwell among your fears and enemies long enough for them to lose their sting. Take captivity captive. Precisely at the point when all seems lost, rejoice greatly. Arise—and then shine.

Hope begins to fail when it becomes no more than wishful thinking, unmoored from reality, but even then, Jennens once wrote, it can be "physick'd"—enlivened, buttressed, brought back to health—by seeing reality in a new light. The *Messiah* was one example of such a cure in action. It was a Christian's account of the purpose of this life and the promise of a world to come. But it continues to move listeners because its lessons are universal. The things we live through are part of figuring out what we live for. If you can imagine the opposite of misery not as joy or happiness but as grandeur and awe—"Blessing and honor, glory and power," as the singers declare together in the final chorus—survival has a bonus. It is the redemption that comes of reasoning not from experience but against it.

"Let us sing of greater things," Jennens had written at the top of the original *Messiah* wordbook. The foundation of hope, he sensed, was not the will to look past awfulness. It was the habit of seeing clearly in the middle of it. In the face of everything life might bring, the truly radical way to forecast the future was to put an assurance up front.

Since 1742 every performance of the *Messiah* has started out with the same two words. Even today, they still sound startling and revelatory—a proclamation, a challenge, and a deliverance all at once, like a coachman's horn on a fogged-in coast road:

Comfort ye

Charles Jennens's
Messiah Libretto

Handel's handwritten score of the *Messiah* has survived down to the present and is held in the British Library. The score from the first Dublin concert, written out by a copyist, is housed at the Bodleian Library in Oxford. Jennens's original pages for the libretto, however, have been lost. The earliest published version is the 1742 Dublin wordbook, printed by George Faulkner, which was so full of what Jennens called "Bulls," or misprints—or possibly other mistakes that Jennens blamed on Handel—that he was disgusted when he saw it.

Copies of the 1742 wordbook are today exceedingly rare. One surfaced in 1891 in Dublin, "among some old books exposed for sale," and is now in the British Library. Another was owned by the godson of the composer Sir Arthur Sullivan (of Gilbert and Sullivan fame), before being gathered into an unparalleled private trove of music manuscripts and letters, the Heineman Foundation Library, and then passing to the Library of Congress.

Jennens might have had a hand in editing a new wordbook produced in 1743 by the printer Thomas Wood for Handel's London performances. This version came to light in the 1970s in Massachusetts and now resides in the collection of the Morgan Library and Museum in New York. It began with the same epigraphs that Jennens had supplied for the Dublin premiere: the Latin quotation from Virgil and the passage laying out the essentials of Christian belief, compiled from New Testament verses in 1 Timothy 3:16 and Colossians 2:3. The main text altered some spellings from the 1742 version and divided the libretto not only into the standard three parts but also into numbered quasi-scenes. It also changed the attribution line on the title page from "Compos'd by" Handel, as the original Dublin wordbook had it, to "Set to Musick" by him. Since Jennens never seems to have sought public credit for his contribution to the *Messiah*, the change might simply have reflected the feeling that no one should claim to have "composed" a work made up of sacred scripture.

With a wordbook in hand, a listener could follow along through the work as Jennens seems to have imagined it: not so much a series of scenes in a plot as legs of a theological and philosophical journey. The 1743 text is somewhat different from how performances of the *Messiah* usually run today, but it is perhaps as close as history can come to Jennens's intentions.

MESSIAH,
AN
ORATORIO.

Set to Musick by George-Frederic Handel, Esq.

MAJORA CANAMUS.

And without Controversy, great is the Mystery of Godliness: God was manifested in the Flesh, justify'd by the Spirit, seen of Angels, preached among the Gentiles, believed on in the World, received up in Glory.

In whom are hid all the Treasures of Wisdom and Knowledge.

PART I.

1.

RECITATIVE, accompanied.

Comfort ye, comfort ye my People, saith your God; speak ye comfortably to *Jerusalem,* and cry unto her, that her Warfare is accomplished, that her Iniquity is pardon'd.

The Voice of him that crieth in the Wilderness, Prepare ye the Way of the Lord, make straight in the Desert a Highway for our God.

SONG.

Every Valley shall be exalted, and every Mountain and Hill made low, the Crooked straight, and the rough Places plain.

CHORUS.

And the Glory of the Lord shall be revealed, and all Flesh shall see it together; for the Mouth of the Lord hath spoken it.

II.

RECITATIVE, accompanied.

Thus saith the Lord of Hosts; Yet once a little while, and I will shake the Heavens and the Earth; the Sea, and the dry Land:
And I will shake all Nations; and the Desire of all Nations shall come.
The Lord whom ye seek shall suddenly come to his Temple, even the Messenger of the Covenant, whom ye delight in: Behold He shall come, saith the Lord of Hosts.

SONG.

But who may abide the Day of his coming? And who shall stand when He appeareth?
For He is like a Refiner's Fire:

CHORUS.

And He shall purify the Sons of Levi, *that they may offer unto the Lord an Offering in Righteousness.*

III.

RECITATIVE.

Behold, a Virgin shall conceive, and bear a Son, and shall call his Name *Emmanuel*, GOD WITH US.

SONG and CHORUS.

O thou that tellest good Tidings to Zion, *get thee up into the high Mountain: O thou that tellest good Tidings to* Jerusalem, *lift up thy Voice with Strength; lift it up, be not afraid: Say unto the Cities of* Judah, *Behold your God.*
Arise, shine, for thy Light is come, and the Glory of the Lord is risen upon thee.

RECITATIVE, accompanied.

For behold, Darkness shall cover the Earth, and gross Darkness the People; but the Lord shall arise upon thee, and his Glory shall be seen upon thee.
And the *Gentiles* shall come to thy Light, and Kings to the Brightness of thy Rising.

SONG.

The People that walked in Darkness have seen a great Light; they that dwell in the Land of the Shadow of Death, upon them hath the Light shined.

CHORUS.

For unto us a Child is born, unto us a Son is given; and the Government shall be upon his Shoulder; and his Name shall be called Wonderful, Counsellor, The Mighty God, The Everlasting Father, The Prince of Peace.

IV.

RECITATIVE.

There were Shepherds abiding in the Field, keeping Watch over their Flock by Night.

SONG.

And lo, an Angel of the Lord came upon them, and the Glory of the Lord shone round about them, and they were sore afraid.

RECITATIVE.

And the Angel said unto them, Fear not; for behold, I bring you good Tidings of great Joy, which shall be to all People:
For unto you is born this Day, in the City of *David*, a Saviour, which is Christ the Lord.

RECITATIVE, accompanied.

And suddenly there was with the Angel a Multitude of the heavenly Host, praising God, and saying,

CHORUS.

Glory to God in the Highest, and on Earth Peace, Good Will towards Men.

V.

SONG.

Rejoice greatly, O Daughter of Sion, *shout, O Daughter of* Jerusalem; *behold thy King cometh unto thee:*
He is the righteous Saviour; and He shall speak Peace unto the Heathen.

RECITATIVE.

Then shall the Eyes of the Blind be open'd, and the Ears of the Deaf unstopped; then shall the lame Man leap as a Hart, and the Tongue of the Dumb shall sing.

SONG.

He shall feed his Flock like a Shepherd: He shall gather the Lambs with his Arm, and carry them in his Bosom, and gently lead those that are with young.
Come unto Him all ye that labour and are heavy laden, and He will give you Rest.
Take his Yoke upon you, and learn of Him; for He is meek and lowly in Heart: and ye shall find Rest unto your Souls.

CHORUS.

For his Yoke is easy, and his Burden is light.

The End of the FIRST PART.

PART II.

1.

CHORUS.

Behold the Lamb of God, that taketh away the Sin of the World!

SONG.

He was despised and rejected of Men, a Man of Sorrows, and acquainted with Grief.
He gave his Back to the Smiters, and his Cheeks to them that plucked off the Hair: He hid not his Face from Shame and Spitting.

CHORUS.

Surely He hath born our Griefs, and carried our Sorrows:
He was wounded for our Transgressions, He was bruised for our Iniquities; the Chastisement of our Peace was upon Him, and with His Stripes we are healed.

CHORUS.

All we, like Sheep, have gone astray, we have turned every one to his own Way, and the Lord hath laid on Him the Iniquity of us all.

RECITATIVE, accompanied.

All they that see him laugh him to scorn; they shoot out their Lips, and shake their Heads, saying,

CHORUS.

He trusted in God, that He would deliver him: Let him deliver him, if he delight in him.

RECITATIVE, accompanied.

Thy Rebuke hath broken his Heart; He is full of Heaviness: He looked for some to have Pity on him, but there was no Man, neither found he any to comfort him.

SONG.

Behold, and see, if there be any Sorrow like unto His Sorrow!

II.

RECITATIVE, accompanied.

He was cut off out of the Land of the Living: For the Transgression of thy People was He stricken.

SONG.

But Thou didst not leave his Soul in Hell, nor didst Thou suffer thy Holy One to see Corruption.

III.

SEMICHORUS.

Lift up your Heads, O ye Gates, and be ye lift up, ye everlasting Doors, and the King of Glory shall come in.

SEMICHORUS.

Who is this King of Glory?

SEMICHORUS.

The Lord Strong and Mighty; the Lord Mighty in Battle.

SEMICHORUS.

Lift up your Heads, O ye Gates, and be ye lift up, ye everlasting Doors, and the King of Glory shall come in.

SEMICHORUS.

Who is this King of Glory?

SEMICHORUS.

The Lord of Hosts: He is the King of Glory.

IV.

RECITATIVE.

Unto which of the Angels said He at any time, Thou art my Son, this Day have I begotten thee?

CHORUS.

Let all the Angels of God worship Him.

V.

SONG.

Thou art gone up on High; Thou hast led Captivity captive, and received Gifts for Men, yea, even for thine Enemies, that the Lord God might dwell among them.

CHORUS.

The Lord gave the Word: Great was the Company of the Preachers.

DUETTO and CHORUS.

How beautiful are the Feet of them that bring good Tidings, Tidings of Salvation; that say unto Sion, thy God reigneth, break forth into Joy, thy God reigneth!

SONG.

Their Sound is gone out into all Lands, and their Words unto the Ends of the World.

VI.

SONG.

Why do the Nations so furiously rage together? and why do the People imagine a vain Thing?
The Kings of the Earth rise up, and the Rulers take Counsel together against the Lord and against his Anointed.

CHORUS.

Let us break their Bonds asunder, and cast away their Yokes from us.

VII.

RECITATIVE.

He that dwelleth in Heaven shall laugh them to scorn; the Lord shall have them in Derision.

SONG.

Thou shalt break them with a Rod of Iron; Thou shalt dash them in pieces like a Potter's Vessel.

VIII.

CHORUS.

Hallelujah! for the Lord God Omnipotent reigneth.
The Kingdom of this World is become the Kingdom of our Lord and of his Christ; and He shall reign for ever and ever, King of Kings, and Lord of Lords. Hallelujah!

The End of the SECOND PART.

PART III.

I.

SONG.

I Know that my Redeemer liveth, and that He shall stand at the latter Day upon the Earth:
And tho' Worms destroy this Body, yet in my Flesh shall I see God.
For now is Christ risen from the Dead, the First-Fruits of them that sleep.

CHORUS.

Since by Man came Death, by Man came also the Resurrection of the Dead.
For as in Adam *all die, even so in* Christ *shall all be made alive.*

II.

RECITATIVE, accompanied.

Behold, I tell you a Mystery: We shall not all sleep, but we shall all be changed, in a Moment, in the Twinkling of an Eye, at the last Trumpet.

SONG.

The Trumpet shall sound, and the Dead shall be raised incorruptible, and We shall be changed.
For this Corruptible must put on Incorruption, and this Mortal must put on Immortality.

III.

RECITATIVE.

Then shall be brought to pass the Saying that is written; Death is swallow'd up in Victory.

DUETTO.

O Death, where is thy Sting? O Grave, where is thy Victory?
The Sting of Death is Sin, and the Strength of Sin is the Law.

CHORUS.

But Thanks be to God, who giveth Us the Victory through our Lord Jesus Christ.

SONG.

If God be for us, who can be against us?
Who shall lay any thing to the Charge of God's Elect?
It is God that justifieth; who is he that condemneth?

It is Christ that died, yea, rather that is risen again; who is at the Right-Hand of God; who maketh Intercession for us.

IV.

CHORUS.

Worthy is the Lamb that was slain, and hath redeemed us to God by his Blood, to receive Power, and Riches, and Wisdom, and Strength, and Honour, and Glory, and Blessing.

Blessing, and Honour, and Glory, and Power, be unto Him that sitteth upon the Throne, and unto the Lamb, for ever and ever. Amen.

FINIS.

Author's Note

In the eighteenth century, spelling, capitalization, and punctuation were idiosyncratic. I have followed the usage in the original texts unless doing so would create confusion or unnecessary strangeness, such as in reported speech. The same goes for now-outdated labels for categories of people.

The current, or Gregorian, calendar came into use in Britain and its overseas colonies by act of Parliament in September 1752. Before then, Britain was eleven days behind the modern system, which had already been adopted in parts of continental Europe. Moreover, the new year began not on January 1 but on the Feast of the Annunciation, or Lady Day, March 25. Events in the intervening months can thus seem to be off by an entire year from how they would be reckoned today. (That is why Handel's gravesite in Westminster Abbey confusingly gives his birth year as 1684, which, given that he was born on February 23, we would now call 1685.) I have used the calendar appropriate to the place and time of the action, with the exception of the hazy period from January to March, where I give the year as it would be calculated now.

Acknowledgments

This book, a small act of thanksgiving, would not have started without Maggie Paxson, the bravest, kindest, smartest person I know. She talked me through slumps and demonstrated that the cure to a writing problem about the eighteenth century is sometimes the gift of a frilly shirt.

When I began this project, early in what would turn out to be a long pandemic, I couldn't have predicted how reliant I would become on electronic books, digitized documents, and full-text, searchable databases such as the Gale Eighteenth Century Collections, the Seventeenth and Eighteenth Century Burney Newspapers Collection, HathiTrust, Project Gutenberg, SlaveVoyages.org, and many others. I owe deep thanks to the librarians, archivists, curators, programmers, and other creatives who have made these things possible. They have rendered the eighteenth century perhaps the most digitized one outside our own.

My version of the story of Jennens, Handel, Cibber, Coram, and Diallo relies wherever possible on original sources. As the book developed, I racked up debts to many people who gave freely of their time and opened the treasures under their care.

In the United Kingdom, Anita Harrison and Chris Brookes of Belgrave Hall, Leicester, led me to some of the remnants of Jennens's memorial to Edward Holdsworth, now tucked away in a back garden. Liz Baliol-Key of Leicester Museums and Galleries opened a warehouse so that I could see the Roubiliac statue that once adorned the top of the memorial. Vanessa Gaskin, Rita Poulson, and Louis Patterson of St. Giles Church, Nether Whitacre, were my guides to the Jennens family chapel. Clare Hopkins, archivist at Trinity College, Oxford, uncovered materials related to Nicholas Stevens and Robert Jennens. Anna Petre, assistant keeper of Oxford University Archives, Bodleian Libraries, Oxford, located materials on the university proceedings connected with Robert's suicide. Emily Jennings, assistant archivist and records manager at Magdalen College, Oxford, shared a pencil sketch that linked up unexpectedly with the Jacobite conspiracy. Charlotte Hopkins of the London Metropolitan Archives was very helpful with the Foundling Hospital collection. Marion Wallace, formerly lead curator for Africa at the British Library, and Paul Naylor of the Hill Museum and Manuscript Library shared their pathbreaking work on Diallo's extant writings. Lucy Peltz, senior curator of eighteenth-century collections at the National Portrait Gallery, answered my questions about William Hoare's portrait of Diallo. Francesca Tate, assistant archivist at the Honourable Society of the Middle Temple, tracked down further evidence related to the Jennens family and their association with the legal profession.

Colin Coleman, assistant librarian of the Gerald Coke Handel Collection at the Foundling Museum, was indispensable as a guide to the Jennens-Holdsworth correspondence and kindly digitized several sources so that I could view them at a distance. He and Katharine Hogg, head librarian, welcomed me at the museum's annual eighteenth-century music study day in November 2022, which made me wish that all academic conferences had a concert at lunchtime.

I am very grateful to His Grace the Duke of Buccleuch and Queensberry, KT, of Boughton House, Northamptonshire, for permission to use his family's papers. Crispin Powell, archivist at Boughton, was a font of information and insights about the Duke of Montagu, Diallo, and the broader context of patronage and peerage. Kathryn Price, collections registrar at Boughton, showed me around one of Britain's most storied homes and art collections. Claire Davies, deputy director of Handel Hendrix House in London, took me on a tour of 25 Brook Street—in the middle of a full-scale renovation project—which allowed me to see the bare bones of Handel's house as it might have looked when it was first being built.

Finally, Chris Scobie, lead curator of music manuscripts at the British Library, arranged for the original autograph manuscript of the *Messiah*, with its large ink stain, to be brought out of its vault. Martin Holmes, Alfred Brendel Curator of Music at the Bodleian Libraries, Oxford, did the same thing with the original Dublin conducting score. Seeing these priceless artifacts of world civilization is an experience I will never forget.

In the United States, I am very grateful to Margaret Dunham of the Delaware State Archives, who helped lead me through slavery-era materials. Chris Haley, director of the Legacy of Slavery in Maryland Project, Maryland State Archives, answered my questions about slaveholding in colonial Maryland. The professional staff of my local libraries in Washington, D.C.—the Main Reading Room and Performing Arts Reading Room of the Library of Congress, and Lauinger Library at Georgetown University (especially Ted Mallison)—were friendly and helpful as always.

I was fortunate to be able to check some points of fact and have otherwise enlightening email conversations with Paul Boucher, Amy Froide, Mary Margaret Revell Goodwin, Micah Hoggatt of the Harvard Theatre Collection, Jonathan Keates, Joseph Lockwood, Bob Lowe of the Kent Island Heritage Society, Emma Moesswilde, Catherine Molineux, Barbara Paca, Alan Passmore of the Parkgate Society, Carole Taylor, and Dustin Frazier Wood, librarian and archivist of the Spalding Gentlemen's Society. Lorenzo Pagdanganan, a Georgetown undergraduate, provided a beautiful translation of the Latin inscription formerly in the Gopsall Temple.

This book makes use of the published scholarship of historians, musicologists, performance specialists, and Handel experts whose work is cited in the notes. On Handel and the Baroque, they include Donald Burrows, Winton Dean, Jane Glover, David Hunter, Jonathan Keates, Watkins Shaw, and especially Ellen T. Harris, whose deep reading of the finished manuscript went above and beyond the call of scholarly duty. On the Enlightenment, I have been much influenced by the research of Ritchie Robertson and Jonathan Israel. On Atlantic history and enslavement, I have learned to think in new ways from the work of Holly Brewer. Overall, I want to single out Ruth Smith, the pioneering scholar who resurrected Charles Jennens from obscurity and whose writings were an early inspiration to me. Ruth kindly read an early draft of the manuscript and provided invaluable comments on points of fact and interpretation.

For advice and encouragement, I am very grateful to Kate Brown, Henry Louis Gates Jr., Grant Harris, Dana Ivey, Marjoleine Kars, Patrick Radden Keefe, Mark P. Leone, Devoney Looser, Marden Nichols, Ken Opalo, Adam Rothman, Tom de Waal, and Georgina Wilson. Other friends and colleagues—Joshua Cherniss, Hope Harrison, John McNeill, and Shannon Stimson—put aside their own work to read the manuscript and offered thoughtful comments and corrections that made the book better. My home institution, Georgetown University, was generous and supportive as always, and I thank my deans and department chairs over the years—Joel Hellman, Soyica Diggs Colbert, Rosario Ceballo, Carol Benedict, Katharine Donato, and Anthony Clark Arend—for nurturing a community that is both inspiring and kind. A sabbatical and faculty grant from Georgetown allowed me to visit sites and archives in Dublin, Leicestershire, London, Northamptonshire, Scotland, and Venice relevant to the story.

My agent, Rob McQuilkin, was excited about the *Messiah* story and its bigger meaning from the moment I pitched it to him. His reading of the draft manuscript was an astonishing feat of deep and sympathetic editing. I am so thankful to Rob, Maria Massie, and the entire team at Massie & McQuilkin for continuing to have me as part of their community of writers. At Doubleday, I have again had the unbelievable good fortune to work with Kris Puopolo, a dream editor if there ever was one. It has been a privilege to entrust the manuscript to brilliant teams in production, publicity, and marketing, including Ana Espinoza, Kathleen Fridella, Michael Goldsmith,

Sara Hayet, Anne Jaconette, Emily Mahon, Felecia O'Connell, and Cassandra Pappas, and to have Bill Thomas on this project's side from the beginning.

The dedication at the front of this book points toward a woman who taught me more about music and life than just about anyone I have known, the late Pat Ellison. Few people could have coaxed a group of kids from rural Arkansas into working up a folder of Baroque brass music and then taking it on tour to the National Cathedral in Washington, D.C. That was the least of her accomplishments but one that meant the world to a younger me.

Everyone should get the chance to have a high school band teacher. If they're very lucky, they'll have someone like Ms. Ellison.

Notes

Abbreviations used in notes:

Coke	Gerald Coke Handel Collection, Foundling Museum
Deutsch	Deutsch, *Handel: A Documentary Biography*
HCD	Burrows et al., *George Frideric Handel: Collected Documents*
HTC	Harvard Theatre Collection, Houghton Library
LMA	London Metropolitan Archives
Montagu	Montagu Archive, Boughton
MSA	Maryland State Archives
MTA	Middle Temple Archives
NA	National Archives, Kew
OUA	Oxford University Archives, Bodleian Library
Trinity	Archive of Trinity College, Oxford

PROLOGUE

1 "Solyman the Magnificent": Johnston and Owen, *New and General Biographical Dictionary*, 7:384.
1 "puny": Jennens to Edward Holdsworth, June 28, 1746, Coke.
1 He was so afraid: Ibid.
1 "all the Books": Will of Charles Jennens, Dec. 10, 1773, NA PROB 11/993/139.
2 "an impetuosity of temper": Eulogy by Rev. George Kelly Jr., in Nichols, *History and Antiquities*, vol. 1, pt. 2, 861n14.
2 "'Tis impossible": Jennens to Holdsworth, Jan. 20, 1746, Coke.
2 In his drawing rooms: Smith, "Achievements," 169.
3 "lay out his whole Genius": Jennens to Holdsworth, July 10, 1741, Coke.
4 "head is more full": Jennens to Lord Guernsey, Sept. 19, 1738, in *HCD*, 3:427.
4 "The Subject": Jennens to Holdsworth, July 10, 1741, Coke.

INTRODUCTION

7   "technicolor 'Messiah'": Harold C. Schonberg, "'Messiah' Is the Greatest Oratorio of Them All," *New York Times*, Dec. 11, 1977.

8   The earliest documented concerts: Redway, "Handel in Colonial and Postcolonial America," 195–96; Lockwood, "Performance and Reception."

9   "a more numerous Band": Quoted in Burney, *Account*, 6 (Commemoration section).

9   "a *Manu-ductor*": Ibid., 15.

9   "I was at the piece": Adams to Elizabeth Cranch, Sept. 2, 1785, in Adams, *Letters*, 369.

9   "monster performances": Shaw, *Story of Handel's "Messiah,"* 73.

9   "As the master": Ralph Waldo Emerson, "Nominalist and Realist," in *Complete Works*, 4:233; Emerson, *Journals*, 6:479.

10   "I should have sometimes fancied": Adams to Jefferson, June 6, 1785, in Adams, *Letters*, 354.

10   "Oh, that I had cannon!": Quoted in Townsend, *Account of the Visit of Handel*, 103n.

10   According to a blogger: "Hallelujah! Hallelujah! Find a Messiah Sing in Your Area! 2023 Season," Adventures by Katie, accessed Dec. 8, 2023, adventuresbykatie.com/.

12   "unbelieving city": Emerson, *Journals*, 6:480.

12   "When it came to that part": Adams to Elizabeth Cranch, Sept. 2, 1785, in Adams, *Letters*, 369.

14   "We must discover": Martin Luther King Jr., "'Loving Your Enemies,' Sermon Delivered at Dexter Avenue Baptist Church," Nov. 17, 1957, accessed June 9, 2023, kinginstitute.stanford.edu/.

15   "the age of reason": Paine, *Age of Reason*, pt. 1, chap. 1.

15   "recovery of nerve": Gay, *Enlightenment: The Science of Freedom*, 3.

15   "If it is now asked": Immanuel Kant, "An Answer to the Question: What Is Enlightenment?," in *Practical Philosophy*, 21.

16   By the last decade of the century: SlaveVoyages.org.

1 · "THE FAMOUS MR. HENDEL"

23   The Thames was tiled: In addition to cited quotations, my description of George I's journey up the Thames draws from Hogwood, *Handel: "Water Music,"* chap. 2; Coxe, *Anecdotes*, 15–16; Serwer, "World of the *Water Music*"; Burrows and Hume, "George I, the Haymarket Opera Company."

23   "Persons of Quality": *Daily Courant*, July 19, 1717, in *HCD*, 1:379.

23   "You pimps to your own mothers": Ward, *London-Spy Compleat*, 4. On swearing and insults among Thames watermen, see also Saussure, *Foreign View of England*, 94; Misson, *Memoirs and Observations*, 320.

23   "*sans nombre*": Frédéric Bonet to King of Prussia, July 19, 1717, in *HCD*, 1:381.

24   Travelers coming to London: Saussure, *Foreign View of England*, 32.

24   "the finest Symphonies": *Daily Courant*, July 19, 1717, in *HCD*, 1:379.

24   "the famous Mr. Hendel": See, for example, Boyer, *History of the Reign of Queen Anne*, 335.

25   "neither cat nor dog": Wilson, *Europe's Tragedy*, 784–85, 842–43.

25   Some parts of Europe: Ibid., 787.

25   In all, as many as: Ibid., 4.

26   The new household: Hunter, *Lives*, 250.

26 Even in a provincial city: Burrows, *Handel*, 5–10; purchase document for "Zum Gelben Hirsch," June 30, 1666, in *HCD*, 1:4.
26 In later life: Mainwaring, *Memoirs*, 5.
27 At first he practically: Ibid., 4.
27 He would keep some: Burrows, *Handel*, 13.
27 A few years later: Deutsch, 8.
28 "Ein Christliches": "Bestallung vor den Organisten Hendel," March 13, 1702, in *HCD*, 1:33.
28 Ships arrived: Lindberg, "Rise of Hamburg," 641.
28 The city's opera house: Keates, *Handel*, 12.
28 "a *ripieno* violin": Quoted in Burney, *Account*, *2.
28 He occasionally traded lessons: Burrows, *Handel*, 21.
28 Mattheson's rapier: Mainwaring, *Memoirs*, 35; Burney, *Account*, *5.
28 Mattheson would later boast: Mattheson, *Grundlage einer Ehren-Pforte* (1740), in *HCD*, 1:44.
29 To get to a performance: Burney, *Account*, *2n(a); Burrows, *Handel*, 20; Mattheson, *Grundlage einer Ehren-Pforte* (1740), in *HCD*, 1:38.
30 "contaminated laments": Plato, *Laws*, 3.700e, in *Collected Dialogues*, 1294.
30 "So little are they": Mainwaring, *Memoirs*, 43–44.
31 "Some of them had got": Ancillon, *Eunuchism Display'd*, vi. On the history of castrati and women, see Berry, *Castrato and His Wife*.
32 "We have freed ourselves": Handel to Mattheson, Feb. 24, 1719, in *HCD*, 1:412.
32 On a visit to Hamburg: Harris, *Handel as Orpheus*, 37–38.
32 "A sort of intimacy": Mainwaring, *Memoirs*, 39.
33 "no conveniences": Ibid., 41.
33 By 1706: For a discussion of the precise dating of Handel's travels, see Hunter, *Lives*, 153–59; Dean and Knapp, *Handel's Operas*, 78–79; Burrows, "What We Know."
33 He wrote and played: Keates, *Handel*, 22.
33 "tall, strong": Quoted in Burney, *Account*, *5.
33 thought to be Handel: See Marx, "On the Authenticity."
33 "He always had": Quoted in Burney, *Account*, *4.
34 There were close encounters: Mainwaring, *Memoirs*, 50–51; Glover, *Handel in London*, 8; Keates, *Handel*, 15–16.
34 "fire and force": Mainwaring, *Memoirs*, 56.
34 In a social world: See Harris, *Handel as Orpheus*. Speculation about Handel's sexuality ebbs and flows among musicologists and historians, but an answer depends on what one wants to know in asking the question. The category "gay," in its twentieth-first-century sense, did not exist in the eighteenth century, but romantic, erotic, sexual, and intense platonic relationships between same-sex individuals obviously did, even though the legal penalty in Britain and other countries for "sodomy" was, in theory, death. For overviews, see Gary C. Thomas, "'Was George Frideric Handel Gay?': On Closet Questions and Cultural Politics," in Brett, Wood, and Thomas, *Queering the Pitch*, 155–203; Ellen T. Harris, "Homosexual Context and Identity: Reflections on the Reception of *Handel as Orpheus*," in Mounsey and Gonda, *Queer People*, 41–66; Hunter, *Lives*, 307–15.
34 "A graceful youth": Quoted and translated in Harris, *Handel as Orpheus*, 45. See also *HCD*, 1:77.
34 "an old Fool!": Quoted in Dean, "Charles Jennens's Marginalia," 164.
34 "pestered with Swarms": Blainville, *Travels*, 2:394.

Notes

34 One evening the Neapolitan composer: Mainwaring, *Memoirs*, 51; Burrows, *Handel*, 44; Hunter, *Lives*, 154.
34 He was in Rome again: Burrows, *Handel*, 31–52; Hunter, *Lives*, 153–59.
35 *Agrippina* ran: Mainwaring, *Memoirs*, 52.
35 "thunderstruck": Ibid., 52–53.
35 Venetian society was now: Ibid., 53.
35 At the Leineschloss: Keates, *Handel*, 50.
35 It was an opportunity: Mainwaring, *Memoirs*, 73.
36 "Henling": Sophia, Dowager Electress of Hanover, to Princess Sophia Dorothea of Prussia, June 15, 1710, in *HCD*, 1:183.

2 · "AN UNDERTAKING SO HAZARDOUS"

37 After a visit to his mother: Glover, *Handel in London*, 12; Burrows, *Handel*, 80.
37 "Devil-land": See Jackson, *Devil-Land*.
38 "I shall not give you": Erndl, *Relation of a Journey*, 26–27.
38 "a Prodigy of Buildings": Defoe, *Tour thro' the Whole of Great Britain*, 2:85.
38 "Sweepings from butchers' stalls": Swift, "Description of a City Shower."
39 Ever since seeing him: Mainwaring, *Memoirs*, 61.
39 "performed wonders": Mary Delany autobiography, in *HCD*, 1:195.
39 "Let him come!": Mainwaring, *Memoirs*, 83.
39 "to pull down": Baker, *Biographia Dramatica*, 1:xx.
40 "Nor do I dote": Pepys, *Diary*, Feb. 1667.
40 "An imagination as lively": Cibber, *Lives of the Poets*, 5:255.
40 "vast triumphal Piece": Quoted in *Survey of London*, vols. 29 and 30, pt. 1.
41 "spare no Pains": *Rinaldo, an Opera*, n.p.
41 Handel raced: Burney, *Account*, 10.
41 "My little Fortune": *Rinaldo, an Opera*, n.p.
41 The copyist who had written: Burrows and Hume, "George I, the Haymarket Opera Company," 323.
41 As the opening approached: *Daily Courant*, Feb. 13, 1711, in *HCD*, 1:198.
42 According to one source: *Spectator*, March 16, 1711, in *HCD*, 1:208.
42 In the decades that followed: Glover, *Handel in London*, 35.
42 A publisher in the Strand: *Post-Man*, Sept. 6, 1711, in *HCD*, 1:226; Donald Burrows, "John Walsh and His Handel Editions," in Myers, Harris, and Mandelbrote, *Music and the Book Trade*, 80–81.
42 "Signor Georgio Frederico Hendel": *Rinaldo, an Opera*, n.p.
43 "the Best of Nations": Ibid.
43 After her, no monarch: Hoppit, *Land of Liberty?*, 41.
43 "a lady in diamonds": Boswell, *Life of Johnson*.
44 "The Sea already swarms": Quoted in Hoppit, *Land of Liberty?*, 112.
44 After a battle: Ibid., 117.
44 As the war wound on: Glover, *Handel in London*, 27.
45 "extreamly well pleas'd": Abel Boyer, *The Political State of Great Britain* (1711), in *HCD*, 1:196.
45 Yet when Anne expressed: Mainwaring, *Memoirs*, 84.

3 · JACOBITES

46 "It may be": Quoted in Somerset, *Queen Anne*, 92.
46 A future Catholic dynasty: Hoppit, *Land of Liberty?*, 31.
46 When the force eventually arrived: Ibid., 15.
47 Terrified and suffering: Ibid., 18.

47 In late November: Somerset, *Queen Anne*, 102.
48 "*stock* and root": Burke, *Reflections on the Revolution in France*, 24.
48 "excluded because of the Popish Religion": *Genealogy of the Most Illustrious House*, 9.
49 "I have made": Handel to Andreas Roner, July 1711, in *HCD*, 1:223.
49 "contracted an affection": Mainwaring, *Memoirs*, 89.
49 "Mr. Handel . . . [has] been": Kreienberg to Electoral Court at Hanover, June 5, 1713, and Kreienberg to Jean de Robethon, July 3, 1713, in *HCD*, 1:276, 278.
49 "Trusty and Wellbeloved": "Treasury Entry Book of Royal Warrants," Dec. 28, 1713, in *HCD*, 1:285.
49 "constantly at his house": Kreienberg to Electoral Court at Hanover, June 5, 1713, in *HCD*, 1:276.
50 "The main thing": Defoe, *Answer to a Question*, 4.
51 "At the entrance": Partridge, *Merlinus Liberatus*, n.p. (Oct. 1701).
51 "I believe sleep": Quoted in Damrosch, *Jonathan Swift*, 264.
52 They landed at Greenwich: Plumb, *First Four Georges*, 39.
52 "There Hendel strikes": Gay, *Trivia*, 32.
52 Handel was soon informed: Burrows, *Handel*, 95, 99; Hunter, *Lives*, 176.
52 The old pension: For a discussion of Handel's income from royal pensions and salaries, see Hunter, *Lives*, 175–90, and Harris, "'Master of the Orchester.'"
53 "Royal Privilege": Burrows, "John Walsh," 81–82; David Hunter, "George Frideric Handel as Victim: Composer-Publisher Relations and the Discourse of Musicology," in Crawford, *Encomium Musicae*, 684–85; Handel's first Royal Privilege, in *HCD*, 1:489.
53 A few years later: Warrant for the appointment of Handel as Composer of Music for the Chapel Royal (Feb. 25, 1723), in *HCD*, 1:627.
53 "Between 4 and 5": Daily routine of the Royal Princesses (June 9, 1723), in *HCD*, 1:648.
53 That role carried: See *Court Register*.
54 "Inform me once again": Handel to Michael Dietrich Michaelson, Feb. 20, 1719, in *HCD*, 1:410.

4 · GRUB STREET

55 Few societies placed: Plumb, *First Four Georges*, 14. See also Sharpe, *Fiery and Furious People*.
55 "vastly delights this nation": Uffenbach, *London in 1710*, 60.
55 As many as 186,000: Landers, *Death and the Metropolis*, 286.
56 Burials typically increased: Ibid.
56 Whenever demobilized soldiers: Ibid., 298.
56 New, more virulent strains: Razzell and Spence, "History of Infant, Child, and Adult Mortality," 286–87.
56 Catholics were subject: Hoppit, *Land of Liberty?*, 216.
56 The last execution: See Graham, *Blasphemies of Thomas Aikenhead*.
56 The last alleged witch: Gaskill, "Witchcraft and Evidence," 62.
57 But at the time: Hoppit, *Land of Liberty?*, 30, 53; Corfield, *Georgians*, 22.
57 Coffeehouses—more than five hundred: Lillywhite, *London Coffee Houses*, 23.
57 Scholars met: Dale, *First Crash*, 8.
57 Among the wider public: See Smith, *Oratorios*, 178–87.
57 "Patriotism, in Days of Yore": James Miller, *Harlequin Horace; or, The Art of Modern Poetry* (1735), 1:509n, quoted in Smith, *Oratorios*, 181.
58 "England is a Country": Henri Misson, *Memoirs and Observations in His Travels over England* (1719), 203, quoted in Hoppit, *Land of Liberty?*, 178.

58 By one count: Hoppit, *Land of Liberty?*, 194.
58 Innovations in printing: Ibid., 169.
58 "We had no such thing": Defoe, *Journal of the Plague Year.*
58 "my *present* Thoughts": Franklin, *Dissertation on Liberty.*
58 "abominable": Franklin, *Autobiography*, chap. 6.
59 "It fell *dead-born*": Hume, *My Own Life.*
59 "It came unnoticed": Ibid.
59 A change in ticket price: McPherson, "Theatrical Riots," 242.
59 "to banish himself": Baker, *Biographia Dramatica*, 1:xxxvi.
59 A who's who: Burrows, *Handel*, 130–31.
60 By that summer: Ibid., 131.
60 Other investors added: Burrows and Hume, "George I, the Haymarket Opera Company," 329.
60 "Master of the Orchester": Minutes of the Royal Academy of Music Directors' Meeting, Nov. 30, 1719, in *HCD*, 1:450.
60 Women nearly fainted: Mainwaring, *Memoirs*, 99.
61 "addicted to the use": Townsend, *Account of the Visit of Handel*, 23.
61 "You may be a real devil": Mainwaring, *Memoirs*, 110–11n.
61 "Hissing on one Side": *British Journal*, June 10, 1727, in *HCD*, 2:128.
61 "But who would have thought": *The Devil to Pay at St. James's* (1727), in *HCD*, 2:138. The author was reputed to be John Arbuthnot.
61 "Strange all this Difference": The epigram was sometimes attributed to Jonathan Swift but was in fact written by the poet John Byrom. *London Journal*, June 5, 1725, in *HCD*, 1:773.
61 The first act he sat through: Stukeley et al., *Family Memoirs*, 1:59.
63 twenty-five guineas: Burrows, "John Walsh," 97–101.
63 The entire procession: Thompson, *George II*, 73.
63 Inside the abbey, choristers located: Ibid., 74.
63 "The Anthems in confusion": Quoted in Burrows, "Handel and the 1727 Coronation," 471.
64 The new king: Plumb, *First Four Georges*, 71–72.
65 "People have now forgot": Gay to Jonathan Swift, Feb. 3, 1723, in *HCD*, 1:623.

5 · YAHOOS

66 "Though justly Greece": Pope, *To Augustus*, lines 43–46.
67 "My Mother dear": Hobbes, *Life*, 2.
67 "continuall feare": Hobbes, *Leviathan*, chap. 13.
67 "shatterd and giddy": Locke to John Locke Sr., ca. Jan. 9, 1660, quoted in Brewer, "Slavery, Sovereignty, and 'Inheritable Blood,'" 1044.
67 "a condition, which": Locke, *Second Treatise*, chap. 9, sec. 123.
67 "an Appetite": Hobbes, *Leviathan*, 1.6.
67 "an expectation indulged": Johnson, *Dictionary*, s.v. "hope."
68 "affection of the mind": Bailey, *Universal Etymological English Dictionary*, s.v. "hope."
70 "Man is wicked": Bayle, *Dictionary*, 4:94n.
70 "Hope humbly then": Pope, *Essay on Man*, III.
71 A childhood tubercular infection: Mack, *Alexander Pope*, 153–58.
71 "this long disease": Pope, *Epistle to Dr. Arbuthnot*, poetryfoundation.org/.
71 "a mediocrity": Quoted in Robertson, *Enlightenment*, 5.
71 "in any sort terrible": Burke, *Philosophical Enquiry*, 13.
71 Some of the core: Robertson, *Enlightenment*, 93.
72 "to throw persons": Burney, *Account*, 32.

73 "schemes of religion": Swift, preface to *Tale of a Tub*.
73 "die here in a rage": Quoted in Damrosch, *Jonathan Swift*, 279.
74 "the common Scribbles": Swift, *Gulliver's Travels*, 9.
75 "only a heap": Ibid., 122.
75 "opened my Eyes": Ibid., 237.
76 "whether *Flesh* be *Bread*": Ibid., 226–27.
77 "When I thought": Ibid., 255.
77 Victorian publishers: Damrosch, *Jonathan Swift*, 369.
77 "to behold my Figure": Swift, *Gulliver's Travels*, 270.
78 "Grave D[ean] of St. P.": Quoted in Boydell, "Jonathan Swift and the Dublin Music Scene," 133.
78 "I would not give": Quoted in Damrosch, *Jonathan Swift*, 269; Swift, "Directions for Making a Birthday Song," in *Poetical Works of Jonathan Swift*, 2:177.
78 "Supposing now your song": Swift, "Directions for Making a Birthday Song," 177.

6 · THE HYP AND THE PRODIGIOUS

81 He had studied: Admissions record, MTA. I am grateful to Francesca Tate for supplying scans of MTA material.
82 He wrote to a friend: See Stevens, *Two Letters from a Deist*.
82 All that his parents really knew: *Records of Parliament, 1703–1747*, Jan. 26, 1728, MTA.
82 "destroyed himself": William Stratford to Edward Harley, Oct. 23, 1728, in Portland, *Manuscripts*, 7:468.
82 They were later published: Stevens, *Two Letters from a Deist*.
82 "Father, I must": *Infidel Convicted*, 59.
83 "I was much surprised": Saussure, *Foreign View of England*, 196, 198.
83 "the Study of the Mathematicks": Robert Downes to Joseph Spence, Jan. 24, 1728/29, in Spence, *Anecdotes*, 387. See also V. H. H. Green, "Religion in the Colleges, 1715–1800," in Sutherland and Mitchell, *History of the University of Oxford*, 434–38.
83 Robert's correspondent: Matriculation record, Trinity. I thank Clare Hopkins for locating information regarding Stevens's time at Trinity College, Oxford. Records of Oxford University's disciplinary actions are in Case Papers 1728/101:1–3, Chancellor's Court, OUA. I thank Anna Petre for locating these materials. See also Hearne, *Remarks and Collections*, 10:69; William Stratford to Edward Harley, Oct. 23, 1728, in Portland, *Manuscripts*, 7:468.
83 The primary estate: *Dictionary of National Biography*, s.v. "Jennens, Charles."
83 It was first laid out: Nichols, *History and Antiquities*, 4:854.
83 From that point Gopsall: Throsby, *Select Views*, 1:283n.
84 "Jennings": Harrison and Willis, *Great Jennens Case*, 15.
84 "the great iron-master": Nichols, *History and Antiquities*, 4:856.
84 In one year workmen: Ibid.
84 Among them was the storied: Ibid.
84 The proceedings and negotiations: Harrison and Willis, *Great Jennens Case*, 2.
84 He studied law: MacGeagh, *Register of Admissions to the Honourable Society of the Middle Temple*, 1:207.
85 justice of the peace: *Dictionary of National Biography*, s.v. "Jennens, Charles."
85 three daughters and four sons: Smith, *Charles Jennens*, 21.
85 "Member, Non-Performing": Smith, "Achievements of Charles Jennens," 163n22. See also Crum, "Oxford Music Club."
85 For much of his adult life: Smith, "Achievements of Charles Jennens," 166.

85 "ill reception": Jennens to Holdsworth, July 24, 1736, Coke.
85 he could annotate a score: Babington and Chrissochoidis, "Musical References," 78.
85 One of his detractors: Nichols, *Literary Anecdotes*, 3:122.
86 "tender & sensible": Jennens to Holdsworth, June 28, 1746, Coke.
86 "I find my Stomach": Jennens to Holdsworth, Feb. 8, 1746, Coke.
86 "white wine": Jennens to Holdsworth, Nov. 27, 1735, Coke.
86 "your old friend Burgundy": Holdsworth to Jennens, Dec. 7, 1735, Coke.
86 In later life he was said: Nichols, *Literary Anecdotes*, 3:122.
86 "hasty expressions": Kelly eulogy in Nichols, *History and Antiquities*, vol. 1, pt. 2, 861n14.
86 In the letter Robert apologized: Robert Jennens to Charles Jennens, n.d. (ca. 1725), Coke.
87 David Hume took pills: Mullan, "Hypochondria and Hysteria," 147.
87 "an unactive, sedentary": Cheyne, *English Malady*, xx. See also Hare, "History of 'Nervous Disorders.'"
87 "Such a Hyppish Wretch": Jennens to Holdsworth, July 24, 1736, Coke.
87 "She is finely shaped": Holdsworth to Jennens, Oct. 19, 1736, Coke.
87 "a very polite": *New General and Biographical Dictionary*, 6:243.
87 But when Jennens entered: Smith, *Charles Jennens*, 7.
88 That position put him at odds: Smith, "Achievements," 162–63, 172–73. Jennens did have members of his extended family who shared his nonjuring beliefs. I thank Ruth Smith for pointing out this fact to me.
88 "Come, come, Clamour": Cibber, *The Non-juror*, in *Dramatic Works*, 4:311.
89 at Gopsall he assembled: Smith, *Oratorios*, 191.
89 He later painstakingly crossed out: Ibid.
89 London neighborhoods where nonjuring: Smith, "Achievements," 174; Smith, *Charles Jennens*, 6.
89 By contrast Holdsworth: Ferdinand, *Accidental Masterpiece*, 13.
89 "He made more journeys": Spence, *Anecdotes, Observations, and Characters*, 188n.
89 "notoriously attached": Horatio Mann, British diplomat in Florence, quoted in Ferdinand, *Accidental Masterpiece*, 13–14.
89 He might first have met: Babington and Chrissochoidis, "Musical References," 79.
90 "I suppose you have heard": Holdsworth to Jennens, Aug. 24, 1730, Coke.
90 Jennens was said to be: Kelly eulogy in Nichols, *History and Antiquities*, vol. 1, pt. 2, 861n14.
90 "I have but little acquaintance": Holdsworth to Jennens, April 20, 1736, Coke.
90 "But the surest way": Holdsworth to Jennens, Sept. 1, 1737, Coke.
90 "I think myself under": Holdsworth to Jennens, April 20, 1736, Coke.
90 "I know of no Honour": Jennens to Holdsworth, April 27, 1736, Coke.
91 "my lodgings": Jennens to Holdsworth, Dec. 21, 1745, Coke.
91 A piano Holdsworth had sent: Sumner, "Charles Jennens's Piano."
91 "I am sorry that the loose airs": Holdsworth to Jennens, Feb. 13, 1733, Coke.
91 "I had this day": Ibid.
91 In his library and drawing rooms: For a list of Jennens's collection, see Martyn, *English Connoisseur*, 1:117–43.
91 "As you know I am perfectly ignorant": Holdsworth to Jennens, May 4, 1742, Coke.
92 Jennens's music collection: The items were inventoried when they were auctioned in 1918, although other components of the collection had been sold off earlier. See *Catalogue of Valuable Books and Manuscripts* and, for a full discus-

sion, John H. Roberts, "The Aylesford Collection," in Best, *Handel Collections and Their History*, 39–85.

92 Among the treasures preserved: See Talbot, "Some Overlooked MSS"; Talbot, "Vivaldi's 'Manchester' Sonatas"; "Henry Watson Music Library Manuscripts and Rarities," accessed July 13, 2022, www.manchester.gov.uk/.
92 He bound them: Talbot, "Some Overlooked MSS," 942.
92 "the Prodigious": Holdsworth to Jennens, July 11, 1731, Coke.

7 · ORATORIO

93 A few years later: Smith, "Achievements," 165; Burrows, *Handel*, 222–25.
93 "I shall rejoice": Holdsworth to Jennens, Feb. 23, 1734, Coke.
93 "Every thing that has been united": Jennens to Holdsworth, Feb. 19, 1746, Coke.
93 shared with his brother-in-law: Smith, *Charles Jennens*, 6.
94 "delight": Holdsworth to Jennens, Nov. 20, 1734, Coke.
94 "I hope that will raise": Holdsworth to Jennens, April 20, 1736, Coke.
94 probably from an idea: Damrosch, *Jonathan Swift*, 385.
95 The show continued: Jeremy Barlow, "*The Beggar's Opera* in London's Theatres, 1728–1761," in Joncus and Barlow, *"Stage's Glory,"* 170.
95 By the end of the second season: Robert D. Hume, "John Rich as Manager and Entrepreneur," in Joncus and Barlow, *"Stage's Glory,"* 39–40.
95 he had brought along large sheets: Uglow, *Hogarth*, 136–37.
96 For decades to come: Barlow, "*Beggar's Opera*," 170.
96 "gave such a turn": Earl of Shaftesbury's memoirs, in Deutsch, 845.
96 "Ich kan nicht": Handel to Michael Dietrich Michaelsen, Feb. 12, 1731, in *HCD*, 2:417–18.
97 the English text was likely supplied: Burrows, *Handel*, 123.
97 "N.B.": *Daily Journal*, April 19, 1732, in *HCD*, 2:515.
98 made up almost entirely of Italians: Cast of *Esther*, in *HCD*, 2:523–24.
98 George II and Queen Caroline: *Daily Advertiser*, May 3, 1732, in *HCD*, 2:524; Glover, *Handel in London*, 203.
98 "This being a new Thing": Anonymous, *See and Seem Blind*, June 8, 1732, in *HCD*, 2:535; Burrows, *Handel*, 218.
99 Another group of musicians: Glover, *Handel in London*, 201; *Daily Journal*, April 19, 1732, in *HCD*, 2:515.
99 Near the end of the run: *Daily Post*, May 17, 1732, in *HCD*, 2:528; Burrows, *Handel*, 218.
99 In due course the Opera: Burrows, *Handel*, 227.
99 "If I was to see him": Quoted in Plumb, *First Four Georges*, 86.
100 He soon found another venue: Burrows, *Handel*, 232.
100 "Let it suffice": *Craftsman*, April 7, 1733, in *HCD*, 2:609–10.
100 "a *deep Melancholy*": Ibid., in *HCD*, 2:611.
100 The claim was probably: See Smith, *Handel's Oratorios*, 202–10.
100 "pleased our Ears": *Old Whig*, March 20, 1735, in *HCD*, 3:63.
100 "I am sorry to hear": Holdsworth to Jennens, March 23, 1735, Coke.
100 "I left the *Italian* Opera": Anonymous, *See and Seem Blind*, June 8, 1732, in *HCD*, 2:534.

8 · "DYING BY INCHES"

102 Thomas's father and brother had died: Nash, *Provoked Wife*, 6–9.
102 Tom would sometimes borrow: Ibid., 19.

- 103 But Tom would later tell: Ibid., 21.
- 103 There, confidently bowing: Ibid., 23.
- 103 "a thread": Burney, *History of Music*, 2:899; Burrows, *Handel*, 349n28.
- 104 "In grief and tenderness": Davies, *Memoirs of the Life of David Garrick*, 2:111–12.
- 104 "forc'd into the House": Viscountess Irvine to Earl of Carlisle, March 31, 1733, in *HCD*, 2:608.
- 104 close to three thousand performances: Koon, *Colley Cibber*, 191–92.
- 104 "an excellent player": Voltaire, "Letter XIX: On Comedy," in *Letters on England*.
- 105 "a good play": Cibber, *Apology*, 235–36.
- 105 "Antichrist of wit": Pope, *Dunciad*, bk. 4.
- 106 Theophilus had been born: Chetwood, *General History of the Stage*, 118.
- 106 "I pity you": Quoted in Koon, *Colley Cibber*, 145.
- 106 She had an attorney draw up: Nash, *Provoked Wife*, 74.
- 106 She lost a baby girl: Ibid., 77.
- 107 The male lead: Ibid., 93; *Account of the Life of That Celebrated Actress*, 5.
- 107 "I thought her voice": *Tryals of Two Causes*, 7.
- 107 an annual salary of two hundred pounds: Ibid., 8; *Account of the Life of That Celebrated Actress*, 6.
- 107 "the apple of Contention": Hugh Owen to Edward Owen, Dec. 9, 1736, in *HCD*, 3:216.
- 108 He pushed through her door: Nash, *Provoked Wife*, 107.
- 108 He also informed her: Ibid., 109–10.
- 108 Theophilus referred to Sloper: *Tryals of Two Causes*, 24.
- 109 She usually took along her own pillow: Ibid., 22–23.
- 109 In the summer of 1738: *Account of the Life of That Celebrated Actress*, 7.
- 109 His wife and his creditor: Nash, *Provoked Wife*, 112.
- 109 He wrote to his "sweet Numps": Theophilus Cibber to Susannah Cibber, May 21, no year [1738], fol. 1, in John Benjamin Heath scrapbook (1865), HTC. I am grateful to Micah Hoggatt for providing a scan of this document. See also Nash, *Provoked Wife*, 119–22.
- 110 On lazy afternoons: *Tryals of Two Causes*, 5.
- 110 a figure that equaled: Townsend, *Account of the Visit of Handel*, 19.
- 110 "Bless us!": Defoe, "Academy for Women" section, in *Essay upon Projects*.
- 111 Widows and unmarried heiresses owned: Langford, *Polite and Commercial People*, 110.
- 111 *flagellis et fustibus:* Blackstone, *Commentaries*, bk. 1, chap. 15, section III.g.
- 112 A woman sentenced to death: Colley, *Britons*, 238.
- 112 by mid-century perhaps 75 percent: Landers, *Death and the Metropolis*, 47–48.
- 112 Men pushed into trades: Langford, *Polite and Commercial People*, 111.
- 112 "If such are the triumphs": Nihell, *Answer to the Author*, 20.
- 113 "Consult the women's opinions": Rousseau, *Emile*, bk. 1.
- 113 "What nonsense!": Wollstonecraft, introduction to *Vindication of the Rights of Woman*.
- 113 "The laws respecting woman": Ibid.
- 113 "civil existence": Ibid., chap. 9.
- 114 "equal to the best Fowler": Charke, *Narrative*, 29.
- 114 "strange frolicks": *Biographia Britannica*, 3:590n.
- 114 "Gad demme!": Charke, *Narrative*, 22.
- 114 Charles made a serial living: *Biographia Britannica*, 3:590n. See also Shevelow, *Charlotte*.
- 114 "a Nonpareil of the Age": Charke, *Narrative*, iv.

114 Wellborn women could chart: See Vickery, *Gentleman's Daughter*.
114 They were generally considered: On the delicate "economics of celebrity," see Nussbaum, *Rival Queens*, chap. 1.
116 "dying by inches": Susannah's letter has not survived, but its contents can be gleaned from Theophilus's reply. Cibber to Cibber, May 21, [1738], HTC, fol. 1. See also Nash, *Provoked Wife*, 118–19.
116 "private Meetings": Cibber, *Four Original Letters*, 28.
116 "poor unfortunate Family": Ibid., 24.
116 "I chuse to smile": Ibid., 29.
116 "asserting the Husband": Ibid., 26.
116 In early September: My account of the Cibber kidnapping is based on *Tryals of Two Causes*, 15–17, and Nash, *Provoked Wife*, 130–35.
117 "an hundred mob": *Tryals of Two Causes*, 17.
117 That evening, when Theophilus stepped: Nash, *Provoked Wife*, 135.

9 · A DESIGN FOR RESCUING

120 "the honestest": Horace [Horatio] Walpole to Robert Walpole, April 18/29, 1735, in Coxe, *Memoirs of the Life*, 3:243.
120 "without any Art": *Private Virtue and Publick Spirit*, 5.
120 "once he made an Impression": Ibid., 6.
121 Coram would still emphasize: Coram to Benjamin Colman, April 30, 1734, in "Letters of Thomas Coram," 20.
121 Coram watched as German villagers: "Copy of the Affidavits Relating to the Spoyling & Plundering the Ship Seaflower on the River Elbe," LMA, A/FH/M/01/005. See also Wagner, *Thomas Coram*, 55–57.
121 At trustee meetings: Fant, "Picturesque Thomas Coram," 91–93.
121 To underwrite the costs: Ibid., 93.
122 "hundred-year contracts": Arthur and Carpenter, *History of Georgia*, 81.
122 One of his earlier causes: Nash, *Provoked Wife*, 7.
122 "Carolina has above 40,000 negroes": Oglethorpe to Duke of Montagu, ca. 1745, in *Manuscripts at Montagu House, Whitehall*, 1:408, Montagu.
123 When the board took up: Fant, "Picturesque Thomas Coram," 94–95.
123 He walked away: Wagner, *Thomas Coram*, 99. Coram did not formally resign but stopped attending trustee meetings, with his participation fully ending by 1741.
123 "that Wretched Colony": Coram to Colman, Sept. 22, 1738, in "Letters of Thomas Coram," 47.
123 "my Darling Project": Coram to Colman, Sept. 13, 1740, in "Letters of Thomas Coram," 55.
123 "Proud Coaches pass": Gay, *Trivia*, 26.
123 "a melancholy object": Swift, *Modest Proposal*.
124 "morbid morality": John Brownlow, *Memoranda; or, Chronicle of the Foundling Hospital*, quoted in Nichols and Wray, *History of the Foundling Hospital*, 14.
124 In the 1720s, a plurality: Trumbach, *Sex and the Gender Revolution*, 1:96, 116.
125 In one count: Ibid., 279.
125 perhaps 45 percent of infants: Levene, *Childcare, Health, and Mortality*, 49.
125 the figure rising steadily: Paul Laxton and Naomi Williams, "Urbanization and Infant Mortality in England: A Long Term Perspective and Review," in Nelson and Rogers, *Urbanisation and the Epidemiologic Transition*, 126.
125 75 percent of children: Razzell and Spence, "History of Infant, Child, and Adult Mortality," 273.

- 125 "infancy" was itself understood: Landers, *Death and the Metropolis*, 94.
- 125 Four of Susannah Cibber's five siblings: Gilman, *Theatre Career of Thomas Arne*, 33, 60.
- 125 75 percent of girls and boys: Levene, *Childcare, Health, and Mortality*, 50.
- 125 By the 1730s more than a third: Landers, *Death and the Metropolis*, 95.
- 126 "Designe of Re[s]cuing": Coram to Colman, Sept. 22, 1738, in "Letters of Thomas Coram," 43.
- 127 "The inconvenience to be apprehended": Bernard, *Account of the Foundling Hospital*, 8–9.
- 127 "age of benevolence": Langford, *Polite and Commercial People*, 481.
- 128 "for preventing the frequent murders": Bernard, *Account of the Foundling Hospital*, 4.
- 128 One by one, Coram insinuated: Wagner, *Thomas Coram*, 122.
- 128 He noted their names and dates: Coram's pocket notebook, LMA, A/FH/A/01/007/001.
- 129 Over more than a decade: Wagner, *Thomas Coram*, 126.
- 130 "I thank God": Coram to Colman, March 2, 1737, in "Letters of Thomas Coram," 34.

10 · THE BOOK OF JOB

- 131 "I am oblig'd": Holdsworth to Jennens, March 2, 1734, Coke.
- 131 at least a thousand pounds: Holdsworth to Jennens, Dec. 27, 1736, Coke.
- 131 twelve times that amount: Jennens to Holdsworth, Nov. 23, 1745, Coke.
- 132 "the kingdoms, lands, etc.": Quoted in Dale, *First Crash*, 40.
- 132 an enormous debt-equity swap: Ibid.
- 132 A royal charter empowered: Phillips and Sharman, *Outsourcing Empire*, 83.
- 133 nearly 150,000 people: Pettigrew, *Freedom's Debt*, 11.
- 133 a third or more: SlaveVoyages.org. See also Brewer, "Slavery, Sovereignty, and 'Inheritable Blood,'" 1073.
- 133 lobby for protecting, and even escalating: See Pettigrew, *Freedom's Debt*, chap. 1.
- 133 some eight thousand of whom: SlaveVoyages.org.
- 133 Isaac Newton owned shares: See Levenson, *Money for Nothing*; Gleick, *Isaac Newton*.
- 133 John Locke owned stock: For discussions, see Glausser, "Three Approaches"; Brewer, "Slavery, Sovereignty, and 'Inheritable Blood'"; Brewer, "Slavery-Entangled Philosophy."
- 133 "And they offer'd me": Defoe, *Robinson Crusoe*, 33.
- 134 Nearly a third: David Hunter, "Music and the Use of the Profits of the Anglo-American Slave Economy (ca. 1610–c. 1810)," in Morcom and Taylor, *Oxford Handbook of Economic Ethnomusicology*, section "London Opera Supported by Slavery's Profits."
- 134 Chandos's principal family holding: "Jamaica St. Andrew 114 (Hope Estate)," Centre for the Study of the Legacies of British Slavery, accessed July 21, 2022, www.ucl.ac.uk/lbs/.
- 134 Handel himself held: Harris, "Handel the Investor," 522; Harris, "'Master of the Orchester,'" 16.
- 134 Until 1732, he received: See Hunter, "Worlds Apart?," where Hunter's discovery of Handel's Royal African Company connection was originally revealed in 2013, and Hunter, *Lives*, 200–206. For an important debate on the interpretation of Handel's accounts, see Harris, "Handel the Investor," Hunter, "Handel,

Notes

an Investor," Harris, "Handel, a Salaried Composer," and Harris, "'Master of the Orchester.'"

134 a substantial cash account: Harris, "Handel the Investor," 539.

134 The evidence suggests: Harris, "Handel, a Salaried Composer," 544–45; Harris, "'Master of the Orchester,'" 8.

137 twelve and a half million people: Current estimate from SlaveVoyages.org.

137 half of all debt: Brewer, "Creating a Common Law," 833.

137 In granting freedom: Anson and Bennett, "Collection of Slavery Compensation," 1. See also Draper, *Price of Emancipation*, and the Centre for the Study of the Legacies of British Slavery database, www.ucl.ac.uk/lbs/.

137 It was a process: On these points, see Brewer, "Slavery, Sovereignty, and 'Inheritable Blood'"; Morgan, *Reckoning with Slavery*; Green, *Fistful of Shells*, chap. 6; and Gates and Curran, *Who's Black and Why?*

137 in early 1731: Grant, *Fortunate Slave*, 61.

137 In his late twenties: Bluett, *Some Memoirs*, 12.

139 "flowing with milk": Quoted in Gomez, *Pragmatism*, 20.

139 Bundu had been conquered: See ibid., chap. 2; Barry, *Senegambia*, chap. 7.

139 iron, guns, textiles, and silver: Gomez, *Pragmatism*, 3, 53.

139 writing paper: Bluett, *Some Memoirs*, 16.

139 nine slave voyages: Data on the Hunts and the voyages of the *Arabella* are from SlaveVoyages.org.

139 shaved and shackled: Bluett, *Some Memoirs*, 17.

139 167 women, men, and children: Population count from SlaveVoyages.org.

139 Pike had not been interested: Bluett, *Some Memoirs*, 16–17. Diallo apparently sold the boys to a local herder for twenty-eight head of cattle. "Copy of a Letter from Joseph Ames to William Bogdani," in Honeybone and Honeybone, *Correspondence of the Spalding Gentlemen's Society*, 82.

140 twenty-man crew: SlaveVoyages.org.

140 "a parcel of choice Country born": *Maryland Gazette*, Jan. 16, 1752.

140 two weeks: Bluett, *Some Memoirs*, 18.

140 At some point after April 11: Grant, *Fortunate Slave*, 71.

140 On April 18: SlaveVoyages.org.

140 The first person: Morgan, *Reckoning with Slavery*, 141.

140 less than one-twelfth: David Eltis, "Africa, Slavery, and the Slave Trade, Mid-seventeenth to Mid-eighteenth Centuries," in Canny and Morgan, *Oxford Handbook of the Atlantic World*, 273.

141 But things were beginning to change: Ibid., 272.

141 their bodies tossed overboard: Rediker, *Slave Ship*, 37–39.

141 After roughly forty days at sea: SlaveVoyages.org.

141 "the Voices hired": *Maryland Gazette*, Feb. 24–March 3, 1730.

141 husband to Finda and Umm: Naylor and Wallace, "Author of His Own Fate," 369.

142 probably named Alexander Toulson: Grant, *Fortunate Slave*, 78. Grant and other sources give the name as "Tolsey." No contemporary records of a Tolsey seem to exist in Maryland, but an Alexander Toulson, or Tolson, and his family are traceable to Kent Island in this period. See Emory, *Queen Anne's County, Maryland*, 136; Will of Alexander Toulson, Jan. 27, 1736, MSA.

142 Diallo—or Simon: Grant, *Fortunate Slave*, 78.

142 as many as six languages: Naylor and Wallace, "Author of His Own Fate," 367.

142 "increase of the said negro woman": Will of Alexander Toulson, Jan. 27, 1736, MSA.

142 He soon fell ill: Bluett, *Some Memoirs*, 19.

142	The child mocked: Ibid., 20.
143	"shoot, kill and destroy": "An Act to Prevent the Tumultuous Meetings and Other Irregularities of Negroes and Other Slaves" (Sept. 1723), in Dorsey, *General Public Statutory Law*, 1:63.
143	Rewards were offered: Brackett, *Negro in Maryland*, 76.
143	"Run away from Samuel Peel's Quarter": *Maryland Gazette*, May 13–20, 1729.
143	the only words: Bluett, *Some Memoirs*, 21.
143	"By his affable Carriage": Ibid., 22.
144	"I am Ayuba": Quoted in Naylor and Wallace, "Author of His Own Fate."
145	"very willing to part": Bluett, *Some Memoirs*, 23–24.
145	In the spring of 1733: Ibid., 24.
145	Somewhere along the way: "Copy of a Letter from Joseph Ames to William Bogdani," in Honeybone and Honeybone, *Correspondence of the Spalding Gentlemen's Society*, 81.
145	in early May: Grant, *Fortunate Slave*, 102.
146	Thomas Arne Sr.: Nash, *Provoked Wife*, 3–5; Richardson, *Savage and Modern Self*, 25–33.
146	the bey of Tunis to the Duke of Montagu: Grant, *Fortunate Slave*, 103, 106.
146	George II: Bluett, *Some Memoirs*, 31.
147	Many of his patrons: See Harris, "With Eyes on the East."
147	But philosophers and pamphleteers: See Wolff, *Singing Turk*; Malcolm, *Useful Enemies*.
147	Pierre Bayle: Israel, *Enlightenment Contested*, 618.
147	Diallo might even have created: Grant, *Fortunate Slave*, 94; Naylor and Wallace, "Author of His Own Fate," 362.
147	When asked about his homeland: The map is in BL, Add. MS 32556, fol. 239v.
148	He dispatched: Naylor and Wallace, "Author of His Own Fate," 363.
148	He endorsed: Ibid., 361–63.
148	"His Youth was taken up": "Copy of a Letter from Joseph Ames to William Bogdani," in Honeybone and Honeybone, *Correspondence of the Spalding Gentlemen's Society*, 81.
148	He was more likely: Grant, *Fortunate Slave*, 103.
149	Subscriptions "to redeem": Ibid.; Bluett to Sloane, Dec. 3, 1733, BL Sloane 4053, fol. 105.
149	fifty-nine pounds: Royal African Company accounts, Dec. 31, 1733, NA, T70/302, fol. 68.
149	"Simon . . . the Gambia Black": Royal African Company, Court of Assistants Minutes, Dec. 27, 1733, NA T70/93, fol. 284.
149	He wore the new clothing: Grant, *Fortunate Slave*, 106.
149	"Why do some of you": Bluett, *Some Memoirs*, 50–51.
149	"Where slaves once more": Pope, *Essay on Man*, III.

11 · SCORN

151	Handel's principal trumpeter: See Grano, *Handel's Trumpeter*.
151	It was the death: Lillywhite, *London Coffee Houses*, 428.
151	Toward the end of his life: Harris, *George Frideric Handel*, 285.
151	two hundred granted: Townsend, *Account of the Visit of Handel*, 14n.
152	employ a manservant: Luckett, *Handel's "Messiah,"* 17.
152	On at least one occasion: Townsend, *Account of the Visit of Handel*, 25.
152	One of the largest single boosts: Glover, *Handel in London*, 268; Burrows, *Handel*, 262; *Daily Advertiser*, March 28, 1738, in *HCD*, 3:377.

Notes

152 "epicure": George Harris to James Harris, Sept. 14, 1743, quoted in Harris, *George Frideric Handel*, 315.
152 "unwieldy in his motions": Burney, *Account*, 31.
152 "Oh—I have de taught!": Ibid., 32n(a).
152 On most days, however: For discussions of Handel's health, including the possibility of lead poisoning, see Hunter, *Lives*, chap. 6; Harris, *George Frideric Handel*, chap. 10.
152 "Rhumatick Palsie": Earl of Shaftesbury to James Harris, April 26, 1737, in *HCD*, 3:263.
153 "his senses were disordered": Mainwaring, *Memoirs*, 121.
153 lead poisoning: Hunter, *Lives*, 285–96; Harris, *George Frideric Handel*, 315.
153 A cartoon would later: See Chrissochoidis, "Handel, Hogarth, Goupy."
153 "the finest Cruel": Princess Amelia to Princess Anne, Dec. 16, 1737, in *HCD*, 3:326.
153 He was busier than ever: Burrows, *Handel*, 258–61.
153 In the spring of 1738: Ibid., 261.
153 "not a plant": Cibber, *Apology*, 220.
154 Even George II had decided: *London Evening-Post*, Dec. 31, 1737, in *HCD*, 3:334.
154 "He wou'd do very well": Holdsworth to Jennens, March 15, 1737, Coke.
154 "keep off the Hyp": Jennens to Holdsworth, July 24, 1736, Coke.
155 In fact, the first documented: Handel to Jennens, July 28, 1735, in *HCD*, 3:91.
155 He likely helped create a text: John H. Roberts, "Handel, Charles Jennens, and the Advent of Scriptural Oratorio," in Timms and Wood, *Music in the London Theatre*, 228–29.
156 "He opens with the Loves": Knatchbull to James Harris, Dec. 5, 1738, in *HCD*, 3:441–42.
156 "tolerable success": Jennens to James Harris, Dec. 29, 1740, in *HCD*, 3:666.
156 "I could tell you more": Jennens to Lord Guernsey, Sept. 19, 1738, in *HCD*, 3:427.
157 Theophilus Cibber's lawsuit: *Tryals of Two Causes*, 3.
157 "Assaulting, Ravishing": Ibid.
157 "Did Mr. Cibber, the plaintiff": Ibid., 7.
158 "for she grew": Ibid., 8.
158 "'How do you do'": Ibid., 11.
159 "When Mrs. Hopson": Ibid.
159 "I dogged them": Ibid., 13.
160 "After he was gone": Ibid.
160 "I have a closet": Ibid., 11.
160 "to kiss her": Ibid., 11–12.
161 "There is no occasion": Ibid., 12.
161 "the plaintiff had certainly": Ibid., 19.
161 "Mr. Cibber was then very bare": Ibid., 20.
162 "Good night": Ibid., 22.
162 "I thought it no business": Ibid., 23.
162 "resigns his wife to him": Ibid., 24.
164 "Mrs. Archer": Ibid., 31.
164 He had somehow tracked: Nash, *Provoked Wife*, 159.
164 In December 1739: *Tryals of Two Causes*, 25.
164 "Henceforth, business poured in": John, Lord Campbell, *Lives of the Chief Justices of England, from the Norman Conquest till the Death of Lord Mansfield* (London, 1849), 2:308, quoted in Nash, *Provoked Wife*, 147.

12 · FOUNDLINGS

166 He had even identified: Wagner, *Thomas Coram*, 132.
166 "I was in hopes": Coram to Colman, Sept. 22, 1738, in "Letters of Thomas Coram," 43.
167 "gave me very rough words": Notes written on copy of Privy Council minutes, July 29, 1737, quoted in Wagner, *Thomas Coram*, 129.
167 "to have putt doun": Coram to Colman, Sept. 22, 1738, in "Letters of Thomas Coram," 43.
167 "she would by no means": Quoted in Wagner, *Thomas Coram*, 131.
167 "Even People of Rank": *Private Virtue and Publick Spirit*, 15.
167 Instead, he printed five hundred: Wagner, *Thomas Coram*, 130.
168 "the first Foundling": Quoted in ibid., 132.
168 The leadership was to be drawn: Nichols and Wray, *History of the Foundling Hospital*, 345–53.
168 For this sum: The hospital's largest single donor was a sugar trader and plantation magnate named Thomas Emerson. He was not on the original list of governors but joined a few months later. In his will, he left the hospital twelve thousand pounds, more than two million dollars today. Berry, *Orphans of Empire*, 83; Nichols and Wray, *History of the Foundling Hospital*, 354.
169 "I can now rest satisfied": Quoted in Wagner, *Thomas Coram*, 134.
169 "my declining years": Quoted in ibid.
169 A porter was placed: Wagner, *Thomas Coram*, 146.
169 "as if Stupefied": Foundling Hospital Daily Committee Minutes, March 25–June 22, 1741, quoted in ibid., 147.
170 "A more moving Scene": Ibid.
170 Every time a new intake: Wagner, *Thomas Coram*, 151.
170 "The *Hospital Foundling*": *Scandalizade: A Panegyri-Satiri-Serio-Comi-Dramatic Poem* (1750), quoted in ibid., 169.
170 Later versions of the hospital's code: Wagner, *Thomas Coram*, 146.
170 Stories filtered up: Ibid., 155.
171 His last vote: Nichols and Wray, *History of the Foundling Hospital*, 24.
171 He relinquished: Wagner, *Thomas Coram*, 153.
171 "But thou'rt in thy Projects": *Scandalizade*, quoted in ibid., 169.
171 Of the first 30: Wagner, *Thomas Coram*, 149.
171 Of those more than 100: "List of Number of Children Admitted and Whether Dead or Alive, 25 March 1741 to 2 June 1756," LMA, A/FH/A/09/022/001.
171 The tokens would survive: Styles, *Threads of Feeling*, 9.
171 hospital officials created billets: "Note of Tokens," April 17, 1741, LMA, A/FH/M/01/008/009-017.
172 "Very neat": "Note of Tokens," April 17, 1741, LMA, A/FH/M/01/008/009-017 (JB35).

13 · THE RETURN OF A PRINCE

173 A company ship: Grant, *Fortunate Slave*, 108.
173 The considerable gifts: Ibid., 109.
173 Diallo also secured: Ibid., 110.
174 "he might be able": African House to Richard Hull, July 4, 1734, NA, T70/55, fol. 221.
174 by early August: Grant, *Fortunate Slave*, 111.
174 "and one Black Man": Moore, *Travels*, 202.
174 On August 23: Ibid., 203.

- 174 Through a Fulbe man: Ibid., 207–8.
- 174 some of the gifts: Duke of Montagu and Earl of Pembroke to Diallo, April 26, 1736, Montagu; African House to Richard Hull, Jan. 13, 1737, NA, T70/55, fol. 246.
- 174 Finally, in February 1735: Moore, *Travels*, 223–24.
- 175 "wept grievously": Ibid., 224.
- 175 For the next four days: Grant, *Fortunate Slave*, 116.
- 175 "They are more generally": Moore, *Travels*, 30.
- 175 "All the Muslims": Diallo to Duke of Montagu, April 5, 1735, Montagu.
- 176 "promised to buy him": Bluett to Duke of Montagu, May 31, 1735, Montagu.
- 176 a letter from Diallo: Job ben Solomon to Mr. Smith, Jan. 27, 1736, in Donnan, *Documents*, 4:456.
- 176 By 1738: African House to James Fort, Feb. 2, 1738, NA, T70/56, fol. 11.
- 176 "We often think": Duke of Montagu and Earl of Pembroke to Diallo, April 26, 1736, Montagu.
- 176 "In the morning": Thomas Hull journal, Sept. 20, 1735, Montagu.
- 177 "About Noon came home": Thomas Hull journal, Sept. 13, 1735, Montagu.
- 177 Two lines below: *Account of the Gentlemen's Society at Spalding*, app., xxvi.
- 177 "Wore the Alchoran": Note by Maurice Johnson, Aug. 1750, in Honeybone and Honeybone, *Correspondence of the Spalding Gentlemen's Society*, 83.
- 178 "Handel says": Jennens to Holdsworth, July 10, 1741, Coke.
- 178 To the nonjuring community: Nichols, *History and Antiquities*, 4:856.
- 178 Portions of his estate: Ibid., 857.
- 178 "I have been glutted": Jennens to Holdsworth, July 10, 1741, Coke.
- 179 "the most dangerous increase": Quoted in Norton, *King James Bible*, 82.
- 179 "Noah's ark for English words": Ibid., 190.
- 179 "Standard for Language": Swift, *Proposal for Correcting*, 23.
- 180 Jennens would later: Smith, "Achievements," 176.
- 181 "Mr. Handel has his fits": Jennens to James Harris, Jan. 15, 1740, in *HCD*, 3:565.
- 181 "I am sorry you cannot": Holdsworth to Jennens, June 17, 1741, Coke.
- 181 There was Richard Kidder: Smith, "Achievements," 182. See also Marissen, *Tainted Glory*. Erhardt, *Händels "Messiah,"* app. 2, reconstructs the contents of Charles Jennens's library.
- 181 Sometime between the autumn of 1739: The precise year in which Jennens began work on what would become the *Messiah* is unknown. The earliest documentary reference to a "Collection . . . from Scripture" is from late December 1739 (Jennens to James Harris, Dec. 29, 1739, in *HCD*, 3:550), but he did not explicitly name his collection until the summer of 1741 (Jennens to Holdsworth, July 10, 1741, Coke). See also Burrows, *Handel: "Messiah,"* 11, who finds it "plausible," but not certain, that the dating falls toward the end of this time window, in May and June 1741.
- 182 He spread the volumes: Nichols, *Literary Anecdotes*, 3:121, notes Jennens using this technique in later life.
- 182 He copied down: See Marissen, *Tainted Glory*, pt. 3, for an extensive annotation of the connections between Jennens's libretto and contemporary sources, a theme explored most fully in Erhardt, *Händels "Messiah."*
- 182 Their audiences were other theologians: Something of a scandal shook Handel studies in 2007, when the musicologist Michael Marissen, writing in *The New York Times*, argued that the *Messiah* was at base a work oriented against Jews and Judaism. In a later book, Marissen found evidence of an "anti-Judaic" foundation in the *Messiah* text and its "unsettling" composition history, especially Jennens's "rejoicing against Judaism," in Marissen's words, for failing to recognize Jesus as the Messiah.

Part of the evidence for this claim comes from letters written by Holdsworth and Jennens. In an exchange in February 1743, both men referred disparagingly to Handel as "a jew," lowercase in Holdsworth's usage, uppercase in Jennens's reply. From the context, it is clear that Holdsworth meant the word as a slur suggesting cheapness or excessive frugality—that is, that Handel was producing music too quickly and inattentively. In response, Jennens made a joking play on words, saying that if Handel were in fact "a Jew," in a religious sense, his work using biblical texts would have shown more respect for the prophets.

This exchange was without question anti-Semitic. So, too, were most other ways that European Christians thought about, spoke about, wrote about, and behaved toward Jews in the eighteenth century, in the same way that Europeans' views of sub-Saharan Africans were nearly universally racist. It is not surprising to find that people living in a specific historical moment reflect the dominant prejudices of their time.

However, the complex personal and textual origins of the *Messiah* seem hard to square with the idea that the work's principal intention is to be an anti-Semitic or anti-Judaic polemic. Much of the charge depends on what one means by "anti-Judaic." Jennens certainly believed in the universal truth of revealed Christianity. It was foundational to his faith that Christianity was a superior successor to, and the prophetic fulfillment of, Judaism. None of that made Jennens unusual in his time or, for that matter, in ours. The same view is common in most versions of Christianity today except for the most progressive churches and denominations.

See Marissen, "Unsettling History of That Joyous 'Hallelujah'"; Marissen, *Tainted Glory;* and, for thoughtful responses, Heller, "Wendy Heller on Handel's 'Messiah'"; Roberts, "False *Messiah*"; and Smith, "Ruth Smith on Handel's 'Messiah.'"

182 he began to sort: Jennens's original pages have not survived. Some books on the *Messiah* quote passages from a purported "scenic structure" that appear to be attributable to Jennens. However, these in fact belong to a historian from the 1990s, Richard Luckett, whose summary of the *Messiah*'s themes is now mistakenly quoted as Jennens's own. I thank Ruth Smith for calling my attention to this common misattribution. See Luckett, *Handel's "Messiah,"* 78–80.
182 "more to my own tast[e]": Jennens to James Harris, Dec. 29, 1739, in *HCD*, 3:550.
183 "The Subject": Jennens to Holdsworth, July 10, 1741, Coke.

14 · TO THE HIBERNIAN SHORE

187 "I can't help telling you": Jennens to Holdsworth, Dec. 2, 1741, Coke.
187 "faintness, lowness of spirits": Holdsworth to Jennens, March 2, 1734, Coke.
187 "And I am lodg'd": Holdsworth to Jennens, May 1, 1738, Coke.
187 The winter of 1739–40: Post, *Food Shortage*, 23.
188 *bliadhain an áir:* Bardon, *Hallelujah*, 1.
188 "I heard with great pleasure": Jennens to Holdsworth, Dec. 2, 1741, Coke.
188 "It was some mortification": Ibid.
188 A printer: See Burrows and Ronish, *Catalogue*, xxiv–xxxi.
191 "I did think": Townsend, *Account of the Visit of Handel*, 93.
191 At one point: On evidence for and against an "invitation" to Ireland, see Hunter, *Lives*, 360–68.
191 both sides of at least 130 pages: Shaw, *Textual and Historical Companion*, 24.
191 He had completed it: Burrows, *Handel*, 340; Shaw, *Textual and Historical Companion*, 24.

192 "At a Time when Party": *London Daily Post, and General Advertiser*, April 4, 1741, in *HCD*, 3:695–96.
192 a chamber organ: Thomas Harris to James Harris, Dec. 5, 1741, in *HCD*, 3:745.
193 In early November: Townsend, *Account of the Visit of Handel*, 31.
193 probably bringing Smith: Burrows, *Handel*, 346.
193 four days by coach: Probyn, *Jonathan Swift*, 157.
193 the Golden Falcon in Northgate Street: Ibid., 111–14.
193 "You shcauntrel!": Burney, *Account*, 26n(a).
193 "The church and clergy here": Quoted in Damrosch, *Jonathan Swift*, 379.
194 "a straggling confused Heap": Macky, *Journey Through England*, 2:150.
194 "rough, rocky": Quoted in Probyn, *Jonathan Swift*, 157.
194 Handel likely opted: See *HCD*, 3:738n; *Faulkner's Dublin Journal*, Nov. 21, 1741, in *HCD*, 3:739; and Probyn, *Jonathan Swift*, 115–18.
194 Since the packet boats: Probyn, *Jonathan Swift*, 136.
194 the ordeal finally: *Faulkner's Dublin Journal*, Nov. 21, 1741, in *HCD*, 3:739.
194 Around 120,000 people: Fagan, "Population of Dublin," 156.
194 "a fair and well built": Petty, *Geographical Description of the Kingdom of Ireland*, 6.
194 "all noble Buildings": Ibid.
195 "Till He comes": Jennens to James Harris, Dec. 5, 1741, in *HCD*, 3:746.
195 "the joint effects": Burney, *Account*, 25.
195 "drove him": Pope, *Dunciad*, bk. 4.

15 · FISHAMBLE

196 Protestants still held a slim: Fagan, "Population of Dublin," 156.
196 They prided themselves: Barnard, "'Grand Metropolis,'" 187.
196 "papists, converts": K. Conolly to Lady Ann Conolly, Feb. 21, 1747, Irish Architectural Archive, quoted in Barnard, "'Grand Metropolis,'" 188.
196 Medieval records: Townsend, *Account of the Visit of Handel*, 1, 4.
197 Neale was a music publisher: Boydell, "Venues for Music," 30; Townsend, *Account of the Visit of Handel*, 33.
197 He and his associates: Townsend, *Account of the Visit of Handel*, 32n.
197 in mid-December: *Faulkner's Dublin Journal*, Dec. 12, 1741, in *HCD*, 3:751.
197 Featuring some of his older work: Burrows, *Handel*, 348.
197 "so that I needed not": Handel to Jennens, Dec. 29, 1741, in *HCD*, 3:758.
197 "composed (besides the Flower)": Ibid.
198 "You are welcome home": Burney, *Account*, 27n(a).
198 "As for the Instruments": Handel to Jennens, Dec. 29, 1741, in *HCD*, 3:758.
198 His mail was routinely: Damrosch, *Jonathan Swift*, 347.
198 Frequent bouts of vertigo: Ibid., 274.
198 "My giddiness": Quoted in ibid., 461.
198 "rage and rancour": Quoted in ibid., 464.
199 "And Whereas it has been reported": Swift to Sub-dean and Chapter of St. Patrick's Cathedral, Jan. 28, 1742, in *HCD*, 3:775–76.
199 But since the end of the run: Burrows, *Handel*, 348.
199 Before long Handel's attention: Ibid., 349.
200 Susannah Cibber had come: *Faulkner's Dublin Journal*, Dec. 5, 1741, in *HCD*, 3:745.
200 The invitation to appear: Nash, *Provoked Wife*, 167.
201 Yet just at the point: Bardon, *Hallelujah*, 163–64.
202 "For the relief": *Faulkner's Dublin Journal*, March 27, 1742, in *HCD*, 3:801.

- 202 In addition to Cibber: Burrows, *Handel*, 348–51; Bardon, *Hallelujah*, 168.
- 202 For the choir: Burrows, *Handel*, 347.
- 202 Matthew Dubourg would serve: See Hunter, *Lives*, 99–112.
- 203 "not to come with Hoops": *Faulkner's Dublin Journal*, April 13, 1742, in *HCD*, 3:808.
- 203 "Lords, Justices": *Faulkner's Dublin Journal*, April 20, 1742, in *HCD*, 3:813.
- 203 more than seven hundred people: *Faulkner's Dublin Journal*, April 17, 1742, in *HCD*, 3:812.
- 204 "MAJORA CANAMUS": Wordbook for first performance of *Messiah*, April 13, 1742, in *HCD*, 3:809.
- 206 Near the top of the second part: Reconstructing who sang what in the first performance is tricky, since the only direct evidence is a few penciled notes by an audience member on a surviving wordbook. Handel's own notes on the first conducting score were added for a later performance. But Cibber's interpretation of "He was despised" was so widely reported that it seems to be one of the things we know with certainty about the Dublin performance. For detailed studies, see Shaw, "Handel's *Messiah*"; Shaw, *Textual and Historical Companion*, chap. 2; and Burrows, "Autographs and Early Copies."
- 207 A later account would place: Nash, *Provoked Wife*, 175, 342n16.
- 207 He had ordered: Bardon, *Hallelujah*, 174.
- 208 "Woman, for this": Schoelcher, *Life of Handel*, 249. Schoelcher is apparently the only source for this story, which he said came from an "old album" in the British Museum containing cuttings from newspapers of the day, this one "taken out of a journal, of which the collector gives neither the name nor the date." However, a version of the same story was circulating already in the 1780s. See Davies, *Memoirs of the Life of David Garrick*, 2:113, who attributes the outburst to "a certain bishop." Burrows finds the attribution to Delany "not implausible" given that Delany was in fact in Dublin in that period. Burrows, *Handel: "Messiah,"* 21.
- 208 "If God be for us": Shaw, "Handel's *Messiah*," 210.

16 · "HOPE IS A CURTAIL DOG"

- 209 "The whole is beyond any thing": Edward Synge, Bishop of Elphin report, enclosed with Handel to Jennens, Sept. 9, 1742, Coke.
- 209 "elevated, majestick": *Faulkner's Dublin Journal*, April 17, 1742, in *HCD*, 3:812.
- 209 In the end 1,223 pounds: *Faulkner's Dublin Journal*, Jan. 14, 1744, in *HCD*, 4:147.
- 210 "Paraletic stroke": Memoir by Redmond Simpson, n.d. [1742], in *HCD*, 3:843.
- 210 "O! A German": Laetitia Pilkington, *The Third and Last Volume of the Memoirs of Mrs. Laetitia Pilkington, Written by Herself* (1754), in *HCD*, 3:842.
- 210 "behold the Ruins": Ibid.
- 210 He refused to eat: Damrosch, *Jonathan Swift*, 466.
- 210 On August 13: *Dublin News-Letter*, Aug. 15, 1742, in *HCD*, 3:845.
- 210 "It was indeed": Handel to Jennens, Sept. 9, 1742, Coke.
- 211 "O wondrous girl!": *Gentleman's Magazine*, March 1742, in *HCD*, 3:803.
- 211 She began the journey: *Faulkner's Dublin Journal*, Aug. 24, 1742, in *HCD*, 3:845.
- 211 On the packet boat: Nash, *Provoked Wife*, 181.
- 211 What was more, she had news: Ibid., 177.
- 211 They brought suit: Susannah Cibber and Anne Arne complaint, NA C11/1572/15.
- 211 The money was long spent: Nash, *Provoked Wife*, 177.
- 212 "She eloped from this Defendant": Theophilus Cibber answer to complaint, NA C11/1572/15.
- 212 That autumn Mrs. Cibber appeared: Nash, *Provoked Wife*, 183–84.

Notes

- 212 "a burst of applause": *Account of the Life of That Celebrated Actress*, 11.
- 212 Although still only his mistress: Nash, *Provoked Wife*, 185.
- 212 He cast Cibber: Ibid., 186; Cast list for *Samson*, Feb. 18, 1743, in *HCD*, 4:44.
- 213 "For my part": Walpole to Horace Mann, March 3, 1743, in Walpole, *Letters*, 1:231.
- 213 "is more esteemed": *Faulkner's Dublin Journal*, March 15, 1743, in *HCD*, 4:60.
- 213 "His Messiah by all accounts": Jennens to Holdsworth, Oct. 29, 1742, Coke.
- 213 "His Messiah has disappointed": Jennens to Holdsworth, Jan. 17, 1743, Coke.
- 213 "being set in great haste": Ibid.
- 213 "full of Bulls": Jennens to Holdsworth, Feb. 21, 1743, Coke.
- 214 "& I dare say": Jennens to Holdsworth, Jan. 17, 1743, Coke.
- 214 "I am a profess'd Lover": *Universal Spectator, and Weekly Journal*, March 19, 1743, in *HCD*, 4:65.
- 214 "clamour about Town": Jennens to Holdsworth, Feb. 21, 1743, Coke.
- 214 Given the uproar: Burrows, *Handel: "Messiah,"* 28–29. See also James Beattie to William Laing, May 25, 1780, in *HCD*, 4:68.
- 215 At some point, he had marked up: Burrows, "Autographs and Early Copies," 207; Burrows, *Handel: "Messiah,"* 35.
- 215 "He & his Toad-eater": Jennens to Holdsworth, March 24, 1743, Coke.
- 215 "a Farce": Ibid.
- 215 Handel managed only two: Burrows, *Handel*, 357.
- 215 "But partly from the Scruples": Earl of Shaftesbury's memoirs, in Deutsch, 848.
- 215 "a girl without": Walpole to Horace Mann, Feb. 24, 1743, in Walpole, *Letters*, 1:230.
- 215 By April: Jennens to Holdsworth, April 29, 1743, Coke.
- 216 "I don't yet despair": Jennens to Holdsworth, Sept. 15, 1743, Coke.
- 216 "This is really ungenerous": Holdsworth to Jennens, Oct. 28, 1743, Coke.
- 216 "Handel has promis'd": Jennens to Holdsworth, May 7, 1744, Coke.
- 216 Handel would eventually oversee: Burrows, "Handel's Performances of 'Messiah,'" 334.
- 217 "joining good Sense": *Daily Advertiser*, Jan. 17, 1745, in *HCD*, 4:264.
- 217 "a new & hazardous": Jennens to Holdsworth, Feb. 21, 1745, Coke.
- 217 By May 1745: Burrows, *Handel*, 377–78.
- 217 "Your letter": Holdsworth to Jennens, May 4, 1742, Coke.
- 217 "off Politicks": Jennens to Holdsworth, Dec. 3, 1745, Coke.
- 217 "mind their own business": Holdsworth to Jennens, Dec. 26, 1745, Coke.
- 218 "They are, I am afraid": Quoted in Seward, *King over the Water*, 248.
- 218 more than six hundred horses: Thompson, *George II*, 148.
- 219 "I have brought": Holdsworth to Jennens, June 24, 1742, Coke.
- 219 It was in fact: A copy of what is likely the sketch Holdsworth mentioned—previously thought, mistakenly, to be of Holdsworth himself—is in the archive of Magdalen College, Oxford, MS 766.
- 219 "so fine a youth": Holdsworth to Jennens, Aug. 24, 1730, Coke.
- 220 He departed: Seward, *King over the Water*, 268.
- 220 "I am come home": Quoted in ibid., 270.
- 221 "He never dinn'd": Elcho, *Short Account of the Affairs of Scotland*, 329.
- 222 "If some Politicians": Jennens to Holdsworth, Nov. 23, 1745, Coke. See also Jennens to Holdsworth, Dec. 3, 1745, Coke.
- 222 "Credit will revive": Jennens to Holdsworth, Dec. 21, 1745, Coke.
- 222 "Then, hey my dear Friends": *Music in Good Time: A New Ballad* (1745), in *HCD*, 4:349.
- 223 The government soon began: Jennens to Holdsworth, Jan. 10 and 20, 1746, Coke.

223 "I am glad to hear": Jennens to Holdsworth, Jan. 20, 1746, Coke.
223 Some theaters: Burrows, *Handel*, 387.
223 "You see by some parts": Jennens to Holdsworth, Jan. 20, 1746, Coke.
223 "piercing notes": Quoted in Nash, *Provoked Wife*, 200.
223 Other members of the cast: Nash, *Provoked Wife*, 200.
223 "I desire you": Cibber to Garrick, Nov. 9, 1745, in *Private Correspondence of David Garrick,* 1:38–39.
224 "The universal Applause": *Daily Advertiser*, Sept. 30, 1745, in *HCD*, 4:349.
224 Cibber contributed her pay: *Account of the Life of That Celebrated Actress*, 12–13.
224 "The Rebellion is so far": Cibber to Garrick, Oct. 24, 1745, in *Private Correspondence of David Garrick*, 1:36–37.
224 "He thought himself": Elcho, *Short Account of the Affairs of Scotland*, 332.
225 "a hated Usurper": Ibid.
225 "Damn me, Vaughan": Ibid., 343.
225 "Of a sudden": Quoted in Riding, *Jacobites*, 309.
225 "out of humour": Elcho, *Short Account of the Affairs of Scotland*, 342n1.
225 As many as fourteen thousand: Riding, *Jacobites*, 422.
225 "So that I never Saw": Quoted in ibid., 426.
226 "the rising Generation": "An Act for the More Effectual Disarming the Highlands in *Scotland*," in *Statues at Large*, 6:709.
226 "As Antient Pistol says": Jennens to Holdsworth, Jan. 10, 1746, Coke.
226 "Here I am": Jennens to Holdsworth, June 21, 1746, Coke.
227 Holdsworth had slipped away: Wriothesly Digby to Lord Guernsey, Dec. 30, 1746, Coke.
227 "as his blood appear'd": Ibid.
227 "more sensibly affected": Wriothesly Digby to Jennens, Jan. 29, 1747, Coke.

17 · ANTHEMS AND CHORUSES

229 People planning to attend: Thompson, *George II*, 188.
229 an audience of thousands: See Hunter, "Rode the 12,000?," for estimates of crowd size at an earlier rehearsal and skepticism about contemporary accounts of massive attendance.
229 the nine-hour spectacle: Hogwood, *Handel: "Water Music,"* 96.
229 "fidles . . . and violeens": Duke of Montagu to Charles Frederick, March 28, 1749, in *HCD*, 4:659.
229 The royal family looked on: Greenacombe, "Where Precisely," 2.
229 "Irregular & in Confusion": Quoted in Hunter, "Rode the 12,000?," 23.
229 Falling fireworks: Hogwood, *Handel: "Water Music,"* 95.
229 nearly a full minute: Thompson, *George II*, 189.
230 an annual routine: Burrows, *Handel*, 401.
230 "The old Buck": Earl of Shaftesbury to James Harris, Jan. 3, 1749, in *HCD*, 4:621.
230 In rehearsals he was known: Townsend, *Account of the Visit of Handel*, 122.
230 Audiences could tell: Burney, *Account*, 36.
230 He had conducted it: See Shaw, *Textual and Historical Companion*, chap. 5; Burrows, "Handel's Performances of 'Messiah.'"
230 "made me but a Scurvy return": Jennens to Holdsworth, Sept. 26, 1744, Coke.
231 on fifty-six acres: Nichols and Wray, *History of the Foundling Hospital*, 42–43.
231 Coram had been present: Ibid., 24.
231 The governors even allowed: Wagner, *Thomas Coram*, 167.
231 By the autumn of 1745: Nichols and Wray, *History of the Foundling Hospital*, 44.
232 Women drew colored balls: Ibid., 45.

Notes

232 "drooping and dying": Quoted in ibid., 46.
232 Funding receipts: Wagner, *Thomas Coram*, 165.
232 In the late spring: Ibid., 182.
232 "Sashed and made commodious": Quoted in Burrows, "Handel and the Foundling Hospital," 270.
232 In fact, the Foundling Hospital concert: Burrows, *Handel: "Messiah,"* 37. People were reported standing for some of the choruses by the following year. See Diary of George Harris, May 15, 1750, in *HCD*, 4:854.
233 In the spring of 1750: Circular announcing first Foundling Hospital performance of *Messiah*, May 1, 1750, in *HCD*, 4:843.
233 Paid choristers and boys: See Burrows, "Lists of Musicians."
233 Thousands pushed: Nichols and Wray, *History of the Foundling Hospital*, 202–3.
234 "Two or Three Bishops": George Harris to James Harris, May 1, 1750, in *HCD*, 4:844.
234 He had earlier been left off: Wagner, *Thomas Coram*, 173.
234 Some of his remaining friends: Ibid., 185; *Private Virtue and Publick Spirit*, 23.
234 Coram told a friend: Wagner, *Thomas Coram*, 185.
234 he was buried: Ibid., 188–91; McClure, *Coram's Children*, 57–58.
234 Handel's organ: *HCD*, 4:844n.
234 more than 800 children: Nichols and Wray, *History of the Foundling Hospital*, 46.
234 Within a decade: Ibid., 55.
234 At mid-century the infant mortality rate: Ibid., 62.
235 Nurses and other employees: Ibid., 128.
235 The mortality rate gradually came down: McClure, *Coram's Children*, 261.
235 Many would move: See Berry, *Orphans of Empire*, chap. 5; Nichols and Wray, *History of the Foundling Hospital*, chap. 27.
235 "Annual Musical Festival of Messiah": Burrows, "Handel and the Foundling Hospital," 281.
235 seven thousand pounds: Wagner, *Thomas Coram*, 183; Nichols and Wray, *History of the Foundling Hospital*, 204; Miscellaneous notes on Foundling Hospital chapel, LMA, A/FH/A/14/020/001.
235 "It was afterwards": Mainwaring, *Memoirs*, 135.
235 Cibber apparently never participated: *HCD*, 4:330n; Shaw, *Textual and Historical Companion*, chap. 2.
235 The pious tourism: McClure, *Coram's Children*, 71–72.
236 "My Lord": James Beattie to William Laing, citing a conversation with the Earl of Kinnoull, March 23, 1743, in *HCD*, 4:68.
236 Handel performed the *Messiah:* Donald Burrows, "Commentary," in Händel, *Messiah*, 1.
236 "It is needless": Mainwaring, *Memoirs*, 136–37.
236 "the Oratorio": Franklin to Mary Stevenson, May 4, 1759, Founders Online, founders.archives.gov/.
237 "So relaxt": Notation on the score of *Jephtha*, in Deutsch, 701.
237 He started attending prayers: Burney, *Account*, 33.
237 He might give out: Ibid., 30.
237 His fingers had grown puffy: Ibid., 35.
237 "To see him": Ibid., 29–30.

18 · EXALTED

239 He had been able: Burrows, *Handel*, 488.
239 An attempted surgery: Ibid.

239 He had bequeathed: Ibid., 489; James Smyth to Bernard Granville, April 17, 1769, in Deutsch, 818; Memorandum on Handel's will, April 26–30, 1759, in Deutsch, 821; Harris, *George Frideric Handel,* chap. 11.

239 "in a private manner": Quoted in Ellen T. Harris, "Handel and His Will," in Burrows, *Handel's Will,* 18.

239 at least three thousand: *London Evening-Post,* April 24, 1759, in Deutsch, 821; Burney, *Account,* 38.

240 A rumor soon began: Burney, *Account,* 31.

240 "I went to the cathedral": Quoted in Hunter, *Lives,* 55.

240 "And from that time": Burney, *Account,* 27.

240 At the "Hallelujah" chorus: Ibid., 84.

240 At one point or another: Ibid., 85.

240 Much of the income: Ibid., 136.

241 Upon his death, it passed: Burrows, "Royal Music Library and Its Handel Collection," 5.

241 In 1957: Shaw, *Textual and Historical Companion,* 27. See also Burrows, "Royal Music Library and Its Handel Collection."

242 "Explain your self": See Dean, "Charles Jennens's Marginalia." Jennens's copy of Mainwaring's book is in the collection of the Handel Hendrix Museum, London.

242 Wordbooks to the *Messiah:* On Jennens's involvement—or lack of involvement—in the preparation of wordbooks, see Burrows and Shaw, "Handel's 'Messiah': Supplementary Notes."

242 He paid Roubiliac: For a full discussion of the symbolism of the Holdsworth monument, see Smith, "Achievements," 176–81.

243 "He tutored the sophomoric youth": I am grateful to Lorenzo Pagdanganan, a Georgetown undergraduate, for this elegant translation.

243 "There are many circumstances": Jennens to Holdsworth, April 16, 1741, Coke.

244 Each time the hospital moved: See file "Captain Coram's Remains: Papers Relating to Their Removal," LMA, A/FH/A/14/029.

244 "lived above the Fear": *Private Virtue and Publick Spirit,* 28.

245 "This air": Burney, *Account,* 26–27.

245 "No person of sensibility": Sheridan, *British Education,* 417.

246 She earned: Nash, *Provoked Wife,* 265; Chrissochoidis, "Mrs. Cibber's Oratorio Salary," 1.

246 "He knows no more": Burney, *Account,* 33–35.

246 Still, given Cibber's: Nash, *Provoked Wife,* 267–74.

246 Sloper apparently never sought: Shevelow, *Charlotte,* 378; Nash, *Provoked Wife,* 322–23.

246 Catherine would eventually destroy: Nash, *Provoked Wife,* 323.

246 "stomach worms": *Account of the Life of That Celebrated Actress,* 17.

246 Sea bathing in frigid waters: Nash, *Provoked Wife,* 319.

247 The theaters in Drury Lane: Ibid., 318.

247 "By Death's cold Hand": Keate, *Poem to the Memory,* 5.

247 In her will: Susannah Cibber will, NA PROB 11/915/430.

247 Molly would pass her adult life: Nash, *Provoked Wife,* 319.

247 he cast himself: David Mann, introduction to *Plays of Theophilus and Susannah Cibber,* ed. Mann, xliii.

247 He turned in a more serious: *Biographia Britannica,* 3:589n; Baker, *Biographia Dramatica,* vol. 1, pt. 1, 88.

247 He came to believe: Nash, *Provoked Wife,* 220, 236.

248 "Possessed of talents": Baker, *Biographia Dramatica,* vol. 1, pt. 1, 88.

248 That October he boarded: Ibid.

248 "begun, pursued": Ibid.
248 His collection of Handel's music: "Henry Watson Music Library," accessed Nov. 27, 2022, www.manchester.gov.uk/.
248 He would take care: Ruth Smith, "Charles Jennens Revisited," in Vickers, *New Perspectives*, 334.
249 "touching, affecting": Shakespeare, *Othello*, 31nZ.
249 "He imprudently thrust": Johnston and Owens, *New and General Biographical Dictionary*, 7:384.
249 "The chief error": Steevens, quoted in Nichols, *Literary Anecdotes*, 3:121.
249 "what he had once": Ibid., 122.
249 "He is said to have composed": Johnston and Owens, *New and General Biographical Dictionary*, 7:384.
249 On November 20 he called: Kelly eulogy in Nichols, *History and Antiquities*, vol. 1, pt. 2, 861n14.
250 He had helped extend: Grant, *Fortunate Slave*, 160–61.
250 "a Woman-Slave": Moore, *Travels*, 208.
251 "We would have you": Quoted in Grant, *Fortunate Slave*, 198.
253 "a certified detention equipment contractor": Jailcraft Inc., www.jailcraftinc.com/.
253 The Holdsworth temple collapsed: John Matthews, "A Brief History of Gopsall," accessed Jan. 5, 2023, congerstonevillage.co.uk/; Parry, "Temple at Gopsall," 36.

EPILOGUE

257 "physick'd": Jennens commentary in Shakespeare, *Othello*, 45nL.

CHARLES JENNENS'S *MESSIAH* LIBRETTO

259 "among some old books": Culwick, *Handel's "Messiah,"* 5. See also Shaw, "Handel's *Messiah*," 208.
259 Another was owned: Donald MacKinnon to D. MacKinley, July 15, 1903, letter accompanying Library of Congress copy of 1742 *Messiah* wordbook, ML31.H43g.no.3.Case.
259 This version came to light: *Messiah: A Facsimile;* Burrows and Shaw, "Handel's 'Messiah': Supplementary Notes," 366–68.

Bibliography

ARCHIVES, DATABASES, AND PRIVATE PAPERS

Bodleian Library, Oxford
    Chancellor's Court Records, Oxford University Archives
    Messiah conducting score (MS Tenbury 346)
British Library, London
    Joseph Ames Collection
    Messiah autograph composing manuscript (R.M.20.fol.2)
    Hans Sloane Letters
Centre for the Study of the Legacies of British Slavery Database, www.ucl.ac.uk/lbs/
Chrissochoidis, Ilias, ed. Handel Reference Database, web.stanford.edu/~ichriss/HRD/
Delaware State Archives, Dover
    Chancery Court Records
    Land Records
Founders Online, founders.archives.gov/
Foundling Museum, London
    Gerald Coke Handel Collection
Harvard Theatre Collection, Houghton Library, Harvard University
Honourable Society of the Middle Temple, London
    Minutes of Parliament
    Treasurers' Receipt Books
Legacy of Slavery in Maryland, slavery.msa.maryland.gov/
London Metropolitan Archives
    Foundling Hospital Archive
Magdalen College Archives, Oxford
Maryland State Archives, Annapolis
    Chancery Court Records
    Chattel Records
    Land Records
    Will and Probate Records

Montagu Archive, Boughton House, Northamptonshire
    2nd Duke of Montagu Private Correspondence
    Bills of Fare
    Thomas Hull Manuscript
National Archives of the United Kingdom, Kew
    Company of Royal Adventurers of England Trading with Africa Records
    Court of Chancery Records
    Prerogative Court of Canterbury and Related Probate Jurisdictions: Will Registers
Royal Institute of British Architects, London
    David and William Hiorn Designs for Gopsall, Leicestershire
SlaveVoyages 2.0 Databases, SlaveVoyages.org/
Trinity College Archives, Oxford
    Admissions Registers
    Bursary Accounts
    Visitor's Correspondence and Papers

BOOKS, ARTICLES, AND OTHER SOURCES

An Account of the Gentlemen's Society at Spalding. Bibliotheca Topographica Britannica, no. 20. London: J. Nichols, 1784.

An Account of the Life of That Celebrated Actress, Mrs. Susannah Maria Cibber. London: n.p., 1887.

Adams, Abigail. *Letters.* Edited by Edith Gelles. New York: Library of America, 2016.

Ancillon, Charles. *Eunuchism Display'd: Describing All the Different Sorts of Eunuchs; The Esteem They Have Met with in the World, and How They Came to Be Made So.* London: E. Curll, 1718.

Anson, Michael, and Michael D. Bennett. "The Collection of Slavery Compensation, 1835–1843." Bank of England Staff Working Paper No. 1,006 (Nov. 2022). bankofengland.co.uk/.

Arthur, T. S., and W. H. Carpenter. *The History of Georgia from Its Earliest Settlement to the Present Time.* Philadelphia: Lippincott, 1861.

Aspden, Suzanne. *The Rival Sirens: Performance and Identity on Handel's Operatic Stage.* Cambridge, U.K.: Cambridge University Press, 2013.

Babington, Amanda, and Ilias Chrissochoidis. "Musical References in the Jennens-Holdsworth Correspondence (1729–46)." *Royal Musical Association Research Chronicle* 45 (2014): 76–129.

Bailey, Nathan. *An Universal Etymological English Dictionary* (1721). Lexicons of Early Modern English. leme.library.utoronto.ca/.

Baker, David Erskine. *Biographia Dramatica; or, A Companion to the Playhouse.* New ed. 2 vols. London: Rivingtons, 1782.

Bardon, Jonathan. *Hallelujah: The Story of a Musical Genius and the City That Brought His Masterpiece to Life.* Dublin: Gill and Macmillan, 2015.

Barnard, T. C. "'Grand Metropolis' or 'Anus of the World'? The Cultural Life of Eighteenth-Century Dublin." *Proceedings of the British Academy* 107 (2001): 185–210.

Barry, Boubacar. *Senegambia and the Atlantic Slave Trade.* Cambridge, U.K.: Cambridge University Press, 1998.

Bayle, Pierre. *The Dictionary Historical and Critical of Mr. Peter Bayle.* 2nd ed. 5 vols. London: J. J. and P. Knapton et al., 1734–38.

Bayne-Powell, Rosamond. *Travellers in Eighteenth-Century England.* London: John Murray, 1951.

Beecham, Sir Thomas. *A Mingled Chime: An Autobiography*. 1943. Westport, Conn.: Greenwood Press, 1976.
Berlin, Isaiah. *Against the Current: Essays in the History of Ideas*. Princeton, N.J.: Princeton University Press, 2001.
Bernard, Thomas. *An Account of the Foundling Hospital in London*. 2nd ed. London: Thomas Jones and the Foundling Hospital, 1799.
Berry, Helen. *The Castrato and His Wife*. Oxford: Oxford University Press, 2011.
———. *Orphans of Empire: The Fate of London's Foundlings*. Oxford: Oxford University Press, 2019.
———. "Queering the History of Marriage: The Social Recognition of a Castrato Husband in Eighteenth-Century Britain." *History Workshop Journal* 74, no. 1 (2012): 27–50.
Best, Terence, ed. *Handel Collections and Their History*. Oxford: Clarendon Press, 1993.
Bevilacqua, Alexander. *The Republic of Arabic Letters: Islam and the European Enlightenment*. Cambridge, Mass.: Harvard University Press, 2018.
Biographia Britannica; or, The Lives of the Most Eminent Persons Who Have Flourished in Great Britain and Ireland, from the Earliest Ages, to the Present Times. 2nd ed. 5 vols. London: W. and A. Strahan, 1778–93.
Blackstone, William. *Commentaries on the Laws of England* (1765). Project Gutenberg. www.gutenberg.org/.
Blainville, Monsieur de. *Travels Through Holland, Germany, Switzerland, but Especially Italy*. Translated by Dr. Turnbull, Mr. Guthrie, and Mr. Lockman. 3 vols. London: John Noon, 1757.
Bluett, Thomas. *Some Memoirs of the Life of Job, the Son of Solomon, High Priest of Boonda in Africa*. London: printed for Richard Ford, 1734.
Blyth, Alan. "Music from Heaven." *Gramophone* (Dec. 2003): 52–55, 57.
Boswell, James. *Boswell's Life of Johnson* (1791). Project Gutenberg. www.gutenberg.org/.
Boydell, Brian. "Jonathan Swift and the Dublin Musical Scene." *Dublin Historical Record* 47, no. 2 (Autumn 1994): 132–37.
———. "Venues for Music in 18th Century Dublin." *Dublin Historical Record* 29, no. 1 (Dec. 1975): 28–34.
Boyer, Abel. *History of the Reign of Queen Anne, Digested into Annals: Year the Ninth*. London: Thomas Ward, 1711.
Brackett, Jeffrey R. *The Negro in Maryland: A Study of the Institution of Slavery*. Baltimore: Johns Hopkins University, 1889.
Brett, Philip, Elizabeth Wood, and Gary C. Thomas, eds. *Queering the Pitch: The New Gay and Lesbian Musicology*. 2nd ed. London: Routledge, 2006.
Brewer, Holly. "Creating a Common Law of Slavery for England and Its New World Empire." *Law and History Review* 39, no. 4 (Nov. 2021): 765–834.
———. "Slavery-Entangled Philosophy." *Aeon*. Accessed Jan. 4, 2023. aeon.co/.
———. "Slavery, Sovereignty, and 'Inheritable Blood': Reconsidering John Locke and the Origins of American Slavery." *American Historical Review* 122, no. 4 (Oct. 2017): 1038–78.
Brewer, John. *The Sinews of Power: War, Money, and the English State*. New York: Knopf, 1989.
Brockliss, L. W. B. *The University of Oxford: A History*. Oxford: Oxford University Press, 2016.
Burke, Edmund. *A Philosophical Enquiry into the Origin of Our Ideas of the Sublime and Beautiful* (1757). Eighteenth Century Collections Online. quod.lib.umich.edu/e/ecco/.
———. *Reflections on the Revolution in France*. 1790. Oxford: Oxford University Press, 1993.

Burney, Charles. *An Account of the Musical Performances in Westminster-Abbey and the Pantheon in Commemoration of Handel*. London: T. Payne and Son and G. Robinson, 1785.

———. *A General History of Music, from the Earliest Ages to the Present Period*. 2nd ed. 2 vols. 1789. New York: Harcourt, Brace, 1935.

Burrows, Donald. "Autographs and Early Copies of 'Messiah': Some Further Thoughts." *Music and Letters* 66, no. 3 (July 1985): 201–19.

———. *Handel*. 2nd ed. Oxford: Oxford University Press, 2012.

———. "Handel and the Foundling Hospital." *Music and Letters* 58, no. 3 (July 1977): 269–84.

———. "Handel and the 1727 Coronation." *Musical Times* (June 1977): 469–71, 473.

———. *Handel: "Messiah."* Cambridge, U.K.: Cambridge University Press, 1991.

———. "Handel's London Theatre Orchestra." *Early Music* 3, no. 3 (Aug. 1985): 349–57.

———. "Handel's Performances of 'Messiah': The Evidence of the Conducting Score." *Music and Letters* 56, no. 3/4 (July–Oct. 1975): 319–34.

———. "Handel, Walsh, and the Publication of 'Messiah.'" *Music and Letters* 97, no. 2 (2016): 221–48.

———. "Lists of Musicians for Performances of Handel's *Messiah* at the Foundling Hospital, 1754–1777." *Royal Musical Association Research Chronicle* 43 (2010): 85–109.

———. "The Royal Music Library and Its Handel Collection." *Electronic British Library Journal* (2009), Article 2. Accessed Jan. 18, 2023. www.bl.uk/eblj.

———. "What We Know—and What We Don't Know—About Handel's Career in Rome." *Analecta Musicologica* 44 (2010): 97–108.

———, ed. *The Cambridge Companion to Handel*. Cambridge, U.K.: Cambridge University Press, 1997.

———, ed. *Handel and His Will: Facsimiles and Commentary*. London: Gerald Coke Handel Foundation, 2008.

Burrows, Donald, et al., eds. *George Frideric Handel: Collected Documents*. 4 vols. Cambridge, U.K.: Cambridge University Press, 2013–20.

Burrows, Donald, and Robert D. Hume. "George I, the Haymarket Opera Company, and Handel's 'Water Music.'" *Early Music* 19, no. 3 (Aug. 1991): 323–338, 340, 343.

Burrows, Donald, and Martha J. Ronish. *A Catalogue of Handel's Musical Autographs*. Oxford: Clarendon Press, 1994.

Burrows, Donald, and Watkins Shaw. "Handel's 'Messiah': Supplementary Notes on Sources." *Music and Letters* 76, no. 3 (Aug. 1995): 356–68.

Canny, Nicholas, and Philip Morgan, eds. *The Oxford Handbook of the Atlantic World, c. 1450–c. 1850*. Oxford: Oxford University Press, 2011.

Catalogue of Valuable Books and Manuscripts. London: Sotheby, Wilkinson, and Hodge, 1918.

Charke, Charlotte. *A Narrative of the Life of Mrs. Charlotte Charke*. London: W. Reeve, A. Dodd, and E. Cook, 1755.

Chetwood, William Rufus. *A General History of the Stage, from Its Origin in Greece Down to the Present Time*. London: W. Owen, 1749.

Cheyne, George. *The English Malady; or, A Treatise of Nervous Diseases of All Kinds*. London: printed for G. Strahan, 1733.

Chrissochoidis, Ilias. "Handel at a Crossroads: The 1737–1738 and 1738–1739 Seasons Re-examined." *Music and Letters* 90, no. 4 (Nov. 2009): 599–635.

———. "Handel, Hogarth, Goupy: Artistic Intersections in Early Georgian England." *Early Music* 37, no. 4 (Nov. 2009): 577–96.

———. "Mrs. Cibber's Oratorio Salary in 1744–45." *Handel Institute Newsletter* 20, no. 1 (Spring 2009): 1–2.

Cibber, Colley. *An Apology for the Life of Mr. Colley Cibber, Comedian.* 1740. London: Whittaker, Treacher, and Arnot, 1830.
———. *The Dramatic Works of Colley Cibber, Esq.* 4 vols. London: printed for J. Clarke et al., 1760.
Cibber, Theophilus. *Four Original Letters.* London: T. Read, 1739.
———. *The Lives of the Poets of Great Britain and Ireland, to the Time of Dean Swift.* 5 vols. London: R. Griffiths, 1753.
Cohen, Mitchell. *The Politics of Opera: A History from Monteverdi to Mozart.* Princeton, N.J.: Princeton University Press, 2017.
A Collection of Remarkable Trials. London: Tom. Tickle, 1739.
Colley, Linda. *Britons: Forging the Nation, 1707–1837.* London: Pimlico, 2003.
Coopersmith, J. M. "A List of Portraits, Sculptures, etc., of Georg Friedrich Händel." *Music and Letters* 13, no. 2 (1932): 156–67.
Corfield, Penelope J. *The Georgians: The Deeds and Misdeeds of 18th-Century Britain.* New Haven, Conn.: Yale University Press, 2022.
The Court Register. London: printed for R. Amey, 1744.
Coxe, William. *Anecdotes of George Frederick Handel and John Christopher Smith.* 1799. New York: Da Capo Press, 1979.
———. *Memoirs of the Life and Administration of Sir Robert Walpole.* 3 vols. London: T. Cadell, jun., and W. Davies, 1798.
Crawford, David, ed. *Encomium Musicae: Essays in Memory of Robert J. Snow.* Hillsdale, N.Y.: Pendragon Press, 2002.
Crum, Margaret. "An Oxford Music Club, 1690–1719." *Bodleian Library Record* 10 (1973–78): 83–99.
Culwick, James C. *Handel's "Messiah": Discovery of the Original Word-Book Used at the First Performance in Dublin, April 13, 1742; With Some Notes.* Dublin: University Press, printed for private circulation, 1891.
Curtin, Philip E., ed. *Africa Remembered: Narratives by West Africans from the Era of the Slave Trade.* Madison: University of Wisconsin Press, 1967.
Dale, Richard. *The First Crash: Lessons from the South Sea Bubble.* Princeton, N.J.: Princeton University Press, 2004.
Damrosch, Leo. *The Club: Johnson, Boswell, and the Friends Who Shaped an Age.* New Haven, Conn.: Yale University Press, 2019.
———. *Jonathan Swift: His Life and His World.* New Haven, Conn.: Yale University Press, 2013.
Davies, Thomas. *Memoirs of the Life of David Garrick, Esq.* 3rd ed. London: printed for the author, 1781.
Dean, Winton. "Charles Jennens's Marginalia to Mainwaring's Life of Handel." *Music and Letters* 53, no. 2 (April 1972): 160–64.
Dean, Winton, and John Merrill Knapp. *Handel's Operas, 1704–1726.* Woodbridge, Suffolk: Boydell Press, 2009.
Defoe, Daniel. *An Answer to a Question That Nobody Thinks Of, viz., But What If the Queen Should Die?* London: J. Baker, 1713.
———. *An Essay upon Projects* (1697). Project Gutenberg. www.gutenberg.org/.
———. *A Journal of the Plague Year* (1722). Project Gutenberg. www.gutenberg.org/.
———. *Robinson Crusoe.* 1719. London: Penguin, 2001.
———. *A Tour thro' the Whole Island of Great Britain.* 1724–27. 3rd ed. 4 vols. London: J. Osborn et al., 1742.
Dennison, Matthew. *The First Iron Lady: A Life of Caroline of Ansbach.* London: William Collins, 2017.
Deutsch, Otto Erich. *Handel: A Documentary Biography.* New York: W. W. Norton, 1955.

Dickinson, H. T. "The Eighteenth-Century Debate on the 'Glorious Revolution.'" *History* 61, no. 201 (1976): 28–45.
Diouf, Sylviane A. *Servants of Allah: African Muslims Enslaved in the Americas*. New ed. New York: New York University Press, 2013.
Donnan, Elizabeth, ed. *Documents Illustrative of the History of the Slave Trade to America*. 4 vols. New York: Octagon Books, 1965.
Dorsey, Clement. *The General Public Statutory Law and Public Local Law of the State of Maryland, from the Year 1692 to 1839 Inclusive*. 3 vols. Baltimore: printed by John D. Toy, 1840.
Doughty, Oswald. "The English Malady of the Eighteenth Century." *Review of English Studies* 2, no. 7 (1926): 257–69.
Draper, Nicholas. *The Price of Emancipation: Slave-Ownership, Compensation, and British Society at the End of Slavery*. Cambridge, U.K.: Cambridge University Press, 2013.
Dussinger, John A. "Fabrications from Samuel Richardson's Press." *Papers of the Bibliographical Society of America* 100, no. 2 (June 2006): 259–79.
Elcho, David, Lord. *A Short Account of the Affairs of Scotland in the Years 1744, 1745, 1746*. Edited by Evan Charteris. Edinburgh: David Douglas, 1907.
Eltis, David, Frank D. Lewis, and Kenneth L. Sokoloff, eds. *Slavery in the Development of the Americas*. Cambridge, U.K.: Cambridge University Press, 2004.
Emerson, Ralph Waldo. *Complete Works of Ralph Waldo Emerson*. quod.lib.umich.edu/e/emerson/.
———. *Journals of Ralph Waldo Emerson, 1820–1872*. 10 vols. Cambridge, Mass.: Riverside Press, 1909–14.
Emory, Frederic. *Queen Anne's County, Maryland: Its Early History and Development*. Baltimore: Maryland Historical Society, 1950.
Erhardt, Tassilo. *Händels "Messiah": Text, Musik, Theologie*. Bad Reichenhall: Comes, 2007.
Erndl, Christian Heinrich. *The Relation of a Journey into England and Holland, in the Years 1706, and 1707*. London: John Morphew, 1711.
Fagan, Patrick. "The Population of Dublin in the Eighteenth Century with Particular Reference to the Proportions of Protestants and Catholics." *Eighteenth-Century Ireland* 6 (1991): 121–56.
Fant, H. B. "Picturesque Thomas Coram, Projector of Two Georgias and Father of the London Foundling Hospital." *Georgia Historical Quarterly* 32, no. 2 (June 1948): 77–104.
Ferdinand, Christine. *An Accidental Masterpiece: Magdalen College's New Building and the People Who Built It*. Oxford: Magdalen College, 2010.
Flower, Newman. *George Frideric Handel: His Personality and His Times*. Rev. ed. New York: Charles Scribner's Sons, 1948.
Foster, Joseph. *Alumni Oxonienses*. 4 vols. Oxford: Parker, 1888–91.
Foster, R. F. *Modern Ireland, 1600–1972*. London: Allen Lane, 1988.
Franklin, Benjamin. *Autobiography* (1793). Project Gutenberg. www.gutenberg.org/.
———. *A Dissertation on Liberty and Necessity, Pleasure and Pain* (1725). Founders Online. founders.archives.gov/.
Gant, Andrew. *The Making of Handel's "Messiah."* Oxford: Bodleian Library, 2020.
Garrick, David. *Private Correspondence of David Garrick*. 2 vols. London: Henry Colburn and Richard Bentley, 1831–32.
Gaskill, Malcolm. "Witchcraft and Evidence in Early Modern England." *Past and Present* 198 (2008): 33–70.
Gates, Henry Louis, Jr., and Andrew S. Curran, eds. *Who's Black and Why? A Hidden Chapter from the Eighteenth-Century Construction of Race*. Cambridge, Mass.: Belknap Press of Harvard University Press, 2022.

Gay, John. *Trivia; or, The Art of Walking the Streets of London.* 2nd ed. London: Bernard Lintott, 1716.
Gay, Peter. *The Enlightenment: The Rise of Modern Paganism.* New York: W. W. Norton, 1966.
———. *The Enlightenment: The Science of Freedom.* New York: W. W. Norton, 1969.
The Genealogy of the Most Illustrious House of Brunswick-Lunenburgh. London: Richard Parker, 1701.
Gikandi, Simon. *Slavery and the Culture of Taste.* Princeton, N.J.: Princeton University Press, 2011.
Gilman, Todd. *The Theatre Career of Thomas Arne.* Newark: University of Delaware Press, 2013.
Glausser, Wayne. "Three Approaches to Locke and the Slave Trade." *Journal of the History of Ideas* 51, no. 2 (1990): 199–216.
Gleick, James. *Isaac Newton.* New York: Pantheon, 2003.
Glover, Jane. *Handel in London: The Making of a Genius.* London: Macmillan, 2018.
Gomez, Michael A. *Pragmatism in the Age of Jihad: The Precolonial State of Bundu.* Cambridge, U.K.: Cambridge University Press, 1992.
Graham, Michael F. *The Blasphemies of Thomas Aikenhead: Boundaries of Belief on the Eve of the Enlightenment.* Edinburgh: Edinburgh University Press, 2008.
Grano, John. *Handel's Trumpeter: The Diary of John Grano.* Edited by John Ginger. Stuyvesant, N.Y.: Pendragon Press, 1998.
Grant, Douglas. *The Fortunate Slave: An Illustration of African Slavery in the Early Eighteenth Century.* Oxford: Oxford University Press, 1968.
Gray, J. M. *A History of the Gambia.* London: Frank Cass, 1966.
Green, Toby. *A Fistful of Shells: West Africa from the Rise of the Slave Trade to the Age of Revolution.* London: Allen Lane, 2019.
Greenacombe, John. "Where Precisely Was the 'Fireworks Machine' in 1749?" *Handel Institute Newsletter* 27, no. 1 (Spring 2016): 2–4.
Greig, Hannah. *The Beau Monde: Fashionable Society in Georgian London.* Oxford: Oxford University Press, 2013.
Hämäläinen, Pekka. *Indigenous Continent: The Epic Contest for North America.* New York: Liveright, 2022.
Händel, George Friedrich. *Messiah, HWV 56, Autograph.* Commentary by Donald Burrows. Kassel: Bärenreiter, 2009.
Hare, Edward. "The History of 'Nervous Disorders' from 1600 to 1840, and a Comparison with Modern Views." *British Journal of Psychiatry* 159 (1991): 37–45.
Harris, Ellen T. "Courting Gentility: Handel at the Bank of England." *Music and Letters* 91, no. 3 (Aug. 2010): 357–75.
———. *George Frideric Handel: A Life with Friends.* New York: W. W. Norton, 2014.
———. *Handel as Orpheus: Voice and Desire in the Chamber Cantatas.* Cambridge, Mass.: Harvard University Press, 2001.
———. "Handel the Investor." *Music and Letters* 85, no. 4 (Nov. 2004): 521–75.
———. "Handel, a Salaried Composer: A Response to David Hunter." *Music and Letters* 103, no. 3 (2022): 541–48.
———. "'Master of the Orchester with a Sallary': Handel at the Bank of England." *Music and Letters* 101, no. 1 (2020): 1–29.
———. "With Eyes on the East and Ears in the West: Handel's Orientalist Operas." *Journal of Interdisciplinary History* 36, no. 3 (Winter 2006): 419–43.
Harrison and Willis, Messrs. *The Great Jennens Case: Being an Epitome of the History of the Jennens Family.* Sheffield: Pawson and Brailsford, 1879.
Healey, Jonathan. *The Blazing World: A New History of Revolutionary England, 1603–1689.* New York: Knopf, 2023.

Hearne, Thomas. *Remarks and Collections of Thomas Hearne*. Edited by C. E. Doble et al. 11 vols. Oxford: Clarendon Press for the Oxford Historical Society, 1885–1921.

Heller, Wendy. "Wendy Heller on Handel's 'Messiah.'" *New York Times*, April 23, 2007.

Hill, Christopher. *The World Turned Upside Down: Radical Ideas During the English Revolution*. New York: Penguin, 1972.

Hobbes, Thomas. *Leviathan* (1651). Project Gutenberg. www.gutenberg.org/.

———. *The Life of Mr. Thomas Hobbes of Malmesbury* (1680). Early English Books Online. quod.lib.umich.edu/e/eebogroup/.

Hogwood, Christopher. *Handel: "Water Music" and "Music for the Royal Fireworks."* Cambridge, U.K.: Cambridge University Press, 2005.

Hogwood, Christopher, and Richard Luckett, eds. *Music in Eighteenth-Century England*. Cambridge, U.K.: Cambridge University Press, 1983.

Honeybone, Diana, and Michael Honeybone, eds. *The Correspondence of the Spalding Gentlemen's Society, 1710–1761*. Woodbridge, Suffolk: Boydell Press, 2010.

Hoppit, Julian. *A Land of Liberty? England, 1689–1727*. Oxford: Clarendon Press, 2000.

Hume, David. *My Own Life* (1777). Hume Texts Online. davidhume.org/.

Hunter, David. "Handel Among the Jacobites." *Music and Letters* 82, no. 4 (Nov. 2001): 543–56.

———. "Handel, an Investor in Slave-Trading Companies: A Response to Ellen Harris." *Music and Letters* 103, no. 3 (2022): 532–40.

———. "Handel Manuscripts and the Profits of Slavery: The 'Granville' Collection at the British Library and the First Performing Score of *Messiah* Reconsidered." *Notes* 76, no. 1 (Sept. 2019): 27–37.

———. "Handel's Ill Health: Documents and Diagnoses." *Royal Musical Association Research Chronicle* 41 (2008): 69–92.

———. "Handel's Students, Two Lovers, and a Shipwreck." *Early Music* 39, no. 2 (May 2011): 157–64.

———. *The Lives of George Frideric Handel*. Rochester, N.Y.: Boydell Press, 2015.

———. "The Publishing of Opera and Song Books in England, 1703–1726." *Notes* 47, no. 3 (March 1991): 647–85.

———. "Rode the 12,000? Counting Coaches, People, and Errors En Route to the Rehearsal of Handel's *Music for the Royal Fireworks* at Spring Gardens, Vauxhall in 1749." *London Journal* 37, no. 1 (2012): 13–26.

———. "Worlds Apart?" *Opera* 66, no. 12 (Dec. 2015): 1546–50.

Hunter, David, and Rose M. Mason. "Supporting Handel Through Subscription to Publications: The Lists of *Rodelinda* and *Faramondo* Compared." *Notes* 56, no. 1 (Sept. 1999): 27–93.

The Infidel Convicted; or, A Brief Defence of the Christian Revelation. London: J. Roberts, 1731.

Israel, Jonathan. *Democratic Enlightenment: Philosophy, Revolution, and Human Rights, 1750–1790*. Oxford: Oxford University Press, 2012.

———. *Enlightenment Contested: Philosophy, Modernity, and the Emancipation of Man, 1670–1752*. Oxford: Oxford University Press, 2006.

———. *A Revolution of the Mind: Radical Enlightenment and the Intellectual Origins of Modern Democracy*. Princeton, N.J.: Princeton University Press, 2010.

Jackson, Clare. *Devil-Land: England Under Siege, 1588–1688*. New York: Penguin, 2021.

Johnson, Samuel. *A Dictionary of the English Language* (1755). johnsonsdictionaryonline.com/.

Johnston, William, and William Owen. *A New and General Biographical Dictionary: Containing an Historical and Critical Account of the Lives and Writings of the Most Eminent Persons*. 12 vols. London: printed for W. Strahan et al., 1784.

Joncus, Berta, and Jeremy Barlow, eds. *"The Stage's Glory": John Rich, 1692–1761*. Newark: University of Delaware Press, 2011.
Kant, Immanuel. *Practical Philosophy*. Edited and translated by Mary J. Gregor. Cambridge, U.K.: Cambridge University Press, 1996.
Keate, George. *A Poem to the Memory of the Celebrated Mrs. Cibber*. London: J. Dodsley, 1766.
Keates, Jonathan. *Handel: The Man and His Music*. New ed. London: Pimlico, 2009.
———. *"Messiah": The Composition and Afterlife of Handel's Masterpiece*. London: Head of Zeus, 2016.
Kielmansegge, Friedrich, Count. *Diary of a Journey to England in the Years 1761–1762*. London: Longmans, Green, 1902.
Killeen, Kevin, Helen Smith, and Rachel Willie, eds. *The Oxford Handbook of the Bible in Early Modern England, c. 1530–1700*. Oxford: Oxford University Press, 2015.
Kimbell, David. *Handel on the Stage*. Cambridge, U.K.: Cambridge University Press, 2016.
Koch, Klaus-Peter. "Handel's Family." *Handel Institute Newsletter* 19, no. 2 (Autumn 2008): 1–3.
Koon, Helene. *Colley Cibber: A Biography*. Lexington: University Press of Kentucky, 1986.
Landers, John. *Death and the Metropolis: Studies in the Demographic History of London, 1670–1830*. Cambridge, U.K.: Cambridge University Press, 1993.
Landon, H. C. Robbins. *Handel and His World*. Boston: Little, Brown, 1984.
Lang, Paul Henry. *George Frideric Handel*. New York: W. W. Norton, 1966.
Langford, Paul. *A Polite and Commercial People: England, 1727–1783*. Oxford: Clarendon Press, 1989.
Lee, Jonathan Rhodes. "From Amelia to Calista and Beyond: Sentimental Heroines, 'Fallen' Women, and Handel's Oratorio Revisions for Susanna Cibber." *Cambridge Opera Journal* 27, no. 1 (March 2015): 1–34.
"Letters of Thomas Coram." *Proceedings of the Massachusetts Historical Society* 56 (Oct. 1922–June 1923): 15–56.
Levene, Alysa. *Childcare, Health, and Mortality at the London Foundling Hospital, 1741–1800*. Manchester: Manchester University Press, 2007.
———. *The Childhood of the Poor: Welfare in Eighteenth-Century London*. Basingstoke: Palgrave Macmillan, 2012.
Levenson, Thomas. *Money for Nothing: The Scientists, Fraudsters, and Corrupt Politicians Who Reinvented Money, Panicked a Nation, and Made the World Rich*. New York: Random House, 2020.
Lillywhite, Bryant. *London Coffee Houses: A Reference Book of Coffee Houses of the Seventeenth, Eighteenth, and Nineteenth Centuries*. London: George Allen and Unwin, 1963.
Lindberg, Erik. "The Rise of Hamburg as a Global Marketplace in the Seventeenth Century: A Comparative Political Economy Perspective." *Comparative Studies in Society and History* 50, no. 3 (July 2008): 641–62.
Locke, John. *Second Treatise of Government* (1690). Project Gutenberg. www.gutenberg.org/.
Lockwood, Joseph. "The Performance and Reception of Handel's Music in Revolutionary North America." PhD diss., Oxford University, 2023.
Luckett, Richard. *Handel's "Messiah": A Celebration*. New York: Harcourt Brace, 1992.
MacGeagh, Henry F. *Register of Admissions to the Honourable Society of the Middle Temple: From the Fifteenth Century to the Year 1944*. 3 vols. London: Butterworth, 1949.
Mack, Maynard. *Alexander Pope: A Life*. New Haven, Conn.: Yale University Press, 1985.
Macky, John. *A Journey Through England*. 2nd ed. London: J. Hooke, 1722.

Malcolm, Noel. *Useful Enemies: Islam and the Ottoman Empire in Western Political Thought, 1450–1750*. Oxford: Oxford University Press, 2019.
Mann, David, ed. *The Plays of Theophilus and Susannah Cibber*. New York: Garland, 1981.
Marissen, Michael. "Rejoicing Against Judaism in Handel's *Messiah*." *Journal of Musicology* 24, no. 2 (Spring 2007): 167–94.
———. *Tainted Glory in Handel's "Messiah": The Unsettling History of the World's Most Beloved Choral Work*. New Haven, Conn.: Yale University Press, 2014.
———. "Unsettling History of That Joyous 'Hallelujah.'" *New York Times*, April 8, 2007.
Marshall, Ashley. "The '1735' Faulkner Edition of Swift's *Works*." *Library* 14, no. 2 (June 2013): 154–98.
Martin, Adrienne. *How We Hope: A Moral Psychology*. Princeton, N.J.: Princeton University Press, 2013.
Martyn, Thomas. *The English Connoisseur*. 2 vols. London: L. Davis and C. Reymers, 1766.
Marx, Hans Joachim. "On the Authenticity of Christoph Platzer's Handel Portrait (*c.* 1710)." *Early Music* 45, no. 3 (2017): 459–65.
Matthews, John, and Mike Foley. *Gopsall: A Millennium of Influence*. Congerstone, UK: Independent Publishing Network, 2021.
McClure, Ruth K. *Coram's Children: The London Foundling Hospital in the Eighteenth Century*. New Haven, Conn.: Yale University Press, 1981.
McGeary, Thomas. "Handel and Homosexuality: Burlington House and Cannons Revisited." *Journal of the Royal Musical Association* 136, no. 1 (2011): 33–71.
———. "Handel as Orpheus: The Vauxhall Statue Re-examined." *Early Music* 43, no. 2 (May 2015): 291–308.
———. "Handel in Rome: The Homosexual Context Reconsidered." *Early Music* 44, no. 1 (Feb. 2016): 59–75.
———. *The Politics of Opera in Handel's Britain*. Cambridge, U.K.: Cambridge University Press, 2013.
Messiah: A Facsimile of the 1743 Wordbook. Edited by Christopher Hogwood. Boston: Handel and Haydn Society, 1995.
Mintz, Sidney W. *Sweetness and Power: The Place of Sugar in Modern History*. New York: Viking, 1985.
Misson, Henri. *Memoirs and Observations in His Travels over England. With Some Account of Scotland and Ireland*. London: D. Browne, 1719.
Mittleman, Alan. *Hope in a Democratic Age: Philosophy, Religion, and Political Theory*. Oxford: Oxford University Press, 2009.
Molineux, Catherine. *Faces of Perfect Ebony: Encountering Atlantic Slavery in Imperial Britain*. Cambridge, Mass.: Harvard University Press, 2012.
Monod, Paul, Murray Pittock, and Daniel Szechi, eds. *Loyalty and Identity: Jacobites at Home and Abroad*. Basingstoke: Palgrave Macmillan, 2010.
Moore, Francis. *Travels into the Inland Parts of Africa*. London: printed by E. Cave, 1738.
Moore, William. *The Gentlemen's Society at Spalding: Its Origin and Progress*. London: William Pickering, 1851.
Morcom, Anna, and Timothy D. Taylor, eds. *The Oxford Handbook of Economic Ethnomusicology*. Oxford: Oxford University Press, 2020.
Morgan, Jennifer. *Reckoning with Slavery: Gender, Kinship, and Capitalism in the Early Black Atlantic*. Durham, N.C.: Duke University Press, 2021.
Mounsey, Chris, and Caroline Gonda, eds. *Queer People: Negotiations and Expressions of Homosexuality, 1700–1800*. Lewisburg, Pa.: Bucknell University Press, 2007.

Mullan, John. "Hypochondria and Hysteria: Sensibility and the Physicians." *Eighteenth Century* 25, no. 2 (1984): 141–74.

Myers, Robin, Michael Harris, and Giles Mandelbrote, eds. *Music and the Book Trade from the Sixteenth Century to the Twentieth Century*. New Castle, Del.: Oak Knoll Press; London: British Library, 2008.

Nash, Mary. *The Provoked Wife: The Life and Times of Susannah Cibber*. Boston: Little, Brown, 1977.

Naylor, Paul, and Marion Wallace. "Author of His Own Fate? The Eighteenth-Century Writings of Ayuba Sulayman Diallo." *Journal of African History* 60, no. 3 (2019): 343–77.

Nelson, Marie C., and John Rogers, eds. *Urbanisation and the Epidemiologic Transition*. Uppsala: Family History Group, Department of History, Uppsala University, 1989.

A New and General Biographical Dictionary, Containing an Historical, Critical, and Impartial Account of the Most Eminent Persons in Every Nation of the World. New ed. 8 vols. London: n.p., 1795.

Nichols, John. *The History and Antiquities of the County of Leicester*. 4 vols. London: J. Nichols, 1795–1811.

———. *Literary Anecdotes of the Eighteenth Century*. 2nd ed. 6 vols. London: printed for the author by Nichols, Son, and Bentley, 1812–16.

Nichols, R. H., and F. A. Wray. *The History of the Foundling Hospital*. London: Oxford University Press, 1935.

Nicolson, Adam. *God's Secretaries: The Making of the King James Bible*. New York: HarperCollins, 2003.

Nihell, Elizabeth. *An Answer to the Author of the Critical Review, for March, 1760. Upon the Article of Mrs. Nihell's Treatise on the Art of Midwifery*. London: A. Morley, 1760.

Norton, David. *The King James Bible: A Short History from Tyndale to Today*. Cambridge, U.K.: Cambridge University Press, 2011.

Norwich, John Julius. *A History of Venice*. New York: Knopf, 1982.

Nussbaum, Felicity. *Rival Queens: Actresses, Performance, and the Eighteenth-Century British Theater*. Philadelphia: University of Pennsylvania Press, 2010.

———, ed. *The Global Eighteenth Century*. Baltimore: Johns Hopkins University Press, 2003.

Orr, Clarissa Campbell. *Mrs. Delany: A Life*. New Haven, Conn.: Yale University Press, 2019.

Owen, Dorothy M., ed. *The Minute-Books of the Spalding Gentlemen's Society, 1712–1755*. Lincoln, U.K.: Lincoln Record Society, 1981.

Oxford Dictionary of National Biography. www.oxforddnb.com/.

Pagden, Anthony. *The Enlightenment and Why It Still Matters*. New York: Random House, 2013.

Paine, Thomas. *The Age of Reason, Part I and II* (1796). Project Gutenberg. www.gutenberg.org/.

Parry, Timothy. "A Temple at Gopsall Park." Bachelor's thesis, Victoria University of Manchester, 1981.

Partridge, John. *Merlinus Liberatus: Being an Almanack for the Year of Our Blessed Saviour's Incarnation 1701*. London: R. Roberts, 1701.

Pepys, Samuel. *The Diary of Samuel Pepys, M.A., F.R.S.* London: George Bell and Sons, 1893. Project Gutenberg. www.gutenberg.org/.

Pettigrew, William A. *Freedom's Debt: The Royal African Company and the Politics of the Atlantic Slave Trade, 1672–1752*. Chapel Hill: University of North Carolina Press, 2013.

Phillips, Andrew, and J. C. Sharman. *Outsourcing Empire: How Company-States Made the Modern World*. Princeton, N.J.: Princeton University Press, 2020.

Pincus, Steve. *1688: The First Modern Revolution*. New Haven, Conn.: Yale University Press, 2009.

Plato. *The Collected Dialogues of Plato*. Edited by Edith Hamilton and Huntington Cairns. New York: Pantheon, 1961.

Plumb, J. H. *The First Four Georges*. London: Collins, 1956.

Pope, Alexander. *Dunciad* (1728–43). Project Gutenberg. www.gutenberg.org/.

———. *An Essay on Man* (1733–34). Poetry Foundation. www.poetryfoundation.org/.

———. *To Augustus* (1737). Project Gutenberg. www.gutenberg.org/.

Portland, W. John Arthur Charles James Cavendish-Bentick, et al. *The Manuscripts of His Grace the Duke of Portland: Preserved at Welbeck Abbey*. 10 vols. London: Eyre and Spottiswoode for the Royal Commission on Historical Manuscripts, 1891–1919.

Post, John D. *Food Shortage, Climatic Variability, and Epidemic Disease in Preindustrial Europe: The Mortality Peak in the Early 1740s*. Ithaca, N.Y.: Cornell University Press, 1985.

Private Virtue and Publick Spirit Display'd. In a Succinct Essay on the Character of Capt. Thomas Coram. London: J. Roberts, 1751.

Probyn, Clive. *Jonathan Swift on the Anglo-Irish Road*. Leiden: Brill, 2020.

Rackham, Oliver. *Trees and Woodland in the British Landscape: The Complete History of Britain's Trees, Woods, and Hedgerows*. Rev. ed. London: Phoenix Press, 1990.

Razzell, Peter, and Christine Spence. "The History of Infant, Child, and Adult Mortality in London, 1550–1850." *London Journal* 32, no. 3 (2007): 271–92.

Rediker, Marcus. *The Slave Ship: A Human History*. New York: Viking, 2007.

Redway, Virginia Larkin. "Handel in Colonial and Post-colonial America (to 1820)." *Musical Quarterly* 21, no. 2 (April 1935): 190–207.

Richardson, Robbie. *The Savage and Modern Self: North American Indians in Eighteenth-Century British Literature and Culture*. Toronto: University of Toronto Press, 2018.

Riding, Jacqueline. *Jacobites: A New History of the '45 Rebellion*. London: Bloomsbury, 2016.

Rinaldo, an Opera: As It Is Perform'd at the Queens Theatre in London. London: Tho. Howlatt, 1711.

Roberts, John H. "False *Messiah*." *Journal of the American Musicological Society* 63, no. 1 (Spring 2010): 45–97.

Robertson, Ritchie. *The Enlightenment: The Pursuit of Happiness, 1680–1790*. New York: Harper, 2021.

Rothschild, Emma. *The Inner Life of Empires: An Eighteenth-Century History*. Princeton, N.J.: Princeton University Press, 2011.

Rousseau, Jean-Jacques. *Emile; or, Education* (1762). Liberty Fund. oll.libertyfund.org/.

Ryan, Alan. *On Politics: A History of Political Thought from Herodotus to the Present*. New York: Penguin, 2012.

Saussure, César de. *A Foreign View of England in the Reigns of George I and George II*. London: John Murray, 1902.

Scanlan, Padraic X. *Slave Empire: How Slavery Built Modern Britain*. London: Robinson, 2020.

Schoelcher, Victor. *The Life of Handel*. London: Trübner, 1857.

Serwer, Howard. "The World of the *Water Music*." *Händel-Jahrbuch* (1996–97): 101–11.

Seward, Desmond. *The King over the Water: A Complete History of the Jacobites*. Edinburgh: Birlinn, 2021.

Shakespeare, William. *Othello, the Moor of Venice: A Tragedy*. Edited by Charles Jennens. London: W. Bowyer and J. Nichols, 1773.

Sharpe, James. *A Fiery and Furious People: A History of Violence in England*. London: Random House, 2016.

Shaw, Watkins. "Handel's *Messiah*: A Study of Selected Contemporary Word-Books." *Musical Quarterly* 45, no. 2 (April 1959): 208–22.

———. *The Story of Handel's "Messiah."* London: Novello, 1963.

———. *A Textual and Historical Companion to Handel's "Messiah."* London: Novello, 1965.

Sheridan, Thomas. *British Education; or, The Source of the Disorders of Great Britain*. Dublin: Faulkner, 1756.

Shevelow, Kathryn. *Charlotte: Being a True Account of an Actress's Flamboyant Adventures in Eighteenth-Century London's Wild and Wicked Theatrical World*. New York: Henry Holt, 2005.

Shklar, Judith N. "The Liberalism of Fear." In *Liberalism and the Moral Life*, edited by Nancy L. Rosenblum, 21–38. Cambridge, Mass.: Harvard University Press, 1989.

Smith, Ruth. "The Achievements of Charles Jennens." *Music and Letters* 70, no. 2 (May 1989): 161–90.

———. *Charles Jennens: The Man Behind Handel's "Messiah."* London: Handel House Trust, 2012.

———. *Handel's Oratorios and Eighteenth-Century Thought*. Cambridge, U.K.: Cambridge University Press, 1995.

———. "Ruth Smith on Handel's 'Messiah.'" *New York Times*, April 25, 2007.

Somerset, Anne. *Queen Anne: The Politics of Passion*. New York: Knopf, 2013.

Spence, Joseph. *Anecdotes, Observations, and Characters, of Books and Men: Collected from the Conversation of Mr. Pope and Other Eminent Persons of His Time*. Edited by Samuel Weller Singer. London: W. H. Carpenter, 1820.

The Statutes at Large from Magna Charta to the Last Session of Parliament, 1225–1763. 9 vols. London: M. Basket et al., 1763–65.

Stern, Philip J. *Empire, Incorporated: The Corporations That Built British Colonialism*. Cambridge, Mass.: Belknap Press of Harvard University Press, 2023.

Stevens, Nicholas. *Two Letters from a Deist to His Friend, Concerning the Truth and Propagation of Deism, in Opposition to Christianity*. London: James Roberts, 1730.

Stukeley, William, et al. *The Family Memoirs of the Rev. William Stukeley, M.D., and the Antiquarian and Other Correspondence of William Stukeley, Roger & Samuel Gale, etc*. 3 vols. Durham, U.K.: Andrews, 1882–87.

Styles, John. *Threads of Feeling: The London Foundling Hospital's Textile Tokens, 1740–1770*. London: Foundling Museum, 2010.

Sumner, Brenda. "Charles Jennens' Piano and Music Room." *Handel Institute Newsletter* 22, no. 2 (Autumn 2011): 1–3.

———. "Gopsall Hall: 'Look on My Works, Ye Mighty, and Despair.'" Master's thesis, University of Leicester, 2009.

Survey of London. 47 vols. London: London County Council, 1900–2008. www.british-history.ac.uk/.

Sutherland, L. S., and L. G. Mitchell, eds. *The History of the University of Oxford: The Eighteenth Century*. Oxford: Clarendon Press, 1986.

Swift, Jonathan. "A Description of a City Shower" (1710). Poetry Foundation. www.poetryfoundation.org/.

———. *Gulliver's Travels* (1726). New York: Penguin, 2001.

———. *A Modest Proposal* (1729). Project Gutenberg. www.gutenberg.org/.

———. *The Poetical Works of Jonathan Swift*. 3 vols. London: W. Pickering, 1853.

———. *A Proposal for Correcting, Improving, and Ascertaining the English Tongue*. London: Benj. Tooke, 1712.

———. *A Tale of a Tub* (1704). Project Gutenberg. gutenberg.org/.

Talbot, Michael. "Some Overlooked MSS in Manchester." *Musical Times* 115 (Nov. 1974): 942–44.

———. "Vivaldi's 'Manchester' Sonatas." *Proceedings of the Royal Musical Association* 104 (1977–78): 20–29.

Taruskin, Richard. *Music in the Seventeenth and Eighteenth Centuries*. Oxford: Oxford University Press, 2010.

Thompson, Andrew C. *George II: King and Elector*. New Haven, Conn.: Yale University Press, 2011.

Timms, Colin, and Bruce Wood, eds. *Music in the London Theatre from Purcell to Handel*. Cambridge, U.K.: Cambridge University Press, 2017.

Townsend, Horatio. *An Account of the Visit of Handel to Dublin; With Incidental Notices of His Life and Character*. Dublin: J. McGlashan, 1852.

Trumbach, Randolph. *Sex and the Gender Revolution*. Vol. 1, *Heterosexuality and the Third Gender in Enlightenment London*. Chicago: University of Chicago Press, 1998.

The Tryals of Two Causes, Between Theophilus Cibber, Gent. Plaintiff, and William Sloper, Esq.; Defendant. London: printed for T. Trott, 1740.

Uffenbach, Zacharias Conrad von. *London in 1710*. Edited and translated by W. H. Quarrell and Margaret Mare. London: Faber and Faber, 1934.

Uglow, Jenny. *Hogarth: A Life and a World*. London: Faber and Faber, 1997.

Van den Heuvel, Steven C., ed. *Historical and Multidisciplinary Perspectives on Hope*. Cham, Switzerland: Springer, 2020.

Vickers, David, ed. *New Perspectives on Handel's Music: Essays in Honour of Donald Burrows*. London: Boydell and Brewer, 2022.

Vickery, Amanda. *The Gentleman's Daughter: Women's Lives in Georgian England*. New Haven, Conn.: Yale University Press, 1998.

Voltaire, François-Marie Arouet de. *Letters on England* (1733). Project Gutenberg. www.gutenberg.org/.

Wagner, Gillian. *Thomas Coram, Gent., 1668–1751*. Woodbridge, Suffolk: Boydell Press, 2004.

Walpole, Horace. *The Letters of Horace Walpole, Earl of Orford*. Edited by Peter Cunningham. 9 vols. London: Bickers and Son, 1877–80.

Walvin, James. *The Zong: A Massacre, the Law, and the End of Slavery*. New Haven, Conn.: Yale University Press, 2011.

Ward, Ned. *The London-Spy Compleat*. London: J. How, 1700.

Williams, Peter, ed. *Bach, Handel, Scarlatti: Tercentenary Essays*. Cambridge, U.K.: Cambridge University Press, 1985.

Wilson, Peter H. *Europe's Tragedy: A New History of the Thirty Years War*. London: Allen Lane, 2009.

Wolff, Larry. *The Singing Turk: Ottoman Power and Operatic Emotions on the European Stage*. Stanford, Calif.: Stanford University Press, 2016.

Wollstonecraft, Mary. *A Vindication of the Rights of Woman* (1792). Project Gutenberg. www.gutenberg.org/.

Index

Pages numbers followed by *n* refer to notes.

abolitionists, 135, 251
Acis and Galatea (Handel), 97, 99–100, 197
Act of Proscription (1746), 226
Act of Settlement (1701), 46–47, 50–53, 55–56
Adams, Abigail, 9–10, 12–13
Adams, John, 9
Africa, 16, 132, 136–37
Age of Reason, 15, 137
Agrippina (Handel), 35
Aix-la-Chapelle, Treaty of (1748), 228
Albemarle, Earl of, 129
Almaami elite, 138–39
American colonies, 16, 84, 119, 129–30
    first *Messiah* performances in, 9
    slavery and, 19, 133, 136–37, 141
    women's equality and, 136
American Revolution, 16, 137
American Revolution Museum, 252
Ames, Joseph, 148
Anglicans. *See* Church of England
Anglo-Dutch army, 46–47
Angola, 141
Annapolis, Maryland, 141–42, 252
Anne, Queen of England, 19, 43–51, 63, 66, 73, 112, 131–32, 135, 142, 146, 151, 218
    death of, 51

Anne (ship), 121
antimiscegenation laws, 137
Arabella (slave ship), 138–42, 144, 148, 168, 173, 219
Arabic language, 147–48
Arbuthnot, John, 49–51, 66, 97, 146, 155, 284n
Arne, Anne, 102–3, 106, 112, 117, 125, 211
Arne, Edward, 122
Arne, Susannah. *See* Cibber, Susannah
Arne, Thomas, Jr., 102–3, 107, 117, 134–35, 211, 224, 228
Arne, Thomas, Sr., 102–6, 138, 146
asiento de negros, 132
Athens, ancient, 30
Athlone, Battle of, 51
Atterbury, Francis, Bishop, 64
Augustan age, 66–67, 104
Aungier Street Theatre (Dublin), 196, 199–200
Austria
    War of the Austrian Succession and, 218
    War of the Spanish Succession and, 44
Avolio, Christina Maria, 197, 202, 206
Aztecs, 136

Bach, Johann Ambrosius, 27
Bach, Johann Sebastian, 27, 237, 239
Bahamas, 123
Bailey, Nathan, 68
Baltic Sea, 28
Baltimore, Calverts, barons of, 142
Bank of England, 121
Baroque period, 19, 31–32, 92, 257
basso continuo, 30–31
Bavaria
    Thirty Years' War and, 25
    War of the Austrian Succession and, 218
    War of the Spanish Succession and, 44
Bayle, Pierre, 70–71, 75, 82, 147
BBC Chorus, 7
Bedford, Duke of, 129
Beecham, Thomas, 7
Beggar's Opera, The (Gay), 94–98, 123, 214, 224
Behn, Aphra, 146
Belle, Dido Elizabeth, 136
Bellini, Giovanni, 91
Belshazzar (Handel), 216
Benin, Bight of, 140
Biafra, Bight of, 140
Bible. *See also specific books and biblical figures*
    Esther and, 97–99
    Jennens librettos and, 179
    King James, 179–82, 189–90, 256
    Messiah and, 11–12
    New Testament, 3, 5, 182, 260
    Vulgate, 179
Birmingham ironworks, 84
black servants, in Britain, 135
blasphemy, 56, 83
Bleak House (Dickens), 84
Blenheim, Battle of (1704), 44
Blenheim Palace, 44
Bloomsbury, 89
Bluett, Thomas, 143–46, 148–49, 173, 176, 251
Bolton, Anne Vaughan, Duchess of, 129
Bolton, Charles Powlett, Duke of, 95
Bononcini, Giovanni, 61
Book of Common Prayer, 182
Bordoni, Faustina, 61
Boston, Emerson on *Messiah* in, 9–10, 12
Bourk, John de, 152
Boyne, Battle of the, 51

Braunschweig-Lüneburg family, 35–37, 52
Brazil, 133, 141
Bristol
    triangular trade and, 133
    Wesley on *Messiah* in, 240
Britain, 19–20
    abolition of slavery in, 137–38
    Africa and, 132
    American Revolution and, 16
    Catholics vs. Protestants and, 19, 46–47, 50
    contemporary concerts of *Messiah* and, 10
    empire and, 16
    Glorious Revolution and, 46–47
    Handel's first visits, 37–39
    Jacobite rising of 1745–46 and, 218–23
    national debt, 16
    Norman invasion of 1066, 83
    Protestant Succession and, 50
    Restoration and, 38–40
    Royal Fireworks and, 230
    Seven Years' War vs. France, 228
    slavery and, 136
    sodomy laws and, 281n
    War of the Austrian Succession and, 218–20, 228
    War of the Spanish Succession and, 44
British Library, 147, 241, 252
British Museum, 147, 178, 241, 298n
British Parliament, 16, 38, 44, 47, 56–57, 115, 129, 137, 226, 230
    House of Commons, 57, 218, 219
British Royal Navy, 16, 49, 194
Brydges, James. *See* Chandos, Duke of
Buckingham, Duke of, 160
Buckingham Palace, 160, 241
Bundu, 139–42, 144, 148–49, 174–76, 178, 251
Burke, Edmund, 48, 71
Burlington, Dorothy Boyle, Countess of, 129
Burlington, Richard Boyle, Earl of, 59–60, 129
Burney, Charles, 103, 193, 195, 237, 240, 245
Burrows, Donald, 295n, 298n
Byrom, John, 284n

Cádiz, 44
Calvert family, 142
Calvinists, 25, 48

Canaletto, 38
Candide (Voltaire), 69
cantata, defined, 30
Canterbury, Archbishop of, 64, 168
Caravaggio, 91
Caribbean, 49, 133–38, 141, 219
Caroline, Queen of England, 52–54, 64, 98–99, 146, 176
  death of, 153–54, 166
Carroll, Lewis, 61
Carter, Mrs. (trial witness), 162
Caruso, Enrico, 7
castrati, 31, 40, 42, 281n
Catholics, 25, 46, 50–51, 56–57, 73, 89, 98, 142, 179, 196
Ceeser (enslaved person), 142
censorship, 115, 198, 217
Chandos, James Brydges, Duke of, 60, 97, 131, 134, 169
Chapel Royal, 9, 233
Charitable Music Society, 197
Charke, Charlotte/Charles Cibber, 113–14
Charke, Richard, 114
Charles I, King of England, 38
Charles II, King of England, 38, 46–47, 124, 129, 132
"Charlie, Bonnie Prince." *See* Stuart, Charles Edward
childbirth, 112
Charlie Brown Christmas, A, 12
child mortality rates, 125
child poverty and neglect, 15, 123–26, 231–32. *See also* Foundling Hospital
Christ Church Cathedral (Dublin), 194, 196, 201–2, 207
Christianity, 5
  Charles Jennens and, 178–83
  Islam and, 147
  Judaism and, 296n
  minorities in England and, 56
  Robert Jennens and, 82–83
  slavery and, 137
  themes in the *Messiah*, 182–83
Christian missionaries, 121, 178
Christmas, 11–12
Churchill, Winston, 44
Church of England (Anglican Church), 2, 56, 73, 81, 179, 182
Church of Ireland, 72
Cibber, Charlotte/Charles. *See* Charke, Charlotte/Charles Cibber
Cibber, Colley, 19, 104–7, 114, 119, 153, 157, 169, 223, 248

Cibber, Molly (daughter of Sloper and Susannah Cibber), 164–65, 200, 212, 247
Cibber, Susannah Arne (Mrs. Cibber), 18, 101, 104, 106–10, 113–20, 125, 134, 149, 151, 248
  aftermath of Dublin *Messiah* concerts and, 245
  death of, 247
  deaths of siblings and children of, 125
  Delaney exclaims sins forgiven, 208
  early life of, 102–4
  fame of, post 1745, 246
  health problems of, 246
  Handel friendship and, 246
  letter to Theophilus and, 116, 289n
  marries Theophilus Cibber, 104–8
  Messiah performances and, 235, 245–46
  Messiah Dublin premiere and, 199–203, 206–8, 211–12, 255–56, 298n
  Messiah London premiere and, 213–15
  musical education of, 102–4, 138
  performs in Handel's *Samson*, 213
  performs in Voltaire's *Zara*, 107–8
  performs with Garrick in *King John*, 223–24
  prenuptial agreement with Theophilus and, 107–8, 112
  return to London after *Messiah* premiere and legal case vs. Theophilus, 211–13
  secret hideaway with Sloper, 252
  sings "God Save the King," in Jacobite rising and, 224
  stars in *Provoked Wife*, 246–47
  trial and flight with Sloper and, 157–65
Cibber, Theophilus, 105–10, 113–19, 136, 149, 157–66, 181, 200, 211–12, 226, 247–48
  death of, 248
Cibber v. Sloper trial, 157–65
civil strife, 55–56, 66–72. *See also* child poverty and neglect; Jacobites; slavery
  Swift's *Gulliver's Travels* and, 74–77
Clive, Kitty, 104, 107–8
coffeehouses, 57
Colossians, Epistle to the, 260
Commentaries on Hosea, Joel, Micah, and Malachi (Pococke), 181
Commentary on the Book of Common Prayer (Nicholls), 181

concertmaster, defined, 32
concerto, defined, 30
conspiracy, 83, 90, 92
Coram, Eunice Waite, 121, 125, 167
Coram, Thomas, 19, 135, 151, 212, 289n
  child welfare and Foundling Hospital cause of, 19, 123–30, 138–39, 144, 146, 166–72, 231–34, 236, 244–45, 256
  death and grave of, 234, 244
  early life and career, 121–22
  Georgia plan and, 120–23, 125, 136, 145, 160, 218
  Hogarth portrait of, 233, 245, 253
  poverty of, in old age, 234
  statue of, 245
Coram Foundation, 245
Corelli, Arcangelo, 29
Corinthians, first epistle to, 205
Covent Garden, 93, 100, 102, 105, 160, 178, 211–12, 247
COVID-19, 5–6
Craftsman, The, 100
Cristofori, Bartolomeo, 32, 91
Crocus (enslaved person), 142
Cromwell, Oliver, 38, 39, 55
Crown Estate, 253
Cugoano, Ottobah, 136
Culloden, Battle of, 225–26
Cumberland, Duke of, 224–26, 228
Cuzzoni, Francesca, 60–61

Daily Advertiser, 217, 224
Daily Journal, 97–98
Darkey (enslaved person), 142
Davies, Thomas, 298n
Deborah (Handel), 104
debtors' prisons, 102, 120, 122, 151, 209, 233
Decline and Fall of the Roman Empire (Gibbon), 72
Defoe, Daniel, 38, 50, 58, 110, 113, 133, 218, 248
Deidamia (Handel), 156
Deism, 56, 82–83, 180–81
Delany, Mary, 39
Delany, Patrick, 207–8, 212, 298n
Denton, Vachel, 140, 142, 144–45, 149, 176, 251
Dettingen, Battle of (1743), 218
Devonshire, William Cavendish, Duke of, Lord Lieutenant of Ireland, 192, 194, 197

Diallo, Ayuba bin Sulayman "Simon," 19, 138–51, 168, 173–78, 219, 250–53, 256, 291n
  Bluett memoir of and, 251–52
  Haley's *Roots* and, 251–52
  Hoare portrait of, 149, 252
Diallo, Sulayman, 174, 175
Dickens, Charles, 84
Dictionary of the English Language (Johnson), 58, 67
Dissenters, 73, 83
Dolphin (ship), 173–74
Domkirche (Halle cathedral), 28
Dorset, England, 121
Dover, Pennsylvania, 143, 144
Drury Lane Theatre, 40, 104–5, 107, 117, 157, 169, 200, 247
Dublin
  child beggars in, 124
  Handel concerts of 1741 in, 192–202, 209–10
  Messiah performance in, by Cibber, grows famous, 245–46
  Messiah premiere of 1742 in, 18–19, 201–10, 245–46
  Messiah score by copyist and, 259
  Messiah wordbook of 1742 and, 259
  Swift in, 73, 123–24
Dubourg, Matthew, 197–98, 202, 214, 255
Dunciad, The (Pope), 105, 195
Dutch. *See* Netherlands
Du Teillay (ship), 220

Easter, 12, 192
East India Company, 121
eBay, 6–7
Edinburgh, 221
Egypt, ancient, 136
Elbe River, 25, 28
Elcho, Lord, 221, 224
Elisabeth (ship), 220
Elizabeth II, Queen of England, 241
Emerson, Ralph Waldo, 9–10, 12
Emerson, Thomas, 294n
English civil war, 16, 38, 55, 56, 67
English common law, 137, 163
English language
  Beggar's Opera and, 95–97
  Esther and, 97–98
Enlightenment, 15–18, 20, 137–38, 257
en travesti, defined, 31
Equiano, Olaudah, 135–36
Erhardt, Tassilo, 295n

Erndl, Christian Heinrich, 38
Essay on Man, An (Pope), 70–71, 149–50
Essays of Theodicy (Leibniz), 69
Essay upon Projects, An (Defoe), 110
Esther (Handel), 97–99, 155, 121, 197, 201
"Eternal Source of Light Divine" (Handel), 49
Europe, 16
   Holdsworth and grand tours of, 89–90
Exodus, Book of, 155

Farinelli (castrato), 19, 99, 110
Faulkner, George, 201, 204, 213, 259
Faulkner's Dublin Journal, 201, 213
fear, 67–71, 257
Fenton, Lavinia, 95
Fife, Mr. (henchman), 116
Finlandia (Sibelius), 7
Fishamble Street music hall, 196–97, 201, 203–4, 209
Fleet Prison, 122
Fleetwood, Charles, 157–58
Florence, 29, 33–34, 89
Fontenoy, Battle of, 220
Foppington, Lord (Colley Cibber character), 105, 117
foster families, 234
Foundling Hospital, 125–30, 138–39, 144, 146, 166–72, 173, 231–36, 239–40, 244–45, 252–53, 294n
"Foundling Hospital Anthem" (Handel, with recycled "Hallelujah" chorus), 232–33
Foundling Museum, 253
France, 16, 51, 173
   Jacobites and, 45, 219–21, 228–29
   Peace of Utrecht and, 49
   War of the Austrian Succession and, 218–20, 228–29
   War of the Spanish Succession and, 44
   Seven Years' War, 228
Franklin, Benjamin, 58–59, 236
Frederick, Prince of Wales, 99, 129, 232
French privateers, 194
Fulbe people, 139, 174–75, 251
Fulfulde language, 142
Fund for Decay'd Musicians (*later* Royal Society of Musicians), 151–52, 239–41
Futa Jallon highlands, 175

Gabrieli, Giovanni, 29
Gainsborough, Thomas, 233
Gambia River, 140, 145, 173–74, 219, 250
Garrick, David, 104, 211, 223–24, 246, 248
Gay, John, 19, 52, 65, 66, 94, 123
   Beggar's Opera and, 94–97
   Handel's *Acis and Galatea* and, 97
Gay, Peter, 15
Gentleman's Magazine, 211
George I, King of England (*formerly* Georg Ludwig of Hanover), 19, 23–24, 52–53, 55, 58, 60, 146, 151, 280nn
   crowned as King of England, with death of Anne, 50–52
   death of, 63
   Handel as Kapellmeister to, in Hanover, 35–37, 47–50
   Handel naturalized by, 63
   Handel's pension and, 52–53
   Jennens refuses to swear loyalty to, 88–89
   relations with son Georg August (later George II), 54
George II, King of England (*formerly* Georg August), 13, 19, 52–54, 66, 98–99, 108, 119–20, 146, 149, 154, 166, 229
   Coram's Foundling Hospital and, 168
   coronation of, 63–64, 206
   Handel appointed music master to daughters of, 53, 152
   Jacobite uprising and, 218, 224–25, 28
   London premiere of *Messiah* and stands for "Hallelujah" chorus, 214
   War of the Austrian Succession and, 218–19
George III, King of England
   Handel collection received from Smith Jr. by, 241
   Messiah Westminster performance of 1784 centenary of Handel birth, 240
Georg August, Prince of Hanover and Prince of Wales. *See* George II, King of England
George, Prince of Denmark (consort of Queen Anne), 43
Georgia
   Coram and Sloper colony in, 119–23, 125, 127, 129, 136, 145, 171, 218
   slavery and, 122
   women's rights and, 123, 136

Georg Ludwig, prince-elector of Hanover, 35–36, 47–50. *See also* George I, King of England
German lands, 25, 35
Ghana, 136
Gibbon, Edward, 72
Gibraltar, 44, 49
Gideon (biblical hero), 40
Giulio Cesare (Handel), 62–63
Glorious Revolution (1688), 46–47, 50, 56–57, 72, 88
Gluck, Christoph Willibald, 246
Gopsall Hall (Jennens country home), 1–2, 83–85, 89, 91, 94, 154, 180–81, 222, 226–27, 242–43, 249
    Handel at, 210, 242
    ruins of and temple at, 253–54
Gospels, 205
government, 73, 83, 257
    rethinking of, 15–16
Grainger, Percy, 7
Grano, John, 151
Grant, Douglas, 291n
Great Ormond Street (Jennens town house at), 89, 123, 252
Great Storm of 1703, 106, 181
Greece, ancient, 66
Green Park, 229
Grub Street, 59, 61, 73–74, 100, 164, 170–71
Guadagni, 31
Guinea, 133
Gulliver's Travels (*Travels into Several Remote Nations of the World*) (Swift), 74–77, 81, 86, 147, 193, 198, 207, 244

Hagar, 233
Haggai, prophet, 205
Haley, Alex, 251
Halle, Saxony, 25–28, 30, 35, 37, 48, 84, 96
Halley, Edmond, 2
Hamburg, 28–30, 32–33, 53, 121
Hamlet (Shakespeare), 249
Hamlin's Coffee House, 149
Hammond, Henry, 181
Händel, Dorothea Taust (mother), 26, 35, 37, 54, 84, 96
Händel, Georg (father), 25–27, 84
Handel, George Frideric
    advertisement demanding respect and, 217
    appearance of, 33–34, 152, 230, 238
    arias of, as uplifting, 71
    Beggar's Opera and, 94–97
    birth and early education of, 25–28, 84
    British citizenship granted to, 63
    British musical sensibility shaped by, 236
    British royal family as patrons of, 8
    Brook Street home of, 62–63, 93, 152
    Brook Street home of, as museum, 252
    Cardinal Pamphili and, 34
    charities supported by, 151
    "Charming Brute" cartoon of, 153
    composes *Acis and Galatea* to English text by Gay, 97
    composes anthem for funeral of Queen Caroline, 153
    composes *Belshazzar* oratorio with Jennens, 216
    composes birthday ode to Queen Anne, 48–49
    composes coronation music for George II, 63–65
    composes *Deborah* oratorio with Susannah Arne in secondary role, 104
    composes *Deidamia*, as last Italian opera, 156
    composes *Esther* with English text, 97–98, 121
    composes operas *Giulio Cesare*, *Tamerlano*, and *Rodelinda*, 62–63
    composes *Israel in Egypt*, 156
    composes *Judas Maccabaeus*, 228
    composes *L'Allegro, il Penseroso ed il Moderato*, 156
    composes *Music for the Royal Fireworks*, 229–30, 232
    composes *Radamisto* as opera seria, 60–61
    composes *Rinaldo*, 41–42, 44, 48
    composes *Samson*, 212–13
    composes *Saul*, 156
    composes *Serse*, 153
    composes *Water Music*, 24–25, 53
    compositional method and speed and, 10, 153, 192
    compositions of, after *Messiah*, 216
    copyists and, 62, 191
    copyright on printed music and, 53, 63, 152

Coram and, 123
Covent Garden opera house and, 153
death and funeral of, 8, 239–40
death of father and, 27
death of mother and, 96
death of Queen Anne and rise of George I and, 52–53
de' Medici invitation to Italy and, 32–33
divine inspiration for "Hallelujah" chorus and, 191
dowager electress Sophia and, 45, 48–49
Dublin concerts of 1741–42, 192–202
duel with Mattheson survived by, 28
earliest audiences of *Messiah* and, 20
early music career in Halle and, 28
early music career in Hamburg and, 28–29, 32
England visit of 1710 and, 37–39, 55
English language ability of, 52
English texts first set to music by, 60, 97
essence of wonder captured in *Messiah* by, 9
finances of, 10, 35, 49, 52–53, 63, 65, 134, 136, 151–52, 217, 246, 283n
Foundling Hospital *Messiah* performances and, 232–37, 244
Foundling Hospital organ donation and, 234
as Foundling Hospital trustee, 234
friends hold benefit concert for, 152
Fund for Decay'd Musicians and, 151–52, 240–41
George I and, 52–53, 59–60
George II and, 13, 65
Gopsall Temple and, 254
as gourmand and overindulgence by, 152
Grub Street attacks on, 100–101
"Hallelujah" chorus's popularity and, 232–33
Hanover career of, as Kapellmeister for future George I, 35–37, 48–49
harpsichord playing and, 34, 36, 39, 42
Haymarket return of, 153
health problems of, 19, 152–53, 210, 215–16, 237–38, 293n
Hudson portrait of, 237–38
Italian musical style and innovations of, 8, 30–32, 154–55
Italian-style works of, premiered in King's Theatre, 52–53
Italian years of, 30–36
Jennens's admiration for and friendship with, 92–94, 154–56, 237–38, 248
Jennens and Dublin premiere of *Messiah* and, 197–98, 210
Jennens collaboration ends, 230–31
Jennens dispute on *Messiah* and disavowal of, 213–16
Jennens largely forgotten in memoirs about, 242
Jennens suggests librettos for, 155–56
Jennens text for *Messiah* and, 3–4, 8, 18–19, 178–83, 188
Jennens texts for other oratorios and, 178–79, 181
King's Theatre commission lost by, 99–100
letters to brother-in-law, 54
letters to Jennens, 197–98
London career of, and rise of George I, 59–60
London commissions for Queen's Theatre and, 48
London mid-career decline and, 94, 99–101
London returned to, after Dublin year of 1741–42, 210
London returned to, after Hanover visit of 1712, 48–49
Mainwaring biography on, published, 241–42
Messiah criticized for mixing stage and scripture and, 214
Messiah Dublin premiere and, 8, 19, 201–10, 255–56, 259, 298n
Messiah handwritten score and, 20, 259
Messiah London premiere and, 213–16, 236
Messiah manuscript left to Smith Sr., 241
Messiah performances and, 216, 230, 236
Messiah recycles melodies from previous compositions of, 11, 189–90
Messiah text by Jennens set to music by, 8, 18–19, 178–83, 188–92
Messiah 20th-century concerts resemble those in lifetime of, 10

Handel, George Frideric *(continued)*
  Mrs. Cibber's performance in *Messiah* and, 200–201, 206–7, 245
  Mrs. Cibber (Susannah Arne) and, 104, 246
  musical education of, 8, 26–27, 30
  music master to daughters of George II, 53, 152
  music paper used for manuscripts by, 188–89
  Opera of the Nobility vs., 99
  operas of, and Islamic landscapes, 147
  operas of, and Italian style, 66–67
  operas of, and reordering of world, 81
  oratorios and, 98, 131
  organ playing and, 28, 39
  patron Brydges and, 60
  patron Montague and, 135, 146
  patrons and, 10, 124
  performances by, in old age, 237
  performances staged by, 10
  personality of, and dry wit, 33–34, 72, 197
  personality of, and flashes of anger, 152
  Pope on, 195
  Queen Anne and, 44–45
  romantic attractions and sexuality of, 34, 281n
  Roubiliac memorial statue of, 239–40
  Roubiliac statue of, at Vauxhall, 153–54
  Royal Academy of Music and, 60–62, 74
  Royal African Company and, 134, 290n
  royal family and, 53, 166
  servants and, 152
  slave trade investments and, 134, 136
  social circle of, 19, 66, 72, 133–34
  South Sea Company and, 134
  as spy for Hanover heirs to British throne, 49–50
  Swift and, 72
  Swift impedes Dublin concerts of, 198–202, 210
  Swift poem on, 78
  Thomas Arne and, 102–3
  Vittoria Tarquini and, 34
  volume and spectacle and, 10
  Westminster Abbey 1784 centenary of birth of, 9, 15, 240–41
  will of, 239

Hanover, 35
  Handel as Kapellmeister of, 35–37, 41, 48
  Handel returns to, from London in 1711, 45
  War of the Austrian Succession and, 218, 220
Hanoverian dynasty, 16, 35–37, 47–48, 229
  as heirs to British throne, 48–52, 56, 58
  Holdsworth and, 87–88
  Jennens and, 89
  Leibniz and, 69
  Swift and, 198
Hanover Square, 62
Harlot's Progress, The (Cibber), 247
Harris, Ellen T., 290n
Hatton Garden, Foundling Hospital in, 169, 171, 231, 244
Hayes, Mr. (trial witness), 109–10, 159–61, 163
Hayes, Mrs. (trial witness), 158–59
Haymarket, 40–41, 93–94, 99, 178
Hebrew scriptures, 3, 5, 182
Heineman Foundation Library, 259
Help for the More Easy and Clear Understanding of the Holy Scriptures (Wells), 181
Hendrix, Jimi, 62
Herrenhausen country estate, 35, 45
Hill, Aaron, 40–44, 106–7, 120, 155
Historical and Critical Dictionary (Bayle), 70, 82
Hoare, William
  portrait of Ayuba Diallo, 149, 252
Hobbes, Thomas, 67–68, 71, 73, 75, 183
Hogarth, William, 19, 95
  Beggar's Opera painting and prints and, 95–96, 129
  Coram's Foundling Hospital and, 168, 170, 233
  Foundling Hospital chapel concert tickets and, 233
  Foundling Hospital uniforms, 235
  Gin Lane, 124, 126
  March of the Guards to Finchley, 233
  paintings of black servants, 134, 149
  portrait of Coram, 167, 253
  portrait of Coram and Foundling Hospital, 231, 233
  Strolling Actresses Dressing in a Barn, 115

Index

Hoggatt, Micah, 288n
Holdsworth, Edward, 87–94, 100, 131, 133, 136, 154, 178, 183, 187, 213–14, 216–17, 219–20, 222–23, 226–27, 231
   death of, 227, 230, 242–44
   temple built by Jennens for, 253, 299n, 302n
Holyhead packet boats, 193–94
Holy Roman Empire, 25, 35, 37, 48
Honourable Society of the Middle Temple, 81, 82, 84–85
Hope Estate (Jamaica), 134
Hopkins, Clare, 285n
Hopson, Anne (trial witness), 158–62
Horace, 86, 250
Horne, Janet, 56
Hudson, Thomas
   portrait of Handel, 237–38
Huguenots, 28, 70
Hull, Thomas, 176, 177
Hume, David, 15, 59, 67, 71, 87
Hunt, Henry, 139–41, 144–45, 149, 251
Hunt, William, 139–42, 144–45, 149, 168–69, 251
Hunter, David, 290n
hyp, defined, 86–87
hysteria, 87

India, 16, 147, 219
infant mortality, 125, 234–35
influenza outbreak of 1918, 7
Inns of Court, 81–82
Ireland, 19, 38, 47, 51, 188
   Ascendancy and, 196
   civil war and, 16, 55
   Handel travels and concerts in, 192–95, 209–10
   Jacobites and, 51, 220
   parliament, 196
   Swift in, 73–78
Iroquois, 146
Isaiah, Book of, 11, 13, 14, 17, 190, 205–6, 255–56
Ishmael, 233
Islam, 147. *See also* Muslims
Israel, 64
Israel in Egypt (Handel, with libretto by Jennens), 156
Italian musical form and style, 29–32, 35, 59, 98–99, 154, 156, 189–90, 203, 222
   Beggar's Opera as parody of, 94–96
   Handel in London and, 52–53
   Rinaldo and, 41–43

Italy, 19, 89–90
   Handel in, 29–36, 53, 155
   Holdsworth and, 89, 187

Jacobites, 50–52, 54–55, 57, 64, 88, 90, 180, 196, 198, 233, 243
   rising of 1745–46 and, 218–29
Jailcraft Inc., 253
Jamaica, 134
James Fort, 173–76
James I and VI, of England and Scotland, 37, 47
James II, King of England, 46–47, 50, 72, 132
   ouster of, 88
James Island, Africa, 138, 140, 174, 219, 250–51
Jarndyce v. Jarndyce, 84
Jefferson, Thomas, 10
Jenkins, Robert, 122
Jennens, Charles Jr., 1–4, 91
   art collection of, 2–3, 91
   Baroque period and, 92
   begins work on *Messiah* text, 3–4, 295n
   beliefs of, 180–81
   birth of, 2
   brother Robert and, 86, 88
   charities and, 178
   Christianity and Judaism and, 296n
   Christian texts in library of, 181
   Coram and, 123
   death and burial of, 249–50, 253
   death of father and inheritance of, 242
   death of Handel and, 239, 248–49
   death of Holdsworth and, 227, 230–31, 242–44
   desire to produce librettos for Handel, 154–56
   Diallo and, 177–78
   education of, 85, 155
   family background of, 85
   first meets Handel, 93
   Gopsall Hall after death of, 253
   Great Ormond Street town house and, 252
   Handel collaboration ended by, 230–31
   Handel in Dublin and, 195, 197–98, 210
   Handel librettos by, 181, 217, 231
   Handel music collected by, 92, 248
   Handel's *Belshazzar* and, 216
   Handel's career decline and, 100, 154

Jennens, Charles Jr. *(continued)*
   Handel's *L'Allegro, il Penseroso ed il Moderato* and, 197
   Handel's *Saul* and, 178–79
   Handel visits, in London, 93–94
   Holdsworth friendship and, 87, 89–91, 93–94, 131, 133, 178, 187–88, 226–27
   Holdsworth temple built by, 253
   Hudson portrait of Handel and, 237–38
   hyp and agitated melancholy of, 86–87, 128, 154, 181, 216
   Jacobite rising and, 219–20, 222–23, 226, 243
   Jewish people and, 295n–96n
   King James Bible and, 180
   letters censored, 217
   letter to Holdsworth includes title "Messiah," 183
   library of, 3, 91–92, 181, 214, 242, 295n
   lifestyle of, 85–86
   Mainwaring's biography of Handel annotated by, 242
   on *Messiah*, to Holdsworth, 243–44, 296n
   Messiah contribution cast in doubt, 249–50
   Messiah disavowed by, 213–14
   Messiah dispute with Handel over libretto revisions, 215–17
   Messiah Dublin premiere and, 201, 203–8, 210, 255–56, 259–60
   Messiah epigraphs and, 204, 258, 260
   Messiah Foundling Hospital concerts and, 235–36
   Messiah London premiere and, 214–15
   Messiah music composed by Handel for "Scripture Collection" of, 188–93
   Messiah "Scripture Collection" created and sent to Handel by, 3–4, 18–19, 178, 181–84, 257–60, 295nn–96nn
   Messiah wordbook fails to credit, 204
   Messiah wordbook for London concerts and, 259–60, 302n
   Mrs. Cibber's interpretation of *Messiah* and, 245
   musical knowledge of, 85
   music collection of, 2–3, 91–92, 155, 286n–87n
   nonjurors and, 88–89, 104, 155, 178, 180, 217, 226, 286n
   personality of, 86–87
   possessiveness toward Handel and, 154
   Queen Square house and, 169, 252
   Roubiliac and, 154
   Roubiliac temple for Holdsworth and, 242–44
   Royal Academy of Music and, 93
   Shakespeare project of, 248–49
   South Sea annuity and, 131, 133, 136
   Spalding Gentlemen's Society and, 177
   Steevens shapes future perceptions of, 249
   will of, 1–2
   winter of 1739–40 and, 187–88
Jennens, Charles Sr., 84–85, 88
Jennens, Elizabeth, 85
Jennens, Humphrey, 84
Jennens, Robert, 81–82, 86, 88, 147
   suicide of, 82–83, 85, 91, 94, 180, 183
Jennens, William, 84
Jesuits, 50
Jesus Christ, 11–12, 68, 182, 207, 233
Jews and Judaism, 28, 97, 182, 295n–96n
Jim Crow laws, 137
Joar, Africa, 138–39, 174–75
Johnson, Hester "Stella," 73, 198
Johnson, Maurice, 177
Johnson, Samuel, 43–44, 57–58, 67, 249
Journal of the Plague Year, A (Defoe), 58
Judas Maccabaeus (Handel), 228
Julius Caesar (Shakespeare), 249

Kant, Immanuel, 15
Keate, George, 247
Kennedy Center for the Performing Arts, 10
Kent, Duke of, 129
Kent Island, Maryland, 142, 144, 253, 291n
Kidder, Richard, Bishop, 106, 181–82
Kielmansegg, Sophia von, 53
Killiecrankie, Battle of, 51
King, Martin Luther, Jr., 14
King John (Shakespeare), 223
King Lear (Shakespeare), 249
King's Bench Court, 157

King's Theatre (*formerly* Queen's Theatre), 52, 59, 65, 74, 96–100, 102
Knatchbull, Katherine, 156
Königstreu, Mehmet von, 53
Kreienberg, Christoph Friedrich, 49–50
Kunta Kinte, 251–52

L'Allegro, il Penseroso ed il Moderato (Handel ode, with Jennens libretto), 156, 197
Lamb's Conduit Field, 231, 234
latitudinarians, 56
le Blond, Peter, 152, 192
Lee, William, 157, 161
Leibniz, Gottfried Wilhelm, 69–70
Leicester House, 54
Leicester Museum, 253
Leicestershire, 83–84, 178
Leineschloss Palace, 35, 41, 48–50
Lent, 98
Letters of the Late Ignatius Sancho, An African, 135
Leviathan (Hobbes), 67, 73
Library of Congress, 259
Licensing Act (1737), 115
Lichfield, Frances Lee, Countess of, 129
Lilliputians, 77
Limehouse (enslaved person), 143
Lincoln Center, 10
Lincoln's Inn Fields, 40, 94, 156
Liverpool, 133
Lives of the Poets (Cibber), 247
Locke, John, 15, 67, 71, 113, 133
London, 20
  Charles Edward Stuart and, 222–26
  child begging and, 123–24
  civil strife in, 55–56, 66–67
  Diallo in, 252
  Great Fire of 1666 and, 38
  Handel first visit of 1710, 38–39
  Handel return of 1712, 48–49, 53
  Jennens arrival and, 93
  Messiah contemporary concerts and, 10
  Messiah premiere in, 213–15, 231, 236
  Messiah wordbook of 1743 for, 259–60
  procession of 1717 of George I, 23–24
  Royal Fireworks of 1749, 229–30
  theater and, 39–41, 104–5
  triangular trade and, 133
  vulgarities of public life in, 57–59
  winter of 1739–40 in, 187–88
London Bridge, 38
London Daily Post, 192
London Underground, 241
Louis XIV, King of France, 46, 50
Louis XV, King of France, 218, 220–21
Lover, The (Theophilus Cibber), 247
Luckett, Richard, 296n
Luke, Gospel of, 12
lupus, 43
Lutherans, 25, 35, 48

Macbeth (Shakespeare), 249
Maclaine, Mrs. (singer), 202
Mainwaring, John, 30, 32, 34, 49, 235–36, 241–42
Malinke (Mankinka) people, 139–40
Manchester, Duke of, 129
Manchester, Isabella Montagu, Duchess of, 129
Mansfield, William Murray, 1st Earl of, 136, 162, 164
Mantua, 29
Marissen, Michael, 295nn
Marktkirche (Halle), 26–27
Marlborough, John Churchill, Duke of, 44, 135
Marlborough, Sarah Churchill, Duchess of, 43–44, 63, 135
marriage, women's rights and, 112–13
Marshalsea Prison, 102, 120, 151
Martin, David
  portrait of Dido Elizabeth Belle, 136
Mary II, Queen of England, with William of Orange, 46, 56
Maryland, 141–43, 148, 176, 253
Maryland Gazette, 141, 143
Masham, Abigail, 43
Massachusetts, 121, 130
Mattheson, Johann, 28–29, 32–33
Medici, Ferdinando de', Grand Prince of Tuscany, 32, 34
Medici, Gian Gastone de', 32–33
Memoirs of the Life of the Late George Frederic Handel (Mainwaring), 241–42

Index

Messiah (Handel, with libretto by Jennens). *See also specific individuals; venues; and concerts*, 9
- Abigail Adams on, 9–10, 12–13
- Beecham recording of 1927 of, 7
- Boston concert of 1843 of, 9–10
- Burney on, 240
- as Christmas tradition, 11–12
- combines grand choruses and arias, sacred and profane, 11
- copyists turn manuscript into full score, 192
- criticized for mixing scripture with stagecraft, 214
- dispute between Handel and Jennens over revision of, 215–16
- early performances of, in secular spaces, 11
- Easter and, 11–12
- Emerson on, 12
- Enlightenment and, 15–18
- essence of faith for first audiences of, 8
- familiarity of, 11
- final fugue of chorus and "Amen" at end, 14
- first American performances of, 9
- form and subject matter of text, 8
- Foundling Hospital annual performances of in 1750s, 231, 233–37, 245
- Foundling Hospital Anthem recycles "Hallellujah" chorus of, 232–33
- Franklin on, 236
- "Hallelujah" chorus brings audience to feet, 12–13, 17, 214–15
- Handel and sacred texts created by Jennens, 18–19
- Handel composes musical score following Jennens scenario, 8, 188–92
- Handel fails to publish full score, 230
- Handel finishes and scribbles title, 191
- as Handel's greatest creation, 236
- Handel letter to Jennens on Dublin premiere, 210
- Handel performances of, post 1742, 8, 216, 230, 236–37
- Handel performs at Foundling Hospital, 233–34
- Handel placard at Gopsall Temple ruin and, 254
- Handel premieres in Dublin, 8, 18–19, 192–93, 199–202, 201–10, 255–56
- Handel premieres in London, 213–15, 231, 236
- Handel revises Jennens text in Dublin, and prepares for Cibber, 201–2
- Handel Roubiliac memorial statue with page of, 240
- Handel's changes in, to suit circumstances, 10
- Handel's death before performance of 1759 and, 239
- Handel's score connects disparate threads, with Jennens's text, 205–6
- Hudson portrait of Handel and, 238
- iconic nature of sung text of, 11
- ink spilled on manuscript of, 191
- Jennens and London premiere, 231
- Jennens disappointment and disavowal of connection with, 213–14
- Jennens letters to Holdsworth while working on, 243–44
- Jennens libretto and themes of, 258
- Jennens libretto reproduced, 261–70
- Jennens not credited in wordbook of, 204, 242
- Jennens's role largely forgotten, 210, 242, 249–50
- Jennens writes libretto for, as "Scripture Collection," 3–4, 179–83
- Martin Luther King Jr. speech and, 14
- mass secular audience and, 5
- Mrs. Cibber's performance in Dublin premiere and, 206–8, 211
- orchestras and, 5
- original manuscript of, 20, 241
- as participatory art, 5–6
- *Peanuts* TV special and, 12
- performances following Handel's death, 8–9, 240
- pirated copies and, 230
- popularity of, 10–11, 241
- shadow geography of, 252
- sing-alongs, 10–11
- soloists and, 5
- themes of hope, pain, survival, and redemption and, 5, 11, 13–14, 17–18, 20, 67–70, 172, 204–5, 207, 257, 257–58
- themes reflecting eighteenth century struggles resonate today, 16–20
- twentieth century performances and orchestra and choir size, 10

as unlike any other works by
  Handel, 8
 weirdness of form of, 11
 Westminster performance of 1784
  on centenary of Handel's birth, 9,
  240–41
 wordbook epigraphs added by
  Jennens, 204
 wordbooks of 1742 and 1743, 259–60
Methodism, 122, 240
Methodist Central Hall, Westminster, 7
Middle East, 147
Middle Passage, 251
midwives, 112, 125
Milton, John, 55, 155–56
Modest Proposal, A (Swift), 124, 127
Momo (castrato), 31
Monmouth, James Scott, 1st Duke of,
 124, 129
Montagu, John Montagu, 2nd Duke of,
 122, 129, 146–47, 168–69, 175–76, 178,
 229, 250
Montagu, Mary Churchill, Duchess
 of, 135
Montesquieu, 147
Monteverdi, Claudio, 29
Montgomery, Alabama, 14
Moore, Francis, 174, 175
Morgan Library and Museum, 259–60
Moses, 233
Murray, William. *See* Mansfield, 1st
 Earl of
Muscogee Confederacy, 120
music. *See individual works; musicians;
 styles*
Music for the Royal Fireworks (Handel),
 229–30, 232
Muslims, 147, 173, 175–76, 251–52

Naples, 29, 34
*Narrative of the Life of Mrs. Charlotte
 Charke, A*, 114
National Guard, 6
National Portrait Gallery, 252
Native Americans, 120–21, 123, 146
Neale, William, 197, 207, 256
Near East, 147
Netherlands, 28, 37, 67, 70, 132
 War of the Austrian Succession and,
  218, 220
 War of the Spanish Succession and, 44
Nether Whitacre chapel, Jennens burial
 at, 249–50

New Englanders, 123
New France, 119
Newton, Isaac, 2, 61, 69, 133, 148
New York
 contemporary concerts of *Messiah*
  and, 10
 Messiah performance of 1770 in, 9
New York Times, 7, 295n
Nicholls, William, 181
Nicolini (castrato), 31, 42
Nigeria, 136
Nihell, Elizabeth, 112
Nonconformists, 56
Non-juror, The (Colley Cibber), 88, 104,
 223–24
nonjurors, 88–89, 92, 155, 178, 180, 217,
 222–23, 226, 229, 286n
North America, 49
 War of the Austrian Succession and,
  219

O'Carolan, Turlough, 78
Oglethorpe, James, 121–22, 145, 149,
 218
"Ombra mai fù (Handel's Largo)," 153
Opera of the Nobility, 99, 153
opera seria, 60
Orange Coffee House, 151
oratorio, defined, 98–99, 131
Oroonoko (Southerne), 146
Orpheus, 34
Othello (Shakespeare), 212, 249
Ottoboni, Cardinal Pietro, 34
Ottoman Empire, 25, 31, 40, 53, 136
Ovid, 97
Oxfordshire, 44
Oxford University, 81–82, 85, 87–88
 Balliol College, 85
 Bodleian Library, 82, 259
 Magdalen College, 87–88
 Trinity College, 81, 83, 285n

Pagliacci (Leoncavallo), 7
Paine, Thomas, 15
Palazzo Bonelli, 34
Palazzo della Cancelleria, 34
Palazzo del Re, 89, 90
Pamphili, Cardinal Benedetto, 34
Paradise Lost (Milton), 55
*Paraphrase and Annotations upon the
 Books of the Psalms* (Hammond), 181
Park, Mungo, 139
Parkgate packet boats, 193–94, 210

Pasqualini (castrato), 31
Paul, apostle, 11, 204–5, 208
Pauluccio (castrato), 31
Paxson, Maggie, 6–7
Peanuts Christmas special (TV show), 12
Peel, Samuel, 143
Pepusch, Johann Christoph, 95
Pepys, Samuel, 40
Persian Letters (Montesquieu), 147
Peter the Great, Tsar of Russia, 40
"Peter the Wild Boy," 146
Petrie, Anna, 285n
Philis (enslaved person), 142
piano, evolution of modern, 32, 91
pifferari (bagpipers), 33, 206
Pike, Stephen, 139–40, 144, 147–48, 173, 251
Pistol, Ancient (character), 105–6, 117, 163, 226
plague, 26, 58
Plato, 30
Pococke, Edward, 181
Pompey (enslaved person), 142
Pope, Alexander, 19, 66, 70–71, 97, 99, 105, 148–49, 195, 198
    Handel *Esther* libretto and, 155
Portland, Duke of, 129
Portugal, 132
    slave trade and, 140
Poussin (artist), 91
Prague, defenestration of (1618), 25
Prestonpans, Battle of, 221
prostitution, 124
Protestants
    Act of Settlement and, 46–48, 50
    Dublin and, 196
    nonjurors and, 89
    sects of, 56
    Thirty Years' War and, 25
Provoked Wife, The (play), 246–47
Prussia
    War of the Austrian Succession and, 218, 228
Psalms, 3
    second, 13, 205
    twenty-fourth, 205
public-private partnerships, 132
Puritans, 38–39, 55, 73, 104

Qatar, 252
Quakers, 73
Queen Square, Jennens's town house in, 89, 93, 123, 169, 226–27, 252
Queen's Theatre, 40–41, 43, 48, 52. *See also* King's Theatre
Qur'an, 145, 147–49, 252

Rachmaninoff, 7
racialized enslavement, 136–38
Racine, Jean, 97
racism, 6
Radamisto (Handel opera), 60–62
Raphael (artist), 91
Rebecca (ship), 122
refugees, 257
    refugiés and origin of term, 71–72
religion
    Jennens family and, 83
    Swift on, 73
    warfare and, 16
    See also Christianity; Islam; Muslims; Jews and Judaism
Rembrandt, 91
Renaissance, 29
Revelation, Book of, 190, 205
Reynolds, Joshua, 233
Rhine River, 25, 44
Rich, John, 94, 96–97
Richmond, Duke of, 129
Richmond, Sarah Lennox, Duchess of, 129
Rinaldo (Handel)
    Beggar's Opera and, 95
    librettist and, 155
    revivals of, 48, 52
    wordbook of, 42
    written and first performed, 41–42, 44–45
Robinson Crusoe (Defoe), 87, 133
Rodelinda (Handel), 63
Romans, Epistle to the, 208
Rome, 3, 29, 33–34, 38
    Holdsworth in, 89–90, 187
    James Stuart the Old Pretender in, 89, 219, 222
Rome, ancient, 48, 66
Romeo and Juliet (Shakespeare), 247
Roots (Haley), 251
Roubiliac, Louis-François, 91
    Gopsall Temple statue for Holdsworth, 242–43, 253
    Handel Westminster memorial statue, 239–40, 242
    statue of Handel in Vauxhall Gardens, 153–54
Rousseau, Jean-Jacques, 15, 112–13

Royal Academy of Arts, 252
Royal Academy of Music, 60–63, 74, 93, 96, 127, 132, 134
Royal African Company, 132–34, 136, 138, 144–46, 148, 173–76, 250, 290n
Royal Albert Hall, 10
Royal Mail, 194
Royal Society of Musicians (*formerly* Fund for Decay'd Musicians), 241
Rubens (artist), 91
"Rule, Britannia" (Arne and Thomson), 16, 134–35, 228
Ruspoli, Francesco Maria, 34

Sancho, Ignatius, 135
satire, 81, 96
Saul (Handel, with libretto by Jennens), 155–57, 178–79
Saxe-Weissenfels, Duke of, 26
Saxony, 25, 35, 69
Scarlatti, Domenico, 34, 39
Schoelcher, Victor, 298n
Schulenburg, Melusine von der, 53
science, 15–16
Scotland, 19, 37–38, 188
　civil war, 16, 55
　James Stuart and Jacobite rising of 1715 and, 50–52, 64
　Jacobite rising of 1745–46 and, 220–22, 225–26
Scottish parliament, 44
Scriblerus Club, 66
scrofula (tuberculosis), 43
Seaflower (ship), 121
Second Treatise of Government (Locke), 67
"See, the conquering hero comes" (*Judas Maccabaeus*), 228
segregation, 137
Senegal River, 139
Senegambia, 140, 148, 251–52
Senesino (castrato), 19, 60, 98, 99
Sephardic Jews, 28
Serse (Handel), 153
Seven Years' War, 228
Shaftesbury, Earl of, 96, 215
Shakespeare, William, 58, 105, 223, 226
　Jennens editions of, 248–49
Sheridan, Thomas, 207, 245–46
Sibelius, 7

slavery, 15–16, 19, 122, 130, 132–50
　African voices against, in Britain, 135–36
　afterlife of, 137–38
　becomes racialized, 136–37
　Bluett pamphlet on Diallo and, 251–52
　Britain enters trade in, 132–36
　Diallo and, 138–50
　Georgia and, 122
　Maryland and, 141–42
　opposition to, 135–36
　play *Oroonoko* and, 146
　Pope on, 149–50
　South Carolina and, 122
　transoceanic trade and, 16, 132–36, 138–41, 177, 250–52
　value of trade in, 141
Sloane, Hans, 147–48, 169, 175–77, 250, 252
Sloper, Catherine, 108, 246
Sloper, William, Jr., 108–10, 115–17, 119–20, 136, 157–65, 200, 211, 246–47, 252
Sloper, William, Sr., 108, 119–21, 160, 171, 218
　death of, 212
smallpox, 56, 90, 106, 235
Smith, John Christopher, elder, 62, 191–93, 200, 210, 215, 239, 241
Smith, John Christopher, younger, 62, 235, 237, 241
Smith, Ruth, 286n, 296n
Smock Alley Theatre (Dublin), 196, 248
Some Memoirs of the Life of Job (Bluett), 251
Somerset, Charlotte Seymour, Duchess of, 128, 168
Somerset, Henrietta Paulet, dowager duchess of, 129
Soninke people, 139
Sophia, dowager electress of Hanover, 36, 45, 47–48, 69
　death of, 1714, 51, 69
Sophia Dorothea of Celle, Queen of England (wife of George I), 36, 54
South Carolina, 119–20, 122
Southerne, Thomas, 146
South Sea Company, 131–33, 136, 222, 240–41
Southwark, 55

Spain
  Armada and, 46
  colonies of, 122, 132
  Florida and, 119–20
  War of the Spanish Succession and, 44
Spalding Gentlemen's Society, 148, 177, 250
St. Andrew's Church (Holborn), 244
Steevens, George, 249
Stevens, Nicholas, 83, 285n
St. George's Church (London), 62, 237
Stint, Mr. (candle snuffer), 117
St. James's Palace, 52, 229
St. Martin-in-the-Fields Church, 160
St. Patrick's Cathedral (Dublin), 73–74, 77–78, 194, 198
  choristers, 78, 201, 202, 210
  Swift burial at, 210
St. Paul's Cathedral, 9, 39, 58
St. Philip Neri, Oratorians of, 98
Strange, John, 157
Stuart, Charles Edward (the Young Pretender, "Bonnie Prince Charlie"), 90, 219–26, 229
Stuart, James Francis Edward (James III, the Old Pretender), 46, 50, 52, 57, 64, 88–89, 121, 196, 124, 218–22
Stuart dynasty, 16, 19, 37–38, 47–48, 57, 88, 89. *See also* Jacobites; Stuart, Charles Edward; Stuart, James Francis Edward
  attempt at restoration of 1745, 218–26
Sue (enslaved person), 142
Sullivan, Arthur, 259
Sweden, 25
Swift, Jonathan, 19, 38, 51, 183, 193–94, 207, 214, 244, 284n
  as administrator at St. Patrick's, Dublin, 73–74, 77–78
  on child poverty, 123–24, 126–27
  collected essays of, 73
  death of, 210
  Dublin and, 123–24
  early background of, 72–74
  essay on "the hyp," 86
  Gay and, 94
  Gulliver's Travels and, 74–77, 81, 86, 147
  Handel satirical poem on, 78
  King James Bible and, 179–80
  Messiah premiere in Dublin and, 198–99, 201–2, 210, 255
  music disliked by, 78
  Tale of a Tub and, 73
Sympson, Richard (pen name of Jonathan Swift), 74
Synge, Edward, bishop, 209–10

Tale of a Tub, A (Swift), 73
Tamerlano (Handel), 63
Tarquini, Vittoria, 34
Tate, Francesca, 285n
Taylor, John, 239
Teatro San Giovanni Grisostomo, 35
Te Deum (Handel, celebrating the end of conflict with France and Spain), 49
Te Deum (Handel, on George II's victory at Dettingham), 219
Thames River, 23–24, 38–93, 187, 280n
Theatre Royal (Covent Garden), 214
Thirty Years' War, 16, 25–26, 28–29, 35, 139
Thomas Coram Foundation for Children, 245
Thomson, James, 135
Timothy, First Epistle to, 204, 260
Tintoretto, 91
Titian, 91
Tories, 57, 61, 90, 122, 219, 228
Toulson, Alexander, 142–45, 149, 251, 291n
Tower of London, 39
Trafalgar Square, 252
Travels into the Inland Parts of Africa (Moore), 175
Treatise of Human Nature, A (Hume), 59
Trinity Church (New York), *Messiah* performance of 1770 at, 9
Trinity College (Dublin), 194, 196, 207
Trivia (Gay), 123
Tunbridge Wells, 237, 239
Tunis, bey of, 146
Tuscany, 32–33, 98
Two Crowns and Cushions, 102, 146

United Kingdom, creation of, 16, 44. *See also* Britain
United States. *See also* American colonies; American Revolution
  abolition of slavery and, 137–38
  Messiah performances in, 10–11

Universal Etymological English Dictionary (Bailey), 68
Utrecht, Peace of (1713), 49, 132

Vanbrugh, John, 40
Vauxhall gardens
  Handel statue by Roubiliac, 153–54
Venice, 3, 29, 33–35, 37, 39, 91, 136
Veronese, Paolo, 91
Vindication of the Rights of Women, A (Wollstonecraft), 113–14
Virgil, 154, 243, 260
Vivaldi, Antonio, 91
  Four Seasons, 92
Voltaire, 69, 104, 107, 247

Wales, Prince of. *See* Frederick, Prince of Wales; George II, King of England
Walpole, Horatio, 120, 213, 215
Walpole, Robert, 120, 168, 218–19
Walsh, Antoine, 220
Walsh, John, 42, 63
Walter, Lucy, 124
War of Jenkins' Ear, 122, 218
War of the Austrian Succession, 218–20, 228
War of the Spanish Succession, 44, 49, 55–56, 120, 132
Washington, D.C.
  Messiah concerts and, 10
Washington, George, 228
Water Music (Handel), 24, 53, 95
Watson, Mr. (henchman), 116
"ways of Zion do mourn, The" (Handel; funeral anthem for Queen Caroline), 153
Wells, Edward, 181
Wesley, John, 122, 240
West Africa, 84, 175–77, 251
  Diallo map of, 252
  Islam and, 147
  slave trade and, 133, 138, 140–41, 145, 147–48
  War of the Austrian Succession and, 219
West End, London, 39–41
West Indies, 84
Westminster Abbey
  Anne coronation and, 43
  George II coronation and, 63
  Handel centenary of 1784, and *Messiah* concert, 9, 15, 240–41
  Handel grave at, 239, 247
  Mrs. Cibber buried at, 247
Westphalia, Peace of (1648), 25, 35
Whigs, 56, 57, 61, 73, 88, 95, 100, 108, 120, 219, 221, 228
wife beating, 111–12
Wild Court (Holborn), 101, 109, 160
William, Prince of England, 43
William Augustus, Duke of Cumberland, 218
William III, King of England and Prince of Orange, 46–47, 51, 56
William the Conqueror, 83
Windsor Castle choir, 9
witch trials, 25, 56
Wollstonecraft, Mary, 15, 113
Wolof, 139, 142–43
women
  charitable societies and, 111
  death sentences and, 112
  education of, 110–11, 113
  equality of, in Georgia, 136
  hysteria and, 87
  marginalization of, 15
  marriage and, 111–12
  out-of-wedlock pregnancy and, 124–25
  performing by, 42, 111, 114–15
  poverty of, 124
  rights of, 110–14, 123
  violence vs., 56
  witchcraft and, 25, 56
Wood, Thomas, 259
workhouses, 126
World War II, 241, 253
Wren, Christopher, 39

Xerxes, King of Persia, 153

Yahoos, 76–77, 244
Yellow Stag (Halle), 26
Yoai, Loumein, 139–40, 176

Zachow, Friedrich Wilhelm, 27, 30
"Zadok the Priest" (Handel; coronation of George II), 64, 97–98, 190
Zara (Voltaire), 107

ILLUSTRATION CREDITS

Canaletto Westminster Bridge: Yale Center for British Art, Paul Mellon Collection, B1976.7.94
George Frideric Handel by Denner: © National Portrait Gallery, London
Jonathan Swift by Jervas: © National Portrait Gallery, London
Gopsall Hall: Digital image courtesy of the Paul Mellon Centre, PA-F05886-0007
Charles Jennens by Hudson: Courtesy of Handel Hendrix House
Susannah Cibber by Hudson: © National Portrait Gallery, London
William Hogarth, "Strolling Actresses": Author's collection
"Pistol's a Cuckold": TCS 61, folder 102, Harvard Theatre Collection, Houghton Library, Harvard University
William Hogarth, "The Beggar's Opera": Author's collection
William Hogarth, "Gin Lane": Author's collection
Thomas Coram by Hogarth: © The Foundling Museum, London
Ayuba Diallo by Hoare: OM.762, Qatar Museums / Lusail Museum, Doha, Qatar. Photography © Qatar Museums / Lusail Museum, Doha, Qatar
Ayuba Diallo map: British Library, Add.MS.32556, fol. 239v. / Bridgeman Images
"The Charming Brute": Prints and Photographs Division, Library of Congress
Messiah ink stain page: British Library, R.M.20.fol.2 / Bridgeman Images
"Hallelujah" chorus manuscript page: British Library, R.M.20.fol.2 / Bridgeman Images
Old Music Hall: Gerald Coke Handel Foundation
Messiah wordbook: Performing Arts Reading Room, Library of Congress
Prince Charles Edward Stuart by Blanchet: Royal Collection Trust / © His Majesty King Charles III 2023
William Hogarth, "March of the Guards to Finchley": Author's collection
Battle of Culloden: Courtesy of the Council of the National Army Museum, London
Coram with baby: Gerald Coke Handel Foundation
Foundling Hospital: Author's collection
Foundling Hospital tokens: © The Foundling Museum, London
Royal Fireworks: Gerald Coke Handel Foundation
Edward Holdsworth memorial ruins: Photograph by the author
Edward Holdsworth memorial allegorical statue: Photograph by the author
Charles Jennens by Chamberlin: Gerald Coke Handel Foundation
George Frideric Handel by Hudson: © National Portrait Gallery, London

penguin.co.uk/vintage